DATE DUE		

KURT WALDHEIM
A CASE TO ANSWER?

KURT WALDHEIM
A CASE TO ANSWER?

JACK SALTMAN

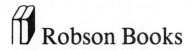 Robson Books

in association with
Channel Four Television Company

To Lynne, my long-suffering wife

First published in Great Britain in 1988 by Robson Books Ltd, Bolsover House, 5–6 Clipstone Street, London W1P 7EB.

Copyright © 1988 Jack Saltman

Photos and extracts from the Inquiry © Thames Television
Other photos courtesy of Thames Television

Sketches by Bill Palmer

British Library Cataloguing in Publication Data

Saltman, Jack
   Kurt Waldheim : a case to answer.
   1. Austria. Waldheim, Kurt, 1918– . Biographies
   I. Title
   943.6'053'0924

ISBN 0–86051–516–8

Edited by Nancy Duin

Typeset by Action Typesetting Ltd, Gloucester
Printed in Great Britain by
Billing & Sons Ltd, Worcester

Contents

Acknowledgements

So many people helped to make the *Waldheim* programme and, in their way, made this book possible that, hard as I might try, I would probably miss out someone if I attempted to name them all. Therefore, to everyone who worked on or contributed to *Waldheim* – thank you.

However, I must pay particular tribute to Ed Braman, who ran our research effort (involving an incredible amount of work) in a masterly fashion. And to Peter Smith, Susie Harrison and Chrissie Cocks, the other members of the original *Waldheim* team, as well as Bill Palmer, whose set was superb and who has kindly allowed me to reproduce some of the 'impressions' he drew during the recording – very many thanks.

I also owe a great deal to my wife and family, who not only lost me during the months of making the programme, but also through the very many additional hours spent writing this book.

My thanks are also due to the senior members of Thames TV in London and Home Box Office in New York and to Channel 4 – not to forget Cheryll Roberts of Robson Books and Liz Brown, who had the original idea of turning the programme's progress into a book, and Jeremy and Carole Robson who always had faith in the idea and whose encouragement was much appreciated.

Finally, to Nancy Duin, my editor, who helped turn what was a stream-of-consciousness manuscript, badly typed on my venerable Olivetti, into what I hope you will find an interesting book, I owe a deep debt of gratitude.

Introduction

Waldheim – made by Thames Television as a co-production with the USA's biggest cable home entertainments company, Home Box Office – was always going to be a very special programme.

From its inception on the 13th floor of a New York mini-skyscraper and its nine days of recording at Teddington studios on the banks of the River Thames to its final trans-mission in June 1988, it was a voyage into the unknown. No one had ever charted the waters of a Commission of Inquiry held by two television companies with real judges, real lawyers, real witnesses and no script. And the person who was to be, metaphorically, in the dock was a real man who also happened to be a former Secretary-General of the United Nations and was now President of Austria.

The problems were multitudinous – most of them without precedent – and the programme makers had to plot their own course with great care, for the subject was too important to get wrong. The participants were men and women of high repute – eminent judges from five countries and lawyers who included a former British Attorney-General and a former US Justice Department special prosecutor and director of the Office of Special Investigations.

But, most of all, the programme was important for the man whose past was to be examined – Kurt Waldheim. He had brushed aside accusations of his alleged involvement in war crimes in the Balkans between 1942 and 1945. Then the US had put him on their 'Watch List', effectively barring him from entering the country, their decision being based on secret evidence which, they claimed, showed that he had been involved in war crimes. A Commission of Historians, set up by the Austrian government, frankly disbelieved some of Waldheim's statements about his activities during World War II, but they refused to be judgemental.

9

It was commonly acknowledged that the evidence against Kurt Waldheim would never be tested in open court. This convinced Thames Television and Home Box Office that this unique four-hour programme should be made, and transmitted, on the same night, in the United Kingdom, in the United States and in many other countries around the world.

The first meeting about the programme took place in June 1987, and the programme itself was transmitted 12 months later. This book is my personal account, as the producer of *Waldheim*, of one extraordinary year in my life, and of one extraordinary programme. I have tried to tell, as honestly as my memory and the laws of libel allow, how it evolved and developed; of the people who were keen to criticize and stop it; and of those who supported and helped to make it happen. Always hanging over our heads was the accusation that we were involving Dr Waldheim in a 'trial by television'. This I absolutely refute, and it was a suggestion equally denied by our eminent jurists: no programme will ever be more fairly made.

Waldheim was made at a cost of £1.5 million. Few other television programmes will ever be produced in the same way. This, then, is the inside story.

Part I

The Production

1

In the Beginning

Vienna was blisteringly hot, even for the middle of July, and as Barrie Sales, Ed Braman and I got out of the taxi, the Hofburg Palace seemed to shimmer in the heat. It certainly was impressive, the centre of the Habsburg empire for almost 400 years, and I felt a strange contradiction between the beautiful old building and the modern medium that I represented.

We were expected, and directed up a flight of stairs. Confronted by what appeared at first to be a long corridor, I realized as we walked through it that this was actually a series of sumptuously furnished and decorated rooms − complete with elegant chandeliers and lush red velvet − separated from each other by double doors, the type that, in the best films, open mysteriously as the camera tracks down. If this had been a film, we would have been met in the last room by the Tsar of All the Russias or the King of Siam − but we had to settle for a young woman typing efficiently on a very modern machine.

We were told that the meeting would take place in a few minutes. We retraced our steps by a room or two and, nervously, sat down to wait.

Certainly nothing in my almost three decades in television had prepared me for this − for when the door to that end room opened again, I had to explain to the man we would then meet that I, a British TV producer, was going to hold a commission of inquiry to look into allegations of war crimes against him: that man, until recently the Secretary-General of the United Nations, was now Austria's President.

The proposal for this inquiry had come my way in June 1987,

during the week that Margaret Thatcher humiliated the Labour Party for the third time. I was one of the two producers for Thames Television's pre-election coverage. I was sitting with Barrie Sales, director of news, current affairs and documentaries, and reporters Graham Addicott and Bill Wigmore, discussing two films comparing the affluent south and the less-than-affluent north of England, when the director of programmes, David Elstein, burst into the office.

'I need a producer for this great idea – the trial of Kurt Waldheim!'

I can't remember whether it was David or Barrie or both who pointed in my direction. Either way, that was how I began on what was to become the most challenging, frightening, difficult, demanding and probably most important programme that I had ever produced.

The election over, I had returned to my post as editor of *Reporting London*. I also turned my thoughts to the proposed 'trial'. I suppose it was a natural progression from the various programmes with a legal format that been produced in both Britain and the US over the years. In all of these, there were counsel for the prosecution and counsel for the defence, as well as juries – juries made up of the studio audience or of the viewers at home, who had to ring or send in their judgements based on the arguments presented in the programmes.

A few years ago, London Weekend Television had had the brilliant idea of 'trying' Lee Harvey Oswald for the murder of President John F. Kennedy. Given that Oswald was, in turn, murdered by Jack Ruby before he could stand trial, and that arguments still rage over how many shots were fired and by whom, it was a clever way of turning back the clock and holding the only form of trial that there could be. The producer had done everything he could to make the proceedings real and valid. A US Federal judge and American attorneys had been brought to London, together with real witnesses who had been in Dallas in November 1963. And they had run it for real.

The defence attorney for the Oswald 'trial' had been Gerry Spence, one of America's most brilliant advocates, with a unique capacity for making juries see things his way. It is said that, in his time, Spence has defended more than 2000 cases and has not lost one – except for the Oswald trial. After this experience as a television lawyer (and despite his failure to get a posthumous verdict of 'innocent' for Oswald), he had come up with the idea of trying Kurt Waldheim for war crimes, with himself as prosecuting counsel. He had put this to the American cable network, Home Box Office, who were, to say the least, intrigued. It was at this point that HBO brought Gerry Spence's idea to Thames, asking us to produce the programme; HBO flatteringly believed that, on this side of the Atlantic, there is a lot of expertise in making heavyweight investigative programmes.

Thames Television productions are transmitted on commercial channels – either Independent Television (ITV) or Channel 4, the independent TV channel that has, since it began in November 1982, built up a reputation for being innovative and courageous. While some on the Thames board of directors had argued that, if the Waldheim programme were shown on the more commercial ITV channel, it would get a much larger audience, the estimated four-hour transmission time simply proved too heavy for ITV to bear. However, in Channel 4's eyes, an inquiry of this kind was certainly innovative television, and when Thames offered it to Liz Forgan, then a Channel 4 commissioning editor (now Director of Programmes), the project was guaranteed a British transmission.

Thames' contract with Home Box Office runs to a modest 50-odd pages. It took some time to negotiate, and in the end, for their portion of the original budget – £1.5 million – Thames guaranteed to deliver the programme as discussed and agreed, including the 'regular in-person, first-call services of Jack Saltman as producer'.

Now that I was committed to producing the programme, I kept coming back to the original idea. As I mulled over the concept of 'trying' Kurt Waldheim, I realized that it couldn't be as simple as Gerry Spence had put it. This 'trial' wouldn't be hypothetical; no long-dead figure's ghostly presence in the dock. On this programme, the defendant, even in his absence, would be Kurt Waldheim, who was very much alive. Besides, 'trial by television' had a very unsavoury ring to it – even though I knew that the very process of investigative journalism is, in effect, a trial. The question remained: could we

15

create a form of inquiry that was morally acceptable and also containable within a television format?

It was with the help of one of Britain's finest judges that I began to find some of the answers. Over lunch at his home in the Hampshire countryside, I discussed the problem with Lord Devlin, who before his retirement had been one of the Law Lords – the final court of appeal in the United Kingdom.

He agreed that the idea of a trial was a non-starter. 'But,' he asked, 'why not a committal proceedings, or something along the lines of an American grand jury? In these, what is being looked at is not the innocence or guilt of the person, but rather it is the evidence that is on trial. Is there sufficient *prima facie* evidence to warrant, were it a real judicial process, sending the accused to trial? Does that person have a case to answer?

'This way,' Lord Devlin continued, 'you'd be testing the evidence. And because so much has already come to light and so many allegations have been made in the media, this would be a way not only of looking at such evidence but of testing it in an adversarial manner.'

At a subsequent discussion about the format with Lord Elwyn Jones, Lord Chancellor in a former Labour government and a member of the British legal team at Nuremberg, Lord Devlin's idea of testing the evidence rather than the man became even more refined. Lord Elwyn Jones felt that even a quasi-committal proceedings was too close to the real legal process for comfort. He suggested instead a tribunal with terms of reference along the lines of: To look into the allegations of the culpability of Kurt Waldheim in connection with war crimes...

But why Waldheim anyway? And what were these 'crimes' of which he stood accused, at least by much of the world's media? Before I could presume to find out if Waldheim had a case to answer, I had to satisfy myself that, behind all the headlines and accusations, there was enough genuine controversy to warrant HBO's and Thames' involvement in an inquiry.

Combing through a pile of some of the thousands of newspaper stories that had been written about Waldheim over the previous few years, and reading the transcripts of interviews he had given, it was possible to get a general overview of his life and the controversy surrounding his wartime career.

Kurt Waldheim had been born near the provincial capital of Tulln in Austria in 1918, grandson of a blacksmith and son of the mayor's daughter and a local schoolteacher. In 1937, at the end of a year's conscription with the Austrian cavalry, he began his law studies at the University of Vienna and also registered at the Consular Academy. Founded in the 18th century during the reign of Maria Theresa and taking no more than 40 students at any one time, the Academy had a high reputation for training diplomats.

Then, on 13 March 1938, *Anschluss* – Germany annexed Austria, Hitler arrived in Vienna the next day and the Austrian army was merged with the German *Wehrmacht*. It is at this point, I found, that Waldheim's version of his subsequent history begins to differ from that of historians and other researchers.

Just 19 days after the first German troops crossed the Austrian border – on 1 April 1938 – documents show that Kurt Waldheim joined the National Socialists' *Studentenbund* ('student organization'). Waldheim maintains that he joined to make life easier for himself and his family, that his joining did not mean that he, in turn, joined the Nazi Party, and besides, all the other students had become members of the *Studentenbund*, too.

On 18 November 1938, other documents show that Waldheim became a member of the *Reiterstandarte Sturm-Abteilung*, the riding club of the SA, the Nazi 'storm troopers'. Waldheim claims that, when he'd joined the club, it hadn't had any connections with the SA, and when it was absorbed into that organization, he no longer took part in its activities.

A few weeks before Britain and France declared war on Germany after its invasion of Poland, Waldheim was called up (15 August 1939). He was sent on an officer cadet course, then went to fight in France for a brief time, followed by service with the Upper Austrian Division. After Germany invaded the Soviet Union on 22 June 1941, he was ordered to the Eastern Front, and on 3 July, he was awarded the Iron Cross, second class, plus two other decorations. Five months

17

later, on 20 December, as he reached the area south-west of the Orel salient in the central Russian uplands, he was wounded in the leg by a grenade splinter. When the wound became infected, he was taken to a field hospital near Minsk, then to Frankfurt an der Oder, and finally to the army hospital in Vienna. Although discharged in February 1942, on 7 April he was registered as 'unfit for active duty'.

In the English-language version of Waldheim's autobiography *The Eye of the Storm*, his wartime experiences end here. After some months, he wrote, he applied for permission to resume his law studies and, to his surprise and undisguised relief, this was granted; he obtained his master's degree and, in 1944, his doctorate, and also married Elizabeth Ritschel, all the while being paid as an army lieutenant. It was only in early 1986 that Waldheim publicly admitted the remainder of his wartime record. He'd left it out of his autobiography, he says, because he'd thought it was unimportant.

The newspaper articles I read told a different story. In April 1942, Waldheim arrived in Plevlje in Montenegro (now in south-west Yugoslavia). Together with the Croatian Ustachi (the local Fascists) and the Italians, the German army was committed to the annihilation of the partisans and the pacification of the whole area. It came as no surprise to learn that the means used were both ruthless and draconian: hangings; homes, towns and villages burned; hostages taken; partisans shot; prisoners sent to concentration camps or deported for slave labour.

Because he spoke some Italian, Waldheim had been assigned to the operations staff of *Kampfgruppe* ('battle group') Bader to provide liaison with the Italian 5th Mountain Division known as the 'Pusteria'. His job was to report back to his own headquarters, telling them what the Italians were up to − or, to the annoyance of the Germans, *not* up to − and to convey messages and requests to the Italian commanding general, Esposito.

With little help from the Italians, the Germans with the Ustachis completed what had become known as Operation Trio. However, many of the partisans had slipped through the net to Sarajevo, Foca and Goradze, and further 'cleansing operations' were required. An encirclement campaign was

18

planned by the *Wehrmacht*, and despite the Italians' lack of enthusiasm, Operation Foca went ahead, resulting in hundreds of dead, wounded and prisoners.

On 20 May 1942, the quartermaster of *Kampfgruppe* Bader reported that nearly 500 prisoners had been handed over to the SS and sent on to slave labour camps in Norway. It was alleged, not least by the US Justice Department, that Waldheim had been involved in this handover of prisoners.

The partisans under Tito had regrouped around a thickly wooded plateau in the Kozara hills. By now, they had become a positive danger to the German occupation forces, attacking installations and even threatening the Belgrade-to-Zagreb railway line. The Ustachis failed to secure the area, and the newly formed *Kampfgruppe* West Bosnia was told to 'take out' the partisans. It was to this battle group that Waldheim was then sent.

In May, Waldheim was posted, first, to Sarajevo, and then to Croatia (now in north-west Yugoslavia). At Banja Luka at the foot of the Kozara hills, where the *Kampfgruppe* had its

19

headquarters, he became an 'O2' officer – assistant adjutant to the quartermaster – on the face of it, strange sort of work for someone who had so recently been running a liaison/intelligence operation. However, in a document of June 1942, the quartermaster for the Nazi commander in Belgrade stated that among the duties of the quartermaster's department of *Kampfgruppe* West Bosnia was prisoner deportations. The battle group was instructed to reach an agreement with the Nazi puppet state of Croatia to send prisoners to Belgrade; once there, they were sent to death camps in the surrounding area.

During the 45-day Kozara campaign of June/July 1942, when 25,000 Axis troops swept through the mountains, capturing and killing, more than 130 villages were put to the torch. It is estimated that a total of 68,000 Croatians – partisans and civilians – died in battle or in the concentration camps to which they were sent after capture.

On 25 March 1986, when an Austrian TV interviewer asked him whether Kozara had been a massacre, Waldheim replied, 'That's ridiculous. It was nothing like a massacre, but there was heavy fighting...' In April, he told a Belgrade newspaper: 'I made a mistake when I said I was in the Kozara area. My son and I have analysed everything and have come to the conclusion that I was in Plevlje at that time. Later, I saw that this area was some geographical distance from Banja Luka and Kozara where the great battle of 1942 took place.' Finally, in November 1986, Waldheim asserted that he wasn't involved in any fighting, and that, as a quartermaster, he'd have had nothing to do with operational matters.

On 22 July 1942, Waldheim was awarded (according to his paybook) the King Zvonimir medal in silver with an oak cluster by the Croatian Fascist leader Ante Pavolic. The citation, signed by General Friedrich von Stahl (the notorious officer largely responsible for the Kozara massacre), stated that the medal had been awarded 'for heroic bravery in the battle against insurgents', and Waldheim's name appeared third on the citation list. It was alleged that the awarding of Waldheim with this medal at this level is significant, that the oak cluster meant that he'd been involved in the fighting. Waldheim, however, has said that it was a minor medal, 'handed out like chocolates', and he pointed out that there were 915 other names on the citation list and it was also given to the doctor and the chaplain.

Waldheim's paybook shows that, by 26 September, he'd been transferred to Arsakli, a town in the mountains some four miles from Salonika in north-west Greece and headquarters of the German Forces South-east, which covered all of northern and southern Greece. Waldheim's duties involved serving as an interpreter. This assignment didn't last long for, on 19 November, he returned to Vienna for a study leave of 4½ months, until (again according to his paybook) 31 March 1943.

It was alleged that *Oberleutnant* Waldheim – he had been promoted to first lieutenant on 1 December – returned to Salonika at the beginning of April 1943. His return then would have coincided with the major deportation of tens of thousands of Jews from that city to Auschwitz, which had started on 15 March and continued until August. Waldheim has denied this. He told a US news programme on 7 March 1986, 'Never until this day have I heard or been informed about the mass arrest of Jews in Salonika.' In his statement to the US Department of Justice of 12 April 1986, he claims that he was assigned to the German liaison staff to interpret for the Italians in Tirana, the capital of Albania: 'I was away from Arsakli both for the whole of the terrible deportation atrocities and preceding events in Salonika in 1943 (departure in mid-November 1942; returned via Tirana in early July 1943).'

However, an earlier form of the same statement, dated 6 April 1986, read: '...(departure in mid-November 1942; returned *April 1943*)' [my italics]. Yet a third version of this chronology was reported in *Der Spiegel* on 14 April 1986:

WALDHEIM: Our staff HQ were in Arsakli, in a mountainous area 6 kilometres from Salonika...We were isolated there, it was like living in a cloister. The deportation of the Jews wasn't even talked about in the officers' club.

DER SPIEGEL: That's strange – the Jews were deported from Salonika between mid-March and May 1943 at the time you were stationed there.

21

WALDHEIM: No, between November 1942 and sometime in April 1943, I was on study leave back home. It's in the documents...I couldn't have known anything. I saw very little of the town itself and definitely no Jewish deportations.

Waldheim's critics pointed to the differences between the dates given – the paybook date of 31 March and Waldheim's recollection of both early July and April – all of which were crucial in determining whether or not Waldheim was in Arsakli during this period and, thus, whether or not he knew about the deportation of the Jews. None of this meant that Waldheim was necessarily involved in any way – but, I thought, it would be interesting to know why he denied knowledge of the deportation and why he changed his story.

On 15 May 1943, Operation *Schwarz* ('Black') began, with the aim of destroying the remaining partisans in Montenegro and East Herzogovina. A battle took place, involving the Italians, Croatian Fascists and the much-feared German Prinz Eugen Division. It was a particularly vicious campaign – the excesses of the Prinz Eugen Division were so great that even a German officer complained about them – and it was alleged that 16,000 partisans and civilians died.

On 22 May, Waldheim travelled with the liaison staff to Podgorica (now Titograd) in Montenegro. Here he was photographed with SS *Obergruppenführer* Arthur Phleps (commander of the Prinz Eugen Division), *Oberst* Joachim Macholz and the Italian general, Escola Roncaglia. It was alleged that, after these three met, Operation *Schwarz* increased in intensity. Waldheim claims that he was just there as an interpreter, ironing out differences of opinion between the Italians and the Germans. He totally denies involvement, saying in his statement to the US Department of Justice, 'I was involved neither in Operation Black nor in "Operation White".'

On 19 July 1943, Waldheim was in Athens with the German/Italian liaison staff. He had now become assistant adjutant to the operations officer Lt Colonel Bruno Willers, and his name appears as the keeper of his unit's war diary. Many entries in this daily secret diary relate to reprisals – for example:

Greece

Appropriate instructions are being sent to the 1st Mountain Division concerning treatment of bandits [partisans]. According to a new order from the Führer, bandits captured in battle are to be shot. Others suspected of banditry, etc. are to be taken prisoner and sent to Germany for use in labour details.

Under international law and the Nuremberg principles, the deportation of civilians for slave labour is defined as both a war crime and a crime against humanity. The onward transmission of the orders to the 1st Mountain Division would have to have come from either Waldheim or his superior Willers. Waldheim claims that the keeping of the war diary did not constitute a power of command – his role was strictly clerical.

On 8 September 1943, Waldheim's war changed radically, for on that day, General Eisenhower announced that, five days earlier, the Italians had surrendered to the Allied forces. On 22 September, Waldheim signed a report of a phone briefing. This gave a 1st Lt Frey at Army Group E headquarters in Arsakli details of the plans for the removal of what were now Italian prisoners-of-war, and included the fact that 4500 Italians were to be retained in Athens as a labour detail. Significantly, he informed Lt Frey how many trains would be necessary to complete the deportation of the rest of the Italians, who numbered in the tens of thousands.

Waldheim maintains that he was merely a functionary, and did not initiate the orders. He further claims, in a November 1986 document, that the operations with which he has been linked were 'evacuations', not 'deportations'. However, his denials were regarded with scepticism by many. In the report to Lt Frey, he employed the phrase 'for use as labour' when referring to the 4500 Italians to be detained in Athens.

By Christmas Day, Waldheim was back in Arsakli. Although he was diagnosed as suffering from a thyroid condition on 15 January 1944, he remained at his desk. Four days later, he initialled a document marked 'Secret Command Business' and, in his own handwriting, altered some of its contents. Where it stated that the Greek resistance comprised 40,000 'fighters', he crossed out 'fighters' and replaced it with 'men'. In further handwritten, initialled remarks, he stressed that Greek resistance was less formidable than the report indicated: 'Strengths of reserves with 40,000 men *possible*, but cannot be counted on as combatants, as weapons lacking. Also with regard to the 30,000 described as sufficiently armed.' He also commented that certain Greek forces were anti-Communist, and noted his personal agreement with some of the intelligence assessments in the report. These alterations and comments were thought by many to be highly significant, since they showed him to have been something more than the functionary and clerk that today he says he was.

On 25 February, Waldheim went on sick leave. Shortly after he returned to duty, on 14 April, he travelled to Austria to be awarded his doctorate by the University of Vienna. Waldheim returned to Arsakli two days later, and rejoined the Ic/AO — i.e. intelligence/counter-intelligence *(Abwehr)* — section. According to a duty roster dated 1 December 1943, which describes job breakdowns, Waldheim's duties included 'prisoner interrogation' and '*Sonderaufgaben*' ('special tasks'). The latter usually referred to reprisals (i.e. executions) and propaganda duties. Waldheim claims that he was definitely not an *Abwehr*

24

officer, he never interrogated anyone, and was merely a 'paper pusher'. He says that he never even conversed with the *Abwehr* officers.

Between 24 March and mid-July, messages were sent from Waldheim's unit in Arsakli to German intelligence units operating in the Aegean. Some of these messages were signed by Waldheim, and all of them were stamped by the Ic/AO section. In addition, there were other types of paperwork. In a July monthly report, initialled by Waldheim, Ic/AO duties are outlined, including 'interrogation of these prisoners from the Anglo-American Military Mission in Greece'. Other documents also refer to these prisoners, saying that those no longer required for interrogation should be turned over to the SD *(Sicherheitsdienst*, 'security police') for 'special treatment' – i.e. execution.

In his evidence to the US Justice Department of April 1986, Waldheim said: 'On the documents, my signature can be clearly seen under the letters "FDR" – that is to say, "*Für die Richtigkeit*", or "copy certified correct". Anyone who works in an office can tell you what that means.'

During that period, Allied commandos were captured by the Germans in the Aegean. For example, on 7 April 1944, seven Special Boat Service commandos (six British and one Australian) and three Greek partisans were caught and sent to Rhodes. Americans were also captured, among them James Doughty, who today is one of the few survivors of these seaborne missions, and who claims to have been interrogated at Arsakli. Waldheim says that he himself never interrogated prisoners, and that no interrogations were carried out at Arsakli.

From May to August 1944, thousands of Jews from Rhodes, Crete and Corfu were deported to concentration camps. Various documents concerning these deportations passed through Waldheim's office as evinced by the 'Ic/AO' stamp on them. One, dated 22 September, speaks of the deportation of Jews '...upon instruction of the High Command of Army Group E Ic/AO'. This would tend to suggest that, at the very least, Waldheim was aware of the deportations. However, he now denies any knowledge of deportations of Jews from the Greek islands.

On 11 August, Waldheim signed a document that contained a report of Operation *Kreuzotter* ('Viper') involving activity between partisans and German troops on Crete: 'During operations in south-west Iráklion, numerous arrests. Two partisan villages destroyed, 20 hostages shot to death...' This document was used at Nuremberg during the prosecution of 12 officers charged with the mass murder of hostages.

Waldheim put all this unpleasantness behind him when, on 19 August, he returned to Baden to marry Elizabeth ('Cissy') Ritschel. He returned to Arsakli on 3 September. That autumn, the tide began to turn against the Germans, and the army in the Balkans started its retreat. On 12 October, Waldheim signed two reports concerning partisan activity in the towns of Stip and Kocane, about 160 kilometres (100 miles) from Arsakli, in southern Yugoslavia. On 13/14 October, the headquarters of Army Group E moved from Arsakli to Stari Trg in Macedonia. It was on these dates that German reprisals are thought to have taken place against three villages on the Stip-Kocane road – a result of partisans attacking German targets. Villagers were lined up by the side of the road and shot, and men, women and children were herded into their houses, which were then burned down.

The Yugoslav government alleges that Waldheim was responsible for the intelligence directives that initiated these reprisals. In his defence, Waldheim maintains that he and his fellow officers flew from Arsakli to Pristina, 130 kilometres (80 miles) from the Stip-Kocane road, and then completed the journey to Stari Trg by road. 'I can assure you,' he said on 3 March 1986, '...I couldn't have taken part in the burning of villages or reprisals – to say nothing of executions.' To the US Justice Department in August 1986, he stated, 'This incident was not a massacre or a reprisal. It was simply a military operation designed to facilitate an orderly German retreat.'

By 15 November, Army Group E headquarters had withdrawn even further from the Allied advance – to Sarajevo. On 3 December, a packet of propaganda material was received by Waldheim's Ic/AO section. This material was to be dropped in enemy areas, and contained at least two virulently anti-Semitic leaflets, one of which included the phrase 'Kill the Jews and come over to us.' Waldheim's initials appear on a receipt stamp on the covering letter.

Fighting continued to go against the Germans in the Balkans, and by March 1945, Army Group E had withdrawn to Zagreb, 100 kilometres (60 miles) from the Austrian border. Somehow, Waldheim managed to return home to his family in Vienna. He was then posted to a fighting unit, but had not yet made contact with it when he heard that Hitler was dead. He returned to Vienna and later gave himself up to a US documentation centre, where he was kept for a time. When he was released, he obtained signed affidavits that stated that he had always been anti-Nazi, and he then applied for government work.

It is widely believed that, at the end of the war, Waldheim was in the hands of the Americans, and most probably dealt with the Office of Strategic Services (OSS), the forerunner of the CIA. He was helped to get his first job with the new democratic Austrian government by Fritz Molden, one of the Allies' top agents who had worked with the OSS. This no doubt resulted from the best of motives, and in the belief that, with his background at the Vienna Consular Academy and his languages, Waldheim would be very useful in the world of diplomacy.

He occupied various posts for his government in Paris before becoming Ambassador to Canada. In 1955, he led Austria's first delegation to the United Nations, was appointed Director General for Foreign Affairs in 1960 and, in 1964, became Austrian Ambassador to the UN. Between 1968 and 1970, he served as Federal Minister for Foreign Affairs before returning to the UN as Permanent Representative. The following year, he entered Austrian politics by running, unsuccessfully, for President as the right-wing People's Party candidate.

Also in 1971, the Secretary-General of the UN, U Thant, retired, and the superpowers began to line up their candidates to fill the job. Initially, the United States supported someone from Latin America, whereas Britain and France proposed Max Jacobson, the Finnish ambassador, who was eminently well qualified for the position. Surprisingly, it was the Soviet Union that put forward the name of Kurt Waldheim −

surprisingly, because a former Yugoslav spy by the name of Kolendic still claims that, in 1947, he had handed a file to the Soviets, which alleged war crimes by Waldheim.

This may be the same as or similar to the Odluka, the war crimes file compiled by the Yugoslav government immediately after the war; this claimed that, among others, Waldheim was a Category A war criminal for his involvement in murder and the execution of hostages. The Odluka was sent to the War Crimes Commission in London, and in December 1947, the WCC passed their documentation on to the UN.

It is difficult not to speculate that the United States, too – through the OSS and then the CIA – knew about Waldheim's war record at the time of the UN negotiations for the new Secretary-General. Why then did the US eventually join with the Soviet Union in supporting Waldheim for the top UN job?

Kurt Waldheim remained Secretary-General from 1972 to 1982. In that role, he could fairly be described as the top civil servant in the world, but one with no actual executive power – a fact that increasingly frustrated him as the years passed. During his time in office, he saw the Yom Kippur war and the tragedy of the Lebanon, the Turkish invasion of Cyprus and the Soviet invasion of Afghanistan. He oversaw the world while the painful war in Vietnam burned itself out, and tried without success to persuade the Iranians under the ayatollahs to release the US embassy hostages. And he met the heads of state and government of most of the 158 member countries of the United Nations.

To the world at large, Kurt Waldheim was a model public servant. He was described as hard working and conscientious, but he seemed to have a great difficulty in making decisions. Some of the UN staff that I spoke to said that he was icy and distant to all but his very top staff, yet would be effusively charming to important heads of state when they came to visit. He was particularly worried about the image he presented to the world.

During his career at the UN, there was only one hiccup. In 1980, US Congressman Stephen J. Solarz of New York wrote to Waldheim asking him about his record in World War II. Solarz was told that, as he was a representative of one of the countries on the War Crimes Commission, he was entitled to see Waldheim's file, but despite promises, he was never given access to it.

Others had made allegations about Waldheim's war record, but every time the Secretary-General repeated the narrative that would eventually find its way into his autobiography – that, for him, active service had ceased that day in December 1941 when he was injured on the Eastern Front. Sir Brian Urquhart, former Under-Secretary-General of the UN and someone who worked closely with Waldheim for many years, has said, 'Waldheim invariably and strongly reaffirmed this story. For lack of evidence to the contrary, we all accepted this version.' Solarz did not pursue the matter, and things went quiet for another five years or so.

Then Waldheim's decision to run again for the Austrian presidency precipitated a veritable deluge of accusations. Many came from the World Jewish Congress (WJC), whose motivations are not difficult to deduce, but others came from sources without such an obvious axe to grind. For example, when Yugoslav journalists unearthed the Odluka file from the archives in Belgrade, they put the charges found in it to Waldheim. His staff and the presidential candidate himself denied everything, maintaining that virtually all members of the *Wehrmacht* who had served in Yugoslavia during the war had found themselves on the Yugoslav government's 'wanted' list, and that the latter's accusations had also been part of a political plot against the emergent democracy in Austria. In addition, according to Waldheim, the Yugoslav evidence was based on the false testimony of Joachim Mayer, a German who had been a prisoner-of-war in Yugoslavia. Waldheim says that Mayer later told his wife that he'd only made this statement to get himself returned to Germany, and had chosen to accuse Waldheim because he knew that the Austrian had already left the country and was, therefore, untouchable. Waldheim also claimed that the man was later convicted of petty crimes in Germany. Who, he asked, could believe such a man's testimony?

Waldheim has consistently denied any evidence that might implicate him in anything – evidence gathered not only by the WJC, the Yugoslav government and journalists, but also by academics such as Professor Irwin Cotler of McGill University in Montreal and Professor Robert Herzstein of the University of South Carolina, and others such as the British historian and Member of Parliament, Robert Rhodes James. His detractors maintain that Waldheim has consistently lied during this period. Waldheim, in his defence, says that, initially, when he was asked for an instant response to events that had happened over 40 years before, he had given answers off the top of his head. Later, after some research, he understandably had to change his answers slightly. This didn't convince his former deputy, Sir Brian Urquhart. In his autobiography *A Life in Peace and War*, he denounces his erstwhile boss:

Waldheim, it has now become clear, lied for nearly 40 years about his war record, presumably believing that the truth would stand in the way of his relentless pursuit of public position and office. Waldheim emerging as a living lie has done immense damage not only to his own country but to the United Nations.

Nor did it convince the US government. After investigating Waldheim for over a year, the Justice Department (through its Office of Special Investigations) placed Waldheim on the so-called 'Watch List' on 27 April 1987. This is maintained by the US Immigration and Naturalization Service through an automated visa lookout system, and alerts consular officials that the individuals named on it are ineligible for a US visa. This effectively prohibits Waldheim from entering the United States − a shocking thing to happen to someone who was (and is) the president of a friendly country.

In conformity with the Holtzman Amendment (which forbids actions against people on the grounds of race, religion, national origin or political opinion), the Office of Special Investigations placed Waldheim on the 'Watch List' because, it claimed, he had 'participated in activities amounting to persecution... of Jews and others in Greece and Yugoslavia during World War II... [and] had assisted or otherwise participated in the persecution of persons because of race, religion, national origin or political opinion.' The OSI cited his involvement in: the use of civilian prisoners by the SS for exploitation as slave labour; the deportations of civilians, including those from Yugoslavia and Jews from the Greek islands, to concentration and death camps; the use of anti-Semitic propaganda; the turning over of Allied prisoners to a branch of the SS; and the harsh Nazi policies that terrorized the Greek population through mass deportations and reprisal executions.

The decision to ban Waldheim from the United States affects Dr Waldheim only as an individual, not as a head of state. It would be possible for the US government to extend an invitation to Waldheim as President of Austria, but it is difficult to imagine this ever happening.

As I looked through the relevant newspaper cuttings and read transcripts of Waldheim's answers to various radio and television interviewers, it certainly appeared that he'd changed his story. His opponents said that there was a distinct pattern, similar to that of past known war criminals. First, a flat denial. Then, when more evidence was available, denials of any responsibility. Finally, in the face of yet more evidence, the suggestion that what had happened was merely part of a war, and all wars are nasty.

However, all these accusations and denials ignore one vital question: what is the degree of culpability of any young man or woman thrust into a war through no fault of his or her own?

Before World War II, Waldheim seems to have been known more for his serious attitude towards his studies than for either his sporting or combative activities. He was forced into an army that, by its nature, was particularly brutal. He was aged between 23 and 25 during the years in question. He was a lieutenant and then a first lieutenant; he was neither a general dictating the direction that the war would take, nor was he a front-line soldier who perhaps took pleasure in individual acts of brutality.

Apart from the obvious one of whether or not he deliberately did anything that led to breaches of the Geneva Convention or other humanitarian criteria, other questions had to be asked. If he hadn't liked the orders he was given — perhaps because he thought they were morally wrong — could he have refused to obey them without being taken outside and

31

shot? Faced with such a dilemma, how many other young men of his age and rank would have refused to be a party to such illegal actions?

We did know that there were men in the German army who did refuse orders for moral reasons, and there was evidence that at least some of them were merely moved to other divisions or to the front and were not punished. But whether Waldheim was aware of this was, so far, unknown.

It could be argued that he was, after all, only a young man who had been drafted into the army and ended up with a job that he felt he had to do to keep alive and for the sake of his family. As a result of his duties, he found himself in a position of knowing some unpleasant facts — facts that he certainly wouldn't want to make public many years later when, as he saw it, he was making a major contribution towards world peace. None of us, I suspect, would rattle our family skeletons unless we had a very good reason to do so. However, most of us are not public figures, models of behaviour to the rest of the world.

These were difficult questions, and ones that, in my mind, had to be addressed by any Waldheim inquiry that we might come up with. But first, we had to evolve a judicial form that would accommodate both the moral issues and the evidence, and be acceptable to our co-producers Home Box Office, to Gerry Spence, and to the other eminent lawyers we would be approaching.

2

Take Off

I was accustomed, in the general run of television current affairs programmes, to persuading people to take part in studio discussions, getting them to agree to straight interviews on some topical and controversial subject, or even getting them to defend or attack one side of an argument. But for this programme, I would be asking senior counsel and extremely eminent judges to commit themselves for weeks and months to a project on which could rest jealously guarded reputations painstakingly built up over decades. It wasn't going to be easy.

However, before I could approach anyone of the necessary calibre, the format of the programme had to be much further refined, and to that end, David Elstein arranged a meeting in New York with Thames' co-producers, Home Box Office and Gerry Spence, for 19 June 1987.

David Elstein, Thames' director of programmes (and the man who got me into this in the first place), and I set out from London that morning. We had an uneventful flight, paid a brief visit to the office of Thames' New York agent Don Taffner, and then made our way to HBO's offices on the Avenue of the Americas. We had time only to admire the marvellous view of the Empire State Building outside the windows before we were introduced to Bridget Potter, senior vice president in charge of original programming. My first impression of Bridget was of a hard-working, effective, hard-negotiating New York lady; little did I know then what a tower of strength, help and support she was to become. Also there to meet David and me was Colin Callender. Colin is British and has his own production company in London, but he was then working for HBO as an executive producer and was very involved in our project.

And there was Gerry Spence, exactly as I'd remembered him from LWT's *Trial of Lee Harvey Oswald*: well over six foot tall, laid back with a slow drawl, dressed in jeans with an open-necked sports shirt and (particularly impressive to me) a fringed suede jacket, snakeskin belt and matching high-heeled cowboy boots. With him was his agent Tony Fantozzi, a charming, amusing character whom I instinctively liked.

The preliminaries over, we settled down to tackle the judicial side of the programme. I told my colleagues about the discussions I'd had with various eminent legal minds, and that the concept of laying charges against Waldheim in a trial was, from the beginning, a non-starter.

The same could be said for having a jury, I continued. The background of World War II against which the case would be decided — and which remained fresh in the memories of many — made it vitally important that Waldheim be dealt with fairly and as an individual. Our programme must not be seen as a way of making him pay for the sins of others. Because of this, I firmly believed that what we required, only professional judges could give. Their training, experience and skill would ensure, as far as humanly possible, that their judgement would be based, not on their emotions, no matter how appalling the evidence, but on the facts — and only as they applied to the accused. And if this were true in any run-of-the-mill criminal case, it would have to be even more so in the context of our programme.

We talked about all of this at length, and during our discussion, I was happy to discover that Telford Taylor, whom HBO had contracted to act as a consultant on the programme, shared my qualms about having a jury. Once a brigadier general and now a professor of law, Telford Taylor had also been on the US prosecution team at the Nuremberg trials, and today is perhaps the world's leading authority in the area of war crimes. He had recommended a commission of inquiry as a format for our programme.

Gerry Spence eventually accepted these arguments, even though he was, in effect, relinquishing an opportunity to display his powerfully persuasive effect on a jury. However, this inquiry was going to be unique, something out of the experience of all of us, and it required a different approach. We agreed that, to give breadth to the bench, we should have five judges, all from different countries. We would also need to appoint a defending lawyer of the highest calibre – Gerry was, of course, lined up to take the prosecution. Once we'd overcome these hurdles, we would call a meeting, probably in London, which both counsel and either the chairman of the judges or all of them would attend. There, they would decide the rules of procedure, rules of evidence, what was or was not admissible, and how evidence could be procured. For example, it could be that a 75-year-old witness in Upper Bavaria was too ill or infirm or was simply not prepared to come to London for the recording. In that case, would they accept an affidavit sworn locally, or could we record on tape or film – in the presence of, say, junior counsel – a statement and cross-examination taken *in situ*?

In addition, the judges and lawyers would have to decide which definition of 'war crimes' they would apply to the evidence. There were many alternatives. As well as the Geneva and Hague conventions, there was the London Charter that led to the four charges of Nuremberg, including crimes against humanity and crimes against peace; there was also the Holtzman Amendment in the United States. Finally, the legal minds would have to decide their own terms of reference – the style of the inquiry and the wording of their own briefs.

If people of the calibre I hoped to persuade to take part in the programme were to make these decisions, I said, I had no fear of others denigrating the methodology or integrity of our project. I could then truthfully say that it was not television that had 'tried' Kurt Waldheim.

We then turned our attention to the political impact the programme could have. If the judges found that, at the very least, there was a *prima facie* case for Waldheim to answer, would he be forced to resign as President of Austria? He might sniff at all the evidence emanating from the World Jewish Congress, evidence that was appearing almost daily in the world's newspapers – none of it was conclusive, none of it proved anything beyond a reasonable doubt, none of it remotely resembled a 'smoking pistol'. He could shrug off all of this, saying it was the work of his enemies or of the enemies of his country.

However, if all the evidence — what we might find following a massive trawl, plus all that was already available — were presented in a cogent form, together with witnesses who could back it up, even under cross-examination, what then? Could it still be challenged as media hype, even if the job were done properly, with an impeccable defence counsel and a panel of five very senior, dispassionate judges who, on the evidence alone, found that there was, in effect, a case to answer? Would the Austrians still want President Waldheim?

Conversely, what if, despite all these efforts, the inquiry were to find Waldheim clean as a whistle, that none of the evidence was sufficiently damning to warrant anything other than a total clearing of his name? Would the US Department of Justice remove his name from the 'Watch List', or would this force them to publish their own evidence? Would such a judgement from our inquiry end Waldheim's status as the pariah of Europe? So far, with the exception of the Vatican, no single Western state had invited him to visit in his role as president. Would all this change?

These were the heavy thoughts that occupied us through much of the afternoon. In addition, there was talk of distribution rights, back-end adjustments, up-front money, slices off the top and a plethora of other co-production minutiae that simply passed over my head. I was too aware of the magnitude of the task that had been entrusted to me, of the responsibility that was resting on my shoulders.

Oddly enough, I was also euphoric. At that first meeting of the founding mother and fathers of the Waldheim project, there was an enthusiastic belief that we were going to do something that was momentous in the history of television. We talked about making a film of the making of the programme (with accompanying book); we even airily discussed putting whatever money the programme might make into a fund to encourage other adventurous uses of television. At that moment, we certainly believed that we were breaking new ground.

At seven o'clock, an air-conditioned limousine was waiting to take David and me to Kennedy to catch a flight back to

36

London. It had been a long way to go just for a meeting – 7000-odd miles there and back. However, I felt that, given the importance of the project we were about to undertake – a television programme that could literally alter history – it would have been worth travelling around the world.

Back in London, our next port of call was the offices of Channel 4 on Charlotte Street, to meet Liz Forgan and our new commissioning editor David Lloyd. David Elstein and I reported on our meeting at Home Box Office, and the conclusions that had been reached concerning the legal format of the programme. It was not difficult getting the agreement of Channel 4. Liz had believed in the programme from the first moment, but David Lloyd needed a bit more convincing; like many others, he was worried about the moral aspects. After much discussion, however, he too accepted our reasoning and our methodology.

By this time, I had also asked a leading libel lawyer for his opinion on the likelihood of Thames and HBO facing either an injunction or, after transmission, a libel action.

It was the view of our barrister that, provided we set up the programme fairly, and particularly if Waldheim's defence counsel were a balanced match for the prosecution, then an injunction stopping transmission would not be granted. Our main concern, however, revolved around the possibility of a libel action being taken out by Waldheim after transmission. Fortunately, it was the view of our lawyer that if Waldheim were to sue, we could mount a successful defence, given the way the programme was to be constructed.

Another hurdle vaulted.

Even as I was conferring with our co-producers in New York, the Waldheim project research network was beginning to take shape under the direction of our chief researcher Ed Braman. Asking him to take on this was the best decision I made during the year that it took to make the programme.

After getting a degree in English from Cambridge University, Ed had worked in local radio, finishing up at London's top commercial station, Capital Radio. Now Capital is better known for its pop music than for its intellectual content, and when

Ed came to Thames Television to be interviewed for a job as researcher on *Reporting London*, which I was then editing, I'd been dubious about his professional experience. However, within five minutes of his coming into the room where the appointments board was sitting, there was little doubt that he had got the job. What I didn't suspect then was that this was a man who was tailor-made for a programme that, at that stage, was only a twinkle in Gerry Spence's eye.

Ed is still half an academic with a mind that is orderly, organized and massively hard working. He has good contacts in both the academic and the post-graduate worlds, and he knows his way around computer programs – expertise that I, being completely computer illiterate, badly needed. He also speaks fluent German, and, finally, was young and enthusiastic enough to throw himself into the Waldheim project as if nothing else in life existed. And for him, for the next eight months, very little else did!

Our research effort was to be spread over half-a-dozen countries. In terms of archive material and witnesses, it would be principally based in West Germany, Austria, Yugoslavia, Greece and Italy, although we would also be seeing what we could find in East Germany and Albania. In Italy, for example, we would be looking for men who had been in the Pusteria Division of the Italian army, with whom Waldheim (in his role of interpreter and liaison officer) might have had dealings. Some former Italian soldiers might also have been among those who had been deported as POWs or for use as slave labour. Israel, the Soviet Union, Britain and the United States would not escape our searches – in fact, we would hunt wherever we thought witnesses and documents might be found.

The researchers that Ed found were a mixture of academics and journalists. The former were either post-graduate students – some doing research in this area for their doctoral theses – or fully fledged historians of high repute who agreed to work with, and sometimes for, us when our work coincided with their own or simply because they were interested in the subject matter. Of the journalists, many were natives of the countries in which we were searching for evidence, but academics and journalists alike were contracted because they filled the same two basic requirements: total fluency in the local language and a determination to leave no document unread, no witness uninterviewed.

By now, the name and person of President Waldheim had become part of my everyday life. He appeared in everything I read. He intruded into even the most trivial of conversations. My life had begun to revolve around the man. I decided that, in fairness to him, he should be told in detail – and by me – what was going on... provided, that is, he was prepared to see me.

We were now into July. Ed Braman had spent the early part of the summer working in Austria with a brilliant young journalist, Hubertus Czernin, who was covering the Waldheim story for the Austrian magazine *Profil*. Together they had been finding out everything about Waldheim that was in the public domain.

In the course of his research, interviews and meetings, Ed had met Dr Gerhard Waldheim, the President's banker son. He told Ed that, if he wanted any contact with the elder Waldheim, he would have to go through official channels. This turned out to be the President's personal secretary, Dr Ralph Scheide.

I rang Dr Scheide in Vienna and told him that I wanted to meet the President, to tell him in person about the programme. Scheide already seemed to know quite a few details about the project, but asked me to send a letter outlining it as a preliminary to a meeting. Once this had been sent, I received a letter granting me an appointment for the afternoon of Wednesday, 15 July 1987, at the Hofburg Palace, Waldheim's official residence.

That morning, Ed Braman, Barrie Sales and I flew into Vienna airport and took a taxi to the world-famous Hotel Sacher, one of Mozart's favourite haunts. It was easy to imagine that, no matter what upheavals had occurred outside its walls, very little had changed inside. I only had time for a brisk wash and a quick look at my notes before Barrie, Ed and I got into the taxi that would take us to the Hofburg. Ed had tried unsuccessfully to convince us that, while it was a ten-minute taxi ride to the Palace, it was only a five-minute walk.

What with the hot weather and my own tension, the last thing I wanted was to arrive in a pool of sweat.

As we waited in the ante-chamber, I desperately tried to rehearse what I was going to say. But before I had time to do more than go over the basics, a door opened and there stood President Waldheim. He apologized with great politeness for keeping us waiting, and held open the door for us to enter his office. It was a room to wonder at − elegant and comfortable, it has probably seen more history than any gathering of historians.

Barrie, Ed and I sat, not in front of the President's desk, but around a small rectangular conference table, where we were joined by Dr Waldheim and his secretary Dr Scheide. After accepting the President's very much appreciated offer of some cold, fresh orange juice, I took a deep breath and began explaining in detail exactly what our programme would be attempting.

Waldheim listened in silence. When I'd finished, he stated that the whole thing was a conspiracy. 'It's part of the Waldheim industry,' he said, and complained that only the evidence against him ever hit the headlines; his side of the story was either ignored or under-reported.

'That,' I pointed out, 'is why we have decided to make the programme in the style that I have explained. We wish to be totally fair. We believe that, by making the programme in this way, no wild accusations can remain unchallenged. No evidence that is unsupported will carry any weight.' I continued by saying that I believed that this was the fairest possible way of looking at the evidence both for and against him.

'It may well be the fairest programme that is ever made on the subject,' he replied. But then he added, and for the first time, his coldly polite manner was replaced by a not-so-cold anger, 'However, only the Austrian people have the right to "try" me − and this, in effect, is what they have done by voting me in as President.' He pointed out that, in a recent opinion poll, support for him had risen to over 60 per cent. 'Besides,' he added, 'the Austrian government has commissioned a group of historians to look into the allegations. I don't need television − even well-intentioned television − to make programmes like the one you are suggesting.'

As the tension became almost palpable, Barrie and Ed remained silent. I continued by saying, as politely as I could, that more than anyone President Waldheim would know of his own innocence if that were the case, and a programme like ours could only exonerate him. (It didn't seem apposite at that moment and in that place to mention the other possible result!)

With some temerity, I went on: 'Not only are you condemned by the press at the moment, but a lot of the evidence that the papers are using is coming from historians − the very people who will be informing posterity about their views on your guilt or innocence. Your commission of historians may indeed come down heavily on your side, but will anyone believe it, given that it has been set up and paid for by *your* government and is answerable to them? However, because our inquiry is going to be totally dispassionate, absolutely objective, a result in your favour will do you immense good.'

'If you were to search for a hundred years, Mr Saltman,' President Waldheim replied, 'you will find no evidence that will reveal me as a war criminal.'

And that brought the 45-minute conversation to an end. We rose, and the President walked over to the door and held it open for us. We solemnly shook hands with the greatest civility and took our leave of the man who would fill my waking (and, undoubtedly, my dreaming) hours for the next 11 months.

Dr Sheide walked us back through the endless series of museum-like rooms, and then paused as we reached the top of the staircase leading outside. We talked there for a further 20 minutes, Waldheim's secretary assuring us that any reasonable requests for information would be sympathetically dealt with. Then, on the best of terms, we left.

We returned to the Sacher, this time on foot. I undid my tie in the merciless sun. It had been a strange meeting.

When I told friends in London about my encounter with President Waldheim, they all wanted a quick assessment of his reaction. Then, I said, 'It was 43 minutes of restrained fury, and for two minutes, it was unrestrained.' However, looking

41

back, I now think that 'fury' was the wrong word.

Waldheim is nothing if not a massively proud man — the words 'arrogant' and 'overbearing' are frequently used to describe him. He must have been hugely affronted to have to listen to a mere television producer telling how a British and an American television company intended, with or without his permission, to examine allegations against his good name.

That for most of the interview he maintained an icy, very reserved but absolutely correct posture reflected his years as the world's top civil servant. Here was a man, the grandson of a blacksmith and the son of a school teacher, who had risen to the top, not only of his own country, but of the 158 countries that comprise the UN. And all this achievement was to be totally ignored, while a mere three years — in a lifetime of almost 70 — were to be questioned, not by the due process of law, but by television.

3

Early Problems

The rest of the summer was spent sending researchers around Europe in pursuit of evidence. Holidays were dispensed with in our determined attempt to gather all the information already available about Kurt Waldheim, and to make an assessment of what might become available given enough time and money.

The tip of the iceberg was to be found in computer libraries: these held over 5000 stories culled from newspapers around the world. However, many of them were merely re-writes of what other journalists had written, and as I plodded through story after story, it soon became apparent which writers had done some actual legwork − for example, visited someone with an original line − and which had written their stories from what are known in the trade as 'cuts' - press cuttings.

Throughout July, August and September, the file built up, and we came closer to the day when we could make our own judgement as to whether there was enough evidence to make an inquiry into Waldheim's war a feasible proposition. It was also soon time to test the water − to talk to some of the key people we would want to involve in the programme.

I'd first met Lord Rawlinson of Ewell some years earlier when he'd defended Thames Television's interests during a protracted high court case − the company had faced various contempt charges related to a well-intentioned *TV Eye* programme involving a wardship and adoption problem. Therefore, when I approached him with my idea of a Waldheim inquiry, he was already aware that our programmes are well thought out, carefully prepared and transmitted with a great deal of respect for the law.

Lord Rawlinson's own reputation is unimpeachable. A Queen's Counsel (QC) of vast experience, he had been Attorney-General in Edward Heath's Conservative government of 1970-74.

He very kindly agreed to see me at his London home, and it was with a considerable feeling of apprehension and responsibility that, on that Wednesday morning, 14 October, I began to explain our idea in detail. I outlined the concept of the inquiry, and told him that I wanted to persuade five judges to sit and take evidence and then deliver a judgement. Ideally, I wanted one each from the US and the UK, and the remaining three from countries that had remained neutral during World War II – perhaps Ireland, Sweden and Switzerland. I explained the nature of the research teams that we were setting up and the importance that we placed on the research itself. Lord Rawlinson immediately agreed that the very crux of the programme would be the thoroughness of the research.

I next got down to the timetable. We were now in the middle of October. The main thrust of the research would be in place and working by, I hoped, the beginning of November. This would give us four months or a bit more (excluding the two weeks around Christmas and the New Year), taking us to mid-March. I wanted to go into the studio on 11 April to record the inquiry in action for a full nine days. There would then be about a month to edit the final programme, ready for transmission some time in June.

One of my great worries was how we were going to prevent the result of our inquiry leaking to the media before we transmitted it, given that it would have been recorded some weeks before. As I explained to Lord Rawlinson, I thought the solution would be, initially, to record only the bulk of the inquiry in April, and then to summon the entire panel of judges back two or three days before transmission, to deliver judgement. This would give me a couple of days to edit the result of the judges' deliberations on to the rest of the programme.

Lord Rawlinson had the solution – something so obvious that neither I nor my colleagues had thought of it. 'Why not broadcast the result live?' he asked. 'That way, there could be no leaks, and the tension relating to the judges' decision would continue right up to the end.'

I was delighted – for two reasons. First, because I thought his idea was excellent, and second, because he was clearly becoming involved enough in the programme to suggest ways of improving the format.

After that, I shouldn't have been surprised when he added, 'I assume that you're going to ask me to take the role of defence counsel.'

I'd actually been slowly working up to that, but I had my doubts about whether he would take the defence. Perhaps unfairly, I'd thought that most advocates would prefer to prosecute (I use that word only as shorthand), and Gerry Spence had already made it clear that he wanted that role.

I admitted that, yes, I'd been about to ask him to be the defence counsel. I explained that it was crucially important, given Waldheim's own non-appearance, that we provide him with the best defence lawyer possible. I spoke truthfully when I said that I felt we could find no one better than himself.

After some hesitation and many more questions, Lord Rawlinson agreed to take on the role. Not only that, but he also agreed to help with our approaches to various former high court judges, both in the UK and in the US. I was sure that, when it became known that he was actively working for the programme, enlisting the participation of these eminent people would be that much easier.

An hour and a half after entering Lord Rawlinson's book-lined study, I left to head back to the studio. I felt that I'd taken the first real step towards the ultimate transmission of the programme.

Two weeks later, Ed and I were preparing to make a second trip to Vienna, to interview and hand over contracts to the academics and journalists whom we – on the advice of Hubertus Czernin – were considering to take on as our German-speaking researchers. The job descriptions for both types of researchers were very clear. The academics were to hunt through archives, mainly in West and East Germany: Freiburg, Koblenz, Bonn, Berlin, Dresden, Aachen, among many others. First, they were to find names – of officers and men who had served with Waldheim during his Balkan period – and second, to pursue the documents that would point to either his innocent or his guilty involvement.

The documents would be given to our teams of lawyers. The names – the *real* people, all now in their late 60s, 70s or even older – were to passed on to the journalists, who were to interview them, take statements and (we hoped) persuade them to take part in the programme. For many, it would not be easy to tell what they knew; it could mean self-incrimination. We had no idea whether any of them would cooperate. But one thing was sure: if we didn't get real people to testify about their activities during the war, which many of them would rather forget, we would have a very dry programme.

Throughout the afternoon, we interviewed our prospective researchers at the Marriott Hotel, and at the end of the long, tiring day, we were joined for dinner by Hubertus. There were few people in the world who had spent as much time in the pursuit of the truth about Waldheim as Hubertus Czernin – for him, it had become a crusade. This intense, serious aesthete was widely admired for his academic determination to get to the bottom of the Waldheim affair. Not that you'd know it by looking at him: as he cycled about Vienna in his round, untrendy glasses, open-necked shirt and patched jacket, or when he was playing soccer at weekends, it was difficult to imagine that here was a veritable powerhouse of research and, for us, an incalculably valuable source of information and leads. As fortunate as we were that Hubertus had decided to be so generous of his time and interest, his agreeing to help us was primarily because of Ed Braman who, like the Austrian, was now a member of the exclusive band of Waldheim *cognoscenti*.

However, as we ate dinner, my pleasure at the help Hubertus was giving us was dramatically diminished when he dropped a bombshell. 'I have,' he said nonchalantly, 'trawled up to 95 per cent of all the archives, and I don't believe that it's worth spending any more time working in that direction.' My heart sank. All my hopes that our team of researchers, even now beavering away, would find loads of undiscovered information were dashed.

And as if this weren't enough, Hubertus then informed us that he had met Professor Manfred Messerschmidt – a member of the Austrian government's Commission of Historians, who were, coincidentally, also meeting in Vienna – who had hinted fairly strongly that they had discovered a previously unknown witness and that, despite certain pressures, they had every intention of coming out with a very strong conclusion.

This flew in the face of everything we had been led to believe about the Commission. We'd thought that, while they comprised an international group of distinguished historians under the chairmanship of Professor Doctor Hans Rudolph Kurtz of Switzerland, they had neither the funds at their disposal nor the time to investigate the allegations as deeply as they would have wished. And, because the Commission had been set up and paid for by the Austrian government, we'd found it difficult to imagine that the historians – regardless of their very real integrity – would, in the end, deliver any major criticisms of Waldheim's war record.

After Ed and I returned to our suite, having said good-night to Hubertus, we carried on talking about the Commission of Historians. It seemed that we had underestimated their independence. It was just possible that what they had found was dynamite and that, against all the odds, they were going to deliver conclusive proof of Waldheim's guilt. I'd never believed that there was a 'smoking pistol' just waiting to be discovered. But if there were one, and someone else got to it before we did, this could wreck our programme. It was after two o'clock by the time I got to bed, and I woke at three, four and five. It was one of those nights.

After a gloomy breakfast, Ed and I returned to our colossal sitting-room and began another round of interviews. Throughout the morning, a steady stream of would-be researchers passed through our suite. We asked each one for an assessment of what he or she believed might still be found. Not one agreed with Hubertus's depressing prediction. I felt a tiny corner of the gloom lifting.

By lunchtime, we'd given contracts to four historians and one journalist. Because none of the people we had put on the team was in a position to start immediately, we knew that, far from this being the definitive set-up visit to Vienna, we were going to have to return in a couple of weeks for a full day's conference. We believed that, despite Hubertus's statement to the contrary, a systematic search of all available archives had still to be carried out. Together with our Austrian and German researchers, we would have to analyse everything that was known about Waldheim and plan who went where.

Meanwhile, in an attempt to discover what the Commission's position really was, Ed had made contact with its British member, Gerald Flemming, a former Professor of German at the University of Surrey and author of an excellent book on Hitler. They would meet at 5.00 p.m. that afternoon. I, on the other hand, headed for the airport and home.

Fighting off feelings of cold panic had proved exhausting, and I knew that what I really needed was a good night's sleep. However, some time after getting into bed and turning out the light, I was wide awake as the phone rang. It was Ed, reporting that, despite a two-hour meeting with Professor Flemming, he was not much wiser as to what the Commission had found out or how pungent their report was going to be.

November 2 was a Monday. It was also my birthday, but there was little time to celebrate. The day was packed with making final preparations for my next visit to the United States, this time accompanied by Ed. It was going to be one of those 'If it's Wednesday, it must be Washington' sorts of trips.

That day was also significant for an increase in the home-based team's size from three to four. Until then, there had only been myself, Ed and Susie Harrison who, as our production secretary, did everything the two of us hadn't or couldn't do. Susie also spoke German and was our organizer and touchstone. Now we welcomed our fourth member, Peter Smith, a barrister who had previously worked for Thames as our in-house libel lawyer. He was to be our legal coordinator, acting as a kind of arbitrator between the two legal teams and as an adviser to me. He was a welcome sight − I have encountered few lawyers who have understood journalism's needs and the law as well as Peter.

Amid all the preparations for the US trip came a phone call from an Austrian journalist who had interviewed me the previous week. 'I know this is a silly question,' he said apologetically, 'but could you confirm that your production is independent of the World Jewish Congress?'

'Yes,' I replied, 'we are entirely on our own, objective and dispassionate. But we'll take evidence from anyone who has it to give — evidence on either side, and that includes getting material that we know exists in the files of the WJC.'

I wasn't surprised at the journalist's question. President Waldheim had made little attempt to hide his dislike of the WJC, which he chiefly blamed for the position in which he now found himself. He saw this organization as his pursuer and persecutor, and it was certainly true that it had harassed him relentlessly in the media: during his fight for the Austrian presidency, there had been rarely a day when it didn't offer yet another document that, it alleged, was the definitive proof of his guilt. It also seemed, on examination, that the World Jewish Congress had overstated its case not a little.

Waldheim had reacted to all this angrily, but he had also tried to mount a defence of his own, which included the various statements that his lawyers had sent to the US Justice Department on his behalf after he'd been put on the 'Watch List'. In addition, in September he'd had published what would come to be known as the 'White Book' (because of its white cover); now, two months after its first publication, we'd finally got a translation from the German. Entitled *Kurt Waldheim's Wartime Years: A Documentation*, this had been compiled by a 'task force' that included former Austrian foreign minister Karl Gruber, Waldheim's personal secretary Dr Ralph Scheide and Waldheim's son Gerhard. It contained, said Waldheim, his 'absolutely conclusive answers to all allegations', and although not an official Austrian government publication, it was widely available through Austrian government sources. It would prove to be extremely valuable to us because, more than any other statement from Dr Waldheim, the 'White Book' gave his side of the story — and a lot of information besides.

That night, I got home just before 9.00 p.m. My wife Lynne (short for Marilyn), who had been looking forward to a mild celebration to mark my 51 years, was just a touch disgruntled.

As on so many occasions in our life, work had thrust itself massively between us.

Apologies and a bottle of champagne went a small way towards bringing a smile, but the thought of my trip to the US cast something of a blight over what was left of the evening. For most of my married life, I have travelled. My wife has put up with it, but she doesn't like it. Leaving her to take care of the multitudinous chores and decisions that made up our busy and complex lives and those of our three children has never been something that she has easily accepted. I understand her position; I believe she is right. My problem is that this is my career; I have no other. It is also a job that I love.

But at least this time, unlike other trips I had taken to such places as war-torn Vietnam or murder-and-kidnap-rife Beirut, there was a fair chance of my coming home on schedule and in one piece.

Ed and I landed at Logan airport and took a taxi to the Hilton, more or less on time for a meeting with Allan A. Ryan, Jr. He had kindly agreed to see us in Boston before he flew to a conference of law professors in Montreal, the subject of which was 'the prosecution of war criminals'!

Although now an attorney in the office of the General Council of Harvard University, until a few years ago Allan Ryan had been the Director of the Office of Special Investigations (OSI) of the US Department of Justice. He was also extremely knowledgeable about Waldheim and the many allegations against him.

As we sat in the Hilton's deserted dining-room, having finished our lunch, I asked him bluntly: 'Do you think, if you were the prosecutor in a real trial, you could get a conviction against Waldheim?'

'Yes,' came the unequivocal answer.

Although I valued his opinion, I had other, more practical reasons for meeting Allan. I'd begun to wonder whether Gerry Spence was the right person to act as our prosecution counsel – not because I questioned in any way his undoubted talents as an advocate, but simply because he was so busy. Could he,

I wondered, afford to devote the time that this programme would require?

These doubts had begun to make themselves felt almost three months before, in August, when David Elstein and I had flown over to HBO's offices in Denver, Colorado. We'd travelled from New York with Bridget Potter, and had been met at the airport by Colin Callender. Together, we were wafted to HBO in the sort of American limo you can get lost in. Gerry Spence, resplendent in his enormous Stetson, was waiting for us there, together with his (silent) partner Ed Moriarty.

In preparation for this meeting, Ed Braman and I had written a document which, arranged in chronological order, compared the allegations against Waldheim with his known defence and the counter-arguments against this. It included the research that Ed and Hubertus Czernin had carried out in Austria during the summer, as well as contributions by others. Frank Symmonds had retraced his steps in Yugoslavia where he had previously done research for a *TV Eye* programme about Waldheim and the election, and Angela Lambert had done some digging in Greece; in addition, we'd added some of the information that had come from a freelance researcher whom I had put into the archives of the World Jewish Congress in New York. The package was completed with maps and diagrams.

Bridget and David had already read the document on the flight to Denver, and as I handed it out to the others, it was weakly suggested that it would help if Gerry read it first before we began. He didn't think so. As a result, the meeting meandered, with no positive direction or progress.

Despite the fact that we'd already agreed not to pursue it, Gerry still felt that we should have a jury and a straight-forward innocent or guilty verdict. There was, therefore, an enormous gulf between his approach and my personal reservations about a 'trial by television', not to mention the completely different outlook taken by his opposite numbers in Britain — whom I had yet to persuade to take part in the programme.

During the meeting, Ed Moriarty slipped the occasional

note to his partner. Obviously a system they'd worked out during the many hours they'd spent together in court, it seemed irrelevant in the context of a meeting of like-minded people all working towards the same end.

After a mere 2 hours, the meeting was brought to an abrupt end when David Elstein had to leave to catch a plane to London, Bridget had to fly to Los Angeles and Colin had to get back to New York. However, before Ed Moriarty and Gerry Spence set off in the former's private jet for Gerry's home in Jackson Hole, Wyoming, we had time for a meal.

When we'd finished eating, I tried to get us to agree on a few issues, something the meeting had failed to achieve. As well as the aforementioned document, I'd also brought a load of information that I felt was vital for Gerry to get to grips with: various works by historians, all of whom reckoned that Waldheim was more or less guilty; the presentation made by Waldheim's lawyers to the US Department of Justice protesting his innocence; and a variety of definitions of what exactly constituted a war crime. However, as late that night I left Gerry and Ed at the private airfield where Gerry's pilot and jet waited, I had no great belief that, at least in the short term, he would have time to read any of this.

As the weeks went by after the Denver meeting, I'd become increasingly concerned that, even if Gerry were finally to agree to the format that the programme was now taking, his heavy schedule would simply not allow him to have time to do all the homework required to 'prosecute' properly. He is one of the most sought-after attorneys in the United States – not surprising, given his success rate.

However, to take part in the programme would require an enormous amount of reading. The prosecution counsel would have to familiarize himself with the nature of the German army, the structure of its commands, the direction of its paper flow, who answered to whom. He would have to understand the role of German intelligence: the relationships between the various groups, such as 'Ic' (intelligence) and AO (the *Abwehr*, or counter-intelligence); who carried out interrogations and who signed documents, who just rubber-stamped orders and who initiated them. And all this was before he

52

got down to the specific allegations against Kurt Waldheim!

It finally struck me that it would be prudent − in case, further down the road to recording, Gerry found himself unable to fulfil this role − to find a first-class alternative. Allan Ryan was my choice, and when I put it to him in Boston, he seemed more than happy to take over if that was what we wanted. I would have to discuss this with Gerry when I saw him later in the week.

Taking our leave of Allan, Ed and I made our way back to Logan and a flight to New York. As we rode in the taxi from La Guardia and saw once again the wonderful skyline of New York lit up against the evening sky, I was filled with excitement. Even the continuing problems of the programme seemed to shrink as we headed for Seventh Avenue and our hotel.

I woke up to an item on NBC's early-morning *Today* television programme, about the opening of the United Nations' archives on war crimes. Appearing in the studio with the Israeli ambassador to the UN was Chuck Ashman, a journalist on a Chicago newspaper, who claimed that the new evidence revealed definite proof of Waldheim's culpability, and that it confirmed evidence already in the hands of the US Justice Department.

Despite Ashman's transparent certainty that his allegations were true (and this wouldn't be the last time we would be hearing from him), I doubted that the UN documents revealed anything of the sort. The UN file on Waldheim had been leaked some time earlier; however, some people believed that it had already been 'sanitized'. Who knew? We would certainly be putting someone into the UN archives − but only with a list of very specific names to look for and questions to ask.

New York was sweltering in an Indian summer as Ed and I made our way to the offices of the World Jewish Congress, where we were received with a mixture of suspicion and mistrust. We had arranged to meet Elan Steinberg of the WJC, who was accompanied by Beata Klarsfelt, Nazi hunter *extraordinaire*. She and her husband Klaus had been responsible for locating Klaus Barbie, the 'Butcher of Lyons', and having

53

him extradited so that he could be put on trial in France and faced with his victims. A redoubtable woman indeed.

Throughout the long discussion, she made it plain that she was totally against our programme. Steinberg, although sympathetic to our plight, had almost as many reservations – primarily, that no programme would do justice to the evidence. My worry was to get the evidence to *do* justice, our previous research at the WJC having been less successful than I'd hoped.

Steinberg was fairly hard on us. We remained polite. I simply wanted any documentary evidence the WJC might have – certainly not any public support for our project, which could negate any chance we had of appearing objective and non-aligned, even though that was just what we were. Fortunately, Steinberg equally had no desire to get any closer to us. He made it clear that, whatever he might in the end give us, there were many people in the higher echelons of the WJC who felt that we should be totally ignored.

At the end of a long and sometimes not over helpful meeting, we were told that we might get some material. We were also told that there was a lot more at the US Justice Department, but we would never get that!

I think I understood the WJC's dilemma. If, at the end of the day, our inquiry showed that the evidence against Waldheim did not hold water, he would be, in effect, exonerated before the world. If the WJC had given us evidence, they would have in some way contributed to this result, one that would be most undesirable to them. If, however, they did not supply whatever they had, and Waldheim was 'cleared', it could be said that this was only because the WJC evidence had not been seen.

Ed and I were joined at breakfast the next morning by Telford Taylor, whom HBO had been fortunate enough to enlist as our legal consultant. Although nearly 80, his mind was as sharp as a razor. One of the great privileges of my job has been to meet not just famous people, or even great people, but also those who have played a crucial part in recent history. Professor Taylor had done just that when he'd been one of the US prosecutors at the Nuremberg trials, where he'd had to deal with some of the worst villains ever known – men such as Goering, Streicher, von Ribbentrop, Kaltenbrunner, Sauckel and Keitel. Having read about Professor Taylor since my youth, I was deeply impressed to meet him in person.

He was here to advise us on the legal/technical aspects of our programme. He told us what Bridget Potter of HBO had already revealed was his position: that he agreed with our view that the programme had to take the form of a commission of inquiry, and that a jury was out of the question. An approximation of a US grand jury or a British committal proceedings was, according to Professor Taylor, the ideal.

The next stop on our itinerary was Washington, D.C. where, in contrast to the hyped-up energy of New York, we found laid-back sophistication.

Our first appointment was with Robert Wolfe, the chief military archivist of the US Archives, located in a massive, white marble building facing the greensward of the Mall, between the Capitol and the Washington Monument.

Mr Wolfe said that he would give us all the help he could, but then he explained the Catch 22: any information on German officers who appeared in their microfiche copies of wartime German documents would be at our disposal ... provided they were dead; if, however, they were still alive (and so of some use to us as potential witnesses), then he couldn't help. There was this little matter of confidentiality.

Mr Wolfe also pointed out that, after the war, the US had taken all the available documents from occupied Germany, but that after being copied, they'd all been returned to various archives in West Germany. It seemed that we'd have to put more research effort into both places.

That evening, I paid a personal visit to the Israeli ambassador to the United States. Moshe Arad has been a friend of mine for the past 20 years, ever since I'd met him during his first diplomatic posting as a press attaché at the London embassy. As good as it was to see my old friend again, it obviously wasn't the best time to renew old acquaintance: he'd exhausted himself preparing for an official visit by the Israeli president that would take place only two days later. (I thought of that other president of a friendly country, who would not be allowed beyond passport control. . .)

Before I took my leave after a brief chat, I asked Moshe if there was any evidence in the hands of the Israelis that might possibly be of use to the programme. He believed that there wasn't: whatever they had was all, by this time, in the public domain.

The following morning I was granted a quick half-hour with Neal Sher, who, having been Allan Ryan's assistant, had now taken over his old boss's job as director of the Office of Special Investigations of the Justice Department. I sat tantalizingly close to a safe in which, Mr Sher assured me, was a 72-page document (with 262 footnotes) that 'contains conclusive proof of Waldheim's culpability'. Two other people had copies of this. One was Secretary of State George Shultz, and the other was US Attorney-General Ed Meese – and they weren't talking.

Neither was Neal Sher, but he was kind and considerate: before telling me that he thought the idea of the programme was rubbish, he asked if I minded if he were straight with me!

'Why don't you just make a documentary on the subject?' he asked.

'If I did that, I would be counsel for both the defence and prosecution, as well as judge and jury. Surely,' I argued, 'this is a far fairer way of looking at the evidence?'

'Only a judicial process can try Kurt Waldheim.'

'We're going to be holding an inquiry to look into the *evidence*, not trying Waldheim himself,' I rejoined, feeling a decided sense of *déjà vu*. I sometimes wondered if the lawyers' objections to this sort of proceedings had more to do with their own restrictive practices than to any concept of morality.

As I came out of Mr Sher's office and raised my arm to summon a taxi, one did a U-turn in the middle of the road and screamed to a halt in front of me – oh, that American entrepreneurial spirit. We made Georgetown and my hotel in about five minutes flat. It was a relief to get out, fetch my suitcase and settle down in a taxi driven by a much more placid Nigerian driver, on my way to Dulles airport, and then, via Salt Lake City, to Jackson Hole.

* * *

Darkness was falling as the 737 swooped down and I took my first steps on the friendly soil of Wyoming. Gerry Spence's secretary Rosemary was waiting and whisked me off to the modest seven acres on which Gerry's beautiful house, designed by his wife, stands − 'modest' when compared to the more than 30,000 acres he owns in another part of the state, peacefully grazed by 4000 head of cattle. Gerry and his wife Imogin were there to greet me. Dinner plus all the travelling I'd done soon made me ready for an early bed. It had been a long day.

The next morning, refreshed and breakfasted, I joined Gerry in his 'den' - an enormous room occupying one end of the house, self-contained with its own bathroom and coffee-making facilities, as well as a breath-taking view of the Rockies. We soon got down to work.

I told him of my problems and worries about his time constraints, explaining over and over again that our chances of finding any 'smoking pistols' were virtually nil. I also pointed out that the prosecution was his responsibility, not mine. In my role, I could not help one side − neither the prosecution nor the defence − more than the other in any way.

In reply, Gerry explained his own working methods, how he employed not only a number of lawyers, but also para-legal people, investigators and others. Like most people at the top, Gerry expected a lot of the groundwork to be done by juniors. The trouble with this project was that the prosecution counsel not only had to know the facts of the specific case backwards, he also had to learn a lot about European history, the history of the Nazi Party and many other things as well.

At this point, I told him about my discussions with Allan Ryan.

'I'm glad to hear that you've found a possible substitute prosecutor,' he said. 'If I decide that my workload really is too much, that means that I can pull out without letting the prcgramme down.'

This sounded ominous. I continued to explain my belief that the prosecution would depend on a painstaking building up of evidence, based on the 3000 documents relating to Waldheim's war that were already in the public domain, and many others still to be discovered. These would be supplemented by expert witnesses — historians interpreting the documents, explaining how things worked, where documents went to and what resulted from them — and, we hoped, eye witnesses — who could tell us what they remembered actually happening.

As far as I could determine at this early date, I told Gerry, it seemed that our judges would make up their minds on the basis of a balance of probability as to whether or not, in certain instances, Waldheim initiated action, as opposed to being merely a rubber stamp.

None of this was welcome news to Gerry. As the morning rolled on, our discussion became more and more worrying. Deep down, I sensed that he still felt that there was a magic key that would unlock absolute proof of Waldheim's guilt — and that, somehow, I had been remiss in not having found it.

However, on the positive side, I found Gerry to be a good listener. Having initiated the project and been closely involved from the outset, he as much as anyone was aware of the many problems of getting the programme on the air, and he sympathized with my own private nightmares.

Despite this, we seemed to be getting nowhere, so we broke for lunch and then climbed into Gerry's jeep and drove into surrounding wilderness to get some fresh air. He stopped at the foot of some hills, saying, 'Let's take a walk in the woods and look at the elk.' He loaned me some trainers, and up we climbed. Gerry insisted on silence, so trying to keep my laboured breathing as quiet as possible, I mounted the hill in his footsteps, climbing over, round and sometimes under trees, fallen, leaning, rotting and crumbling.

It was wonderful. After the pressure-cooker atmosphere in Gerry's den, combined with my own particular neuroses and anxieties, the air, cool and smelling of pine, cleared the brain admirably and I found my worries evaporating. In the silence and beauty surrounding us, against the backcloth of the magnificent Rockies, my troubles dwindled.

Occasionally, we got a whiff of animal scent but, despite our silent progress, not a sight of any other living creature. Finally, an hour or so after we'd set out, and as darkness was beginning to fall, we found our elk. There, grazing in the distance, was a small herd of about 30 of these magnificent animals. As we crept forward, they seemed not to notice us, but when we were about 100 yards away, the grey, ghostly shapes heard or smelled something and all their heads came up, listening carefully. We froze. They looked at us and we looked at them. If we moved forward, they would disappear. We let them get on with their meal, retraced our footsteps to the jeep and headed for the airport to pick up Ed Braman, who was joining us.

From Washington where I'd left him Ed had headed for Columbia, South Carolina to talk to Professor Robert Herzstein at the university there. Herzstein was widely acknowledged as one of the best-informed sources on Waldheim anywhere in the world. As a result of their meeting, Ed now had a number of new angles on the evidence, but we asked him to keep them to himself until after dinner.

Back in the den, Ed − surrounded by an enormous pile of documents, mostly in German − began to explain some of the minutiae of the case. As the night wore on, Gerry became more tired and, I thought, more worried. As Ed described his papers − their relevance, the background to some of the allegations − Gerry began to understand the real nature of what the programme entailed. It was going to make the life of the prosecutor extremely difficult.

'Here, look at this document,' said Ed, totally absorbed by his discoveries and oblivious to Gerry's look of increasing concern. 'It's signed by Waldheim and appears to suggest that there was an insurrection of the Jews in Jannina in Greece. Herzstein claims that there were five copies of this, two of which would have gone to the secret police − the SD − and the SS.

'If it were possible to prove that there was no insurrection nor was there ever likely to be one, *and* if Waldheim knew this, then the prosecutor could argue that, since it was well known that the SS required very little reason to deport Jews to the gas chambers, Waldheim could be said to have knowingly started the process. If that were the case, then the evidence might be getting nearer to revealing one example of a war crime. . . but, of course, there will have to be a lot more hard work before that stage is reached, supposing it's true in the first place.'

Gerry appeared to realize just how tenuous was the case he would be handling, and how laboriously it would have to be built up. He was now plainly worried. As time passed, voices were raised and the pressure increased.

'This is the reality,' I said to Gerry. 'There is no smoking pistol. If you can't accept that, then there are really only two alternatives: either we kill the programme right now, or if you don't think you can prosecute, you can pull out. Allan Ryan has already said that he believes he can prosecute and, in his view, "get a conviction".'

By now, it was after midnight. Ed and I went to bed, leaving Gerry to watch a heavyweight boxing match on television, and the issues unresolved. It was not one of my better nights: I was wide awake before 4.30, bathed and packed by 5.15.

Despite the early hour and his own lack of sleep, Gerry was back to his normal, imperturbable self. It was as if the previous night had never happened. As we drove through a still-dark Jackson Hole on our way to catch the early commuter flight to Denver, he suggested that perhaps I could knock out a concise ten-page brief on the strength of the prosecution case.

'You know I can't,' I replied. 'My role is a neutral one. I can supply the material to both legal teams, but I can't suggest lines of prosecution. That's *your* role. However,' I continued, trying to placate him, 'we are about to appoint our two solicitors – the lawyers who will help both counsel prepare their cases – and if you still want to do the prosecution, I can send one of them out to you.'

There was no more to say. As our aircraft lifted out of Jackson Hole, we left Gerry behind but took with us all our unresolved problems.

Returning to London was a mind-wrenching experience, not least because I immediately had to attend a meeting with the Thames lawyers about a libel allegation made against us for a programme on Northern Ireland that I'd produced some two years earlier.

When I finally got back to the Waldheim project offices, I had a phone call from Gerry Spence. He suggested that perhaps he should speak to Allan Ryan, to see if he would help him with the evidence or even work as his junior counsel.

As I set up a phone meeting between the two, I was under no illusions that Allan would agree to play a supporting role to anyone, not even Gerry Spence. But that was for them to sort out.

After they'd talked, Allan rang to fill me in on the latest. He'd turned down Gerry's proposition, but had said that he might be prepared to help – but only as Gerry's co-prosecutor, sharing the same fee and having the same right to interrogate, as well as dividing up the opening and closing statements between them.

Now I waited to hear Gerry's response.

4

Here Comes the Judge

'You can hear the sound of the British Establishment closing the door,' said Peter Smith. Our legal coordinator and adviser had put his finger on it.

I'd approached a brace of former Law Lords, asking if they would act as judges for our inquiry. Extremely politely, Lord Wilberforce had turned me down. Lord Scarman, on the other hand, had seemed more likely to accept — or so I thought. In an elegant room in the House of Lords, he'd told me, 'It's the most exciting project I have heard of for many years.' However, despite this show of interest, his Lordship declined my request some days later.

We also tried Lord Havers, who'd only recently resigned after an extremely brief stint as Lord Chancellor — 'for reasons of poor health', according to Prime Minister Thatcher. He, too, declined our approach, through the Central Office of the Conservative Party.

Then we were told by our 'Deep Throat' within the dark recesses of the House of Lords that some of their Lordships had discussed the programme! What decision they had come to was becoming increasingly obvious, so it was plain that we needed to do some lateral thinking.

Despite the closing of ranks among the British judiciary, at least we had persuaded one judge to cooperate with the programme. This was Mr Justice James d'Arcy, a former High Court judge in the Republic of Ireland. Unfortunately, he'd been in bad health recently, and had been in and out of hospital. However, he said that, as long as his health stood up to it, he would participate in our inquiry.

I also seemed to be having luck with our Swiss choice: when

I'd first contacted Judge Huber, a recently retired federal judge, he'd given the impression that he might join the programme. However, when I rang to confirm a meeting with him, his wife read me a letter that he'd left behind. It was polite, well reasoned and completely negative. I next approached another Swiss judge, Otto Kaufmann. He grasped the idea immediately, and then said he wanted a week to think it over. So, too, did Judge Lagergrün, Sweden's judge at the International Court of Human Rights in Strasburg, who was on the verge of retirement. So I would just have to wait until the following Monday, 16 November.

The search for our American judge was continuing. After about four weeks of trying, I finally reached former Chief Justice Warren Burger. Despite my using (with his permission) Lord Rawlinson's name, Burger told me that, although he was interested, he couldn't afford the time. Another retired Justice, Lewis Powell, also turned me down, because, although retired from the Supreme Court, he still acted as a judge and, under the circumstances, didn't think it right to involve himself in such an inquiry. Finally, Allan Ryan suggested that I try Judge Herbert Stern, but preparations for my trip to Belgrade the next day prevented me from contacting him myself and I had to leave that task to Peter.

There was one other problem (one of thousands!) that had to be dealt with. The morning before I left, a Lord Caccia had written to *The Times*, complaining bitterly about the concept of the programme and, in the course of his letter, describing wartime Austria as 'struggling with great courage to end foreign occupation'. To us in the Waldheim project office, immersed as we were in the period, this appeared a *slight* rewriting of history. Although the *Anschluss* had been a disaster for some Austrians, for many others it had been a very happy moment – in fact, in Hitler's plebiscite, over 99 per cent of those who had voted had supported it. Even Waldheim's father, who hadn't liked German Fascism, had supported Chancellor Kurt von Schuschnigg, leader of the Clerical Fascist Austrian Fatherland Front. The *Anschluss* had not been an act of rape. Rather, a touch of seduction – perhaps even a willing liaison.

We looked up Lord Caccia in *Who's Who* and discovered

that – surprise! – he'd been the British Ambassador in Austria just after the war and had, at one time, been involved in Anglo-Austrian relations. Was this, I asked myself, the beginning of subtle pressure from Waldheim, via his friends? There was no way of knowing.

In reply Thames Television's managing director Richard Dunn wrote a strong letter to *The Times*, to correct 'any false impressions that Lord Caccia may have created about the nature of the programme.' We knew that the whole programme was in a delicate state. We had to continue to incubate it, and keep it well clear of the Establishment, lest we create too many enemies too soon.

Ed Braman and I were both flying out on that Thursday but to different places. Ed was going to Vienna to chair the second meeting of our historians and journalists, to make sure that our research in Austria and the two Germanys was as coordinated and thorough as planned. I, on the other hand, was making for Yugoslavia where our research effort, although not as large and wide-ranging as the Vienna-based one, was still very important. Everyone in the United States, and quite a few of our Austrian and German academics, believed that important material lay hidden in the archives in Zagreb or in other smaller archives around the country – perhaps in places such as Ljubljana, Titograd (formerly Podgorica), Stari Trg and Skopje.

I was met off the aircraft by Yela Yevramovic, who had been helping us for some weeks. An editor of a political magazine in Belgrade and a brave and fearless journalist, we'd got to know of her because of the many articles she'd already written about Waldheim.

That evening, she filled me in on the material that she'd already gathered. For example, she'd interviewed one eyewitness, now in his late 50s, who claimed to remember Waldheim when the latter was at Plevlje in charge of a radio truck complete with tall transmitting aerial. Indeed, the witness, who had been only 16 at the time, said that he'd spoken to the tall German officer regularly, and had taught Waldheim a little Serbo-Croat. In addition, he said that Gestapo informers would arrive nightly at the house in which Waldheim was billeted, to be debriefed by him. Yela had arranged to tape a statement from him the following week. (As was sometimes the case, this witness later radically modified his previous testimony.)

Yela had also struck what might turn out to be a mine of untouched information – perhaps the last virgin World War II archives in the world. These were in Tirana, capital of that closed society, Albania. Because Albanian had virtually cut itself off from the rest of Europe (and from the Eastern Bloc – they had aligned themselves with the People's Republic of China), everyone had just about forgotten that it existed. However, Waldheim had been stationed in Albania for a brief time during the war, and we had been led to believe that the Tirana archives held much material relevant to the case. Yela thought that, as a Yugoslav, she just might be able to get into Albania and into the archives. Whether this would lead to revelatory evidence or be just another blind alley, there was only one way to find out.

The following day, Yela introduced me to Colonel Antun Miletic, head of the Yugoslav military archives. An old partisan himself, he had a lot of sympathy with the project. Although he'd searched the Zagreb archives and was fairly convinced that he'd found everything that was worth finding, he did admit that the archives were in some disarray and that there might well be things left undiscovered. He implied that he'd help us all he could; if that were so, he'd be an invaluable friend.

I couldn't get Yela and myself seats on the afternoon flight to Zagreb, so I hired a car to drive the 300 miles on the worst road I've ever tried to navigate. It was a sort of vehicular roulette, with cars, lorries and vans dodging in and out of the single lanes of traffic going either way. Bad as it was in daylight, as night fell it was even worse.

I was eager to meet the second member of my Yugoslav research team. Pierre Vicary had an impressive *curriculum vitae*: fluent in English, French, German and Serbo-Croat, he had been born in England, emigrated to Australia and then moved to Zagreb, where he'd spent the last couple of years working for Australian television searching in all the local archives for information on Nazis who might have fled to Australia after the war. He knew his way around the very places where we desperately needed just that sort of expertise. In addition, he was enthusiastic and full of drive.

He had booked Yela and me into the enormous and classy Esplanade Hotel, which is to Zagreb what the Sacher is to Vienna. The rooms were the size of the suites found in most chain hotels; the entrance hall seemed as big as a football stadium.

Everything went well right from the start. As I registered, I received a telex from Susie, telling me that Peter Smith had successfully spoken to Judge Stern: he'd accepted in principle. What a relief. That night, Pierre, Yela and I dined at a delightful little restaurant and planned our operation in Yugoslavia. After so many setbacks, it was a welcome change to be doing something positive.

Back in the office early on Monday morning, arriving before any of the rest of the team, I read the notes that Peter had left me about our new potential American judge. Now a young 51, Herbert J. Stern, a former Federal judge from Newark, New Jersey, had retired from the bench relatively early and had gone back into private law practice. But his had not been a run-of-the-mill judicial career, for in 1979, he had shot to international fame because of one very strange case.

In that year, an East German man, together with a young woman and her child, had successfully escaped to the West by hijacking a Polish civil airliner *en route* to East Berlin, and forcing it to land at Tempelhof airport in West Berlin. The West German government chose not to try the hijackers, and persuaded the US government, still one of the three occupying powers of West Berlin, to convene a special court for the purpose. Faced with possible embarrassment − on the one hand, understanding and even applauding any German's right to flee East Germany, but on the other, not wanting to condone a hijacking − the US government were eager for the case to be dealt with expeditiously.

Judge Stern had been given the unique appointment of US Judge for Berlin. Determined to run his court on US constitutional grounds, he bravely refused to obey the order of his own State Department that the trial be held without a jury − especially a jury composed of West Berliners who would

Lieutenant Waldheim with officers of the Italian Pusteria Division, including its commanding officer, General Esposito. Lieutenant Waldheim was the liaison officer and interpreter. This picture has not previously been published.

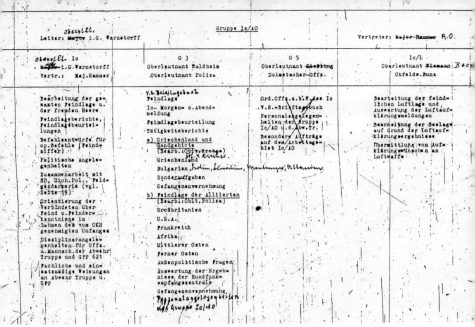

Organizational chart with job descriptions, dated 1 December 1943. This shows 1st Lieutenant Waldheim as the 03 (first assistant) to the head of the Ic/AO Colonel Warnstorff. Waldheim has always maintained that he worked only for the Ic (intelligence) side and not for the AO (the *Abwehr,* counter-intelligence) at Army Group E headquarters based at Arsakli (near Salonika), Greece.

Organizational chart, dated August 1943. This shows 1st Lieutenant Waldheim as the assistant to Lt Colonel Willers, who was head of the 1a (operations) section of a small liaison unit the 'German General Staff' with the Italian 11th Army based in Athens.

Oberkommando Heeresgruppe E
Gruppe Ic/20.   H.Qu. den 18.7.1944.

Betr.: Engl. Commando-Unternehmen gegen die Insel Calino in der Nacht von 1/2.7.44.

In der Nacht vom 1./2.7.44. wurde der Stützpunkt "Morgenrot" auf Calino von einem engl. Cdo-Trupp überfallen. Nach einem Gefecht von etwa 25 Min. Dauer wurde der Gegner zum Rückzug gezwungen.

Eigene Verluste: 1 Leichtverwundeter.

Sachschaden: Steege der Zahnradleitung zwischen Stützpunkt und Kp.-Gefecht wird bereits vor Beginn des Überfalles.

Feindausfälle: 3 Gefangene:

1.) Sergeant John Dryden, geb. 25.10.19, in Newcastle, verwundet, am 5.7. nach Athen überflogen. Wird gemäss Führerbefehl dem SD übergeben.

2.) Private Fishwick, nähere Personalien unbekannt, nach Athen überflogen, dort im Kriegslazarett verstorben.

3.) James Doughty, Sanitäter, geb. 26.3.18., ledig, wohnhaft Ipswich, Essex/USA. Am 17.7. des Tages Saloniki überstellt zwecks Weiterleitung nach Deutschland in ein Kgf.-Lager. Am Kampf nicht beteiligt und ohne Waffen.

Vermutlich mehrere Verwundete vom Gegner mitgenommen.

Vernehmungen: Anl. 1: Serit. John Dryden, verwundet am 11.7.44 in Athen.
Anl. 2: James Doughty, Vernehmungen auf Calino und Leros am 2.7. und durch 4.Gr. E am 17.7. in Saloniki.
Anl. 3: Aussagen des Kriegsgef. Doughty über Verhältnisse in den USA.

Beute:
1 engl. MG mit Muni u. Magazin
1 ital. Pi.
3 Gewehrgranaten
1 Buschmesser (wird gesondert übersandt)
Verschiedene Brieftaschen und Papiere (ebenfalls gesondert übersandt).

Der vom dt. Stützpunktführer gemeldete Einsatz von le Gr wurde von Doughty in Abrede gestellt.

Nach festgestellten Fusspuren waren die Cdo-Angehörigen mit Gummischuhen ausgestattet.

Durchführung des Cdo-Unternehmens: Aus der Vernehmung des Doughty und aus nachträglichen Feststellungen des Sondertrupps konnten bisher folgende Einzelheiten über die Durchführung des Unternehmens gewonnen werden.

b.w.

Zugehörigkeit: Der Cdo-Trupp gehörte zum wahrscheinlich in Unmittelbarer Nähe von Alexandrien in einem Zeltlager stationierten "W"-Detachment des Special Post Squadron (SPS) an. Es handelt sich um 22 Engländer und um den Amerikaner Doughty. Diese gehört dem Royal Medical Corps (engl. Truppe./) an.

Führer: engl. Hptm. Bethany.

Anmarschi: etwa zweite Juli-Woche.

Abmarschweg: Alexandrien - Cypern - türk. Küste, Mytha Bethany. Die Fahrt von den Stützpunkten aus geschah, nach Aussagen von Cypern wahrscheinlich mit MTB gesamt. (Schnellboot). Abfahrt von Cypern wahrscheinlich 26.6.44. Eintreffen auf Calino wahrscheinlich am 26./27.6.44. Dort 5 Tage im unbesetzten Teile der Insel untergebracht. In Freien übernachtet.

Örtlich ohne Zelte. Lagerplatz durch Spähtrupp am 3.7. festgestellt, 60 verbrauchte Konservendosen vorgefunden. Mitgenommener Munitrans. der WTB und Funkgerät angeblich nicht mitgeführt. Die Boote wurden von WTB an Land gesetzt. Das Führerpriss Schiff vermutlich zurückgeführt. Abmarsch: Vermutlich in der Nacht 1./2.7. da gegen 2330 Uhr Motorengeräusche auf See gehört wurden.

German Wehrmacht document dated 18 July 1944, which deals with the captured Allied commandoes, James Doughty (who gave evidence to the Commission of Inquiry) and Sergeant John Dryden. This report from the Ic/AO Army Group E is initialled 'W' (Waldheim), and says that 'commando officer Dryden . . . wounded . . . flown to Athens . . . is to be handed over the SD [security police].' There had been some confusion as to whether or not Sergeant Dryden survived the war. However, James Doughty later told us that he had a drink with Dryden in London shortly after the end of the war.

UN Secretary-General, Kurt Waldheim.

taken before World War II, during his time with the Austrian First Cavalry Regiment (Dragoons).

Ic - Abendmeldung Okdo.H.Gr.E vom 17.12.1944

Luft-und Seelage: Am 16.12.verstärkter all.Lw.-Einsatz mit Bomben-
u. Bordwaffentreffen auf Kol.u. Verkehrsziele im Raum Podgorica -Mate-
sevo - Kolasin. 17.12.vormittags 4 Feindjäger über Mostar ohne gemeldete Kampfhandlungen.
Nach LB vom 16.12. S-Spitze Insel Silba 1 le.Kreuzer ("Dalmacija"2360 t),
Hafen Insel Ist 2 Minenleger ("Galeb"-Klasse 330 t), 1 Segelboot, 1 MS,
9 Hafenschlepper, 1 Prachtkahn u.25 kl. Boote. Hafen Insel Molat 1 Minenleger ("Buccari".Kl.530 ') u.16 Fischerboote, vermutl.keine engl.
Schiffseinheiten in gelichtbildeten Häfen.

Ostfront: Gegen Sporrirol NW Sjenica setzten Teile 22.Tito-Div. von SO
u.vermutl. Tle,37.Div. (IV.u.V.Sandschak-Brig.?) von N erfolgl. Angrif-
fe am gestrigen Tage fort. Feindverluste: 32 Tote, 1 MG, 13 Gewehre.
Gegen Sperrstellung im Raum Biosca fühlten Tle. 25.Div. von SO vor; anhaltend starker Feinddruck von Tln. 2.u.17.Tito-Div. aus N. Im Drina-
Abschnitt herangeschoben stärkerer Feindkräfte Tle. 38. u. 28.Tito-Div.
an Bijeljina. Branjevo (20 NNO Zvornik) vom Feind genommen. Ortsrand
Bijeljina unter fdl. Artl.-Feuer. An syrm.-, Donau- u.Drau-Front nur
örtl. Gefechtstätigkeit. Feindvorstoß von Teilen 223.SD auf Oratevo (9
SO Vukovar) blieb erfolglos. Feindverluste: 42 Tote, 2 Gefangene.

Truppenfeststellungen: XII./25. Tito-Div. im Raum 15 SW Uzice. Stärke
4 Batle.je 400 Mann. Zahlreiche Zwangsrekrutierte aus Raum Zajecar -
Kraljevo. Bewaffnung mässig. Brigade soll gegen Kroemn-Paß (6 WSW Biosca)
eingesetzt worden (alles G.v. Ausg.). VII./1.Div. nach Überläuferauss.
i) Borak (14 S Vukovar).

Montenegro: An Sperrstellung S Spuž zunehmender Feinddruck u. rege
fdl. Art.-Tätigkeit. Anhaltend starker Feinddruck von Tln.1.u.2. alban.
Div. u.Tln. 3.Tito-Div. gegen Strasse Biosca - Lijeva Rijeka. Vor eig.
Vorstoß aus Kolasin nach N Tle. II.u. VI. mo.Di.Div. bis Zovacko (8 N
Kolasin) zurückgezogen. Höhengelände SW Mojkovac von Tln. 3.Div. nach
Widerstand geräumt.

Kroatien: Feindbild im Raum Mostar bis auf örtl. Bewegung 29.Div.
SO Lisa unverändert. Nach zuverlässiger Abw.-Meldg. Tle. serb.Cetnik-
Verbände aus Raum Gerarde (5000 Mann) zu Kalinovic-Brig. nach Trnovo
in Marsch gesetzt, um diese im Kampfe gegen dortige Tito-Kräfte (XI./
29.Div.) zu unterstützen. Vor Sperrstellungen Busovaca Feind (XI./4.u.
Tle. VII./10.) in ausgebauten Stellung N u.SW des Ortes (Erdaufkl.).
Nach Abw.-Meldg. stärkere Teile Tito-Kräfte aus Raum W Zenica (VI.u.
VIII./4.) in Richtung Busovaca abgezogen. Meldungen unterstreichen Feind-
absicht Strasse Busovaca - Travnik unter starkem Kräfteeinsatz zu sperren.
Konzentration stärkerer Tle. 10.u.4. Div. im Raum um Travnik (Erdaufkl.)
in diesem Zusammenhang von Bedeutung. Verstärkte Bandentätigkeit (vermutl.
Tle.bosn. Div.) im Raum Maglaj - Doboj. Strassenbrücke S Doboj unter
Feindbeschuss. Mit zunehmenden Feinddruck durch Heranführung weiterer
Tle. V.Tito-Korps gegen Verkehrswege in Abschnitt Zepce - Derventa ist
zu rechnen. Vor eig. Säuberungsunternehmen im Raum W Lapac Tle.35. Tito-
Div. nach z.T. heftigem Widerstand nach W u.N ausgewichen. 20 gezählte
Tote. Im Raum Karinjou gegen eig. Kpfr. sich von S lfd.verstärkender
Feind (vermutl.Tle.35.Div.). Lebhafte Bandentätigkeit im Raum Cazin -
Ostrozac (13 bzw. 18 NNO Bihac) durch vermutl. Tle.7.Tito-Div.. Durch
Einw.-Auss. fdl. Angriffsabsicht auf eig. Stützpkte. im dortigen Raum er-
neut gemeldet.

P.A.R.

Oberleutnant
Be...

Okdo.H.Gr.E - Ic/AO
Nr. 18095/44 g.v. 17.12.44
(Warnstorff, Ob.ratlt.i.G.)

One of the many daily reports signed by 1st Lieutenant Waldheim in his role as the
assistant to the head of the Ic/AO, Colonel Warnstorff (Army Group E, Arsakli, Greece).

Waldheim as a young soldier.

1st Lieutenant Waldheim in Sarajevo, Yugoslavia, December 1944, with the Army Group E high command, including the commanding officer, General Löhr (subsequently hanged for war crimes by the Yugoslavs), and General E Schmidt-Richberg, chief of the General Staff.

The now famous photograph of Waldheim in his role as interpreter at Podgorica (now Titograd, in

undoubtedly sympathize with any East German who'd escaped the repressive regime beyond the Wall. Instead, Judge Stern empanelled a jury which, in turn, acquitted the man on all but one of the charges. The judge, who had already ruled as inadmissible the evidence against the woman and had released her, now released the man on the basis that he had already spent nine months in custody.

Judge Stern had upheld the rule of common sense, liberality, humanity and Western idealism. As a result, when he departed from his US government post, it was never filled again. He seemed a good choice for us.

I then turned my attention to the search for our other three judges. First, a call to our Swiss judge-to-be – except that it soon became obvious that he was not going to be. Over the weekend, he'd talked to Judge Huber. Word had got around. 'Thank you but no,' he said. It appeared that the Establishment in Switzerland, like that in Britain, was closing ranks.

A second phone call to a potential Swedish judge brought an identical result, but for a different reason. He told me that he was in the process of arbitrating a border dispute between Egypt and Israel and the recording of the programme would occur right in the middle of his taking evidence. I suppose even the Waldheim programme couldn't take precedence over an international border row! Fortunately, the Swedish judge offered me the name and phone number of a former Supreme Administrative Court colleague, Gustav Petrén.

Acting on this immediately, I was lucky to catch the judge at home. He was interested from the start, asked a number of penetrating questions, and then said that he would like a couple of days to think it over. I'd heard that before...but where there's life, there's hope.

When the other team members arrived, I learned of an article about the programme which had appeared in the previous day's *Sunday Telegraph*, written by no less a person than Sir John Colville, former secretary to Winston Churchill and biographer of the great wartime prime minister. I hope he was more accurate about Sir Winston's life than he was about the programme, for the article was ill-judged and grossly inaccurate. It was also probably libellous, for he implied that

67

someone (me!) was going around offering large sums of money to people to get them to participate. This was a total fabrication.

Not only did Sir John have a go at the programme, but he also involved the US Justice Department, which, he said:

On the unsubstantiated accusations of the World Jewish Congress and its chairman Dr Edgar Bronfman chose to conduct an investigation based on allegations supplied by the Congress and then decided to ban Dr Waldheim from entry into the United States. . . It did so under pressure from Zionist zealots and on the basis of an amendment to the American Immigration and Nationalities Act.

I was so angry at the article, and particularly at what appeared to me to be its anti-Semitic overtones, that I forced myself to wait until the next day before going through it again and deciding whether to take any action. Then, on Tuesday, I faxed a copy of the article over to Neal Sher to find out his views on the extraordinary allegation against the US Justice Department, and drafted a reply rebutting Sir John's article for our director of programmes, David Elstein, to send to the *Sunday Telegraph* under his name. At that moment, I felt some sympathy for Dr Waldheim, who had been faced with many similarly ill-judged and equally inaccurate attacks.

My gloom was substantially lightened that afternoon. Peter Smith had arranged for the two of us to go to one of the Inns of Court to see a retired senior judge, Sir Frederick Lawton, at his home set high above some barristers' chambers. A Lord Justice of Appeal since 1972 had retired from the Court of Appeal in 1986 after a lifetime in the law.

I explained the nature of the programme in great detail, interrupted only by some very pertinent questions from Sir Frederick. After I'd talked for half an hour, he said, 'Then to summarize, let me confirm two points. One, you are looking for your inquiry to find whether or not there is sufficient *prima facie* evidence to show *only* that there is or is not a case to answer − and nothing more?'

'Yes.'

'Two, you are not being pressured or underwritten by any

religious or political group, and the programme will be entirely objective and fair?'

'Yes.'

'Then I'll do it.'

I felt as if someone had suddenly removed a yoke from around my neck, as if someone had just turned on the light. As I metaphorically floated on air, Peter and I chatted a little more with Sir Frederick, going over some of the details. Then we left − but not before I warned the judge that the Establishment was baying outside our door. He gave me the impression that it would take more than a quiet word in his ear in the smoking-room of a London club to make him change his mind, and as the car wafted me back to Thames' offices, I offered silent prayers.

Sir Frederick's acceptance seemed to herald a turn in our fortunes. On Thursday morning, the 19th of November, Judge Petrén rang from Sweden to say that, after much consideration, he would be pleased to take part in the programme. He added that he would be coming to London the following week, and we could tie up any loose ends then.

I sat in the office and beamed. Judge Petrén was eminently suitable for our inquiry. A judge of the Swedish Supreme Administrative Court from 1972 until his retirement in 1985, he was also a member of the International Institute of Humanitarian Law and had been a Professor of Administrative Law at the University of Stockholm since 1949. Now we had four out of our five judges: d'Arcy of Ireland, Stern of the US, Lawton of Britain and Petrén of Sweden.

Our research effort continued. Ed Braman flew off to West Germany, this time to Freiburg, via Basel in Switzerland, to see Professor Messerschmidt of the Commission of Historians. We hoped he would be a bit more forthcoming about what they were up to than Gerald Flemming, the British member, had been.

While Ed was still in the air, we received a call from Yela in Yugoslavia saying that she had a very large pile of documents for us, which contained some very interesting information concerning deportations. It sounded as if the first real fruits of our carefully set up research were finally being harvested.

69

How to get them was the question. Poor Ed: he hadn't even touched down in Basel yet and we were briefing the airport to call him over the public address system on his arrival. He would have to divert on his way home and pick up the material in Belgrade. I was informed that the diversion could only be achieved if Ed first flew from Basel to Vienna, then to Belgrade and finally to London. I knew that he and his family had some plans for that weekend, and my heart went out to him. When Ed rang in from Basel, he took the news stoically: if the job required it, he would make the necessary apologies to his family and spend some time in Belgrade.

Later in the day, he rang again to tell me that his meeting with Messerschmidt had been extremely useful. He also said that if we wanted the Professor as an expert witness, that was a possibility.

With this good news, I faced a task that was less pleasant. David Elstein had sent me his amended letter in reply to the *Sunday Telegraph* article – amended because, in the interim, Sir John Colville had died. Reading through David's letter, I felt my anger bubble up again, but it was now academic. I agreed the draft and returned it to David.

The next day, Peter approached a Dutch judge, and I followed this up with a *cri de coeur*. He said that he'd consider it over the following week and would then let me know. However, he did say that he was 75 and wasn't sure if he felt able to take part – with a laugh, he pointed out that he had more life behind him than in front. He added that if, in the end, he turned us down, he would suggest an alternative.

The week had also seen a major step forward on another legal front: we'd finally appointed our two solicitors. Tim House, a 28-year-old solicitor from one of London's most established law firms, had agreed to work for the defence, while Susan Aslan, a year older and from an equally impressive firm, was going to work for the prosecution.

Peter Smith, Tim, Susan and I held a meeting at which some of the more esoteric legal problems were put on the table. (We would wait and fill in Susan and Tim on the minutiae of Waldheim's war activities when they joined us fulltime on 1 December.) What was the precise nature of the charges, given that we were going to hold a sort of committal proceedings? Should we be able to lead the witnesses? What should the rules of evidence be? At what stage should we reveal documents? Would the solicitors have the right to go chasing their own evidence and, if so, to keep it secret? Should we agree the authenticity of documents in advance? Would we be using the British system of presentation of evidence, or would we take rebuttal evidence after both sides had presented their main cases, as is done in the States? And a whole lot more.

I followed most, but by no means all, of the arguments; some of the legal jargon went right over my head. Every now and then, I had to remind the others that the television audience would have to understand the proceedings as well. But for the most part, it was a successful meeting. All our lawyers understood my problem – that, as well as the programme being workable in the context of a quasi-legal setting, it also had to work as a piece of television.

Peter had been working on a document that we hoped to present to our judges and senior counsel as the basis for the final rules of our programme. As 3.00 p.m. became 6.00 and then 10.00, Peter, Tim and Susan thrashed out a second draft. While this was going on, I rang Gerry Spence and, over the telephone, introduced him to Susan. As they chatted, I wondered yet again whether Gerry would be prepared to do the necessary groundwork or whether, now that Susan had joined us, he was hoping she would present him with an easy-to-work-to brief. If that were so, he was in for a big disappointment. Susan struck me as a hard-working and very clever woman, but I felt sure that she would want Gerry to tell *her* the nature of the case he wanted to prosecute.

Monday morning, and we still needed a fifth judge. To start off the week with a whimper, we received a telegram from the nice, friendly Dutch judge. A mere two lines dashed my hopes. However, it did say that a letter was to follow – maybe a suggestion or two?

In the meantime, Peter and I indulged in a bit more lateral thinking. As a result, he rang the Commonwealth Institute in London to ask if they knew of any retired judges who could be

71

approached. They suggested one name – that of a former Chief Justice of India.

Ed had staggered into the office that morning, still suffering from his whirlwind tour of Switzerland, West Germany, Austria and Yugoslavia. His diversion to Belgrade had resulted in his having to fly in not three but five aircraft in one day. However, he'd returned to the office with some deeply fascinating material. At least, we *believed* it to be deeply fascinating: given that it was in Serbo-Croat, we'd have to await its translation before making a final judgement.

Ed started straightaway on a series of meetings with various research teams who were about to head out into the field. The first was a trio heading for Germany: the son of a German aristocrat, Felix Moreau; a serious and very attractive young woman, Alexandra ('Nana') Wiessler; and a very British but fluent German speaker, Dr Nicholas Goodrick-Clarke. Ed told them, as he was to tell all the others, of the need for witnesses, that they'd have to explain the aims of the programme and try to persuade them to take part – at least in principle. He loaded them down with hundreds of pages of material already discovered, books that had already been written (including Waldheim's 'White Book') and about 170 names that we already had on the computer.

But it was one thing to give them the names and quite another for them to find these people and try to persuade them to appear as witnesses. With some, like Colonel Warnstorff who had been in charge of the Ic/AO section during Waldheim's time at Arsakli, we already knew where they were. With others, however, we had no idea where to begin looking. Obvious starting points such as military archives, old regimental associations and the Red Cross were considered, but whether they'd help us, we'd have to find out. In the course of the next four months, we'd chase hundreds of names of people who had served with, known or somehow got entangled with Kurt Waldheim between the crucial dates of 1942 and 1945.

By this time, the research had already entered the realms of the esoteric. Was Waldheim in the 'Ic' (intelligence) or the '1b' (transport and supply) part of intelligence during certain periods? Did it matter? According to at least one historian, the

'1b' took actions based on information supplied by the '1c'. And what was the role of the ordnance officer, which Waldheim claimed he had been in Greece in 1943? Did he just look after munitions or was he responsible for the deportation of POWs? And, if he was, does 'responsible' mean just signing documents or does it include organizing or even instigating such deportations? The fine detail was becoming a matter of great importance.

Our researchers were told repeatedly how vital it was for them to keep us informed of their whereabouts. They were to tell us of everyone they interviewed, and not to leave a location before we had a copy of any statements taken. This, we explained, would enable our teams of lawyers to come back to them with more questions for the interviewees if they felt it worthwhile.

Advances on expenditure and on daily allowances were organized. Chrissie Cocks, who had now joined the team as programme manager, was busy agreeing fees and getting contracts signed. We purchased tape recorders for those without them: 'Please,' we pleaded, 'try and get recorded statements from people who are willing to talk to you.' Names of possible witnesses were given. Geographical areas were divided up; Bonn, Hamburg and other German cities became bases. I felt as if I were in an old war film, sending agents out into the field. The one difference was that I had every hope of getting all my agents back in one piece.

In the afternoon, Ed was once again briefing a team, this time the Greek one. Mark Mazower and Ariana Yakas were about to be despatched to occupied Greece − 'occupied', that is, by a lot of people who had already been interviewed by a veritable regiment of journalists and historians. And we were asking them to seek and find new evidence! However, because they were young and energetic and had a belief in the programme, I had hopes. I couldn't help believing that somewhere − in Salonika, Rhodes, Corfu, Jannina − they would find strong evidence for or against Waldheim. No one can tread a path without leaving at least the trace of footsteps − or can they?

Duly armed with non-exploding tape recorders and tapes, drachma, phone numbers (overt, not covert) and such crucial modern journalistic weapons as our fax and telex numbers and cable address, our Greek team left the office carrying the hopes of the programme makers with them.

This was the day – 24 November 1987 – I will always remember for Peter's comment when I walked into the office. 'Today,' he stated assuredly, 'is the day when our fifth judge is going to agree to the programme.'

Peter had contacted the Law Faculty at the School of Oriental and African Studies as well as Michael Zander, professor of international law at the London School of Economics and legal correspondent for the *Guardian*, and asked them for their opinion of the Indian judge who had been referred to us by the Commonwealth Institute. Both highly recommended Justice P. N. Bhagwati, the former Chief Justice of India and a legal expert with an international reputation. Peter began the long telephonic chase to track him down in India, a task that was complicated by the time difference. Finally, in Delhi, he made contact.

I held my breath; Ed was even persuaded to stop communing with his computer. Once again, the long explanation. Once again, the pauses while penetrating questions were asked about the programme. Once again, the inevitable answers – and then, slowly, a big grin lit Peter's face. A thumb went up in the air.

'That's excellent,' said Peter. 'Would you like to speak to the producer?' And then I was on the phone, explaining a bit more and listening to Justice Bhagwati say that he found the idea very interesting and that he'd be glad to take part. I thanked him, and said that we'd follow up the call with a formal letter and we'd be in touch again in the near future.

Our fifth and final judge – what a weight off my mind. And what an impressive panel! I'd always thought that the quality of the programme and the integrity of the concept depended on getting five top-class judges. Now we'd done it, despite the reactionary Establishment forces lined up against us.

5

Christmas Shopping

Those forces launched another broadside against us the following morning. In a letter to *The Times*, Lord Hailsham, Lord Havers' predecessor as Lord Chancellor, added his considerable weight to the arguments of the project's opponents.

His complaints appeared to centre on two issues: one, that the defence counsel would not be able to consult his client (i.e. Waldheim); and two, his objection in principle to the procedure that we had proposed. He asked in his letter:

> And what is to be the function of the 'panel of five internationally eminent jurists' if they are not actually to adjudicate? Are they just to act as dummies or have they the duty of ruling on the admissibility of evidence or attempting to keep the 'respective counsel' in order?

Lord Hailsham had never, to my knowledge, contacted anyone on the programme to discuss his worries, and in his letter to *The Times*, he seemed to be basing a great many judgements on very few facts. Surprising for a man who had been head of the British judiciary! As well as my own grievances against his Lordship for muddying the waters yet again, I also felt that he was being deeply insulting to our judges, who had made their decisions to take part only after they had the full facts of how the programme was going to be set up.

David Elstein asked me to draft a reply. I knew what I felt like writing, but I supposed that it wouldn't be politic, and so I wrote a relatively polite response instead.

My faith in at least some of the members of the legal profession was restored that evening, when Peter and I went to the

Swedish Embassy to meet Judge Gustav Petrén. We were joined by the Ambassador, and together they read Lord Hailsham's remarks with not a little amusement.

Judge Petrén wanted to know what law we would be using, and we explained that that would be for the panel of judges to work out for themselves. In Sweden, he explained, judges would listen to most types of evidence – hearsay evidence and other sorts considered inadmissible in British courts – but they would only give it the merit they thought it was worth, discounting it according to its source, reliability and so on. I quite liked the idea of that, and I was impressed with Judge Petrén's down-to-earth attitude.

As the week progressed, we began to get a trickle of information from our researchers in the field; this would soon turn into a flood. We had also given our blessing – and tape recorders – to two more 'troops' who then left for Greece and Germany.

Thursday was marked by a not-very-happy conversation with Gerry Spence. I'd planned to send Susan Aslan to the States to meet up with him, and she phoned him to make the arrangements. To her surprise, he said that there was very little point in her coming over until she was in a position to formulate, at least to some extent, the case for the prosecution.

When Susan reported this to me, I rang Gerry back, and we spoke at great length. He told me that, once Susan had worked out the basic prosecution, he would then know in which direction he wanted to devote all his work. I said that I thought it should work the other way around. Given that Gerry had been with the project from the start – indeed, *he* had started it – and Susan was still a 'new girl', I felt that he should give her an outline of the nature of the case he wanted to make. Besides, at this point, we were only just beginning our trawl for new evidence, and it was impossible to tell what we would finish up with. Both the prosecution and the defence had to be fully aware of *all* the evidence available at any one time, so that they could formulate their positions and revise them as necessary. However, on the basis of what he had seen so far, Gerry was plainly unconvinced about the strength of the evidence against Waldheim. I explained my fears – that he would not have the time to put in all the slog that developing the case for the prosecution demanded – and that what I couldn't do was wait until all the research was in before deciding whether or not we had a programme!

'As you know,' I said, 'Allan Ryan has already stated his position concerning the role of the prosecution, as well as his conviction that, even now, he could argue and prove a case against Waldheim. I need that sort of confidence from the prosecution.'

'Well, you as the producer have the right to choose the prosecutor,' he said very fairly – and not for the first time.

'Look, I'll ring you tomorrow and let you know what I think will be best for the programme,' I replied, and with polite goodbyes, we rang off. I needed at least 24 hours to think it all through. I only hoped that, whatever decision I reached overnight, it would not sour the atmosphere of a programme that already had more than its fair share of problems.

The following morning, 27 November, was spent dealing with a variety of administrative jobs. In addition to our team, we had a translator in the office, working on a newly published book on Waldheim that had been written by a Yugoslav and produced in Norwegian (don't ask me why!).

I had a nervous moment when I opened my post and discovered a letter from Lord Rawlinson. He'd just returned from Australia to find Lord Hailsham's letter in *The Times* waiting for him. 'Has anything changed?' he asked.

I spent the next ten minutes on the phone reassuring him that all the promises made would be kept, and explaining that I couldn't be held responsible for any incorrect facts and assumptions that might appear in newspapers. I had sent him, but he had not yet received, all the replies that Thames had made to the other attacking articles and letters that had been printed so far. He seemed satisfied with my answers to his justified worries, and I was convinced that his integrity would be more than enough to withstand these pressures.

Lord Rawlinson assuaged, I could no longer put off a task that I'd been dreading. I'd worried about the prosecutor's role most of the previous evening and well into the night, and it wasn't until the early hours of the morning that I'd made up my mind: in the circumstances, Allan Ryan's unique background made him ideal for this particular job. His knowledge not only of this case but of so much World War II history, his former role as director of the Office of Special Investigations, his experience in preparing cases against alleged 'war criminals' — all this suggested that, if ever there was a man destined for the job of prosecutor in our inquiry, it was Allan.

I was not looking forward to ringing Gerry and telling him my decision, but in the end, it was not as bad as I'd thought it would be. He said that he understood my reasons, and wished me the best of luck with the programme, commenting that it was ironic that he, the man who'd come up with the original idea, was the one not to be involved. The only sad note came when he said that, if he wasn't going to prosecute, he didn't want to be one of the producers either. In reply, I expressed my genuine regrets at this parting of the ways, and my hope that we would meet again in happier circumstances. I knew that Gerry, as well as being a superb advocate, was an original, and life doesn't introduce you to many of those.

As soon as we had finished talking, I phoned Allan Ryan. I'd last spoken to him the previous weekend, when I'd explained the position. He'd said then that he would be delighted to take over if that was how it turned out. Over the telephone now, he reconfirmed his willingness to take on the prosecution. Then I mentioned our inviolate recording dates.

There was silence, then a muttered exclamation. 'I can't make those first few days,' he said. 'That's "Holocaust Remembrance Week" here, and I'm down to give two memorial lectures in Florida.'

I couldn't believe it — sunk without a lifeboat. What to do next? We discussed the problem, but despite agreeing to forgo an intended holiday with his family during part of the relevant time, he felt that his dates in Florida were unbreakable. We left it that both of us would try to think of a solution.

I contacted John White Jones, the head of Thames Television's studios in Teddington on the outskirts of London, to find out how elastic our schedule was — for example, could I work weekends to try and accommodate Allan? Poor John: he was in the middle of sorting out a major industrial problem with his technicians, and here was I messing up his schedules.

'Yes,' he said, after listening to my catalogue of disasters, 'we could work through the weekends if required.'

Well, at least we had one option.

The start of a new month. December 1 saw the Waldheim team almost doubled when Tim House and Susan Aslan joined us fulltime, and we also welcomed our second head office researcher, Veronika Hyks.

It was crucial that everybody familiarize themselves as quickly as possible with all the material we had so far. There was going to be much more coming in and, without a sound grounding in the basics, a lot of it would be meaningless to the newcomers.

To this end, Ed Braman held a seminar, taking Tim, Susan and Veronika through the chronology as dispassionately and objectively as possible. He gave them the background to Waldheim's wartime movements, detailing the agreed dates and places as well as highlighting the various contentious areas, and of the arguments for and against.

It was a slow process, going through the history in such detail, with locations code-numbered to relate to photocopies of some of the key documents we already had in our possession. Ed positively revelled in his role as tutor and all-knowing expert. However, the thousands of hours of work he'd put in so far justified a certain amount of self-satisfaction.

While Ed was marching slowly through Yugoslavia and Greece, I rang Barrie Sales, Thames' director of news, current affairs and documentaries. The previous weekend, the British newspapers had closely resembled a lynching party for the Austrian head of state. The Chicago journalist Chuck Ashman had resurfaced in the *Sunday Express*, claiming a variety of new evidence against Waldheim. However, although I read the story diligently, I'd failed to find anything that I didn't already know. In fact, most of Ashman's 'new' evidence had been in the public domain for the past year or so. Still, I admired Ashman's ingenuity in getting a British national newspaper to run the story so big.

More importantly, his story coincided with a leak from the Commission of Historians. The papers said that a few of its members were of a particularly independent frame of mind, and some of their findings would not be favourable to Waldheim. This came as no surprise to us; Ed had surmised as much during his meeting with Commission member Professor Messerschmidt. But it did lead some newspapers, especially the *Daily Telegraph* that morning, to wonder whether Waldheim was going to resign and even to discuss his possible successor. I myself was extremely sceptical about any talk of resignation. None of this evidence was new, and Waldheim had always said that only the Austrian electorate could remove him.

Later in the day, I phoned Allan Ryan to tell him that we could be a bit more flexible in our recording dates. His reply cheered me up enormously: he had spoken to his lecture organizers and, with just a little bit of luck, he would be released from his speaking engagements and so would be free to keep to our recording schedule. One more small step in the right direction.

One week later, a taxi was taking Susan Aslan and me over the bridge spanning the Charles River that separates Boston from Cambridge, Massachusetts, home of Harvard University. It was like arriving in Father Christmas's grotto: streets decorated in the festive spirit, shops bursting with goodies, carols heard from countless doorways. There was a wonderful warmth and friendliness emanating from everywhere, and, curiously, I felt instantly at home.

I left Susan at our hotel and went to meet Allan to deal with a few contractual matters that had to be sorted out before he and Susan could begin working together in earnest. He took me to a bar and there, 3500 miles from home, I drank some English beer that was only slightly more gassy and ten degrees colder than the same pint in London. We soon finished with the business side, and I filled him in on a lot of small details about the programme – things he'd need to know now that he was to be fully involved.

The following morning, Allan came to our hotel and I introduced him to Susan. That was the last useful thing I could do. Within minutes, the floor was covered with papers – I hadn't any idea that Susan had brought so much with her – and she and Allan were soon into legal minutiae. I crept out and grabbed the rare opportunity to do a little sightseeing and to buy some Christmas presents.

While I was out, I picked up the Boston morning papers. Waldheim was commanding headlines as big as in Britain, and there were further speculations about the results of the Commission of Historians and whether Waldheim would resign.

Before leaving for the States, I'd asked Ed for an analysis of the political scene in Austria from Richard Mitten, a postgraduate student in Austrian politics and one of our researchers there. His assessment ended: 'I don't think ITN [Independent Television News] will be broadcasting Waldheim's resignation story before Thames transmits...' I hoped he was right.

Early the next morning, Susan and Allan resumed detailed work on their papers. They'd established a good working relationship right from the outset, and Susan had told me how impressed she was with Allan's quiet confidence and his quick grasp of many of the complex issues. I left them to go to Logan airport, feeling that the prosecution was in good hands.

The shuttle got me to New York in 45 minutes. Unfortunately, it failed to take my suitcase, and I had to wait at La Guardia for the next shuttle to bring it. This left me no time to go to my hotel before my meeting at Home Box Office, and I arrived there looking like a travelling brush salesman — briefcase in one hand, large suitcase in the other.

I was led into a meeting attended by more vice presidents than even the White House has seen. There were scheduling people, image people (programme image and corporate image), promotion people, production directors and the inevitable lawyers. Everyone seemed friendly enough, but their questions came thick and sharp. I was pressed particularly hard on the likelihood of Waldheim's resignation, but they seemed satisfied when I quoted from Richard Mitten's paper. It was difficult to gauge their response to the programme — were they impressed by what we'd done so far? It was only afterwards, as the meeting broke up, that I heard comments like 'It's an amazingly exciting concept, isn't it?' and other equally gratifying remarks.

I finally made it to my hotel. My room was grubby, badly cleaned and depressing — in fact, just the sort of room in which I'd spent far too much of my life already. But I had no time to go to another hotel or even ask for a room change. I had to get ready for my dinner appointment with Herbert J. Stern, judge *extraordinaire*.

Since I'd last spoken to Judge Stern, I'd read most of his book, *Judgement in Berlin*, which recounted, in confident detail, how he'd defended the US Constitution in the unique case in Berlin, and which had been made into a feature film. I was intrigued to meet him.

Judge Stern was waiting for me when I arrived at the Four Seasons restaurant. He looked even younger than his 51 years, and I wondered how he would get on with the other, much older and far more venerable members of our judges' panel. Over drinks and then some *nouvelle cuisine*, we discussed the programme.

The judge seemed far more interested in the mechanics of the production than in the legal process involved in the inquiry and how the judges would deal with it, although in the course of about five hours' conversation, he did highlight several points that I plainly hadn't thought out sufficiently. However, as the evening wore on, it became all too obvious that I had another major problem on my hands: Judge Stern, having seen his own book turned into a film, was enjoying his relationship with the media.

He'd worked out that, with the exception of the chairman of the judges' panel, the role of the judges would largely be one of listening for most of the proceedings, with relatively little *active* participation. If you wanted to be seen and heard quite a lot on the programme, and to stamp your personality on it, you had to be the chairman.

When the judge asked who the chairman would be, I explained that that would be for the judges themselves to decide − it wasn't up to me. As the hours went by, however, it was plain that this was the role − the *only* role − that Judge Stern envisaged for himself. He argued, not unreasonably, that the inquiry would be taking up a lot of his time, so to make it worthwhile...

It was after midnight when Judge Stern dropped me back at my hotel in his nifty Porsche. Another sleepless night. A decision had to be made. Could I, in conscience, go beyond my self-imposed remit and offer him the position of chairman? Would he fit in with the other members of the panel? I wanted the evidence and what it showed to be the focus of the production. All the participants *had* to be conduits to that purpose.

The phone rang at about eight o'clock the following morning. It was a very brief, polite conversation. And at 8.01, I was back down to four judges.

Two days later, 11 December, I settled my bill at the hotel, asked them to look after my suitcase and caught a taxi down to the very bottom of Manhattan to meet the historian, author and playwright, Dr Rachel Dalven. She had come to the Waldheim team's notice through an organization called The Friends of the Jewish Museum of Greece.

In 1947, she'd returned to her birthplace − the small Greek town of Jannina − to take down evidence about what had happened to the 1950 Jews who had lived there before the Nazi occupation. She told me how the town's Jewish leaders, thinking that they'd be helping their fellow Jews by cooperating with the Nazis, had found instead that all they'd done was made the Nazis' job of rounding them up for deportation that much easier. The Jews had been herded into Larissa, another town, for a short period; while there, 11 young men had escaped, one of whom still lived in Jannina. These men were among the few survivors of the Jewish community in Jannina: after being sent on to Auschwitz from Larissa, 91 per cent of the others had perished.

As appalling as this statistic was, more important to the Waldheim project was Dr Dalven's denial that there had ever been an insurrection among the Jews before their deportation. This seemed to be the kind of evidence that Ed had talked about needing when he'd shown Gerry Spence the document, signed by Waldheim, which suggested that there had been an insurrection. The name of the man who had escaped and who still lived in Jannina would be given to Mark Mazower, one of the researchers in Greece, in the hope that he could find him and interview him.

I returned to the hotel, grabbed a beer and a sandwich and,

suitcase again in hand, went back to Home Box Office. As I entered the building, I heard one of the security men say, 'Here comes that English guy who's always on the move.'

The previous day, at a meeting with Colin Callender, I'd asked him to ask Telford Taylor to suggest the names of some American judges who might be able to replace Herbert Stern. Now I found that Professor Taylor had done his homework — he'd come up with a dozen names, from New York, Boston and all points west. But none of them was better than that of former judge Shirley Hufstedler of Los Angeles. Not only had she been a Circuit Judge for the US Court of Appeals, but in 1979, President Jimmy Carter had made her his Secretary of Education, a position she'd held until 1981. She'd be top of the list when I began phoning the judges on my return to London.

The following Monday found me ground to a halt in London's massive pre-Christmas traffic as I made my way to Thames' Teddington studios. As a result, I arrived late for a full meeting of all the various people who would eventually turn our programme idea into television — the set designer, the senior cameraman, the head of sound, lighting technicians, as well as representatives from wardrobe, make-up and floor services, not to forget the racks engineer (i.e. video engineer) and studio supervisor.

This was not the first time I'd confronted the sheer technical aspects of the programme. Back in October, I'd contacted John White Jones, the man in charge of the studio, who had greeted my proposal with enthusiasm. He was particularly pleased because he and his staff at Teddington had just lost, at least temporarily, a major production. At the 11th hour, a US network had decided to come in on a series about Jack the Ripper that Thames had been about to launch, and this meant that everything had to be put on ice for some months. The Waldheim project, although completely different, would fill in the gap in the studios' schedule quite nicely.

By that time, I had been assigned my set designer: Bill Palmer, who'd also designed the set for the Jack the Ripper series. Together we'd looked at Studio 1 — Teddington's biggest — where we would be recording, and I'd explained in detail the nature of the programme. Bill had already sent away for books on court architecture and for pictures that would show courts, tribunals and other judicial forums from around the world. We talked of the usual production problems as well as one or two that were special to our project. For example, at this stage, I knew that we would need to build in soundproof booths for our instantaneous translators.

By now, I had a checklist of things that had to be dealt with: wardrobe, make-up; autocue for the British and American presenters (still to be chosen); lighting; any special catering arrangements that I'd have to make for the judges, the two legal teams, witnesses and so on; not to mention the security of the set from snoopers as well as nightly security for documents and other important evidence. Later, I would add to the list: wartime library film as well as any original material we might shoot to give an impression of the places that the inquiry would be talking about; graphics; possible music for the opening and closing credits; and, of course, any requirements for the editing. Nine days of recording would have to be condensed to about four hours of television – a classic case of trying to get a quart into a pint pot.

The meeting that day was chaired by Roger Thomas who, a month earlier, had joined us to direct the programme. A dapper dresser, Roger is a first-class director whom I've known for ten years and seen do excellent work on all sorts of programmes, from complex editions of *TV Eye* to national news programmes.

Now, I've been to planning meetings in the past when it seemed as if the only purpose was to provide ammunition for the other participants to throw at you. This meeting was the absolute reverse. Everyone was massively helpful. I outlined the programme idea, and for every problem I had, they seemed to come up with at least three good solutions, even making suggestions on how to overcome problems that I hadn't yet envisaged. I took enormous encouragement from all this goodwill.

When I got back to the office, it was time to start ringing the States. The number that Professor Taylor had given for Shirley Hufstedler proved to be a wrong one. Not a good start, I thought. Sheer laziness drove me to the second name on the list. This was also an incorrect number. Worse and worse. I forced myself to retrace my steps and made a call to international directory inquiries, who gave me a new number for Judge Hufstedler's office.

I got through first time. For what seemed like the hundredth time, I explained the nature of the programme. Again, I was listened to with politeness, and as I finished, the judge asked about the dates and the amount of time required of her. Then, 'Obviously you need a quick answer. I'll let you know by Wednesday at the latest.'

I spent the next two days on tenterhooks, and to keep my mind off Judge Hufstedler's possible refusal, I tried to get through some of the voluminous research that had been coming in.

As each document arrived in the office – through the post, by special delivery, courier, telex and fax machine – it was passed to either Ed or Veronika for initial scrutiny. It was then assigned a number in accordance with the running 'progess sheet' and a pink cover bearing that number. If it were to be translated, a copy was made (and its location noted on the progress sheet), and this was then sent off to Josephine Bacon, who ran the enterprising company that was largely providing us with translations.

When a document returned from one of her multi-lingual translators, the translation was keyed into the computer, together with its file number. Two further copies were then made, one each for Tim and Susan, our solicitors, and the document (the original and the translation) were finally placed in one of our filing cabinets, which were filling at an alarming rate.

Tim and Susan went through all the documents, marking them with that trademark of a solicitor – the hi-light pen. Line after line changed to shocking pink, startling yellow or whatever shade their individual colour-coding called for.

The nature of the material varied widely. For example, here's something that was sent from Greece by Mark Mazower:

X [a contact who was helping Mark] recommended that I see Apostolatos who claims to have seen Kurt Waldheim in

Cefallonia. Apostolatos is a friend of his and X says he will set up a meeting. According to him, Apostolatos knows a lot of people.

X himself was in Cefallonia from summer 1944 onwards, where he stayed next door to the Gestapo. He claims that the Gestapo's interpreter was working for him and that he had a hand in installing him. I explained the crucial importance of interpreters in this sort of investigation and hope that, through X and Apostolatos, we can trace those who were around in Sept. 1943 in Cefallonia and summer 1944 in Corfu. X said at one point, 'I was in the mountains for nearly two years and met almost everyone.'

X was also involved in a Society for Modern Greek History: I get the impression that this is a rather conservative body, devoted to publishing war memoirs of non- and/or anti-Communists, but this may be no bad thing for our purposes since it appears to include a large number of retired generals. When I mentioned my desire to get into the army archives, X was sympathetic and promised help via some of these. This is how it works (or doesn't) here − a slow process!

Another piece of information, dealing with an earlier part of Waldheim's wartime career, came from our man in Rome, James Walston:

Waldheim's time with the Pusteria [Italian army division] in Montenegro, spring 1942. Spoke to ex-corporal Pompeo de Poli, via Pellegrino 35, Belluno. Has a war diary which he is prepared to let us use. Does not remember Waldheim by name but, with the help of Scotti & Viazzi's reconstruction, calculates that the radio officer in Cajnice on the 7th of May 1942 was indeed Waldheim. The German officer was 'tall, thin, fair-haired', he spoke Italian ...Viazzi has an unpublished photo of Waldheim 'with the commanders of the three "allied" [Axis] forces during Operation Trio'. Has also an Alpine engineer officer who remembers Waldheim and will talk to us.

Other documents that arrived included Waldheim's daily war diary entries for a considerable period, and material relating to his time at the Consular Academy in the 1930s which, claimed the Austrian researcher, showed that Waldheim had strong Nazi sympathies at that time. (When we later read the translation ourselves, we found it gave little support to this view.)

In the great tradition of the Balkans, new problems were

surfacing inside Yugoslavia. Our research effort – some of which, even now, must remain a closed secret – was under heavy surveillance. It appeared that the Yugoslav Communist Party was split in its attitude towards the whole Waldheim business. Some of the older Party members had been partisans during World War II and had fought against the Germans; they all wanted to see the truth about Waldheim established and therefore were keen to help us. However, there were others – perhaps younger or closer to Moscow – who were just as keen that we should not get any material, particularly nothing that would, in their eyes, be damaging to their relations with Moscow and even with Austria. Despite this, Yela and Pierre were bravely continuing the legitimate process of trying to get material to us.

By now, we'd located, through the hard work of our researchers, our first three potential eyewitnesses. This was, for me, the most heartening news of all. Another of my recurring nightmares was that, having got everything and everybody in place, we'd have no eyewitnesses. I also knew that, as with opinion polls, the first few approaches to potential witnesses would give us an idea of whether or not people who had actually known and served with Waldheim would actually agree to take part. It now seemed that we were heading for the sort of programme that I'd hoped and prayed to be able to deliver.

That Wednesday, I stayed in the office later than usual in the hopes that I might receive a phone call from Judge Hufstedler. None came, and I finally drove home. Near midnight, my nerve broke. I phoned the judge's office, where it was now almost 5.00 p.m.

'I'm sorry, but the judge isn't here. There's been a storm and her phone line is down – in fact, she's waiting at home for the phone repair man to arrive...Yes, Los Angeles had a terrible storm through the night and a lot of people haven't come into work.'

It was about the best excuse I could have heard – no phone call because no phone. I lived to fight another day.

Thursday passed like Wednesday – waiting for Los Angeles to wake up and get to work. When I arrived home, my wife Lynne told me that the judge's secretary had been on the phone.

'Did you get any feel for the answer?' I pleaded, acting like a child trying to get a glimpse of what was in a Christmas stocking.

'No,' she replied, 'I just spoke to the nice secretary who told me that the judge would be out at lunch between 8.00 and 9.30 p.m. our time.' It was just 8.15 then.

The time passed all too slowly. Finally, on the dot of 9.30, I rang. No, I was told, she wasn't there, but she was due back at any moment. This was becoming an ulcer-making wait. Another 20 minutes and another transatlantic phone call. This time I was put through to the judge herself.

'I've thought a lot about your programme idea...' Mrs Hufstedler said. I inwardly groaned: this was usually the way judges began when they were going to turn me down. '...And I've decided that I will take part,' she concluded.

I breathed out all the air that, subconsciously, I'd been holding in since I'd started dialling.

'I can't make your January meeting but I will be available for the recording in April,' she continued. I thanked her profusely, made a few arrangements to send her some material, and then hurriedly rang off before she had time to change her mind. I then snatched up the phone again, this time to ring Peter with the good news.

The next morning, I gave Chrissie Cocks, our programme manager, the go-ahead to make firm bookings for our seminar on 11 January, when all the judges (except Judge Hufstedler) and the legal teams would meet together for the first time.

By this time, Peter had completed a 50-page tome that would provide an agenda and a working document for the day-long meeting. As well as biographies of all the judges, it contained briefs on the terms of reference − erudite articles on war crimes and criminals, crimes against humanity, murder and ill treatment of prisoners of war and of civilians, slave labour, persecution of the Jews. This was followed by biographies of the legal teams, pleadings, agreed statements of fact and agreed documents, time extensions, pre-trial procedures (including the exchange of research material), the procedures at the actual recording (e.g. time limits, opening and closing speeches), judgement and the rules of evidence (the burden of proof, admissibility of evidence, use of hearsay evidence, character witnesses, how to interview witnesses who might not be able to attend the inquiry).

We despatched this truly impressive document to all the legal people involved in the programme – judges, solicitors, counsel. We hoped that it would provide the basis for what were going to be, in effect, the rules by which the programme would be played. We would be inventing a legal process in only a few weeks – something that most countries achieve only after a long period of evolution – as well as trying to reach unanimity between five different legal systems – those of the UK, the US, India, Sweden and Ireland.

There was one thing I wanted to be sure to do before Christmas. That was to make contact with the man whom I wanted to present the version of the programme that would go out in Britain – Sir Alastair Burnet. (HBO had still to make a decision about the American presenter.)

No one carried more weight on British television than this senior journalist, one of the co-presenters of ITN's *News at Ten* and a former editor of *The Economist* and the *Daily Express*. From my past experience with him on *Panorama* (BBC) and *TV Eye* (Thames), I knew that, as well as being extremely professional, he was also a very easy man to work with. Ever polite, he would listen to the ideas of others and would always be very encouraging. Given the sensitive nature of the Waldheim inquiry, I thought Sir Alastair would achieve just the right balanced and serious approach that I wanted for the introduction and the links between the legal segments.

It was after he came off the air following that Friday's *News at Ten* and just before his departure for a Scottish Christmas that I caught up with him. I launched into my usual description of the programme.

'In principle,' he said, 'I'd be delighted to take part. I will, of course, have to clear it with my editor, David Nicholas, once I have more details.'

After making a lunch date for 8 January, we parted, wishing each other a Happy Christmas.

It all seemed too good to be true. Ever mindful of banana skins, I took nothing for granted, despite my current run of good luck. Let's hope, I prayed, that all the bits of Scotch tape hold through the holidays. January, February and March were going to be pressured months. We still had an enormous amount of work to do — but at least we were in good shape now. I just hoped it would stay that way.

But it was not to be. Our story had one more twist before I was allowed to pack up for Christmas. It was on the Tuesday before the holiday that Peter received a phone call from our Irish judge, James d'Arcy.

We knew that he'd been ill for some time, and he'd constantly warned us that his bad health could prove a problem. However, even though he'd been in hospital for an eye operation, we'd hoped that, by April, all would be well, especially since the judge himself seemed so keen to take part.

Now his wife told Peter that Judge d'Arcy had to return to the hospital in mid-March for another operation, and therefore couldn't take part in our programme. Then the judge came on, apologizing profusely for letting us down. Peter and I both greatly appreciated his concern and thanked him for his past help and kindness, and for his consideration.

Judge d'Arcy's dropping out was not entirely unexpected, and Peter and I had taken the precaution of contacting another Irish judge. Phoning him now, he agreed to see us on 6 January. We could only hope.

Despite this last-minute disaster, I wasn't too despondent. I did have four other judges who were, I hoped, well and truly committed, two first-class legal teams working away, a research effort apparently operating well and productively, witnesses beginning to be identified and a few already agreeing to take part, the seminar booked, the studio booked and the first planning meeting got through successfully.

But in the back of my mind, I couldn't help feeling that the sorts of problems that we'd faced so far were but a beginning, and that between the New Year and our transmission in June, it would feel as if we were on a gigantic roller coaster. Although the pleasures and peaks of this unique programme might prove to be very heady, the troughs and depressions could be very deep indeed.

6

New Year Resolutions

The New Year – 1988 – was only a few days old when our legal coordinator Peter Smith and I flew over to Dublin to have dinner with the man we hoped would be our fifth judge. We stayed at one of my favourite hotels – the Shelbourne, where the Irish Constitution had been drafted and signed. I rather hoped that another agreement would be reached while we were there.

Judge MacWilliam turned out to be a gregarious man with a fine appreciation for food and wine. Socially, the evening was a great success. We talked about everything – the hotel, the food, Irish literature, the politics of the North – and the conversation was further spiced by the judge's dogged determination to avoid discussing any involvement by him in the programme. He was not against the concept in principle – otherwise he wouldn't have agreed to meet us – but every time we brought it up, he changed the subject with lightning speed. In the end, after persuading us to join him for lunch at his club the following day, he was most helpful in suggesting alternative judges, even offering to give us telephone numbers, but he was adamant that he wouldn't take on the role of one of our judges. When he took his leave after midnight, he left a pair of confounded TV men behind.

I was sitting in the bath at eight the following morning when the telephone rang. Luckily, the hotel had been thoughtful enough to provide a phone in the bathroom, so I sat midst the bubbles and listened as Judge MacWilliam suggested another name. 'And what's more,' he added, 'I have the telephone number for this gentleman. Here it is . . .'

'Hang on,' I spluttered. 'I might have a phone next to the

bath, but not a pen and paper. I'll ring you back in five minutes.' I trailed a line of wet footprints back into the bedroom and, armed with writing materials, rang him back.

With yet another number and my hopes high again, I dialled the man Judge MacWilliam had recommended: 'I'm sorry. They lived here until some months ago, but they've moved and I don't know their new number.'

After an hour's detective work by Peter, I rang another number, which this time proved correct. I spelled out the programme for the *nth* time and asked the judge if we could perhaps meet. He replied that he was 'vaguely interested' and that he would come to our hotel in the afternoon.

The judge arrived dead on time. He refused all offers of refreshments and sat, totally self-contained, while we went into details. When we ran dry, he said that he wanted 24 hours to think about it before coming to a decision. Giving nothing away, he shook hands and went off into the cold, wet Dublin afternoon.

I was convinced that he would agree to take part – why else come all that way into Dublin? Peter said that his gut feeling was the reverse. We bet a modest double on it.

Back in the office the next day, we encountered a new and interesting problem. One of Kurt Waldheim's strongest supporters to cross our path so far was Suzanne Lederer, who had been his classmate at the Consular Academy in the 1930s. Interviewed by one of our researchers, she had spoken extensively about the anti-Nazi views of Waldheim and his family, and about a wartime visit that Waldheim had made to her home in Amsterdam. She herself had been a member of a Dutch resistance family.

Then our researcher discovered that Mrs Lederer was separated from her husband and, after some digging, found out where he was and visited him. Mr Lederer told our researcher that his wife had once been engaged to Waldheim! This could account for her stout defence of the man, and even if it didn't, it certainly gave her testimony a curious human angle. As a TV producer, I couldn't stop myself dreaming about her appearing as a character witness for Waldheim and then, in the best *Perry Mason* tradition, Allan Ryan bringing up the fact of her alleged engagement to Waldheim during his cross-examination, to call into question the validity of her testimony.

However, it could never be. Both sides had free access to all the evidence we found, and I had little doubt that, if Lord Rawlinson were to call Mrs Lederer to the stand, he would not fail to mention her previous alleged relationship with Waldheim during his examination.

That evening brought the call from our hoped-for replacement judge. Our conversation was very brief, and ended with my owing Peter a double.

Peter was now convinced that the Irish Establishment was closing ranks with the same speed as the British Establishment had done earlier. I wasn't so sure, but whatever the reason for our Irish candidate's refusal, we were back to four judges and without a clue of what to do next.

Peter and Veronika, our in-house researcher, were left with the problem while I spared a thought for the arrangements that Chrissie Cocks had been making for the seminar for our jurists we were to hold on 11 January at a hotel near Windsor. Our guests, some travelling vast distances to be there, would arrive at different times over the weekend so that they would be fresh for the meeting on the Monday.I'd had too little time to make sure that everything had been arranged properly, but I needn't have worried. Chrissie had done it brilliantly and, with everything taken care of, I was free to look forward to this first meeting of our legal minds.

And while our jurists prepared to travel to the Berkshire countryside from the four corners of the globe, our research went on. The statistics arising out of the programme were already quite impressive: to date, our researchers had provided us with over 600 documents comprising some 7000 pages. Most of them had been in German, but there were also piles of papers in Serbo-Croat, Italian and Greek. They included original *Wehrmacht* material and similar papers from the Italian army and from the Fascist Croatian puppet government set up by the Nazis in Yugoslavia. We had documents originating from the government, police and resistance

94

movements in Greece, as well as material relating to war crimes investigations.

Our teams of researchers had worked in archives in Freiburg and Nuremberg in West Germany and in Cornelia Münster in the East, in those in West Berlin, the US National Archives in Washington, D.C. and the UN archives in New York, as well as others in Belgrade, Zagreb and Ljubljana (all in Yugoslavia), Athens, Tirana (Albania) and, of course, London. They had spoken to former *Wehrmacht* officers, Italian officers, Croatian officials, Yugoslav and Greek partisans and others in ten countries.

They had found witnesses to Waldheim's pre-war and wartime career who, for 43 years, had remained in silent anonymity. We had probably the most detailed account possible of his time in Arsakli/Salonika — through some 300 pages of material, all bearing his name — and were getting close to being able to account for his wartime years more comprehensively than those of any other officer who had fought on the German side.

In November, we had taken over three rooms in a building behind the main Thames Television offices in London's Euston Road. (Because of its relative isolation from Thames, we fondly referred to it as the 'Gulag Archipelago'). At first, with only three of us (Ed, Susie and me), the office had seemed ridiculously luxurious in terms of space — acres of empty floors and walls, enough room for each of us to have a vast room to ourselves. However, within a month, I was sharing my room with Susie, Peter (and his increasing pile of weighty legal tomes), Veronika, and Ed and his computer.

I would watch Ed with fascination. He didn't just work on that machine — he related to it, talked to it. He kept up a half-muttered running conversation while his fingers punched the keyboard, and he rocked backwards and forwards with excitement every time a new intriguing fact was logged in.

Next door was the general office. Here Chrissie sat, only occasionally without a phone at her ear or a calculator in her hand — she always seemed to have a hundred things to do at once. In another corner was Kate Johns, our legal secretary, who had come as a temp but stayed on because she was so good and so popular. She worked fulltime for the two solicitors, doing their confidential work, and had the unenviable responsibility of ensuring that she didn't give away to one what the other told her. Like everyone on the programme, she was determined to do her bit to make sure that President Waldheim had as fair a deal as we could possibly manage. Also based in this office was Roger Thomas, our studio director, and his personal assistant, June Mason.

The third big room belonging to the programme had been divided into two by a hardboard wall. Here Susan Aslan and Tim House maintained their separate and distinct operations. They would soon be joined by an associate producer each, whose job it would be to liaise between their respective legal teams and Roger so that each side could produce its evidence in the way that was best for both television and the judges.

For example, we were then in the process of trying to figure out how we could present the 500 or more separate frames (each showing a document or part of one) that might be required in evidence or during cross-examination. Because it would be impossible to anticipate which would be used and in what sequence, we had to devise some way of recalling them instantly. And not only general shots of the documents, but also close-ups of signatures or particular sentences or paragraphs. We'd also have to provide English translations to be on the screen at the same time.

Filing cabinets were arriving daily and filling almost as soon as they were found a place in the office. The office walls were also used. One was covered with a white board on which were listed the names of our researchers, where they were at any particular time and their current telephone numbers. Another held a bulletin board overflowing with all the latest cuttings on Waldheim from the world's press.

Besides typewriters, we had a photocopier, a shredder and our own fax machine, invaluable for transmitting and receiving documents. And there was our coffee machine, used at least as heavily as any other piece of equipment in the office.

Morning and afternoon, catering staff arrived with trays of rolls to sustain those among us who never seemed to have time for breakfast or lunch. However, no day would have been complete without the arrival of our sandwich delivery boy — a delightful punk with shocking pink hair — who did an excellent line in chicken Waldorf, curry chicken, tuna and mayonnaise and a variety of other imaginative home-made sandwiches. I was finding that worry doesn't necessarily make you lose weight...

The week before the seminar, Bill Palmer, our designer, came into the office with his first model of the set. I'd called a meeting to discuss some of the visual problems we might have with the programme. As well as the set, this included the presentation of the documents, and so Morgan Sendall, our graphics designer who would have to solve that particular dilemma, also attended.

Bill arrived carrying his cardboard construction like a headwaiter presenting a flaming *crêpe Suzette*. As we gathered round, we could see that it was a futuristic concept that could be shot in the round. With something like a 24-metre diameter, it was going to be big and it was going to be impressive. There were a few slight problems, all of which Bill was sure could be ironed out, but overall it was well received, particularly by Roger, and he was the man who would have to shoot it.

Bill would return in a few weeks with a more substantial model incorporating the changes we'd suggested. Morgan would soon be presenting us with some kind of logo or symbol that would eventually hang behind the judges' bench. We'd all agreed that this should be an international concept and in no way 'judicial'.

I'd been asked by a TV magazine, *Video Age International*, to write 750 words on the nature of the programme. This in itself was not a matter of great concern, but one question in the editor's letter did make me stop and think. 'What if,' she asked, 'the judges find him innocent and your evidence in the programme suggests he is guilty?'

Although we weren't, of course, going to have a guilty/innocent result, I still felt that the question was a valid one. What if, in the public's mind, the evidence weighed heavily against Waldheim, but in the narrow areas of judgement that our jurists might choose to use, they found that it didn't add up to a case? Would we have taken man's knowledge any further forward? Or, by using this particular formula, would we merely have added to the already pervasive confusion?

It seemed to me, as I sat down to think things through, that presenting as many facts to the audience as possible was undoubtedly a worthwhile project if it enabled people to have a better understanding of what one small corner of a real war had been like. The programme would look at the nature of war, and at those low-to-middle rank officers who don't start wars but without whom wars could not be fought. It would examine the degree of responsibility that they must share, even with the built-in unfairness that it is usually only the vanquished who have to pay the price.

I thought that the best possible argument for doing the programme was our examination of how responsible we all are for our actions in time of war. Do soldiers have the scope to exercise objections and to make unilateral actions of protest? At what level does responsibility end, if it ever does? And in the same spirit that moved the victorious Allies to institute the Nuremberg tribunals, I thought that, in the Waldheim case, people wanted to see justice done, with the facts brought out and aired before impartial judges. It wasn't a bad motivation.

Late on Friday afternoon, while I was mulling over all this, I had a phone call from Sir Alastair Burnet. We'd had lunch that day and I'd been able to give him more details of the programme. He'd checked with his editor at ITN, and now told me that he would be happy to be the presenter of the British edition, adding that his editor had had no reservations. I was both pleased and relieved: if Sir Alastair had felt that the programme was not going to be equitable, he would have made a very diplomatic excuse for not being able to take part. I felt that we'd just received a much needed vote of confidence.

One of the more inspired decisions I made while putting together the Waldheim programme was my selection of the Oakley Court Hotel near Windsor for the venue of our one-day seminar. Set in 35 acres of its own grounds, with lawns sweeping down to the River Thames, this French-style Gothic château had been built by an Englishman to comfort his homesick French wife. With its arched windows, spires and pinnacles, it had provided a suitable backdrop for a number of films: *Dracula*, Neil Simon's spoof of detective novels *Murder by Death*, Tommy Steele's musical *Half a Sixpence* and the girls'-school farce *The Belles of St Trinian's*.

It seemed particularly fitting for our purposes because it had also been used during World War II for training British and French agents who were to be dropped behind enemy lines. In addition to this appropriate history, all the hotel's rooms are large and beautifully furnished, and the food served in its restaurant is excellent. It was just the sort of place that would provide the right kind of ambience to put everyone attending the seminar in a good mood.

First to discover this were our overseas visitors, who had arrived over the weekend: Judge Petrén from Sweden, Allan Ryan and Professor Taylor from the US, and Justice Bhagwati from India. The latter, whom we had only known as a voice on the telephone, had been met at the airport by Chrissie. She'd phoned me afterwards and told me that I would undoubtedly like this gentle, humorous and very precise man. This sentiment was echoed by Peter when he, too, phoned later in the day. As our legal coordinator, he'd been elected to stay at the hotel as our resident host.

Early on Monday morning, I arrived at the hotel with Barrie Sales, who had come along as an observer, and found that Sir Frederick Lawton and Lord Rawlinson were in the dining-room having breakfast. I joined them nervously, but there was no need to worry. Both were in very good humour − the hotel atmosphere was working.

There was a good reason for my having a quiet word before the meeting. I wanted to raise gently the sensitive issue of whether or not the judges would be prepared to wear gowns during the inquiry. However, Sir Frederick immediately thought this an excellent idea, saying that it would give a sense of unity to the judges' panel. The question of whether they should wear wigs − which had never been a proposition − remained a much-laughed-over joke, particularly by the American contingent who, not fully appreciating our British love of the idiosyncratic, thought wearing wigs in law courts not a little peculiar.

When Sir Frederick and Lord Rawlinson had finished their meal, we joined the rest of our jurists. I greeted those I'd already met, and then introduced myself to Justice Bhagwati.

Both Chrissie and Peter had been right: it was impossible not to warm to the well-travelled, talkative and helpful former chief justice. Age had left few marks on him, and he seemed to have boundless energy as well as enormous enthusiasm for our project.

I also renewed my acquaintance with Judge Petrén. Like many of his fellow countrymen, he was slightly taciturn, but this was softened by his keen sense of humour. In the relaxed atmosphere, he talked easily about the programme and about some of the attacks there had been from the British Establishment. The judge was totally supportive and very keen to give us every assistance.

It was almost 9.30 and time for the seminar to begin. We'd been joined by Tim House and Susan Aslan, our two briefing solicitors; by Susie Harrison, who would be taking notes; by Telford Taylor, our legal consultant; and by Colin Callender from HBO who'd also flown in from the States to be, like Barrie, an observer. Standing at the chairman's table, which I shared with Peter, I called everyone to attention. With this array of very senior legal talent in front of me, and an agenda that included such items as 'terms of reference', 'admissibility of evidence', 'disclosure', 'legal definitions and procedures', it was no wonder that I was somewhat ill at ease and that my knees were gently knocking!

The first task of the morning was to sort out just those terms of reference. Lord Rawlinson and Tim had already submitted draft terms to the judges and lawyers. Now words were added and then taken away; adjectival clauses introduced only to be smitten by someone else's objections; legal arguments bounced back and forth. Finally, the terms of reference appeared:

> Whether this commission − restricting its consideration solely to the statements, documents and submissions presented at the hearing − is of the opinion that there is enough evidence to warrant an answer by Dr Kurt Waldheim to allegations that he wrongly participated in acts which were contrary to the international laws of war.

It had taken nearly 1½ hours to agree this short formula, and I had a sinking feeling that, with all the other items still to be discussed, we were going to be there until midnight. On the other hand, I was grateful that there appeared to be an abundance of goodwill on all sides. We moved on.

Lord Rawlinson argued that, given that he had no client to instruct him, he couldn't be 'defence' counsel – he had no one to defend! Equally, because this wasn't a trial there could be no counsel for the prosecution. It was then agreed that Allan Ryan would be the 'presenting counsel' - i.e. he would present the evidence – and Lord Rawlinson would be the 'challenging counsel' - i.e. he would challenge the evidence presented. It was also formally agreed that the proceedings themselves would be called a 'Commission of Inquiry'.

There was now a very complicated discussion about the basic charge under which Allan Ryan could formulate the specific indictments, and I listened, fascinated, to the arguments. Would the charge be war crimes based on the Nuremberg tribunals? Not according to Professor Taylor; he said that, because charges of 'preparing and waging aggressive war' were plainly inappropriate in the Waldheim case, to rely on Nuremberg would be wrong. He added that, for the most part, 'crimes against humanity' would also be inapplicable: laying charges related to this would raise the issue of the charges being *ex post facto* – that is, this concept had only been introduced *after* the alleged crimes had been committed.

It seems that the concept of 'crimes against humanity' was introduced at Nuremberg because of what Hitler had done to some of his own people – Jews, gypsies, Communists and others. Charges of 'war crimes' only applied when they were committed against an enemy. Plainly, Hitler had not been warring against his own people, but the Allies had thought that what the Nazis had done to millions of their fellow countrymen had been so monstrous that a new type of charge had to be framed and punishment served on those who had been responsible.

There was a general feeling at the meeting that to be too specific on the basic charges could lead to endless wrangling over legal definitions. As Allan Ryan pointed out, 'It is very important that the time of the hearing be devoted to the evidence and not to academic submissions of law which will be of little interest.' However, he could not exclude the

101

possibility of raising charges of crimes against humanity – particularly in the case of 'registration' of Jews, since that was now clearly a defined war crime. Similar problems could also arise from the allegations relating to the deportation of Italian soldiers *after* the Italian capitulation to the Allies but *before* they became belligerents.

In the end, it was decided that the 'indictment' would specify the act alleged, the relevant law which the act was said to violate (either by reference to the London Charter or the Geneva or Hague conventions) and the degree of participation or complicity alleged against Dr Waldheim. While not wanting to be so tied to legal definitions that common sense would be lost, the Commission could not come to a judgement in a legal vacuum. Therefore, their findings would be based on the body of law that had at least created precedents for the measurement of war crimes – such as the definitions of war crimes set out in the London Charter and adopted by the UN General Assembly on 12 December 1950, and the Nuremberg Judgement. For example, the latter states that:

> International law imposes duties and liabilities upon individuals as upon States... Individuals have international duties which transcend the national obligations of obedience imposed by the individual State. He who violates the laws of war cannot obtain immunity while acting in pursuance of the authority of the State, if the State authorizing action moves outside its competence under international law.

Lord Rawlinson assured everyone that he would not wish to make jurisdictional points, and while the facts alleged would be challenged, the *ex post facto* question would be left to the judges to sort out.

There was a general agreement that hearsay evidence would be acceptable; as with the London Charter, the Commission 'would not be bound by technical rules of evidence' and they would admit any evidence that was deemed to have value. This was just what had attracted me when I had talked to Judge Petrén about the Swedish system.

Sir Frederick raised the possibility of introducing a rule against 'double hearsay' - hearsay evidence about hearsay evidence. For example, this would occur if, say, the wife of a

102

long-dead German officer appeared as a witness and told how she remembered her husband talking about what he claimed to have heard Waldheim talking about in the officers' mess.

It was decided that any disagreement at the actual inquiry about what was or was not admissible as evidence would be sorted out by the members of the Commission, and any disagreements that occurred before we recorded it would be settled by Peter as legal coordinator. If he failed to get the parties involved to agree, the problem would then be taken to the 'resident judge', Sir Frederick Lawton, and if agreement failed then, it would be 'red starred' and decided by the full Commission on the day before recording began.

Given that the events we would be examining had occurred more than 40 years before, I'd been worried about the possibility that good witnesses would have to be eliminated from the Inquiry if they were too old, infirm or simply unable to come to London for the recording. I breathed a sigh of relief when it was agreed that any such witnesses could give their testimony and be cross-examined *in situ* with both legal sides represented. Editing of such material would have to be agreed by both sides.

Perhaps one of the greatest problems we encountered during that day was how to deal with statements made by President Waldheim himself, including his two submissions to the US Justice Department and his so-called 'White Book'. Allan raised the issue of calling into question Waldheim's credibility by pointing out any contradictions in statements made by him. Lord Rawlinson said that he could not explain any such contradictions because he had no client to consult as in a conventional case, but Judge Petrén averred that it would be difficult to ignore Waldheim's own account, especially since it was available to the public at large.

Feeling just a touch underqualified, I spoke up. 'It will be difficult for me,' I said, 'to defend the programme if we aren't even going to use Waldheim's own written defence against the many allegations made against him – especially since he won't be there to do it himself.'

We broke for lunch without agreement on this crucial issue. It was a bad moment. However, there was so much goodwill at work that I knew a breakthrough would occur sooner or later.

It was through the good offices of Professor Taylor that a solution was found. After a sandwich lunch, we reassembled, and the former US brigadier general suggested that Waldheim's 'White Book' and any documents to which it referred should be included as exhibits for the Commission itself, which could be used by either side. This appeared to suit everyone.

It was then decided that having a 'Statement of Agreed Facts' would be very helpful. Judge Hufstedler had already suggested this in a letter she'd written to the Commission. By doing this, we could dispense with such non-contentious issues as basic historical background and Waldheim's ranks and particular assignments.

It was felt that leading questions should be left to the discretion of the Commission. In addition, both sides officially agreed to disclose all documents, statements, facts and interviews with witnesses in advance of the recording – something we'd already been doing in anticipation of this decision. We also agreed the order of speeches by counsel; the timing of the proceedings; that the judges would wear gowns but counsel wouldn't; and that the judges would return to deliver their judgement on the night of transmission. It was also decided that witnesses would be asked to undertake a promise on entering the witness box, as follows: 'I solemnly and sincerely promise that the evidence I give shall be the truth.'

It was now my turn to explain and get agreement on the technical arrangements. I told the Commission how I intended to have the Inquiry introduced by Sir Alastair Burnet and his American equivalent (still to be chosen by HBO), and that three or four times during the programme they would give viewers the geographical and historical context in which the next part would be set. The words and pictures to be used during these interpolations would have to be agreed by the two sides and obviously would not imply anything about Waldheim's own part in the events. It was generally agreed that all this would be important for the audience's understanding.

To cover the proceedings, I'd already engaged a company of court shorthand-writers who could offer the latest system of verbatim reporting. Using some American machines just out on the market, the writers touched keys that represented phonetic sounds, and these were fed into a word processor. This computer identified the sounds and turned them into words, which were shown on a visual display unit (VDU). The system did generate a tiny percentage of errors, but these would then be corrected by a second writer. Therefore, within five or six seconds of words having been spoken at the inquiry, they would be visible on VDUs, recallable as required and also able to be turned into printed copy.

All this, I explained, would be available on set. The lawyers seemed duly impressed. It was a far more modern system than anything operating in the UK courts and in most places in the US.

Finally, we spent the rest of the afternoon talking about courtroom practice. In the UK, lawyers remain firmly rooted behind their tables or benches – no histrionics or walking about the courtroom. However, there can be no one in Britain who has not seen, either on film or television, the more individualistic approach of American attorneys, who all seem to gyrate around the courtroom, eyeball witnesses and talk individually to members of the jury while moving slowly along the front of the jury box. It's certainly a much more dramatic way of carrying out justice than our own rather static and perhaps staid way of proceeding.

The discussion raised the question of the disparity between the two legal styles. Allan Ryan obviously wanted the freedom to move about, while Lord Rawlinson, after a lifetime of immobile presentation, was only used to speaking from one spot. In the end, it was decided to permit the procedures and etiquette of both systems, as the two counsels wished. Lord Rawlinson conceded, with tongue well and truly in his cheek, 'Unless I'm prepared to move about as well, Allan Ryan will get all the best shots.'

The Commission now tied up the few loose ends that remained. The judges agreed not to interrupt the counsel during their opening and closing speeches; questions would be addressed at the end. However, they would reserve the right to ask questions of witnesses at their own discretion. Finally, just before we broke for a well-deserved rest before dinner, it was agreed that Sir Frederick Lawton would chair the panel of judges (now to be called 'Commissioners').

That evening, I gave a dinner for my guests at the hotel. With such excellent company, it went extremely successfully, exemplifying the spirit of goodwill that had existed all day.

As the senior members of the Commission departed, either by car for home or upstairs to bed, everyone seemed to be looking forward to April and the recording. Before leaving for home myself, I treated myself to a game of snooker with Tim, Peter and Susie on the hotel's 300-year-old table. I suspected that it had seen few players worse than me, but that night, I really didn't care how many easy pots I missed. Thanks to everybody's hard work, I'd gained a whole bagful of points that day.

7

The Eye of the Storm

The days following the seminar were a bit of an anti-climax. Having climbed successfully over that hurdle, there was no immediate goal in sight — except one.

We were still in desperate need of a fifth judge to replace James d'Arcy. While the rest of us had been at the Oakley Court Hotel, Veronika Hyks had been left with the task of asking a number of High Commissions and embassies for any ideas — and it was through this route that our geographical interest swung to Canada.

Veronika had been given the name of a former Chief Justice of Nova Scotia, and when Peter rang him, he appeared to be very interested. Unfortunately, he was still sitting as a 'supernumerary' judge and didn't know if it would be possible for him to take part. He'd have to speak to the present Chief Justice and get back to us on Friday night.

Friday was also to be my last day at the office before my next visit to the United States, for I'd been invited over to California by Home Box Office to take part in their press launch of the Waldheim project. Never having attended such a gathering, I wasn't sure what to expect. Thames had issued a fairly laconic press statement about the forthcoming programme, but in the US, it was to be launched during a full day's presentation of upcoming Home Box Office attractions to a room full of media editors from across the States.

It seems that these editors gather in Los Angeles twice a year to be battered for days on end by the various networks and TV producers, all hyping their latest projects. On the one hand, I suppose this provides the journalists with a lot of material that they can use over the next few months, and gives them an opportunity to meet programme makers as well as some of the stars in one place and at one time – not a bad reason, given the vast expanse of the United States. On the other hand, I feel that there is perhaps a danger of information overload, as the editors try to take in the hype of one company after another, with the result that all the programmes blend into each other.

By Friday, I'd more or less finalized my schedule for the next week, and my airline tickets had arrived. All that was left to do was to make the call to the Canadian judge.

I wasn't very surprised to learn that, after checking, the former Chief Justice had decided that, while he was still sitting on the bench, it would be improper for him to take part. But we were in luck: he suggested the name of a former colleague – another Appeal Court judge who had retired completely and who might be interested. He gave me the phone number of the Honourable A. Gordon Cooper of Halifax, Nova Scotia, and after thanking him for considering our offer, I rang this new judge straightaway. After another rendition of my much-rehearsed description of the project, Mr Justice Cooper declared a considerable interest. In the course of our conversation, I learned that, as well as having been a judge of the Appeal Division of the Supreme Court of Nova Scotia from 1968 to 1983, he'd also been, in his youth, a Rhodes Scholar and, much later, President of the Canadian Bar Association. He sounded ideal, and I told him that I'd be rearranging my schedule so that I could see him in Halifax before returning to London.

The next morning, I took off from Heathrow for Los Angeles. HBO had kindly provided me with a first-class ticket, and I settled back to enjoy ten hours of luxury.

To my great disappointment, we descended into Los Angeles International – commonly known as LAX – through grey, overcast skies. My waiting HBO hosts drove me in one of those extended cars that look as if the front end starts moving minutes before the back end to the Sheraton Hotel at Redondo Beach, just south of LA, where the conference was going to be held in two days' time.

A good night's sleep sorted out the eight-hour time difference and the stress (even in first class) of the ten-hour flight, and by mid-morning, I was beginning to feel vaguely human again. I decided to go for a walk to clear my head and get my bearings. In front of the Sheraton, beyond the carpark, was the Pacific, today breaking over the sea wall in great spumes of spray. Adjacent to my hotel was another, smaller one – the Portofino Inn – whose very foundations were built right into the ocean. Between the two hotels, the water in the yachting marina rose and fell dramatically, and the air hummed with the sounds of rigging lines and other bits of yachting gear whipping around in the wind. What with the sea and the weather, I was reminded of my childhood visits to Blackpool on the Lancashire coast, and was a little put out that I wasn't experiencing the sunny California that I'd expected.

That afternoon, I returned to LAX with my hosts to meet Telford Taylor, who would also be appearing at the conference. His book on war crimes and the American involvement in Vietnam – *Nuremberg and Vietnam: An American Tragedy* – had provided my reading matter on the flight over. Not only was it extremely learned in its description of the history and evolution of war crimes, but Professor Taylor had not shied away from grappling with the problem of alleged war crimes committed by Americans in South-east Asia. I'd found it immensely informative and, with the Waldheim project coming ever closer to completion, extremely useful. That night at dinner, I was again able to pick the brains of this eminent lawyer, and we discussed the programme and the many problems we still had to contend with. A natural teacher, he imparted information with ease and clarity.

Between our main course and coffee, the peace of the dining-room was shattered by the arrival outside of a helicopter and a cacophonous mixture of police, fire engine and ambulance sirens. The Portofino Inn, now lit dramatically by flashing red lights, had partially slipped into the sea – the crashing waves had undermined parts of the foundations until they simply caved in. A news reporter in a helicopter had picked up the hotel's distress calls on his radio and had been first on the site. He was now in the process of ferrying 50 people, who had made their way up to the hotel's flat roof, over to our hotel and safety.

We all watched aghast as this drama unfolded. Still, it was

difficult not to imagine that it was all a magnificently staged film sequence – after all, this *was* California. When things quietened down a bit and the rescue was over, we said goodnight and went gratefully to our warm, dry beds.

According to the news bulletins the next morning, seven people had died along that stretch of coast the previous night. Breakers up to 25 feet high had slammed into the beaches, destroying 14 seaside restaurants, as well as the six rooms lost by the Portofino. The carpark outside the Sheraton was a sight: a yacht had been thrown from the harbour on to the tarmac, and dozens of cars had been tossed together like discarded toys. Damage was estimated at over $25 million, and the area designated as a disaster zone. It was a turbulent start to the day, and I hoped that it wasn't an indication of what was to come.

I made my way to the Presidential Suite, where I was scheduled to attend a planning meeting. Colin Callender and Bridget Potter came forward to greet me, and together we joined Professor Taylor and a few HBO people I hadn't yet met. Nancy Lesser, director of consumer press information, proved to be massively efficient despite appearing as if she'd just stepped out of the headquarters of a Paris *couturière*. She was accompanied by her immediate boss, Quentin Schaffer, and David Pritchard, a richly funny man whose role was to look after corporate PR for HBO.

The planning meeting was followed by a buffet lunch with the invited journalists. I hoped that they would eat their fill – because of my increasing nervousness, I didn't: (I feel a lot more comfortable behind the camera than in front of it).

Lunch over, a quartet of HBO's top executives gave brief speeches about their respective divisions. Then it was our turn. On the top table were Professor Taylor, Bridget Potter and myself; Quentin Schaffer acted as moderator. The questions flew at us five at a time, and to the great glee of the HBO people, the normally relaxed press corps launched into us with the enthusiasm of Roman lions enjoying a meal of Christians – controversy at its best!

'Is this not, by any other name, trial by television?'

'How are you going to edit down nine days of recording to four hours?'

110

'Is it true that you've spoken to Waldheim – and if so, what did he say?'

'Will Waldheim be taking part?'

'Will Austria be transmitting the programme?'

'Has there been any political pressure on you?'

'How did you get the idea in the first place?'

For 40 minutes, the questions came thick and fast, with reporters shouting from all corners of the room. Finally, Quentin Schaffer called a halt. HBO were already behind their very tight schedule, and it was now time to leave *Waldheim* and go on to *Baja Oklahoma*, complete with preview highlights and a press conference with the writer, producer, director and stars. But the Waldheim project team were by no means finished.

For the next four hours, Professor Taylor and I were bounced between different rooms and interviewed by a myriad of TV journalists, all very polite and very civilized. Throughout this long, wearing process, I was greatly helped by Professor Taylor. Unflagging despite his years, he answered the journalists' questions brilliantly, explaining when required the history of war crimes and some of the legal niceties, and always with the patrician air of a true expert. He was a powerful and comforting figure with whom to share this ordeal.

Finally, we finished. As Professor Taylor and I staggered down to the hotel bar, I remarked that I felt like a well-vacuumed carpet: whatever information had been there, it had long since been hoovered up. Thirstily, the professor downed his vodka martini and I my gin – one drink that I felt I richly deserved. That is, at least for the moment: only tomorrow would tell what sort of result we would get from all those interviews.

When he finished his drink, Professor Taylor returned to his room to pack. He had to take the 'red eye' that night – the five-and-a-half-hour night flight that, because of the three-hour time difference, would get him into New York by mid-morning. From Kennedy airport, he would be going straight to Columbia University to teach one of his law classes. A remarkable man.

As for me, I was off to the HBO dinner. A fleet of very large cars and small buses took the combined gathering of television

111

makers, moguls, stars and critics to the Palos Verdes estate, overlooking the Pacific. 'This is where they made the *Scruples* mini-series,' someone informed me. I was suitably impressed, even though I'd never heard of the *Scruples* mini-series. Through the grand entrance we went, waved in by smartly clad attendants with lighted batons – rather like the ones they use to wave in 747s on a dark night. We touched down in front of an enormous mansion straight out of *High Society* – or even *Scruples*.

During cocktails I spotted Garry Trudeau, the brilliant cartoonist responsible for the *Doonesbury* comic strip (which, in Britain, appears in the *Guardian*), and his beautiful wife Jane Pauly, one of the presenters of a nationwide breakfast TV programme out of New York. However, just as I was trying to get an introduction, they both dashed off to catch the 'red eye' - it seemed to be the thing to do.

After dinner, the limos dropped us back at the hotel, where the HBO staff retired to the Presidential Suite for what they described as an 'inquest'. I was joined in the bar by the one escapee from this doleful task – the anarchic David Pritchard, who said that post-mortems were not for him.

The next morning, the HBO show was all over. I signed my hotel bill, and Nancy Lesser chauffeured me to downtown Los Angeles; she was as keen as I was to meet our American judge, Shirley Hufstedler. After some difficulty in the one-way system, we arrived at the skyscraper where her practice – Hufstedler, Miller, Carlson & Beardsley – is housed.

We got out at the 45th floor and entered a suite of offices, the like of which I'd only previously seen on American soaps like *Dallas* and *Dynasty*. The enormous open-plan central area had the lofty ceiling of a British banking house. Rows of conference rooms faced the cubicles of an apparently endless line of secretaries, all bent over their word processors. It seemed like a extremely large practice to me, but Mrs Hufstedler later said that it was, by American standards, only of moderate size, with 'just 80' lawyers working there.

The former judge greeted us at reception and led us into her office. This occupied one corner of the building, and had breathtaking views towards Hollywood and Beverly Hills; the view of the Pacific was, today, obscured by the Los Angeles smog. An extremely courteous woman of absolute composure, Judge Hufstedler instantly impressed both Nancy and me. After a short talk, she invited us to join her for lunch at her club. In its quiet, professional atmosphere, we got down to the real purpose of our meeting. I'd brought with me the minutes of our seminar at Windsor the previous week, and briefly went through with her the areas of agreement. She concurred with all these points, and gave her own reasons why she thought they were correct.

What impressed me most about Mrs Hufstedler was her complete self-assurance, the result of having worked out all the angles in advance. Despite being extremely busy running her practice as well as carrying out her own appellate court work, she'd obviously been through every legal point at issue, and had formed clear, well-thought-out opinions on them all. Although I had the advantage of having been with the project since the beginning, I was astonished to find that the former judge, having only recently joined us, was already up to speed − she'd considered all the legal implications, all the requirements to make this a fair and balanced procedure, and the basis on which she would take part. New information was instantly assimilated; pertinent questions probed every idea introduced.

I was glad that I'd done my homework. It wasn't difficult to understand why, before she had accepted President Carter's offer of a Cabinet post, many writers on legal matters thought that she had a very good chance of becoming the United States' first woman Supreme Court Justice.

After Mrs Hufstedler promised that it would take an earthquake (not something mentioned lightly in that part of the world) to keep her from appearing on the programme, we took our leave.

As Nancy returned to the hotel to prepare for that evening's Cable Television Awards ceremony, I headed for the airport and the 'red eye' to Boston. Arriving at daybreak, I was only too aware of why that flight has been given that particular name − although, in my case, it should have been 'red eyes'. Then followed a two-hour wait before my flight to Halifax, Nova Scotia was called.

I was amused to see that the aircraft that would be taking me to see our potential Canadian judge was a twin-engined Beechcraft 1900, a great change from the 747s, Tristars and DC10s that I'd been travelling in recently. Besides the pilot and co-pilot, only one other passenger occupied the 20-seat plane, giving the flight a great feeling of exclusivity. With a sigh, I spread out my belongings and myself and fell asleep, only waking briefly as we landed in Portland, Maine for a change of crew.

The temperature in Los Angeles had been nearly 70 degrees when I'd left the previous night. Now, as we approached Halifax, the pilot informed my fellow passenger and me that it was at freezing point outside. I said a silent prayer of thanks as I dragged on my overcoat which, until now, had been so much excess baggage.

As the taxi drove through the countryside towards Halifax, I was reminded of the quiet beauty of Sweden: endless vistas of snow-covered pine forests interspersed with lakes, all frozen over. We dropped down towards Dartmouth on one side of Halifax Harbour, and then across one of the two pencil-slim, elegant bridges into Halifax itself. My hotel room was a welcome sight; I hurried to take a bath, have a shave and change the clothes in which I'd spent the previous night.

No sooner had I performed all these various rites than the phone rang to announce the arrival of Mr Justice A. Gordon Cooper. Over coffee in the hotel lounge, we first exchanged pleasantries. The judge told me that he'd retired from the Canadian bench in 1983 only because it was mandatory to do so on reaching the age of 75; however, even after such a short acquaintance I could see that he'd lost none of his sharpness, nor his sense of humour. Yet, it was his modesty, his unassuming manner, his self-effacing style that made the biggest impression on me.

Finally, it was time to get down to business. Yet again I explained in detail the nature of the programme and how we were intending to make it. The judge sat impassively, listening carefully and (after an apology) smoking.

'That's all extremely interesting,' he said when I'd finished my presentation. 'You're obviously taking great pains to get it right. I'm particularly impressed with the reputations of those

114

already taking part. . .' He paused. I held my breath. '. . . And I would be delighted to join your panel of judges.'

Full of joy, I could breathe again. Every minute of lost sleep, every sticky, uncomfortable moment during my night-time flight had been worth it.

8

A Wild Document Chase

I immediately came up against a problem when I arrived back in the office on Monday. Our researchers in Germany had, by this stage, established very good relations with a number of former *Wehrmacht* officers who'd served with Waldheim. They included Colonel Bruno Willers, *Leutnant* Karl Mang and *Oberst* Joachim Macholz, who had been in charge of the liaison staff with the Italians in Tirana, Albania when Waldheim had been attached to it. According to our researcher Nicholas Goodrick-Clarke, Macholz was prepared to give evidence but, since he was getting on in years, probably only from his own home.

This meant that, somehow, we'd have to arrange for all the relevant legal people to see him there. Unfortunately, as Nick pointed out, Macholz wasn't the most enthusiastic of witnesses and, especially considering his age, it would be all too easy to frighten him off.

I talked to our solicitors, Tim House and Susan Aslan, to see if we could work out how statements could be taken from witnesses in advance of the recording. We wanted to avoid sending a procession of, first, our researcher, then one solicitor followed by the other, and finally, if evidence were to be given *in situ*, both senior counsel and a video crew. We'd have to achieve a sensible compromise if we were to avoid losing valuable eyewitnesses and, at the same time, not disadvantage one side or the other.

While we all contemplated reasonable alternatives in an

116

attempt to find a solution, we received a heart-stopping, ulcer-making shock. We discovered that the military historian and former head of a Yugoslav military archive, Dusan Plenca, had said on Yugoslav television that he had copies of receipts for hostages, personally signed by Waldheim, which were part of the paperwork involved in the hostages' transfer from one German unit to another on their way to extermination.

Plenca's allegations seemed to concern the deportation of civilians from the Kozara region during the German campaign in 1942 when, as well as the thousands of Yugoslavs who were killed outright during the fighting, over 60,000 men, women and children were deported in the 'cleansing' operation – few ever returned. One American newspaper reported that Plenca had said his evidence showed that, while Waldheim did not himself kill people, 'he prepared them for death.'

My first thought was: This is the smoking pistol. I'd always felt that the one thing that could seriously damage the programme would be the discovery of a piece of conclusive evidence. And so it was in something of a panic that we contacted Pierre Vicary in Zagreb and asked him to find out the strength of the story. A number of phone calls later, it was decided that Ed and I would meet him and our other Yugoslav researcher Yela Yevramovic in Vienna the following day.

As Ed and I arrived at the reception desk of the Marriott in Vienna, Yela and Pierre walked through the front door. Almost immediately, we learned that a team from ABC-TV in the States were staying at that very hotel, and were already in hot pursuit of the Plenca story.

The rumour machine had certainly been working overtime. The alleged price for this alleged story had reached £250,000. The story itself had changed considerably: now, it seemed, the communication about the deportees had travelled between a Ustachi (Croatian Fascist) officer and a German officer. Waldheim was only referred to in the text of the message, which supposedly stated that he wanted transport for more than 4000 Yugoslavs. Another refinement was that the actual document was in the hands of Danko Vasovic, a Yugoslavian journalist who had recently written a book about Waldheim. We'd already had this translated but, although we found it

117

interesting, it had seemed to lack the sources — footnotes giving hard evidence, references to more authoritative books — to give it weight. It was said that Vasovic was, even now, in Hamburg negotiating with, among others, the German magazine *Der Spiegel*.

It was 1.40 in the morning when I learned that the rumours had reached HBO in New York. After apologizing for waking me, Colin Callender informed me that Telford Taylor had been approached by ABC-TV who'd asked him if he would be prepared to make an assessment of any evidence they might obtain about the deportation and how it might have contravened the rules of war. Professor Taylor had pointed out that he was working for us and therefore couldn't give them that advice.

I told Colin all I knew of the story so far, and promised to keep him informed. Getting back to sleep wasn't easy!

At an early breakfast, I explained the situation to Ed, Yela and Pierre. Then Yela made a phone call that threw us into total confusion. Dusan Plenca, speaking from his home in Belgrade, swore that he'd never had such a document, nor had he ever seen one. He claimed that he was fed up with having journalists on his back: 'They only want headlines. I don't want to talk to them any more.'

Yela spoke soothingly to him for some minutes. When the conversation ended, she told us that, in his opinion, our methodical approach was the only one to take seriously, and that he'd let us have some material. That, at least, was good news — but the mystery remained.

I returned to London; there was nothing more I could do in Vienna. I received a call from Yela that evening. She reported that she'd been able to speak to Vasovic's mother, who had said that her son had no such document, that he'd been in Vienna, not Hamburg, and that she wasn't aware of her son selling anything.

Friday came and with it a phone call from Ed, who'd remained behind in Vienna. He told me that Nick Goodrick-Clarke had rung him from Berlin to say that he'd been approached by a journalist from *Der Spiegel* who'd asked if he could authenticate a document that, from the German's description, seemed to be the one we'd been hearing so much about. Nick had asked the journalist to fax it to him, but the latter had refused and had gone to someone else for authentification. Nick believed that the source of the document was Vasovic.

'So where,' I asked, 'does that leave us?' The answer was simple: we'd have to wait until Monday to see what *Der Spiegel* printed. In the meantime, Yela was going to see both Vasovic and Plenca over the weekend.

As the Commission of Historians approached the end of their deliberations, accusations about them were flying in all directions. For example, Tom Bower, a famous Nazi hunter in his own right, had suggested in a couple of articles in *The Times* that the Commission were short of money and that the Commission's staff were reporting back to the Austrian government. Replying in a letter to the paper, the Austrian Ambassador to Britain had said that the Commission was not short of anything, and that their staff of two − *two!* − were not spies. It did occur to me that their staff numbers were a little on the small side if, as the Ambassador also stated, the Commission had been offered every facility.

Then it became known that the Commission had given President Waldheim advance notice of all the questions they wanted him to answer at their meeting held the previous Thursday. This had been well publicized − in fact, on the flight that Ed and I took to Vienna, we had met up with the BBC-TV crew on their way to the photo call. Now the press were alleging that the Commission's findings were going to be a total whitewash.

'Not so,' said the Commission. 'We did not give him the questions. We merely told him the areas about which we would be questioning him.'

When Gerald Flemming, the British member, was interviewed, he spoke of the 'ferociously independent' academics, and stated that there would be no whitewash: 'If there had been any such pressure, I for one would have resigned instantly.'

Personally, I didn't doubt the integrity of the academics − although I knew that some were sitting uneasily on the Commission. But I couldn't help remembering Professor

119

Messerschmidt's view that it was not the job of the Commission to be 'judgemental'. 'We are not lawyers,' he had pointed out.

On Monday morning, I eagerly grabbed a copy of *Der Spiegel*, and there, for the first time, was the document that the world's press had been trying so hard to get their hands on. It appeared to be a telegram, dated 22 July 1942, which, just as the rumour had said, had been sent by a Ustachi officer to a German officer, and referred to the deportation of 4224 prisoners following the Kozara mountain campaign. It stated that Waldheim required these deportees to be moved to two centres, presumably for onward transport to concentration camps.

The question was: To what extent did the telegram really implicate Waldheim? If genuine, it certainly indirectly involved him in the transportation, not only of partisan prisoners, but also of women, children and old men (the last comprising 15 per cent of the total, according to the telegram). Like so much else, it allegedly brought Waldheim very close to acts of war criminality without actually proving anything.

No sooner had *Der Spiegel* been published than it was announced that Professor Messerschmidt was flying from Vienna to Belgrade to interview Plenca and see the original document. The Waldheim team had been there already: Pierre Vicary had rung first thing to tell us that he'd seen Plenca and that he, Pierre, had some things he wished to bring over to London – documents that were too valuable to transmit to us in the usual way. He added that there was much to discuss. I heartily agreed with him and looked forward to his arrival the next day.

Before Pierre touched down at Heathrow, Plenca had disappeared from Belgrade. Not only had Messerschmidt not been able to interview him, but no original document had been produced. The professor was reported to be 'furious' and was returning to Vienna – apparently none the wiser.

The international press corps were now filing stories in complete bewilderment. Unfortunately, news of Pierre's imminent visit to London had spread, and I spent the morning fending off calls from disgruntled hacks asking what we knew.

Finally, Pierre arrived with his usual aura of contained energy. It was a relief to have a straightforward conversation with him for once, not like those we'd had over the phone which, by force of circumstance, had to be full of understatements, codewords and evasions.

Among the sheaf of documents that he'd brought was a copy of an obviously genuine telegram that had been sent by the Ustachis. At first glance, we could see that it plainly differed from the one that *Der Spiegel* had printed. Both of the telegrams had been written on similar forms, which had rows of boxes along the top. In the *Der Spiegel* telegram, only the box for the date had been filled in, but in the one that Pierre showed us, *all* the boxes had writing in them – indicating the telegram's routing, where it had come from, who had authorized it and various other things that military forms generally show.

Now Pierre referred us to some other documents that he'd brought. These gave an account of the movement of these same sad deportees, but used a very different sort of language than that employed in the *Der Spiegel* telegram. He also had a copy of a handwritten document that showed the breakdown – by age and sex – of those who hadn't survived the journey to the collection centres.

I found this last document spooky and tragic. In the course of almost two generations, World War II has gradually lost most of its reality until, now, it has become little more than a good setting for novelists and for the film industry. For me, brought up during the war, such a document (albeit a photocopy) brought the horrors of the German occupation almost close enough to touch, and I had to force myself to concentrate on its relevance to our programme.

Pierre also pointed out one clue within the body of the *Der Spiegel* telegram itself which, now that I looked at the text closely, should have been obvious. Whoever had written the telegram had used the words 'Lt Kurt Waldheim'. From my own memories of my national service in the RAF, I knew that the military rarely, if ever, use first names; people are known by their rank and surname – e.g. General Eisenhower, Field Marshal Montgomery. The telegram's writer, we thought, certainly seemed to want there to be no mistaking which

121

'Waldheim' he was referring to.

As we examined Pierre's documents and listened to his theories, we began to indulge in the same sort of speculation then rife in the press. One of the theories that I particularly liked had it that the telegram had been put into the public arena by SUP, the Yugoslav secret police, with the deliberate intention of creating chaos just as the Commission of Historians were due to pronounce their findings, in order to devalue them.

If that *had* been the intention, it was certainly working. The Commission were now being variously quoted as having reached a decision to publish their report on 8 February; as holding it back until they could decide about the value of the *Der Spiegel* telegram; as claiming that, after publication, they would continue to sit and sift through any further evidence; as complaining bitterly about the Yugoslav government...

Later in the week, it was Vasovic's turn to disappear, only for Plenca to pop up from wherever he had been and announce that he was going to produce his document on Yugoslav television on the following Sunday night. The Austrian Chancellor, Franz Vranitzky, was quoted as saying that his Foreign Minister (and Deputy Chancellor), Alois Mock, had written to the Yugoslav government, complaining about their treatment of the Commission and asking what was going on. We were told that the Yugoslavs had answered that they would consider everything and reply in the middle of the following week – days after the Commission were supposed to have presented their evidence.

In the meantime, an opinion poll in Austria showed that Waldheim had increased his popularity to over 70 per cent, despite all the publicity – or perhaps because of it!

On Sunday night, Pierre rang from Zagreb, having watched the programme on which Plenca was to have shown his document. Appearing with him had been Kolendic, the self-confessed Yugoslav spy, who had claimed yet again that he had given the Soviets a copy of the Odluka war crimes file containing evidence against Waldheim. However, Plenca's revelation had turned out to be a damp squib: he'd only shown another copy of the telegram that had been published in *Der Spiegel*, and when asked where the original was, he'd muttered that it was in a place where it couldn't be obtained. So the mystery remained as opaque as ever.

While the Commission of Historians wrung their collective hands, Yugoslavs disappeared and reappeared, and the people responsible – if they'd ever existed – probably rubbed *their* hands with glee, the Waldheim project team continued to work and meet deadlines.

One of the latter was a definite milestone in the programme's history: the delivery of Allan Ryan's preliminary allegations, on which he and Susan had been working furiously hard. These listed the specific areas in which they believed they could convince the five jurists that Waldheim had a case to answer. The allegations started off in good judicial manner:

BEFORE THE INTERNATIONAL COMMISSION OF INQUIRY

In the matter of

KURT WALDHEIM

CHARGES AND SPECIFICATIONS

Presenting Counsel charges that Kurt Waldheim knowingly and wrongfully participated in war crimes and crimes against humanity, in violation of customary international law including the Hague Convention Respecting the Laws and Customs of War on Land of 1907, the Geneva Convention of 1929, Article 6 of the Charter of the International Military Tribunal at Nuremberg, the Judgement of the said Tribunal, and the Report of the International Law Commission accepted by the United Nations on December 12, 1950.

Allan then went on to specify the allegations, although not in chronological order. I knew that, in the interests of clarity, I would have to try to persuade him to work in time order, to avoid confusing the television audience. However, in the order that they were set out, the allegations were:

123

Charge 1: Maltreatment of prisoners of war

This charge alleged that, between April and June 1944, Waldheim, while serving as an intelligence officer in Arsakli, Greece, knowingly and wrongfully participated in the transfer of POWs to the *Sicherheitsdienst* (SD, or security police) for torture and/or murder, pursuant to the Führer Order of 18 October 1942 and to the order of his commander, General Löhr.

Charge 2: Deportation of civilians and POWs

This charge alleged first that, while Waldheim was assigned to the Bader *Kampfgruppe* attached to the Italian Pusteria Division at Plevlje in Yugoslavia, he participated in the planning and execution of deportations of civilians and POWs in the course of and subsequent to Operations 'Trio' and 'Foca'. A further specification of this charge referred to the time when the Italian army had capitulated to the Allied forces, and alleged that Waldheim knowingly and wrongfully participated in the planning of the forcible deportation of Italian soldiers from Greece to slave labour camps in Germany. Also alleged was the seizure and deportation of Greek civilians in the course of Operation *Kreuzotter* (Viper).

Charge 3: Deportation, persecution and incitement to persecution of Jews

This alleged that Waldheim wrongfully and knowingly participated in the planning and execution of the deportation of the Jews of Jannina, Crete, Rhodes and Corfu. It also alleged that, in November 1944, he was involved in the dissemination of propaganda urging persecution of the Jews.

Charge 4: Atrocities, including pillage and reprisal murder

This charge alleged that, during his time in the quartermaster's section of the West Bosnian *Kampfgruppe*, Waldheim participated in the planning and execution of reprisal murders, pillage and other atrocities in the Kozara area; and that he did the same during Operation *Schwarz* in Montenegro. It also referred to the murders committed between the two villages of Stip and Kocane in October 1944.

Because of the rules of our Commission of Inquiry, Allan had to advise the challenging counsel, Lord Rawlinson, of all these charges. However, again in accordance with the agreed rules, he reserved the right to amend or supplement the charges prior to the actual hearing – something that could prove very important, given that we had more than a month of research time left. Who knew what would turn up in that time – or what new 'evidence' might prove, on closer examination, to be completely false?

Finally, as originally promised, the Commission of Historians delivered their conclusions on 8 February. The evening news programmes were full of it.

The historians' report stated that, while Waldheim did not appear to have committed any war crimes himself, he knew that war crimes were being committed, and that he did nothing to stop or try and stop these crimes. Independent Television News emphasized the difference between their penultimate draft and the final document. Apparently, the words 'morally guilty' were deleted from the draft on the insistence of the American and Belgian historians; it was also claimed that Chancellor Vranitzky would only accept the report if this phrase were deleted.

Various members of the Austrian government lost little time in announcing that, having read the Commission's report, they believed that there was no reason for Waldheim to resign, even though the report was stronger than expected. The man himself echoed this sentiment when he was interviewed on Austrian TV. However, besides repeating his constant refusal to resign, Waldheim was also reported as being 'deeply depressed' by the Commission's findings.

It appears that the Commission were just as depressed by Waldheim's own testimony to it. In the report's final paragraph, the historians had stated:

125

Waldheim's version of his military past does not accord with the results of the Commission's work. He made an effort to forget his military past, and as soon as this became possible no longer, he tried to make it appear harmless. In the opinion of the Commission, it has been forgotten so completely that they were unable to take from Waldheim any evidence or clues which might have assisted in clarifying their work.

In other words, according to Professor Norman Stone of Oxford University, writing in the *Sunday Times*, 'The man is a liar.' He continued: 'It is wrong for Austria to have such an incubus. The conservatives in Austria made a mistake in choosing Waldheim to whom the good name of Austria seems to mean nothing.'

While the Commission's conclusions hung over Waldheim's head, the possibility of his resignation hung over ours. Personally, I didn't think that, even if he did resign, it should deter us in our pursuit of evidence nor should it affect the carrying out of our Commission of Inquiry – for us, Waldheim's importance lay in the fact that he had been chosen Secretary-General of the United Nations, not that he had been elected President of Austria. Whether his resignation would affect the thinking of Thames, HBO and Channel 4 was something I hoped I would never have to find out.

As the week drew to a close, and the newspapers remained full of speculation over Waldheim's continued existence as President of Austria, we were entertained by a further revelation in the Plenca document saga.

It appeared that the typewriter used to write the telegram (which, it was now claimed, *Der Spiegel* had paid a modest $100,000 for the privilege of revealing) had been manufactured in Czechoslovakia in 1949 – seven years *after* the message had supposedly been tapped out.

Our research team in Yugoslavia seemed to have won – game, set and match.

9

Will He, Won't He?

During the week of the historians' report, the spotlight turned towards Waldheim's possible involvement in the fate of various British, American, Australian and Greek commandos. It had been alleged that he'd dealt with the documentation relating to those who had landed on a Greek island (either Levítha or Calino; the evidence here is confusing). They were captured by the Germans, and there have been allegations, which Waldheim had consistently denied, that he interrogated them.

There is no doubt, however, that he was aware that some Allied soldiers had been captured. On 17 October 1943, he wrote in the Army Group E war diary that he'd informed the Chief of Staff that, according to a report from the *Luftwaffe*, the latter had captured and disarmed British occupying forces. It has been further alleged that Waldheim knew of a subsequent order: that the Allied 'forces' held by the Germans were to be given 'special treatment' – a euphemism for 'execution' – at the hands of the SD.

There were further allegations about his involvement with other Allied commandos. Members of the Special Boat Service (the aquatic version of the British SAS) were captured by the Germans between the islands of Alimnia and Rhodes on 7 April 1944. A month later, on 6 May, four more British prisoners were taken by the German XXIInd Army Corps near Asproangeli, 20 kilometres north-west of Jannina, in northwest Greece. It was alleged that these four were transferred to the Ic section of Army Group E for interrogation, and that Waldheim had been the supervising officer for those responsible for prisoner interrogation. Finally, on 1 July 1944,

127

three more SBS commandos were captured during an attack on the island of Calino.

While there was not, so far, any direct evidence proving that Waldheim actually took part in the capture, interrogation or deaths of any of these men, his detractors claimed that the unit of which he was an integral part was responsible for what happened to the POWs. Waldheim *was* aware of the illegal order made by Hitler on 18 October 1942, which said that the provisions of the Geneva Convention were not to be applied to any captured Allied commandos, who were not to be sent to POW camps, but instead, handed over to the SD.

In his 'White Book', Waldheim's defenders claimed:

> None of the information, messages or requests transmitted originated from Dr Waldheim, nor did he participate in any of the activities which were the subject of the messages. It should be noted that the British forces were not identified as commandos in the pertinent war diary entries [for which Waldheim was responsible].
>
> The transmission of a request from the Chief of Staff to the *Luftwaffe* to transport British soldiers from Levítha to the mainland can certainly not be interpreted as 'handling of Allied prisoners'. Therefore nothing in the historical record contradicts or even calls into question Dr Waldheim's assertion that he was not involved in the handling or interrogation of Allied prisoners or commandos.

However, among the few commandos who survived the SD's 'special treatment' was the American, James Doughty, who was captured during the attack on Calino. Many journalists had tried to make contact with him, but so far, all had been halted by the impenetrable barrier of his lawyers. Now I asked Allan Ryan to make an approach. It seemed to me that if there were any chance of getting past Doughty's attorneys, it was through another lawyer.

A few days later, Allan rang to say that he'd spoken to the attorneys and they had given him permission to approach Doughty himself. Further, we understood that they had told him that the former commando claimed to have been interrogated at Arsakli; at this stage, we believed that he was going to say that his interrogator had been one Kurt Waldheim.

But Doughty's statement wasn't the only evidence against Waldheim that we were to receive. One of our researchers in Germany, Nana Wiessler, had interviewed Joachim Lützow, a former officer who had served with Waldheim at Army Group E headquarters under General Löhr. Lützow began by telling her his first impressions of Waldheim: 'He caught my eye . . . by his pushiness. Right from the start . . . his manner of always wanting to display his knowledge and give his opinion whereby, without deference to his very reticent and polite superior, he would take the matter upon himself.' The interview continued:

NANA: As an expert, to what extent was Waldheim able to make suggestions on how the problem of the resistance groups or partisans was to be dealt with?
LÜTZOW: That was precisely the major task at the time . . . However, that was certainly his main task, for that was precisely where his expert knowledge lay. He knew exactly what the atmosphere was like in the Serbian Chetnik camp [i.e. the right-wing partisans] or the Croatians and, I believe, also with the Ustachis, and I would say that the close links made with the Ustachis were for the most part his doing.

The former officer went on to say that, in the final months of the war, the decision-making involved in the fighting with the partisans was 'extended much lower down the ranks'.

Another fascinating line of inquiry opened up when our researcher ventured into another area of Waldheim's war.

NANA: It has been said that Waldheim himself had contact with partisans in the last few months of the war, and that he had supervised the taking of prisoners from among the partisans.
LÜTZOW: Waldheim was very often away from headquarters. His mobility was what drew attention to him, it showed in his reports – 'so many days ago I was here or there'. . . .
NANA: Could you explain to me the role of the *Geheim Feldpolizei* [GFP, Secret Field Police]? What was their relationship to the Ic?
LÜTZOW: The GFP were under the authority of the AO [the *Abwehr*, or counter-intelligence; Waldheim has always insisted that he was never involved in their 'dirty' side of the war]. They were there to put down or prevent any unrest – to take prisoners

... The GFP was the long arm of the AO against the civilian population ... Waldheim has always foolishly claimed that there was a separation of roles between the Ic and the AO, but such a separation was unthinkable in this territory.

The former officer then stated that interrogations had been entirely the responsibility of the Ic and, for the most part, took place directly with the *Kampfgruppes* at bases; only special cases would be sent elsewhere. However, his strongest evidence related to what he claimed Waldheim did *not* do:

> NANA: A report lands on Waldheim's desk: 4000 partisan women are to be deported. What could Waldheim have done if he had wanted to prevent this happening?
> LÜTZOW: With this Commander-in-Chief, he could have simply just not done it ... I'll take this on my own head to say this: C-in-C Löhr would have always covered for someone if he concealed these things, acted as if the request had never come in or something along these lines. He [Waldheim] would have got Löhr's sympathy and this would have been his opportunity to make his mark, demonstrate his personal ability − 'Off with you into the woods, go on, run away' - and such like.

Lützow explained that General Löhr − while being loyal to Hitler and, as an Austrian, a supporter of the *Anschluss* − nevertheless saw things from a Christian point of view. Löhr, claimed Lützow, was a humanitarian man and was troubled by what was going on. It was up to his subordinates, the witness said, to help the general by letting certain things happen, by not reporting things − in effect, by sabotaging certain procedures.

> NANA: But with prisoners, it was another matter, since there was always the SS and the SD. You couldn't always just say, 'Right then, off with you into the bushes...'
> LÜTZOW: Yes, it was precisely there that the sabotage had to be done...That's what I hold so strongly against Waldheim. That here, under such a good Commander-in-Chief, such a humanitarian man, suffering personally under such conditions, he [Waldheim] didn't take advantage of the situation himself ... Only this young man, Waldheim, he was too full of his own importance ... He wanted to make his mark, show his mettle, that's how I see it. I feel he has something to answer for.

130

Tim House, briefing solicitor to Lord Rawlinson.

Peter Smith, barrister-at-law and our executive legal co-ordinator. Nobody combines a first-class knowledge of the law with a knowledge of the problems and requirements of television journalism better than Peter.

Ed Braman, who as our head of research, ran a team of historians, journalists and linguists across Europe.

Susie Harrison, my German-speaking secretary and an indispensable member of the team.

Chrissie Cocks, our programme manager. W Chrissie running the logistics, we could win a w

Allan Ryan, 'presenting counsel,' and his briefing solicitor, Susan Aslan, working on the documentation in the Charles Hotel, Cambridge, Mass. Both legal teams had to contend with thousands of pages of documents.

Kate Johns. She was such a 'private' secretary to both sides that neither got a clue of what the other was preparing.

At an 'open day' for the media in Redondo Beach, California. (Left to right) Jack Saltman; Bridget Potter, senior vice-president, original programmes, Home Box Office: and Colin Callender, executive producer, Showcase, HBO.

Professor Telford Taylor, former US prosecutor at Nuremberg and Home Box Office's adviser on the 'Waldheim' programme, at a press conference with Jack Saltman in Redondo Beach, California.

JACK SALTMAN

Lützow's evidence was fairly damning, but in fairness to Waldheim, it must be pointed out that, although General Löhr appears to have been worshipped by his men, he *was* hanged by the Yugoslavs as a war criminal. The transcript of Nana's interview with the former officer also revealed one subtle problem: did Lützow's patent dislike of Waldheim colour his memory? Allan Ryan would, I suspected, need corroboration of these assertions before he would use them to try and convince the judges.

The Commission of Historians' report had acted like a starting pistol. The great game began: will he go or won't he? Every newspaper, almost every news bulletin and certainly every friend asked the same question.

Waldheim was constantly mentioned in the media. One Sunday morning, I switched on the radio at 7.03 and came in on the words: '. . . The Commission of Historians found no evidence that he was guilty of war crimes but . . . ' I lay, frozen, for what seemed like hours. Had he resigned? Then at the end of the news bulletin, the announcer repeated the headlines: it had just been yet another statement from Dr Waldheim that he had no intention of resigning.

The Commission's report was also causing a furore inside Austria, and in an attempt to calm things down, Waldheim went on television and repeated much of what he had been saying for the previous two years. His supporters presumably took heart from this, while his opponents said that they'd heard it all before. However, in the first opinion poll published (in the Austrian newspaper *Die Presse*) after the report came out, Waldheim's support certainly seemed to be slipping. Now, only 46 per cent of those polled agreed he should stay in office, compared with the more than 70 per cent of only two weeks before.

At a cabinet meeting of the Austrian government, it was decided that the coalition would not split, but Chancellor Vranitzky reserved his position as to whether he would resign, as he'd threatened to do if the Waldheim affair continued to occupy so much of his time. The government was decidedly hampered by Austrian law: while Waldheim had the legal right to sack them, if they were to do the same to him, he would have the right to go to the people in a plebiscite.

Already there were stories of people in other countries refusing to buy Austrian goods. One Austrian industrialist I met complained bitterly that every sales meeting he attended started with a protracted discussion about Waldheim. He said: 'I'm fed up with it. I don't need it. It's getting in the way of my business, and what's more, I don't want to be an apologist for that man.'

To add to the programme team's worries, the British government finally decided to get in on the act. The Conservative MP for Cambridge, historian and one-time Principal Officer to Waldheim at the UN, Robert Rhodes James, asked in Parliament what the government knew about his former boss's role in the torture and execution of six British SBS commandos who had been captured in the Aegean during the war. The Prime Minister answered that the British evidence about this episode was to be reviewed.

This came as something of a surprise. It had already been made public that a number of files concerning the commandos, files previously held by the Public Record Office, had subsequently been shredded. The brother of one of the SBS men had told us that he'd spent years trying to get any information out of the government, but had met with total failure. He was, justifiably, somewhat sceptical about their coming up with anything new.

If Her Majesty's Government were to produce new evidence, it would certainly leave open the question of why it had taken so many years to come to light, and why the government hadn't helped the families of the dead servicemen, who had spent so much effort in the past trying to find out exactly what had happened to their sons, brothers, husbands. However, given the resources and forked-tongue approach of all governments in my experience, I wouldn't have been in the least amazed if, with a conjuror's flick of a magic wand, important documents suddenly appeared.

Now, with the British government declaring its interest in at least this aspect of the Waldheim saga, and the Austrian government doing double somersaults over whether he would resign, we felt as if we were in a race to get our programme made and aired before events overtook us.

132

We'd finally resolved the problem of how to get valid evidence from witnesses who could (or would) not attend the Inquiry, without frightening them off with a parade of lawyers and technicians – how to reconcile the requirements of a television inquiry without the right of subpoena to compel witnesses to testify. It was decided that videotaped statements could be taken *in situ*, provided both solicitors were present and both were able to put questions. This videotape would be edited in agreement with both parties and submitted to the Inquiry as evidence during the recording.

However, matters were further complicated by the fact that, according to our solicitors Susan Aslan and Tim House, even witnesses who had agreed to appear would have to be 'proofed' - that is, they would have to be taken through their statements by each of the solicitors to find out what and how they would answer the sorts of questions likely to be put to them during the Inquiry. This could deter them from coming to London. However, it was vastly important to me as producer to have these witnesses (if only on videotape) if our programme was going to be watchable.

Yet again, the lawyers had their way: they'd insisted that they wouldn't call *any* witnesses if they hadn't been proofed. I pleaded with them to speak to the relevant researcher before approaching a potential witness, to get as much background as they could, and please, when they did visit the witness, to be as tactful as possible. Yes, I assured them, all witnesses would have been told that, not only would they be questioned if they came to the Inquiry to give evidence, they would also be cross-examined.

I did win one skirmish. I certainly didn't want witnesses faced with visits by *two* solicitors – representing our 'presenting' and 'challenging' counsel. I got Tim and Susan to agree to ask questions formulated by the other side as well as their own, so that each witness would be left with a little peace before taking his or her place in the witness box at Teddington.

A landmark of a different sort was reached by one of the Waldheim project team on Wednesday, 17 February 1988. Mark Mazower, one of our two hard-working researchers in Greece, left his hunt for evidence and witnesses and returned

133

to Oxford for his 'viva' (oral examination). On successfully completing this, he was awarded his PhD. We were all delighted for him, and it didn't surprise us to hear that he was already being courted to join the teaching staff of Princeton University in the United States.

Two days later, we had cause to return our attention to wartime Greece. The government, expanding on the Prime Minister's verbal reply to MP Robert Rhodes James, announced in an official written Parliamentary answer that they were going to set up a small team of experts to examine a copy of a file held by the Americans, which related to the interrogation and execution of the British commandos.

The following Sunday, that intrepid reporter from Chicago, Chuck Ashman, together with another journalist Michael Toner, claimed in an 'EXCLUSIVE' in the *Sunday Express* that Waldheim had been hunted by the Allies as a top Nazi officer even before the end of World War II, and that the British government had admitted that a secret file on Waldheim did exist.

As I read the story, with its hysterical headline of 'WALDHEIM'S SHOCK FILE COVER-UP', I sighed. Still, I was interested in the government's parliamentary answer, and I rang Allan Ryan to find out if he'd heard anything through his sources concerning material that appeared to have come from the United States. He assured me that his information continued to coincide with what we'd already suspected – that there was no smoking pistol, and that it was only by the building-block approach that he believed he'd get a 'case to answer' result.

After giving me that bit of reassurance, he went on to tell me some good news. He'd spoken to James Doughty, the surviving American commando, and he'd agreed to fly to Boston to see Allan. In addition, Doughty had also agreed, in principle, to take part in the programme.

Congratulating Allan on his persuasive powers – the former commando could prove to be an extremely valuable source – I then raised the problem of how we were going to 'proof' potential witnesses. This had now become a fairly urgent issue. Two key ones in Germany – Helmut Poliza and Joachim Macholz, both former *Wehrmacht* officers who'd served alongside Waldheim during the war — were keen to be visited by Lord Rawlinson, whose reputation and past as Attorney-General obviously impressed them. Fortunately, his Lordship had indicated to Tim House that he was quite prepared to fly out with him to meet them. However, Allan felt that, particularly in these two cases, he wanted to have a 'presence' during the meeting. I agreed that Susan could act as his representative, having first checked with Nick Goodrick-Clarke, the relevant researcher, who'd said that it was unlikely that the presence of an additional person would frighten off either of the Germans.

Unfortunately, we'd so far been unsuccessful in persuading Colonel Warnstorff, third in command at Army Group E and Waldheim's commanding officer in the intelligence section at Arsakli, to take part. He'd told an emissary that on no grounds would his wife agree to his appearing in anything like our programme. However, now that Lord Rawlinson and Tim would be flying to Germany anyway, I asked Tim to make a detour to see Warnstorff in person in a final attempt to persuade this, for us, very important witness.

Obviously, as Waldheim's commanding officer, he'd be in a position to give very strong eyewitness evidence since, presumably, Waldheim would have done very little without Warnstorff's personal agreement or knowledge. In fact, the former colonel had told the Commission of Historians that his 'O3' (Waldheim) had been informed about practically all procedures and events. However, the Austrian president had told the historians that he disputed this 'full knowledge': 'I assure you, I knew nothing of these things. I knew only a fraction of what Warnstorff knew.' On this point, the historians came down heavily on the side of the former colonel:

> The conclusion from the total evidence available arising from these communications, the available reports and dispatches, particularly the ones initialled by Waldheim, is that, in the opinion of the Commission, the O3 of the Army Group E had detailed knowledge of the entire work sphere of the Ic [intelligence section]. Knowledge of numerous 'reprisal' and 'cleansing' actions, knowledge of the command situation/structure in this area.

135

Turning its attention to Waldheim's claims about the separation between the Ic and the AO (the *Abwehr*, or counter-intelligence), the report quoted former *Oberleutnant* Poliza:

'Various matters specific to the narrower AO sphere were probably unknown to him, but that a cooperation with the SD, GFP [Secret Field Police] and Security Police existed is already apparent from the division of labour within the staff of Army Group E.'

When one of our researchers spoke to Hans Rodhammer, who had served in the same division as Waldheim, the German had dismissed the latter's statement that he did not know what Army Group E was doing, and also Waldheim's claim that, as the O3 in Ic, he would not have been aware of what the *Abwehr* were involved in. Rodhammer showed our researcher a duty roster for Army Group E. Although the functions and duties of the various units altered during the course of the war, the roster demonstrates (according to Rodhammer) the close cooperation and slight overlapping of jurisdiction that was accepted practice within the Group. He told us that Waldheim's claim that the *Abwehr* was strictly separated from the Ic in terms of both duties and exchange of information was 'just not credible'.

Rodhammer also derided Waldheim's statement that, while stationed in Greece, he was not aware of a lot of the things going on because of his frequent study leaves and other absences. Our witness said that the first thing that anyone who was responsible for the preparation of intelligence reports would do upon returning from leave would be to acquaint himself with the events that had transpired and the instructions transmitted during his absence. 'It can be completely excluded,' he said, 'that Kurt Waldheim could not have known about events on the Greek islands merely because he was not physically present in Arsakli on the days the reports were received by the Ic.'

A statement that was much more favourable to Dr Waldheim was made to Nick Goodrick-Clarke by former Lt Colonel Bruno Willers, who had been Waldheim's superior officer in Arsakli and Athens before Waldheim was assigned to the intelligence section. Then, Willers claimed, Waldheim's job had been the keeping of the war diary, making out reports on the basis of particulars or instructions from his 'Ia' - i.e. Chief of Staff von Gyldenfeldt and his deputy Willers – taking and recording telephone calls and passing on reports to higher authorities. However, said Willers, 'his principal job no doubt was that of interpreter, in which he directly translated conversations and discussions with the Italians.'

> NICK: Many people have stressed that he was no more than an interpreter?
> WILLERS: He didn't appear to be any more. He was a nice chap and very reserved, a bit green. At 24 years of age . . . he carried out his responsibilities, just the routine activities, where he couldn't do any harm.
> NICK: Your statement is confirmed by your Italian counterpart Lt Colonel Scoti [the Italian Ia officer], in so far as he can't remember anything at all about Waldheim.
> WILLERS: But I do all right, because he was lanky and maybe I would wind him up on occasion – 'Well, what have you been doing all day then?' That was just my way of speaking, in a rather humorous vein. He was always servile. That was his way.

Other insights were gained from a former sergeant-major, Franz Kaupe, who was stationed in Arsakli/Salonika until July 1944. He talked to our researcher about the special relationship that had existed among the Austrians on the head-quarters staff. He said that there had been a strong sense of camaraderie among the Austrians who constituted the over-whelming majority of the lower echelons. (It may be remembered that General Löhr was also an Austrian.) And in perhaps an important turn of phrase, Kaupe explained that 'In the *Wehrmacht* itself, one thought guided all our activities: survival.'

Like Waldheim, who had continually claimed to have been totally unaware of the deportation of the Jews who made up a quarter of the population of Salonika, Kaupe, too, largely pleaded ignorance: 'As far as I know, very few military head-quarters were located in the vicinity of the train station. Everything near the station was residential area.' To the question, 'Did you ever see a Star of David in Salonika?' he answered, 'I can't remember seeing one. I don't remember ever hearing a word said about Jews in the *Wehrmacht*.' He suggested that perhaps the security services had gathered together the Jews secretly, in a night-time operation: 'That's the only way I can imagine it.'

A not-too-dissimilar exchange about the deportation of the Salonika Jews had taken place between President Waldheim, his personal secretary Dr Ralph Scheide and the Israeli professor, Jehuda Wallach, of the Commission of Historians.

WALLACH: Arsakli was only a few kilometres away from Salonika. The Jewish population made up a quarter of the inhabitants. First, these people were forced to wear the Yellow Star [Star of David] and then they disappeared. We have heard that one walked down from Arsakli to Salonika. How is it possible for one to know nothing about this?
WALDHEIM: I was not there at the time . . .
WALLACH: It was the deportation of 50,000 Jews − a quarter of the 200,000 inhabitants of Salonika was therefore suddenly not there any more. Surely it could not escape anyone's notice that, for example, many businesses had suddenly closed down?
WALDHEIM: I have the deepest respect for your opinion and share your horror with regard to these appalling events. Later on, of course, these measures became generally known. During my short stays in Salonika, I never saw any Jews wearing the Star of David.
SCHEIDE: The order to wear the Stars was issued in February 1943. At that time, the President had left Arsakli three months before.

Another of our witnesses revealed further aspects of Waldheim. Former *leutnant* Karl Mang had been a colleague of his in Tirana, the capital of Albania, immediately before Waldheim returned to Arsakli in July 1943. He'd found the future Austrian president 'rather reserved', allowing no one to glimpse his inner character, and that he had 'the aroma of the mysterious highest authority'. Mang added that Waldheim had been 'ambitious, very ambitious' and that everyone knew that he wanted to be a diplomat.

He explained that both he and Waldheim had been working as interpreters between the *Wehrmacht* and the Italians. And while Mang had been primarily restricted to the economic sphere − translating requests from the Germans for specific provisions, payments and other currency matters

138

— Waldheim had seen duty with the higher-ups in the Italian staff. This, said Mang, explains why Waldheim appears in the now-famous photograph taken in Podgorica with SS *Gruppenführer* Arthur Phleps (commander of the Prinz Eugen Division), *Oberst* Joachim Macholz and the Italian General Escola Roncaglia, just before the decisive part of Operation *Schwarz* against the Yugoslav partisans.

Our list of witnesses had begun to grow quickly. Waldheim himself had also begun to grow in my consciousness as I learned more about him. These elderly Germans were all talking about the young man in his 20s with whom they had served: what sort of person he'd been; what had motivated him; how he'd reacted to authority; how he'd carried out his job; what sort of officer he'd been. These and many more insights were beginning to put flesh on the man.

The public persona of Kurt Waldheim began, for most people outside Austria, in 1972. He'd kept his background just *there* — in the background. Now these witnesses had begun to fill out the nature of the man. I felt that, along with the hard evidence about Waldheim's alleged involvement with war crimes, it would make fascinating television to see these carefully constructed layers removed and to discover what he'd really been like before years of political veneer had completely hidden the true Waldheim.

I also drew confidence as each witness agreed to take part in the programme. I started to feel that our lawyers would have real evidence over which to argue — and that there would be sufficient evidence for our judges to be able to come to an informed judgement.

139

10

A Difficult Time

With our recording date coming ever closer, Peter Smith and I started yet another week extremely pleasantly by lunching with Sir Frederick Lawton. We had a few procedural matters to sort out with the chairman of our judges' panel.

Since we'd last seen him, Sir Frederick had been recalled to the Court of Appeal temporarily and was once again sitting as a judge. The donning of his black robe and wig hadn't affected his enthusiasm for our project, which was still as great as ever. In fact, he said that he was finding the whole idea most stimulating, and went so far as to offer to write to the press defending what we were doing if we were again faced with newspaper criticism.

I was concerned that, if I didn't know what the panel's judgement was going to be soon after the recording of the Inquiry, I couldn't be sure that, during the editing, I would include all the salient points they might raise. Sir Frederick said that, after the recording, he and his fellow judges would almost certainly have thought through their judgement by the end of the following day, Saturday. They'd need another couple of weeks to compose a considered opinion, but he was sure that they'd be happy to let me have their respective views before then.

As for the actual recording, I presented a timetable that I thought would enable us to get through the evidence but, at the same time, not put our judges under too much pressure. For those who have never sat for a long time in a TV studio under the intense lights, it is easy to underestimate just how wearing it can be − and with respect, most members of our judges' panel were no longer in the first flush of youth. Sir Frederick agreed to my schedule, although he pointed out that, given the complexity of the case, the ten minutes we'd allowed each counsel for his closing speech would probably not be enough.

We agreed, therefore, that both counsel would be able to make written submissions to the judges dealing with the more complex issues, such as the interpretation of law; then the counsel would give a paraphrased version of these submissions on camera. This way, we could allow each side to go into the detail of its case and the interpretation of law at whatever length it wanted, while still presenting the main points to the audience. This seemed to satisfy both the stringent intellectual standards that our lawyers were rightly insisting upon and the requirements of a television programme to explain, perhaps less minutely, the strengths of their arguments.

The relaxed and enjoyable atmosphere of that long lunch was not to last. That night, the wire services carried a report that Waldheim's People's Party had been asked by the Social Democrats to join with them in selecting another candidate to take over as president. Although the response of the People's Party had been to say that their coalition partners would help to unite the country if they supported Waldheim, panicked phone calls went out from the Waldheim project.

Our constant question was 'Will Waldheim resign?' and we received no positive reassurance that, at least in the foreseeable future, he would not. This had the effect of making us return to the drawing-board and question some of our basic assumptions – not in terms of whether or not the programme should be made, but when it should be transmitted and in what form.

The most attractive of the options we considered was to transmit nightly an edited version of each of the nine days of hearings, ending with the judgement. This would do away with all requirements for secrecy – in fact, we could invite the world's press to attend. We would create an event: each day with new witnesses in the box and the legal arguments unfolding. It would make riveting television, and would generate its own news.

If only I'd thought of this six months ago. If only *someone* had thought of it! However, there were problems. Could HBO and Channel 4 reschedule the programme or, indeed, would they want to? Could we deliver a nightly programme in the time between ending the recording for the day and whatever time was designated for our transmission in the UK? And could my team do without sleep for two weeks?

I put the idea to Colin Callender during one of our many transatlantic phone calls. 'Never mind waiting for an emergency,' he said. 'Why not plan to do it this way anyway?' We left it that we would sound out those who needed to be sounded out, and then get back to each other.

The following day, I had to attend one of Thames Television's occasional editors' meetings, called by the director of programmes, David Elstein. He invited me to report on our Waldheim project first, and I presented the new plan to my fellow editors as well as to David, Barrie Sales and Richard Dunn, our managing director. The consensus was that it was an exciting idea, and although it would certainly create incredible pressures for the production team during the days of the Inquiry, the result should be well worth it.

By chance, I was also scheduled to meet up with David Lloyd, our Channel 4 commissioning editor, after the Thames meeting. I spelled out our alternative scenario over a very quick lunch. The food came and went almost unnoticed: we were both wrapped up in the possibilities and the problems.

David astutely pointed out that one of the dangers of destabilizing the programme from its set pattern was that it could create a situation in which any alternative transmission date could be considered, not just the daily edited highlights. The question could be asked: If a half-hour daily version could be transmitted, why not the full programme, say, a week or, at most, two weeks after the end of recording?

I replied that it was one thing to go live nightly with a quickly put together version – which, because of its immediacy, would be able to carry hasty editing, perhaps the odd mistake or seam showing through – but it was an entirely different proposition to sit down at the end of nine days' recording and start editing perhaps 50 hours of tape down to a 'polished' three and a half hours. Viewers would rightly expect a highly professional programme that reflected the work and talent that had gone into it – not a quickly thrown together, ill-considered one.

'Anyway,' I said, 'that's a risk that I think we should take. I'll have to meet those arguments when and if they come. We should at least offer this option to the various schedulers on both sides of the Atlantic as well as the respective heads of networks.'

David agreed, and said that he, too, would take soundings.

I returned to the office, full of excitement at the prospect of the new format. I must admit that it took a bit of an effort to turn my attention to other less exciting, but equally important programme decisions.

I found a thick document waiting for me on my desk. Right on deadline, Ed (who must have been working all night as well as all day) had produced an historical overview of the Balkans during the relevant years. I'd wanted this so that the judges would have a background to the specific events in which Waldheim had been involved, as well as an awareness of what else had been happening in those areas at the same time. Except to students of Balkan history, that particular theatre of war is hardly well known. But before it could be sent to the judges, Ed's document still had to be agreed by our lawyers, to make sure that it contained no bias. On this programme, nothing was easy!

The newspapers continued to carry reports that ranged from speculations on Waldheim's future as far as the internal politics of Austria were concerned to whether the Pope would actually meet him during his visit to that country in June. (We had checked on the latter possibility; the Vatican said that Pope John Paul II would meet with whoever was the Austrian president at the time.) The London *Daily Mail* appeared to be concentrating on pursuing every surviving commando who had landed on any of the Greek islands and had been captured by the Germans.

One gentleman they interviewed, former captain Charles Bluett (who subsequently agreed to give evidence on our programme), was quoted as saying that he couldn't identify one of the men who had interrogated him because he'd been forced to look straight ahead – every time he'd moved his eyes, he'd been threatened. The story was picked up on that evening's television news. Although the former commando

143

had repeated that he couldn't be certain who his interrogator had been, he was shown a photograph that, the TV news stated, was thought to show Waldheim in uniform.

Our experts had already told us that the photograph revealed to millions that night definitely did *not* show Waldheim. They had good reasons for their conclusion: the man's uniform bore the badges of a different rank from Waldheim's; it carried the wrong medal ribbons; and it also carried the 'flashes' of someone who had fought in World War I. Waldheim was born in 1918.

Thoughts of new formats and new transmission dates were all banished by mid-afternoon on Thursday when I received a call from Allan Ryan in Boston.

'I've heard something on the grapevine that I think could turn out to be a little problem,' he began. As he continued, I realized that the problem was anything but 'little'. In fact, it was exactly what I'd been secretly fearing ever since the Waldheim project had begun – and it was coming from the one source that I'd thought was safe: the US Justice Department.

Allan told me that a meeting was to take place to discuss whether or not to release the material that lay in Neil Sher's safe, the material that the director of the Office of Special Investigations had told me, months earlier, could get a successful conviction against Waldheim, and which was being used as a basis for keeping the Austrian president on the US 'Watch List'.

Allan said that he believed that some of the people who'd been in favour of keeping the material secret had now changed their minds. When he knew the results of their deliberations, he'd get in touch with me straightaway. He added that, if they did intend to make the evidence public, he believed that they would act very quickly, possibly as soon as the following week.

From my point of view, this news was devastating. What worried me was that the evidence that the Justice Department had brought together would, in its entirety, provide the dreaded 'smoking pistol'. And it wouldn't be published by a newspaper looking for a quick headline, or by a group of academics. No, this carefully compiled evidence, brought together with the expressed intention of taking on Waldheim in a court of law if ever required, would be put into the public arena by a first-class lawyer with all the might of the US Justice Department behind him.

Neil Sher of the Justice Department had told me that the release of this evidence would have to be a political decision. Now it looked as if I might have to live with the results of that decision.

Trying to think through the consequences gave me another sleepless night. If the documents were so convincing that Waldheim's 'guilt' was self-evident, was there any point in going on with the programme? If the evidence was not conclusive, what then? We could argue that this was the very reason for the programme − that it would be the only opportunity to 'test' the evidence, complete with cross-examination − and it would be all the more interesting because of this.

But then came the question of timing. There was little doubt that, if the OSI's evidence were published, it would create endless column inches, not to mention wall-to-wall television analysis. If we were to televise the programme soon afterwards, at the very latest in April (when we were scheduled to record), we would still look highly relevant. But not if we waited until June.

All this presupposed an early publication. I wondered, however, whether the US government might not want to hold on to their secrets for a bit longer. Would they want to embarrass the Austrian government just before or even just after the 50th anniversary of the *Anschluss*, which was less than two weeks away, on 11 March? Or would they want to drop the material into the public's lap just before the Pope's visit to Austria in June?

I agonized over all these possibilities (and more) during the weekend. I had no control over nor the ability to influence any of them. I couldn't even pressure my own company to transmit early, since Thames had passed that 'honour' over to Channel 4. I could only harden my suggestions to HBO and Channel 4 in the coming weeks, as soon as I learned the results of the US Justice Department's deliberations.

* * *

145

Over the past months, I'd found that most of the Waldheim project's troubles had little to do with the production problems that normally arise when you make a television programme. We hadn't been faced with any catastrophes to do with facilities, crews, reporters, producers, uncooperative public. It was legal requirements, the reactions of the Austrian government to their own domestic crisis, the response of the British government to the story about the commandos and political decisions taken by bigwigs in the US government that gave us our headaches.

Our research teams were doing us proud, having found vast amounts of evidence and a large number of witnesses. The in-house team – including our newest member, Angela Kennedy, who was helping Chrissie with the logistics of the programme – were working wonderfully well. It was only the problems largely outside our control that constantly threatened not only the success of the programme but its very existence.

I was still on tenterhooks when I arrived back in the office on Monday, but I tried to remain calm and get on with the mountain of work in front of me. Taking a call from Nick Goodrick-Clarke, one of our researchers in Germany, I was told that the meetings in Hamburg and West Berlin between Lord Rawlinson, Tim, Susan and the ex-*Wehrmacht* officers Poliza and Macholz had gone well. Poliza had agreed to take part in the programme – great news! – while Macholz, now in his 90s, had apparently left the door open for a cross-examination to be done *in situ*. And after all the worry about whether sending Susan to represent our 'presenting' counsel would upset the Germans, this hadn't proved to be a problem. In fact, according to Nick, she'd been a positive asset.

However, these glad tidings were somewhat overshadowed by the news that our last attempt to get Warnstorff to take part had failed. Nick said that the former German colonel thought quite highly of the programme – in fact, highly enough to recommend others to participate – but he was adamant that he himself would not.

I turned to the technical aspects of the programme. At least here, I thought, I do have *some* control. Since our last meeting, Bill Palmer had made a few minor changes to the set,

146

and Roger Thomas, our director, had put in a lot of work on the floor plan and was beginning to formulate his ideas on how he was going to shoot the programme.

We would require four video recording machines during the days of the Inquiry. Two would be 'slave-locked' to the output of two cameras, which were going to be permanently trained on the judges and the non-speaking counsel, respectively. This meant that we would have reaction shots and so on that could then cut into the final edited tape. The other two machines would both record the same studio output – comprising shots from all four cameras, chosen by the director from his position in the control room. I'd asked for this output to be duplicated in case one machine or tape developed a fault. This would be one programme that would be impossible to go back and do again!

If the decision was finally taken to transmit nightly, I knew that we would need additional machinery. Then, we would have to start making decisions on the morning's recording by lunchtime each day, and another producer would have to edit throughout the afternoon on yet another pair of machines.

This rapid, almost simultaneous editing would, by necessity, only be very basic, to enable us to go out every night. If we did the programme as originally planned, with about two months between recording and transmission, we would follow different procedures.

Making the arrangements for all these machines and the wizards who work them seemed a dream of a task when compared to Chrissie Cocks' assignment. She had a telephone permanently pressed to her ear as she made the rounds of hotels to find beds for our many guests. It wasn't just a simple question of finding the correct number of rooms for the correct number of bodies. For example, Allan Ryan needed a large room with lots of table space, and the witnesses had to be kept in separate accommodation so that those who had already given evidence wouldn't meet those still to go into (and, indeed, on to) the box.

We'd already arranged for our simultaneous translators, who would be provided by Josephine Bacon's rapidly expanding company, which was already doing most of our written translation. However, to make sure that we got top-quality people, I had to agree in advance to guarantee a certain number of days' work to the Italian, Greek and Serbo-Croat speakers, even though at that point we didn't know on which days we would require them. I wanted the two German speakers for all nine days.

Slowly, the stream of documents was beginning to dry up as most of the archives that we had set ourselves to cover gave up their relevant evidence. Now the hunt for witnesses was beginning in earnest. Every day, it seemed, Felix or Nick or Nana or Pierre or Yela would ring up to offer yet another witness who had agreed to take part.

While working in Israel, Mark Mazower had discovered a survivor from Jannina in Greece who claimed to have been one of the Jewish deportees destined for Auschwitz. He said that, before he escaped, he'd seen Waldheim with the guards, most of whom, he alleged, were Austrian.

In Mark's opinion, the witness was cogent, sure of himself and quite prepared to be cross-examined on his testimony. However, from what we knew of Waldheim's movements, the witness's supposed sighting of him would have occurred some time between 15 January 1943, when Waldheim was diagnosed as having a thyroid illness (as witnessed by his pay-book), and his going on convalescent leave on 25 February. It seemed unlikely that he would have ventured to Jannina during that period, but we still had a gap of a few unaccounted-for days. Of course, the final decision as to whether or not to call this or any other witness would lie with counsel, in this case, Allan Ryan.

We'd also had a report of a Dr Schollen, a former officer in the *Wehrmacht* who'd served in Army Group E in the Ic section from the spring of 1942. He claimed that the Ic had been a pocket of anti-Nazis. 'We were no heroes,' he said, 'but the standing joke every day was "Who still believes in the military leadership abilities of our Führer? OK, don't all shout at once!"'

He'd left the section at his own request when he'd started to have doubts about their activities. He told our researcher Nana Wiessler that, one day, a parcel had arrived in the office: two rucksacks filled with wallets and other personal effects of Italian soldiers. When he'd asked what they were, he was told

148

that they'd belonged to mutinous Italians on the west coast of Greece who had resisted being handed over to the Germans (this episode had occurred after the Italians had capitulated to the Allies); they'd tried to escape by boat to Italy, but had been caught and executed. On hearing this, Schollen had requested a posting to the front, and his superior, Colonel Warnstorff, had agreed, provided Schollen could find a replacement as O3 officer. He did: Waldheim.

According to Nana, Schollen was fully aware that the fact that he'd resigned because of what he was being asked to do could be used as an accusation against Waldheim. 'I don't want to point a finger at Waldheim,' he said, 'just because I had enough common sense to get out. Waldheim's options were limited − after all, he had been declared unfit for front-line service.'

Another interesting witness was traced by Richard Mitten. Wolfgang Sattmann had been a radio operator attached to the AO section of Army Group E for the entire time that Waldheim was in Arsakli and during the retreat through Yugoslavia. In Arsakli, he'd worked in the next room to Waldheim in what had been an American school, and he claimed that his work brought him into frequent contact with the Austrian lieutenant. Indeed, he admitted that he'd taken dictation from Waldheim, which would suggest that there had been at the least some flexibility in the work practices of the Ic and AO. Despite this, Sattmann, a strong supporter of Waldheim, said that there'd been a very strict separation of responsibility between the two staffs.

Sattmann went to some lengths to stress the modesty of Waldheim's role in Army Group E. He claimed that only Colonel Warnstorff in the Ic received copies of his highly secret radio transcripts, and that Waldheim wasn't the officer who filled in for Warnstorff when the latter and his deputy Major Hammer were away; that duty had fallen to the other O3 officer, Lt Poliza. Now that Poliza had agreed to be one of our witnesses, we might at last find out what really happened at Arsakli, not only in respect of this technicality, but in terms of the knowledge and responsibilities of those in the Ic section.

Another piece of the puzzle was supplied to us by Peter von Meissner, another wartime German officer. He hadn't served with Waldheim, but his knowledge of *Wehrmacht* structure, the role played by the Ic and the options open to any officer who didn't like what he was being asked to do all made riveting reading.

Our researcher had asked if, in his experience, Ic officers were given a 'wide berth'. Von Meissner replied:

That is quite correct...The intelligence officers were firstly mainly people who would toe the line...They were mainly people you could expect to know how to play with marked or false cards. Who had few scruples, who had a perfect, or perhaps not-so-perfect, command of infiltration, diversion, using agents...In short, you didn't like being involved with them. They had under them the secret field police, a unit which operated undercover... Ic was a unit which operated mainly outside of legality, if there can be a legality in war, but at any rate, outside the declared aims of a soldier as contained in the German soldier's catechism.

'Did a soldier who was transferred to Ic have any choice?' asked our researcher.

'Of course he did. He did right through the war,' said Von Meissner. He went on to suggest that all the commanders had become even more reasonable towards the end of the war, and added:

It was very easy to act differently and there are plenty of witnesses to prove it...Mr Waldheim could quite easily have done [differently] when there on the Balkan front and [he] saw the cruel, terrible, frightful, devastating things happening on both sides...At any time, he could have said, 'I want a transfer to the Eastern Front.'

This was the statement of a brave man. How many of us, I wondered as I read his words, would have the courage to opt for a transfer to a place where, in all likelihood, we would meet an unpleasant death, when the alternative was to keep our heads down in relative safety and hope to see out the war, no matter how nasty? As Sir Frederick Lawton had told Peter and me, it was difficult to pass moral judgements on someone who'd been a relatively young man during wartime. Sir Frederick wasn't going to make any prejudgements, but he felt that the criterion would have to be: what could *reasonably* be expected of someone of that age at that time and with those responsibilities.

I turned from these grim reminders of the reality of war to the increasingly less-than-serious newspapers of today. The *Sunday People*, not one of Britain's heavyweight national papers, had joined the Waldheim industry with a vengeance. Using the book by the Waldheim expert Professor Herzstein – *Waldheim: The Missing Years* – as their source, it revealed (surprise, surprise!) that the Austrian president's wife had been, like her father, a card-carrying member of the Nazi Party from a very early date. The story was headlined 'EXCLUSIVE' – but, in fact, such details of Mrs Waldheim's past had been known to Waldheim researchers for at least a year.

But it was the *Daily Mail*, in its never-ending search for wartime commandos, who did us no favours. It apparently tracked down and got a brief interview with James Doughty, the former American commando with the Garbo-like penchant for being left alone. The story in the *Mail* suggested that Doughty was not as convinced that his interrogator in Arsakli had been Waldheim as we'd been led to believe. However, until we could get him to Boston where Allan could give him the chance to explain the story himself, I was prepared to reserve judgement. (Later, Doughty found that he was unable to identify his interrogator.)

Our intrepid lawyers finally arrived back in the office from their visit to Germany with Lord Rawlinson. The latter, they said, had been magnificent company – and never more so than when Nick Goodrick-Clarke, who'd driven them to their meetings in Hamburg and West Berlin and acted as interpreter, had ran out of petrol on an *autobahn*!

Allan Ryan finally rang me on Monday night to say that he thought that there was now a distinct possibility that the US Justice Department was going to go public with its evidence. The only hold-up at the moment seemed to be no more than a pause while the US State Department took advice from its ambassador in Vienna, to find out his views not only on whether to release the material but also when it should do so.

I was still left with a distinct – and uncomfortable – feeling of uncertainty.

In the meantime, my hopes for a nightly transmission of our programme were dwindling by the minute. Thames' director of programmes, David Elstein, had put the idea to Channel 4's new controller, Michael Grade, who'd said that he didn't like it. He did ask, however, if it were possible for us to transmit the full programme on 8 May.

This last suggestion did not come as a surprise. Precisely as David Lloyd had warned me, destabilizing the fixed concept was turning out to be a dangerous game.

When I told another of Thames' directors, Barrie Sales, what Michael Grade had asked and that I was considering it, he said that I must be mad. There was no way that I could sensibly cut down 50 hours of material to three and a half hours in two weeks and have a polished programme at the end of it.

I agreed with him, but said that, if that were the final decision, I would bust a gut in the attempt. Anyway, there was no point in worrying about it until HBO had agreed to a new date.

Colin Callender arrived to see me on that Tuesday afternoon. During yet another of his flying visits to the UK, he'd arranged to be brought up to date on the current problems. I went through the options with him, and told him for the first time about my worries over the Justice Department's possible release of their documents. He agreed that 8 May was going to be a tight squeeze, but added that his own schedulers at HBO had not given an opinion on the transmission date since we seemed to have abandoned the previously concrete-set 26 June.

I said that I had reached the stage where, what with all my worries about whether or not we were going to be overtaken by events, I was quite prepared to accept any decision as to when and how the programme was going to be transmitted – as long as there *was* a decision. And this would have to be sorted out between HBO and Channel 4.

Colin methodically went through all his questions about the set, the lighting, whether extras would look like extras (I sympathized with his problem: with so many 'real' people on

152

the set doing 'real' jobs, there was a danger that actors would simply look like...actors). He also wanted to know how we were going to accommodate HBO's requirements to give some limited access to the 'real' press.

It was just possible, I told Colin, that we could allow in feature writers, specially chosen to write 'colour' pieces, for the whole of the first day of recording – when we were going to try out all the systems (sound, lights, cameras, shorthand writers, translators), have a photocall and record the opening statements – without giving away much of our exclusive material. This should go some way towards pacifying Nancy Lesser, HBO's dynamic director of consumer press information, who'd already got vast acres of column inches for the programme in the United States, and who was constantly asking me to give journalists access to the recording.

After Colin left, I returned to my desk and sat deep in thought. Among the long list of problems hovering over us was our awareness that Granada Television's excellent, long-running current affairs programme, *World in Action*, was also on the Waldheim trail. In general, I'm totally in favour of there being a free market in all stories – even the Waldheim story and even if we found ourselves in competition with another commercial British television company. However, I couldn't help being worried about any possible overlap between their programme and ours.

As I pondered our situation – beset by governmental decisions over which we had no control, other programmes competing with us, the Austrians deciding whether or not they wanted to keep Waldheim as president, not to mention the thousand and one problems, both technical and editorial, which could suddenly reach crisis point here at the Euston Road 'Gulag Archipelago' and at Studio 1 at Teddington – I heard a muffled 'POP!'

I looked up, suddenly realizing where I was, to find Chrissie triumphantly holding up a bottle of champagne, which had been graciously provided by Roger Thomas. The bubbly lifted my spirits magnificently. Not because of the incredible efficacy of Mr Mumm's champagne, but because of the kindness of my colleagues who, noticing my apparent depression, had rallied round. When this is all over, and the

153

programme has been transmitted for good or ill, I thought, I will remember most the totally selfless and supportive way that our magnificent team had worked, and without whom not one part of the programme would have been possible.

11

Priming the Charges

The following day revolved around another planning meeting at Teddington, attended by all the people who would turn the Waldheim idea into a piece of television. Sound, cameras, design, lighting, floor services were all there − and, as before, they were being incredibly helpful.

Our director, Roger Thomas, took the chair and explained how he intended to shoot the programme, showing on a floor plan of the set where his cameras would work from and which would get which shots. We went through a whole litany of problems: what sort of monitors would be on each desk on the set; who would need to be 'miked' up; where cables would run; where the computers and printers would be for the court shorthand writers; what sort of sound input and output the interpreters would get; and a lot more besides. We talked about the bread-and-butter issues − or, rather, the coffee-and-tea issues, since a discussion on when and how we would break for these essentials was high on our agenda. (Besides requiring liquid refreshment, we needed a break every 1½ hours or so to change tapes.)

We went on to discuss what sort of crane we wanted for the final day of the shoot, when we were going to do the intros and wide shots. We talked about security. We puzzled over how, if Allan were going to walk around the set *à la* Perry Mason, we could provide him with with earphones that would receive their signal by radio waves − to avoid a trailing cable hampering his movement or even tripping him up.

The meeting lasted for two hours, and once again I was struck by the enthusiasm of the Teddington people: for every problem, they offered ten ways of getting round it. Perhaps after years of working on Thames' most successful comedy programmes – including the long-lived and widely syndicated *Benny Hill Show* – they had become just a little blasé about that side of the business; for them, the Waldheim project was new and different. Whatever the reason, it was a pleasure to work with the Teddington team, to know that, whatever snags we hit (and I was sure that we'd be hitting many more), they'd bust their braces to sort them out.

I returned to the office the next morning to find a letter from David Lloyd of Channel 4, confirming his (and, presumably, Michael Grade's) choice of 8 May as a possible transmission date. My blood ran cold, but I knew that it would still be some time before all the interested parties had agreed an acceptable and workable date.

I also heard from Thames Television International, our sales organization, that we'd had indications of interest in purchasing the programme from Scandinavia (from both an earth-based television company and a satellite service), French-speaking Switzerland, France, Spain, Israel, Zimbabwe, Australia, West Germany and Holland. In addition, RAI, the Italian television company, had expressed an interest but were also worried about how the Italians would come out of the programme; I assumed that this concerned the way in which the Italian army – with which Waldheim liaised in Yugoslavia, Albania and Greece in 1942-3 – would be treated. However, their purchase of the programme was not in any way related to their interest in its editorial content. They very kindly asked if we wanted any help in the collation of documents, and I passed them a message via TTI, saying that all help would be gratefully received.

Later that morning, Tim House surprised me by formally asking for a 'mini-conference'. He explained that he'd been having long discussions with Lord Rawlinson about the way in which the 'challenging' counsel was going to work. 'There are two ways of approaching the role,' he said. 'One is virtually to ignore how "presenting" counsel is proposing to handle his case and, in effect, create our own case to prove Waldheim's lack of culpability. However, it is difficult, if not impossible, to prove a negative. The other route open to us is for us just to challenge everything that Allan Ryan puts up.'

156

I'd already been slightly worried about aspects of the same matter. For example, since there wasn't going to be any 'defence' in the formal sense, how were we going to treat witnesses who were well disposed towards Waldheim? Would Allan Ryan, as 'presenting' counsel, 'present' this type of testimony, and would Lord Rawlinson, as 'challenging' counsel, 'challenge' it? I couldn't really see Allan − who, after all, did have the job of trying to prove Waldheim's culpability − simply allowing a 'friendly' witness to have his or her say; and why should Lord Rawlinson even seek to challenge such evidence, which was useful to his case?

Even if Lord Rawlinson were to call 'friendly' witnesses, Tim continued, when it came to cross-examination they might turn out to be, in the end, more of an evidential asset to Allan than to his Lordship. Because of this, the latter was eager for Tim to spell out to me the reasons why there was an argument for him to call fewer witnesses than he might have done if this were a standard court case.

This was the last thing I wanted him to do − witnesses were going to be the core of the programme. Seeing the look on my face, Tim quickly continued. 'Perhaps all witnesses can be called by the Commission of Inquiry itself,' he said, 'and not by either the "presenting" or "challenging" counsel. This way, virtually everyone who has any relevant evidence to give can be called. We'd also be able to get a lot closer to the whole truth by not limiting ourselves to only those witnesses whose testimony both sides think are going to work best for their own particular cases, and dropping those that they feel may do more harm than good. All witnesses can still be examined and cross-examined.

'Yes,' I said, 'we only have to come up with a way of working out which witnesses will be speaking for which side. Once that's established, they could be led through their testimony by the relevant counsel and cross-examined by the other.'

There was another advantage. If all the witnesses were to be called by the Inquiry itself, we would be able to present the evidence (and counter-evidence) in chronological order. This would mean that all the arguments and, in fact, the whole procedure would be much more easily understandable.

157

Lord Rawlinson came into the office the next day and endorsed everything that Tim had said. The only reservations he had concerned my suggestion that he should 'lead' the examination of some of the witnesses – rather than just challenge their testimony. However, he agreed to leave the matter unresolved until we'd gone through the entire list of witnesses and I was able to put a case for any of them that I thought he should lead.

I spoke to Allan Ryan later that afternoon, and put all this to him. Having already spoke to Susan Aslan, he understood all the ins and outs of this change in direction and, to my profound relief, he agreed to everything.

That settled, I told him that I desperately needed a meeting with him in very soon – to go through the list of witnesses and discuss a lot of other production problems. For example, I needed to know how he intended to go from one charge to another (so that I could plan how to set the scene for the viewer), how many documents and maps he was likely to use, whether he needed any library film.

However, most of all I needed a clear idea of where he was going in the case he was developing. How he chose to present his case also determined how the programme was going to be shaped. Because he and Susan had still to get to grips with about a third of the written material that had come in so far, I knew that they both felt a bit exposed in terms of which charges he was going to bring. But decisions had to be made soon; our rapidly approaching production date was concentrating minds wonderfully, particularly mine.

We made arrangements for Susan and me to fly over the following week, so that she and he could put their heads together and then, a few days later, I'd come along to see if we couldn't come up with some answers.

Late on Friday, Colin Callender rang to tell me that HBO's schedulers were now thinking of running the programme on 5 and 6 June, as two two-hour shows. When they'd first proposed this splitting of the programme, I'd been very much against it, particularly because, then, we were planning for Allan Ryan to 'present' all his witnesses over the first four days or so, followed by Lord Rawlinson 'challenging' their evidence. This would have meant that, in a two-show format, anyone not seeing one part or the other would have received a grossly unbalanced view of the Waldheim case.

Of course, now that we envisaged a much more homogeneous programme, my concern about running it in two parts had largely evaporated. With the two sides weaving in and out together, each two-hour slot would have its own in-built balance (even though I still hoped that the audience would watch it all). I told Colin that if HBO were determined to do it this way, I had no objection. However, I did point out that their suggested dates were about a month later than Channel 4 was hoping to transmit. I suggested that they got together over the telephone to see if they could work out a mutually acceptable date.

It was time to fly in the big silver bird again, and I headed for Heathrow and the land of the dry martini.

Just before I'd left, Lord Rawlinson had − very politely but very emphatically − made the point that he needed to know in detail just what he was going to have to challenge. Would I therefore, using my best offices, get Allan to deliver the specifics? Indeed, I would: I was almost as desperate to know them as his Lordship, for without these important details, I had no idea how I was going to break up the programme into segments to give it its final shape.

Susan Aslan left London the same day, but she was heading straight to Allan's home outside Boston, where the two of them would work steadily for a few days until I could join them. Then, together, we would see how Allan's case was developing. In the meantime, I was on my way to New York. Once HBO and the indefatigable Nancy Lesser had found out that I was coming over, what had been intended as a brief visit had been extended so that I could take in a lightning tour of top journalists, as well as a couple of meetings at HBO itself.

It wasn't until 11 p.m. on Friday night, after a delayed flight from Washington to Boston courtesy of Eastern Airlines (which took a mere 6½ hours instead of the usual 70 minutes), that I finally landed at Logan airport. We drove to our hotel in Scituate Harbor, on the coast south of the Massachusetts state capital and near Allan's home, and I crawled into bed at about two in the morning.

When I'd phoned him from Logan, Allan had suggested a 7.30 a.m. start, but I'd pleaded for just a little more sleep. So at 8.30, he came to the hotel to pick up both me and Susan (who was also staying there), and we headed for his home. He took us via the scenic route, boasting about the beauties of his birthplace. He was certainly justified: as we drove along the coastline, beautiful little harbours and inlets appeared, and clapboard houses, eccentric in their individuality, looked out across the flat, calm sea. Spring was definitely in the air as Allan drove us inland to his house, standing in a glorious woodland setting.

I finally had the pleasure of meeting Nancy Ryan. She was obviously paying a high price for Allan's involvement in our programme. Whiie she did enthuse about the project, she also said that she regretted the amount of his time that it was taking up. Her words and emotions were all too familiar. The time would undoubtedly come when Nancy and my wife Lynne would get together and compare notes – their stories and complaints about their husbands would be identical.

Allan led Susan and me to his office cum study, which was tucked away upstairs in a two-storey barn beside the house. Lined with books and files, it also housed his word processor and a variety of other weapons used by lawyers and writers. I could now understand why, when I'd called Allan from London, there'd always been a long delay after I'd spoken to Nancy before Allan, panting and out of breath, came on the line: it was a sharp dash from the phoneless office to the house.

As we settled down for what was going to be a long head-banging session, Allan spelled out the areas of Waldheim's wartime career that he was going to ignore for lack of evidence. Operation *Schwarz* – the campaign involving the Prinz Eugen Division which resulted in the deaths of 12,000-16,000 Yugoslavs and the capture of another 1500 – was out. 'I just don't have enough evidence to proceed,' Allan said.

I found this particularly interesting because, in a way, it gave credence to one of Waldheim's major complaints. Perhaps the most famous photograph that had come out of the Waldheim affair was the one showing him in uniform on an airfield surrounded by senior officers. It was taken on 22 May

160

1943 at Podgorica (now Titograd) before the beginning of a high-level meeting called to sort out the slow start of Operation *Schwarz*, and involving *Waffen SS* General Arthur Phleps, General Escola Roncaglia of the Italian army and Colonel Joachim Macholz, a deputy of the commander of Army Group E, General Löhr. Within days of the photograph being taken, there was dreadful carnage committed by the combined Axis troops against partisans and civilians.

The juxtaposition of Waldheim appearing in the photograph, the date on which it was taken and the subsequent events had frequently been linked together by the media as cause and effect. However, Waldheim had always claimed, probably correctly, that he'd been there for no other reason than to act as interpreter for the German and Italian generals. Now, using our highly refined criteria, Allan felt that, because of the lack of evidence, he couldn't justify pursuing the matter. The process had begun.

Another area with which Allan had decided not to proceed was the alleged involvement of Waldheim in the deportation of Greek Jews from Jannina, despite the fact that many felt he *was* involved. The evidence we'd been able to uncover was, again, insufficient – either because the memories of those who had given it were not reliable due to age and/or the length of time that had passed since these events, or because there wasn't enough corroboration.

Other allegations were dropped from his original charge sheet or modified. These included any involvement by Waldheim in the so-called 'Stip-Kocane incident', in which Yugoslav villagers were lined up along the road between these two towns and shot as a reprisal measure during the Germans' retreat, and in Operation *Kreuzotter* ('Viper'), which was the codename given to a series of mercilessly executed anti-partisan 'cleansing operations' in Crete.

However, Allan told me, this still left a broad swathe of allegations, ranging in date from March 1942 to November 1944. He handed me a sheaf of papers, and I eagerly ran my eye over the five remaining charges.

Charge 1: Operations Trio and Foca

From about 28 March to about 17 April 1942, Waldheim was assigned by *Kampfgruppe* Bader to the Pusteria Division of the Italian Army in Plevlje. He was the senior officer of the liaison team, and his duties, therefore, went beyond those of a mere interpreter. Those duties included providing intelligence to be sent back to *Kampfgruppe* Bader in Sarajevo, as well as coordinating the German and Italian joint operations Trio and Foca during this period in so far as they related to the Pusteria Division.

As such, Waldheim was aware of the various illegal orders issued by *Kampfgruppe* Bader in relation to these operations; these involved the criminal treatment of the civilian and partisan population and hostage taking. Waldheim was instrumental in the transmission of these orders and complicit in them, in that he would have transmitted information between *Kampfgruppe* Bader and the Pusteria Division to ensure the effective carrying out of these orders, in the following incidents:

(1) The shooting on 26 April 1942 of 15 prisoners without trial who had been captured by the 11th Mountain Regiment of the Pusteria Division.

(2) The shooting of 33 hostages on 4 May 1942 in purported reprisals by the Pusteria Division in Plevlje.

(3) The shooting of 70 hostages at Cajnice in purported reprisals by the Pusteria Division on 7 May 1942, at which Waldheim was present contemporaneously or immediately thereafter.

(4) The shooting of 92 prisoners without trial on 9 May 1942.

(5) The shooting of 47 prisoners without trial on 11 May 1942.

(6) The arrest of at least 488 civilians by the Pusteria Division, and the handing over of these to the SS for deportation to Norway for forced labour.

(7) The indiscriminate burning of villages and arrests of civilians.

Charge 2: Kozara campaign

This related to the time from about 30 May 1942 when

Waldheim was based in Banja Luka, Kostajnica and Novska in Yugoslavia and acted as O2 officer to the Ib (quartermaster), Lieutenant Plume of *Kampfgruppe* West Bosnia. During this period, the battle group was engaged in operations in the Kozara region, and the Ib section was responsible for, among other things, supplying the troops and transporting prisoners.

Waldheim, Allan alleged, would have been aware of the purpose of these operations, which was to destroy the partisans without regard to the laws of war, and similarly to terrorize the civilian population. He would also have been aware of the illegal orders relating to the operations in West Bosnia issued by the *Kampfgruppe*, which provided for and resulted in mass evacuations, imprisonment without trial and deportation of large sections of the civilian population, destruction of villages, the shooting without trial of civilians and of partisans who had surrendered, and the deportation of civilians and partisans to labour camps in Norway. All this resulted in the deaths of at least 4735 people and the imprisonment of at least 12,207.

In addition, Allan continued, as O2 officer to the Ib officer, Waldheim would have assisted in the arrangement for, and so would have been aware of, the deportation of prisoners — including civilians and partisans — from the region of operations to camps.

Such camps [wrote Allan] included Jasenovic, a known forced labour camp, at which a number of partisans and civilians (impossible to specify) were killed or died through starvation or overwork. Other prisoners, both civilian and partisan, were deported — with the assistance and/or knowledge of Waldheim — from Banja Luka, either directly or via Gradiska and Prijedor, to Semlin where they were handed to the SS and thence on to Norwegian forced labour camps where a number (impossible to specify) died of starvation, ill treatment or overwork. At least 7000 prisoners, including civilians, were deported to labour camps, and of these, at least 4000 passed through Banja Luka. The Ib section was responsible for transport from Gradiska and Prijedor to Banja Luka, and was aware of the onward transfer of these prisoners thereafter or arranged such transport itself. As O2 officer, Waldheim would have been aware of and participated in

163

such deportations. He would have also been aware that the deportations were to forced labour camps.

On 31 July 1942, Waldheim was transferred from Banja Luka to Kostajnica following a mopping-up operation in the area. At that point, Kostajnica was very close to (if not actually at the front of) operations, and represented a key link in the deportations of prisoners. As O2 officer of the Ib section, Waldheim's function was to organize the deportations of prisoners captured during the operations, which included *inter alia* all male civilians in the area over the age of 14 years.

On 15 August 1942, Waldheim was transferred to Novska as the Ib O2 officer to coordinate the deportation of prisoners in a further mopping-up operation by the *Kampfgruppe Westbosnien* in the area of the Psunj mountains — including the towns of Pakrac, Banovajruga, Bos Gradiska — in which it was ordered by General Stahl on 12 August 1942 that the male population over 15 years and the villagers supporting the partisans were to be arrested and taken to prison assembly points. Since troops were to carry their own supplies in this operation, the main function of Waldheim as O2 officer to the Ib section in this operation was to arrange deportation of prisoners to prison camps as outlined above.

Charge 3: Athens

Between about 19 July and about 9 September 1943, Waldheim served as O2 officer to the Ia (Operations) section officer, Lt Colonel Bruno Willers, attached to the German Liaison Command with the Italian 11th Army based in Athens and, from 9 September to 4 October 1943, with Army Group Southern Greece in the same position.

3.1: Actions against Greek civilians
During the month of August, the 1st Mountain Division was based in Epirus and reported specifically to the German Liaison Command with the 11th Army in Athens. The German Liaison Command had operational capacity in its own right.

In that region, the 1st Mountain Division were engaged in 'cleansing operations'. This term was used as a euphemism for the wholesale destruction of villages and the indiscriminate killing of civilians suspected of having assisted partisans.

Between 19 July and 21 August 1943, Waldheim kept the war diary of the staff of the German Liaison Command with the 11th Army. In his entry for 8 August 1943, he noted that he had transmitted the Führer order which stated that all 'bandits' (i.e. partisans) captured in battle were to be shot. Because he'd transmitted this order, Allan alleged, he was therefore aware of the circumstances in which the 1st Mountain Division were to conduct their operation.

For example, Waldheim initialled reports from the 1st Mountain Division reporting that partisans were present in a village called Komeno in Epirus. As the O2 officer reporting to the Ia, he would have been part of the decision-making process by which the Ia officer would have formulated authorization to the 1st Mountain Division to begin an operation against the village. On 16 August 1943, members of the 1st Mountain Division entered the village of Komeno at dawn and indiscriminately shot all the inhabitants found there, and set fire to the village. No resistance was offered by the villagers. Later evidence has revealed that 300 civilians were killed that day.

3.2: Italian capitulation

On 8 September 1943, the Italian government surrendered to the Allies. On 15 September, Hitler issued an order that stated that all Italians who did not wish to fight with the Germans were to be deported to forced labour camps. According to Allan:

> Waldheim was aware of, and assisted in, the process of retaining Italians for forced labour. He was also aware of the Hitler order stating that the Italians were to be returned to Germany for forced labour and not to Italy, and assisted in and was complicit in such deportations.

Charge 4: Arsakli/Salonika

From about 4 October 1943 until the end of the war, Waldheim was the O3 officer of the Ic/AO (intelligence/counter-intelligence) section with Army Group E. Until the Germans' retreat, which began on 13 October 1944, Army Group E was based at Arsakli, a few miles outside Salonika in north-east Greece.

4.1: Deportation of Jews from Corfu, Crete and Rhodes

On 23 April 1944, the Ic officer from Corps Group Jannina reported to the Ic/AO department at Army Group E that the deportation of the 2000 Jews of Corfu would alleviate the food problem on the island, and that the SD and *Geheim Feldpolizei* (who were under the command of Army Group E Ic/AO department) were making arrangements for the deportation.

On 12 April 1944, Army Group E agreed to provide transportation for the deportation of Jews from Corfu and Crete, and to authorize the XXIInd Mountain Division to provide 'escort manpower' for the deportation.

On 13 April 1944, Colonel Jaeger, commander of the islands, reported to the Ic section of Corps Group Jannina, which report was passed on to the Ic section of Army Group E, that the deportations of the Jews should be postponed for military and ethical reasons. It is clear that Army Group E over-ruled this recommendation ...

The deportations proceeded with the authorization and agreement of Army Group E and, specifically, the Ic/AO section of which Waldheim was an officer. Waldheim would have been aware of the deportations and assisted in assessing the respective Ic reports forwarded by Corps Group Jannina Ic section as to the effect of the deportations on the Corfu population which led to the decision by Army Group E to authorize the deportations. He was, therefore, complicit in the deportations of the Jews of Corfu and Crete to Auschwitz.

On 13 July 1944, the Jews of Rhodes were ordered to register by order of the Commander of the 999th Division of Storm Division Rhodes, General Lieutenant Ulrich Kleeman. This order stated that the entire Jewish population of Rhodes should congregate in the towns of Tranda, Cremasto and Villanovo by 17 July 1944. On 23 July 1944, three motor vessels with 1651 Jews left Rhodes via Piscopi, and were thence transported to Auschwitz where a number (impossible to specify) died.

This action caused such concern among the soldiers of Rhodes that Kleeman was forced on 16 July to issue an order stating that the Jewish question on Rhodes and its solution were no longer to be the topic of daily conversation among the troops. Although two SS officers had arrived to supervise, it is clear that it was the *Wehrmacht* who controlled the deportations.

The process was identical to that of Corfu and Crete. Army Group E would have given its authority for the deportations, since Storm Division Rhodes reported directly to Army Group E. The Ic section of Army Group E, and Waldheim as O3 officer, would have assisted in assessing the situation on Rhodes to provide information to enable the authority to be given by Army Group E. In addition, the Ic section would have been aware of the 16 July order issued by Kleeman, and the concern expressed by the troops on Rhodes regarding the deportations of Jews generally. Waldheim would have been aware of the deportations and the concern that those deportations raised. Therefore, he was complicit in the deportations of the Jews of Rhodes to Auschwitz.

4.2: Allied commandos

Waldheim was aware of an illegal standing order made by Hitler on 18 October 1942 in relation to captured Allied commandos. *Inter alia*, that order provided that the provisions of the Geneva Convention were not to apply to any captured Allied commandos, who were to be handed to the *Sicherheitsdienst* [SD, security police] and not to be transferred to prisoner-of-war camps. This order had been supplemented for the Balkan and Greek theatre of operations (in which Waldheim was serving) on 28 October 1942 by an order of the OB South-east General Löhr, which provided, *inter alia*, that 'voluntary surrender makes no difference. All encountered enemy forces shall, in all circumstances, be put down to the last man...This is a fight to the death without a halfway house. Ideas of "a peace-loving people's heroism", etc. are misguided. Precious German blood is at stake.'

On 13 April 1944, a directive was issued by Army Group E Ia/Ic sections as follows: 'Recent experiences have demonstrated the necessity of handing over members of commando troops, or prisoners whose membership of commando troops is in doubt, to the High Command Army Group E for interrogation. A preliminary interrogation is to take place beforehand by the division or General Command. The decision about treatment in accordance with the Führer will then be made here.'

This directive demonstrates that Army Group E had specifically abrogated to itself the decision as to whether and in what circumstances to hand captured Allied prisoners to the *Sicherheitsdienst* [SD]. The fact that this directive emanated from

167

the Ic section (although it is accepted that it also had an 'Ia' designation) indicates that those in the Ic section were aware of the previous orders and would be making assessments and recommendations in relation to the handing over of captured Allied prisoners. Waldheim was part of the Ic section.

(a) The Alimnia commandos

On 7 April 1944, a British unit of the Special Boat Service [SBS] was captured by the German Army between Alimnia and Rhodes in Greece. The prisoners comprised:

(1)	Lieutenant Tuckey	(British)
(2)	Captain Blyth	British)
(3)	Sergeant Miller	(British)
(4)	Radio Operator Carpenter	(British)
(5)	Gunner R. E. Jones	(British)
(6)	Gunner L. Rice	(Australian)
(7)	Gunner A. G. Evans	(British)
(8)	Sailor Nikolos Velesaros	(Greek)
(9)	Sailor Michele Laskari	(Greek)
(10)	Sailor Denefos Triadafillio	(Greek)

Prisoners listed 1-7 inclusive were members of the Special Boat Service, a specialist commando unit within the British Army.

(i) Captain Blyth

Captain Blyth was interrogated on 8 April 1944 upon capture by the Ic section of Storm Division Rhodes, who reported directly to the Ic section of Army Group E of which Waldheim was a member. Blyth revealed nothing of military importance during his interrogation and details were referred to the Ic section. Immediately after his interrogation, with the authority of the Ic section at Army Group E, Blyth was transferred to Stalag 7a in Moosberg, Germany, for 'further steps'. On 16 April 1944, the Ic section for Army Group E telexed Moosberg to order that Blyth be handed over to the *Sicherheitsdienst* – 'in accordance with the Führer's order of 18 October 1942' - for further interrogation; up to that point, Captain Blyth had remained silent. Apparently, on the same day as the order to hand over Captain Blyth to the SD was given, he gave detailed information to his interrogators. It is alleged that this information was wrongfully obtained as a result of torture.

168

(ii) Sergeant Miller, Gunners R. E. Jones, L. Rice and A. G. Evans and Sailors Nikolos Velesaros and Michele Laskari

All the above men were interrogated by the Ic section of Storm Division Rhodes on 7 April 1944. Thereafter, they were transferred to the Ic section of Army Group E, of which Waldheim was a member, apparently on the grounds that the prisoners were proving 'very obstinate'.

On 21 April 1944, the Ic/AO section of Army Group E sent records of interrogations of these prisoners to the Army Group F Ic/AO section in Belgrade. The interrogation reports of the three Greeks were signed by 1st Lt Poliza as 'interrogator'; Poliza was the special assistant to Waldheim ...

On 26 April 1944, the Ic section of Army Group E requested permission of Army Group F to deliver all the prisoners — save Radio Operator Carpenter and Sailor Laskari — to the *Sicherheitsdienst* since 'further interrogation ... fruitless'. This request was initialled by Waldheim. In reply, on the same day, the Ic section of Army Group F ordered that, with the exception of Carpenter and Laskari, the remaining prisoners be 'handed over to the *Sicherheitsdienst* for any further interrogation still of interest to them, and for subsequent special treatment in accordance with the Führer's order'. It is alleged, therefore, that further interrogations by the *Sicherheitsdienst*, and possibly earlier interrogations, involved the use of physical torture, and that the subsequent 'special treatment' referred to was a euphemism, in this case, for murder.

(iii) Radio Operator Carpenter and Sailor Laskari

Both the above were interrogated by the Ic section of Storm Division Rhodes, and transferred to the Ic section of Army Group E in Arsakli/Salonika. On 5 June 1944, both were sent for 'special treatment', according to the Führer's order, by the Ic section of Army Group E — which, as stated above, was a euphemism for murder.

... As O3 officer in the Ic section Waldheim would have been aware of the standing orders in relation to the treatment of commandos, which were illegal. As O3 officer, his assistants included Helmut Poliza and 1st Lt Ludwig Krohne, whose duties included the interrogation of prisoners. Waldheim was, therefore, aware of and, indeed, directed the interrogation of prisoners in Salonika, which involved physical ill-treatment.

Waldheim as O3 officer played a part in the assessment of the interrogations and in the decision-making process as to handing the prisoners over to the *Sicherheitsdienst*, and would have been aware of the request for authorization to hand prisoners over to the *Sicherheitsdienst*, and would have been aware that the consequences of such a handing over were that the commandos would be killed.

(b) Asproangeli: Captain Charles Bluett, Captain Hamilton, Private Albert Davis and Private Bennett

On 6 May 1944, four British servicemen were captured by the XXIInd Army Corps near Asproangeli, 20 kilometres north-west of Jannina. On the same day, the Ic section of Army Group E ordered that they be transferred to the Ic section of Army Group E for interrogation. The four were held at the *Geheim Feldpolizei* prison in Salonika under the control of the Ic/AO department of Army Group E. Captain Bluett (and possibly others) was severely mistreated during the course of his interrogation and subsequent imprisonment. Waldheim was the supervising officer for those responsible for prisoner interrogation in the Ic section of Army Group E. He would have been aware of the circumstances in which such interrogations were carried out, and/or present and an active participant in such interrogations.

(c) Calino

On 1 July 1944, three Allied commandos of the Special Boat Service were captured during an Allied attack on the island of Calino. These were:

(1)	Sergeant John Dryden	(British)
(2)	James Doughty	(American)
(3)	Private Fishwick	(Unknown)

Sergeant Dryden

Although severely wounded, he was interrogated on Léros on 2 July 1944, and by the Ic section of Army Group E in Salonika. This interrogation while wounded amounts to ill treatment. Waldheim would have been aware of and, indeed, would have directed such interrogations.

170

4.3: Distomon

On 10 June 1944, the 2nd Company of the SS Panzer Grenadier Regiment 7 shot six Greek civilians on the road between Levádia and Arachowa and arrested a further 12. After coming under attack by partisans earlier in the day, the Company entered the village of Distomon, shot the 12 partisans and all inhabitants – including men, women and children – to be found in the village. Houses in the village were also set on fire. An estimated 300 people were killed ...

Waldheim was O3 officer in the Ic section of Army Group E, and was therefore aware of the events at Distomon and aware that such activity was regarded [by the Commander of the Regiment] as being 'in the spirit' of the reprisal orders then in force. He was therefore aware:

(a) that only minor disciplinary proceedings were recommended for the commander of the company committing the atrocity, and was therefore complicit in this recommendation by his knowledge; and

(b) he was aware that, in identifying areas of partisan activity in intelligence reports, 'cleansing actions' would ensue, involving the murder of civilians. He was part of the process, and he was therefore complicit in that process.

Charge 5: Sarajevo

By 15 November 1944, Army Group E had retreated from Salonika to Sarajevo. Waldheim retained his position as O3 officer in the Ic section of Army Group E.

Anti-Semitic leaflets

Propaganda material was sent under cover of a letter dated 28 November 1944 from Ic section of XXXIV Army Corps to Army Group E Ic/AO section. The leaflets were to be dropped in enemy areas, and included at least two virulently anti-Semitic leaflets, one of which includes the phrase 'Kill the Jews and come over to us.'

Waldheim's initials appear on a receipt stamp, dated 3 December 1944, on the covering letter. Waldheim was, therefore, aware of the activities of the German Army in inciting the local population to murder civilians, and was, therefore, complicit in such activity.

171

This was quite a list of allegations. However, it was still roughly one month before we began recording, and Allan reserved the right to delete or modify his charges right up to the time we started shooting.

During that day, we also went through the eyewitnesses that Allan had finally decided that he might call. There was a potential of nearly 40, even without including any expert witnesses. The latter brought us to one area of disagreement that Allan and Susan wanted me to raise with Tim House and Lord Rawlinson, the 'challenging' side.

Tim had already informed all of us that it was their intention to call as a witness an expert in international law. Because so many facts were not in dispute, he and Lord Rawlinson felt that, apart from challenging witnesses, their best tactic would be to argue that what Waldheim had done was not a war crime by interpretation of international law. To this end, they wanted to call their expert towards the end of the Inquiry.

However, both Allan and Susan held the view that it was for the lawyers themselves to argue the interpretation of Waldheim's actions during this period, together with giving their own opinion of the law and how it applied in these circumstances.

This was just the sort of disagreement that we'd anticipated way back at our seminar in January. We'd then formulated a method for dealing with such eventualities, and I told Allan and Susan that I proposed to activate this. In the first instance, both sides would present their cases to Peter Smith, our legal coordinator. However, I felt sure that, no matter in whose favour he decided, the losing side would want to take it further. The matter would then be considered by Sir Frederick Lawton, who had agreed to act as arbiter in such disagreements. Then, in theory at least, either side could still reject his decision as well, but if they did 'red star' the issue, they would have to wait until the day before recording started to put their case to all five judges. Obviously, this would mean that they would have to make major decisions about their cases, and how they were to be presented, late in the day. In any event, if Lord Rawlinson and Tim were to win this particular argument, I had little doubt that Allan and Susan would want to call in their own expert in international law to offer a counter-

172

argument to that which the 'challenging' side's expert would advocate.

By 6.30, we'd been through Allan's case. It had been a long but productive day, and I felt that the 'presenting' side was up to speed. Once Susan had committed everything to paper, this would, I hoped, satisfy the very reasonable request I'd had from the 'challenging' camp. Equally, I now knew how to begin dividing up the programme into sections.

Following the intro to the programme, Section 1 would go up to Waldheim's posting to Yugoslavia and his roles in Operations Trio and Foca and the Kozara massacre. Section 2 would take Waldheim to Athens in the summer of 1943, and would deal with the allegations concerning partisans and civilians, as well as the deportation of the Italian prisoners-of-war. Section 3 would relate to his period in Arsakli/Salonika, and the deportation of Greek Jews from the islands of Corfu, Rhodes and Crete, the interrogation and later execution of some Greek, British, Australian and American commandos, and finally the allegations about a massacre of Greek civilians at Distomon. Section 4, the final part of the Inquiry proper, would deal with the anti-Semitic leaflets sent to the Ic/AO section of Army Group E for dropping in enemy areas.

On Monday, I was back in New York for a meeting at Home Box Office. They were sticking with 5 June as their date for transmission, but had, as a gesture towards achieving unity with Channel 4, agreed to show the whole programme in one go. What we needed now was a reciprocal gesture from Channel 4.

We discussed how HBO could stimulate interest among special interest groups in the US. Given the polyglot nature of that country, the Italian, Greek, Yugoslav and Jewish communities were obvious targets, and because of the eminence of our judges' panel and the way in which they would be interpreting the law, lawyers were another specialist group on which it would be worth investing some time and resources. We discussed other forms of publicity for the programme, as well as a number of alternative ways that we could stimulate interest.

I'd brought some photographs of the model of the set that its designer, Bill Palmer, had had taken for me. Colin

Callender had already seen the model itself when he'd last been in London, but this was Bridget Potter's first sight. When she said that she liked it, this was music to my ears, but then we hit a slightly discordant note over the presence of extras on the set – the actors I intended would be playing the individuals occupying the press brench and the public gallery. Colin had already mentioned this problem when he had visited me in London, and now Bridget said that she thought having them on the programme was a shame because everyone else was real. I said that everyone contributing to the programme was real and that I didn't feel a few extras would change that. I also thought that since the set had been designed with a press bench and a public gallery, not to fill it then would make it look obviously and embarrassingly empty. The extras would be very useful in the wide shots, just as set decoration, and if we didn't like the cut-in shots of any one person, we could just delete them. I didn't think that the integrity of the programme would be impaired by having a few actors and actresses on the set.

Despite my arguments, there was no doubting the concern in Bridget's mind. Since I was not convinced of the right answer, we left that decision for later. It was yet another thing to ponder in the relatively short time left before we went into the studio. But that aside, I was pleased about the enthusiasm and support that was still emanating from the HBO team. In fact, I'd begun to think of their New York headquarters as my natural second office.

After the night flight from New York, I arrived back in London to a rainy, grey dawn, and I was filled with a familiar sense of anti-climax as I staggered out of the 747. It had been my intention to go home for a bath and a couple of hours' sleep before heading to the office. However, before dropping off, I thought I'd have a quick word with the Waldheim team.

It was Peter who gave me the news that shattered my hopes of a restful sleep. He'd just received a letter from Judge Bhagwati. In it, our Indian jurist apologized profusely before delivering the ultimate blow: for very personal reasons, reasons that he couldn't even put on paper, he would have to withdraw from the programme.

12

'All Rise'

Peter's news was about as bad as any I could imagine. After all the problems that we'd had getting the judges in the first place, it was a bitter blow, especially as we were losing someone of the calibre of Judge Bhagwati, a former Chief Justice of India. I knew that we'd have to start from scratch looking for a replacement, and we had less than a month in which to find one.

Back at the office the next morning, we began our search. Peter got on the phone to Kuala Lumpur to try and track down a Malaysian judge of whom Judge Bhagwati had spoken highly; in the process, he received a lead on another judge and so began making alternate calls to Malaysia and Australia.

Other leads took us in the direction of West Germany, where Veronika Hyks – assisted by Darren Nolan, one of our German-to-English translators – started a 'judge hunt'. Previously, I'd hesitated about considering a German judge because I'd envisaged having to carry out a Waldheim-type inquiry into any potential candidate's wartime career. Between 1939 and 1945, a number of judges in Germany had been only too glad to carry out the wishes of the Nazis, and they'd run courts that were a disgrace to any judicial process.

However, Veronika unearthed a very young judge indeed, born after the end of hostilities. Walter Hübner was, even now, only 42 – the same age as Allan Ryan – but he'd already been a judge, although he'd since gone back into private law practice. In addition, he was prepared to make the time available, and he spoke English. I decided to send Peter and Veronika to Stuttgart on the following Tuesday to talk to him.

175

By now, there was a new atmosphere of controlled panic in the office which affected everyone. It was as if we'd all suddenly looked at our calendars and realized just how little time was left before we had to go into the studio for the recording.

Our solicitors continued to argue about the need for expert witnesses, and for the first time, Peter donned his arbiter's hat. After hearing the arguments on both sides, he ruled in favour of Tim House and Lord Rawlinson for the right to call an expert in international law. Predictably, Susan Aslan objected, and Peter made arrangements for Sir Frederick to adjudicate by setting out for him both sides of the argument on paper. His Lordship also found in favour of 'challenging' counsel. This presented Susan and Allan Ryan with a problem: in principle, they could refer the issue to all five judges on the day before the recording, but this meant that they'd have very little time to engage their own counter-witness if things went against them at that point. Instead, they took Sir Frederick's decision on the chin and began to look for their own international law expert.

Other legal matters were discussed at a long meeting attended by our solicitors as well as Peter and Ed Braman. By now, 'challenging' counsel had read Allan's specific charges, and the fact that he wasn't going to proceed with the allegations surrounding Operation *Schwarz* worried Tim and Lord Rawlinson. They'd intended to use the famous photograph showing Waldheim with the military brass responsible for the carnage resulting from this operation as an example of the sort of disinformation that had surrounded the whole Waldheim affair. Now that Operation *Schwarz* wasn't going to be mentioned, Tim admitted that, in the context of the parts of Waldheim's war that were going to be examined, the photograph had little relevance.

The suggestion was made that Lord Rawlinson could talk about the photograph in either his opening or closing statement by way of a warning – particularly to viewers – to be careful about prejudging Waldheim. Tim said that he'd discuss this with Lord Rawlinson.

Colin Callender rang to say that Home Box Office had finally sorted out who was to be their presenter for the US version of the programme: Eric Sevareid, one of the most famous and well-respected figures in American current affairs television. However, although we'd planned on taping all the introductions and 'links' on the final day of recording (23 April), Mr Sevareid was only available on the 13th and 14th.

I warned Colin Callender about these problems, and he accepted our time constraints. However, after making every attempt to come up with a mutually convenient time for Mr Sevareid and us to get together, Colin realized that it was impossible. Mr Sevareid was also aware of our difficulties and accepted HBO's decision to change presenters. They finally chose the excellent former CBS reporter and anchorman, Morton Dean.

The availability of our judges was another problem. Although Channel 4 had not yet agreed a transmission date, HBO had settled on 5 June, and so, to all intents and purposes, the original date of 26 June had been abandoned. However, that was the date that I'd asked all our judges and lawyers to keep free so that they could return to London for the live transmission of the delivery of the verdict. I didn't know if any of them would be able to extricate themselves from their other commitments so that they would be available on whichever date (or dates) was finally chosen by both television channels. We had to plan what to do if they couldn't be there.

Roger and I thrashed this out. Not only would the judges have to come to a verdict, but they would also have to give their reasons — and there might be a split judgement. In the end, we decided that, if it were a unanimous verdict, Sir Frederick Lawton as chairman of the judges' panel could be brought back to the studio; we would record him against one flat of the original set, and then insert shots of the other judges and the lawyers in the complete set, which we had shot during the recording. If it were a split decision, we'd simply tape one judge from each side giving the reasons for their respective judgements — only Peter, Roger, the judges and I would know which was the minority verdict and which the majority. In both cases, secrecy would be preserved until the final edit, which would be done just hours before transmission.

With two weeks to go before we started recording, the pace in the office seemed to have shifted up a gear or two. Our lawyers suddenly found that they had three or four months of work to fit into the time left. The previous week, Tim House had been in Germany and Austria 'proofing' witnesses, while Susan Aslan had been doing the same in Greece. In a few days, Susan would be off to Yugoslavia, while Tim would be returning to Germany. And there were still the witnesses in Italy to deal with.

Back at the office, each was faced with a two-foot pile of documents in their in-trays. All these had to be read through and absorbed, and decisions had to be taken on which would play a part in their respective cases. But the legal issues weren't the only ones under consideration: both Tim and Susan were under pressure to decide what they wanted in the way of maps, as well as which documents were to go into the stills store of the graphics machine, so that they could be called up on the monitors during the Inquiry. However, coming to their aid were the final members to join the Waldheim team – the elegant Jacqui French and Caroline Blackadder, who would help, respectively, Tim and Susan to translate their cases into television terms.

While the flow of documents had slowed down to a trickle, statements from witnesses had not. In fact, at a quick meeting with the lawyers, we'd decided that we were likely to call between 30 and 40 eyewitnesses from Germany, Yugoslavia, Italy and Greece, as well as another six or seven expert witnesses. My fears about a lack of these had obviously proved groundless, and we owed everything to the dedication and persuasiveness of our researchers.

We certainly couldn't be faulted on the amount of effort and resources we'd put into our research. For the previous five months, we'd had journalists and/or academics working for us in West and East Germany, Austria, Greece, Israel, Italy, Britain, the United States, Canada, Yugoslavia, Norway, Sweden, South Africa, Poland, Switzerland, Albania, Bulgaria, France and Ireland – a total of 19 countries. They'd interviewed over 250 people, locating 13 of Kurt Waldheim's wartime colleagues who had never before spoken in public. They'd visited 29 archives in more than a dozen countries, and had retrieved over 1000 separate documents, some of which

178

had not seen the light of day since they had first been filed. But dealing with dusty papers and ageing eyewitnesses hadn't been our researchers' only problems. Some of their work had had to be done covertly, and two of them had been physically threatened, with the result that we'd had to advise them to take certain security precautions.

On Tuesday, 29 March, Peter Smith and Veronika Hyks had lunch in Stuttgart with Walter Hübner, our prospective fifth judge, to find out more about him and to tell him more about the programme. In London, the afternoon dragged on with no word from our legal coordinator or our researcher. Finally, Peter rang to say that Herr Hübner would be an excellent member of the Commission, and that he was willing and able to join us.

A graduate of Tubingen University, he'd sat on the bench of the Stuttgart Federal High Court of Appeal and, between 1977 and 1979, had worked at the Ministry of Justice in Bonn, involved in the framing of legislation. Finding the bench too restricting, he'd then decided to go into private law practice, and co-founded his own firm of attorneys in Stuttgart. After we'd first phoned him with our proposition, Judge Hübner had checked his availability with his partners, who'd said that they would cover for him during the nine days of our recording.

I breathed a great sigh of relief, then rang the judge to thank him and invite him to a dinner I was giving for all our jurists on the night before the Inquiry began. I was pleased to note that not only was his English excellent, but it was colloquial as well. He seemed a first-class choice.

Another major step forward was taken when I heard from our commissioning editor, David Lloyd, that Channel 4 had decided, in line with Home Box Office, to transmit the programme on 5 June in one four-hour session, starting at 7.45 p.m. At long last, I now had a transmission date and could seriously plan the editing schedule. To this end, Roger Thomas and I had a meeting with Alan Ritchie, who was to be our videotape (VT) editor. Quite simply, he's the best I've ever worked with.

The editing wasn't going to be easy. In addition to the very real problem of reducing 50 hours of tape down to 3½ hours or less, various interested parties required five different versions of the programme. We had to produce two 3½ hour versions (four hours of transmission time, including commercials), one of which would be shown on Channel 4 and fronted by Sir Alastair Burnet, and the other that would be shown on Home Box Office and fronted by Morton Dean. We also had to do three 2½ hour versions: HBO wanted one for their repeats, and Thames Television International (TTI), our sales organization, needed another for any would-be purchasers in the English-speaking market. The third 2½ hour programme would also be for TTI, and would be what is known in the trade as an 'international track', a track without voices speaking English or English translations and captions. The purchasing company could dub any language they wanted over this, and this version would also have a tape with a coded time signal, so that they could drop in captions in the correct language.

Home Box Office were now becoming more interested in the production side of the programme, and as a result, we received a short visit from their director of production, Lynn M. Klugman. She had a number of questions, such as how we were going to light the set, but I was happy to deflect these to our director Roger Thomas and his production assistant June Mason and to our designer Bill Palmer.

HBO were also now expressing further concern about the appearance of the press bench on the set: would it look as if we were having a jury? Finally, we reached an agreement. I spoke to Colin Callender late one night and told him that we'd only have seven or eight seats for the press bench, so that it would look less like a jury, and I promised him that, when they were available, we'd have 'real' members of the press in those seats. I'd decided to allow a trusted few – very few – 'deep' feature writers to watch the proceedings, as long as they signed a legal document guaranteeing not to print anything about what they saw until the programme had been transmitted.

On Thursday, 31 March, the Waldheim project moved lock, stock and computers to Teddington studios. As the contents of the offices at the Euston Road 'Gulag Archipelago' were carried out to the removal vans, the rooms gradually began to look as Ed Braman, Susie Harrison and I had first seen them back in November. There was a distinct air of nostalgia about the place. The research phase, which had at times seemed an end in itself, was finished, and now all our work would be geared to turning what we'd learned into a television programme.

Arriving at Teddington, I found that we seemed to have taken over half of the offices and dressing-rooms, and the vastness of the programme was suddenly frightening. I wasn't the only one who felt this: both Chrissie Cocks and Susie came up during the afternoon of the move and made the same point.

But that Thursday was also the first that I began to feel a renewal of my initial excitement about the programme. I'd lived through many emotional experiences since starting this particular journey, many of which I've described in the pages of this book, but now I had a new sense of expectancy, a great desire to see all our hard work come to fruition.

Eventually, all the desks, filing cabinets, computers and in- and out-trays were in place, and cables were installed that would link us to the studio. The problems that had hung fire while we moved came to the fore again. Our programme film researcher, Alison McAllan, had been diligently contacting her sources all over Europe to get the library film that we needed to illustrate parts of Waldheim's war, but she was having problems with the Belgrade film archive. The copy of the film that she'd requested hadn't arrived — like so often in that country, it had been promised for tomorrow, and then another tomorrow, and another, until our deadline ran out. Finally, in desperation, I authorized Mike Maddison, Thames' senior film researcher, to go to Belgrade with a clean tape, to copy the material and bring it back.

Even now, information was still flowing into the project. For example, Richard Mitten and Felix Moreau, two of our researchers in Germany, had sent in a particularly interesting report, a detailed description of their conversation with Hans Wende, a fully alert and very fit 83-year-old.

Wende had arrived in Arsakli in the summer of 1942 and remained as an expert on Greece and an interpreter in the Ic section of Army Group E until the very end. He'd served under four different O3 officers including Waldheim and a Lieutenant Schollen, who, we hoped, would be another of our witnesses. Wende explained that his duties had included getting the morning situation reports from the various divisions and examining the relevant morning radio traffic so that he could compile a picture of the military situation in Greece. He would then give this to Waldheim or deliver it himself at the daily 11 o'clock briefing of the General Staff. If he gave it to Waldheim, the latter would, in turn, synthesize the various reports into a general situation report, which would then be revised by the head of the Ic section, Warnstorff, prior to the briefing.

Wende would occasionally provide more systematic information, such as a report he wrote on Greek 'bands' (partisans) in November 1943. The fact that it was Wende who'd provided this information, said Richard and Felix, tended to contradict the opinion of other Waldheim watchers, who had always claimed that the source of the compelling intellectual power in the Ic section had been Waldheim.

Wende's evidence was not all good news for Waldheim or, for that matter, for our 'challenging' counsel. Wende had apparently been surprised to learn that there had been any doubt that people were interrogated by the Ic section, although he did say that not many had been. One case in particular had stuck in his mind. He and a colleague, Hans Wollschlager, had been assigned to interrogate two Allied commandos, one of whom, he remembered, was a South African and the other wore a kilt. It seemed likely to us that the former had been Captain Bluett, who'd already agreed to come from South Africa to attend the Inquiry, and the latter might possibly have been Hamilton, another captain who was known to have worn a kilt.

Wende stated that he'd been fully aware of the Führer Order of October 1942 relating to the capture of commandos − that they were to be handed over to the SD (secret police) to be shot. 'Everyone in the Ic department knew that,' he said.

'When he first learned of this order,' wrote Richard and Felix,

Wende was horrified. Not because of any particular belief or knowledge that it violated the Hague or Geneva conventions, but because he considered it inhumane and because it violated his sense of military honour. In the event, knowing that to hand them [the two commandos] over to the SD meant certain death, Wende and Wollschlager decided to hand the two over to the Red Cross.

Wende told Richard and Felix that he'd known that what he and his friend had done violated the Führer Order, but he felt that they'd acted in accordance with what their commander General Löhr would have wanted. This tied in with what another putative witness, Joachim Lützow, had told us – that this attitude towards prisoners was something that would have been condoned by the general. Certainly, neither Wende nor Wollschlager was ever punished for this technical breach of both Hitler's and Löhr's standing orders.

On the morning after our move to Teddington, I was woken by my daughter with the news that President Waldheim had resigned. Then I looked at the date and started to breathe again – it was April Fool's Day.

It was also Good Friday and a holiday, but not for the Waldheim team. I'd called a meeting of everyone, and particularly the two solicitors, to go through the entire list of witnesses. Since we were the only ones in the office that day, there was a relaxed air about the place.

As we worked our way through Allan Ryan's charges, the number of witnesses to be called grew steadily, and by five o'clock, we had a list of 35 who'd agreed to come, another with three or four names of witnesses we still hoped to persuade, and a final one naming six expert witnesses who we'd already signed up. It was an impressive line-up, and just the right number.

All of us spent some time in the office during the rest of the Easter holiday weekend. Except, of course, Ed Braman – he came in every day. Early the following week, Roger Thomas, Bill Palmer and I went to see our nearly completed set in a vast workshop in West London. It was breathtaking – massively authoritative and beautifully finished in oak and ash. Now he had somehow to get this massive structure to Teddington.

That week I also went to hear the 'music' that would play during the opening and closing credits and on either side of the commercial breaks. I say 'music' because what I'd asked percussionist Jim Lawless for was not a theme tune of the usual type. The basic theme for *Waldheim* started with Jim making the sound of a heartbeat on a muffled kettle drum. Four bars later, a snare drum came in, counterpointing the instantly recognizable heartbeat with an equally obvious military rhythm. Three other drums gave the piece depth, while a cymbal gently hissed every other bar. It was just what I'd been hoping for. For me, it seemed to suggest the contradictions of the man in the spotlight, Kurt Waldheim – the heartbeat representing humanity (i.e. his role as Secretary-General of the UN) and the counterpoint suggesting the military background to the many allegations against him.

Allan Ryan arrived in London and set up office in a hotel beside Wimbledon Common. Within hours, jetlag notwithstanding, he'd filled an enormous table with documents, books, files and folders, Susan Aslan had moved into the hotel and the 'presenting' team went into top gear. A few miles away, at Lord Rawlinson's offices in the City, the 'challenging' team were also working flat out, putting the finishing touches to their case. From both teams came a steady stream of requests for information, translations, timetables and so on, and whenever possible, we gave them what they asked for.

Meanwhile, Peter Smith, with Veronika's help, produced what the lawyers called 'the bundles'. These were all the agreed documents (including, where necessary, translations) that the Commission might want to see or that either counsel might want to use as evidence. They amounted to over 2000 pages, split between eight large ring binders, all colour coded and labelled. It was a massive task to compile these, especially since there had to be about 15 identical sets of all these documents.

So far, our graphics designer, Morgan Sendall, had finished creating most of the maps on our computerized graphics machine, the Paintbox, and had fed it all the relevant photographs; now it was the turn of the documents. Jacqui

French and Caroline Blackadder, working for their respective solicitors, were rapidly retrieving the pages that the judges (and viewers) would most likely need to see, as well as sorting out their respective translations. All these – maps, photographs, documents and translations – would, when called up, appear within a second or two on the monitors on set and in the control room. Unfortunately, the Paintbox's stills store could only accommodate 340 items, and what we would do if we couldn't fit all we needed into it, I had yet to work out.

However, the busiest person in the office during this last week before recording was Chrissie Cocks. She'd made arrangements to bring in, from ten different countries, more than 40 witnesses as well as five judges and Allan Ryan. She'd arranged for them to stay in about 35 different hotels around London, and she'd made sure that there were cars and 'minders' to fetch and carry our guests to and from airports and the studio. Her achievement was masterly.

Allan Ryan delivered his latest list of principal allegations. He had reserved the right to modify or delete any of the allegations until the time of recording, and there was one alteration to the charges that he and Susan had given me the previous month: the massacre at Distomon was no longer a separate allegation. The refining process had continued right down to the deadline.

As we went into our final weekend before the recording, last-minute panics inevitably occurred. What should we do about the new documents that our researcher Mark Mazower had told Susan and Allan about? Why wasn't the 'Hitler Order' in the bundles? How should we use one of our witnesses now that Allan had decided not to proceed with the Distomon allegations? We brought a translator into the studio on Sunday to help out, and dragged Peter back to London from a quick trip to see friends in Manchester. The pressure was so great that we all felt as if we were verging on a communal nervous breakdown.

However, on the Saturday, and for the first time in my life, I backed the winner of Britain's top steeplechase, the Grand

National. I won £20, but it wasn't the money that counted; I just hoped that it was a lucky omen.

On Monday night, with less than two days before the recording, we had a dinner at which all our jurists – Sir Frederick Lawton from Britain, Gustav Petrén from Sweden, A. Gordon Cooper from Canada, Shirley Hufstedler from the United States and Walter Hübner from West Germany – met as a group for the first time. It was a particularly good night, everyone in good spirits with plenty of enthusiasm for the project. I left the hotel about 1.00 a.m., feeling (*and* hoping) that everything was on an even keel.

The following morning, I popped into Studio 1 to see how the construction of the set was getting on; in the end, it had taken about seven huge removal vans to get it to Teddington from the workshop. It still made an enormous impact on me. It was, I reflected, like some kind of celestial court: when the good times are over and I go to that great television producers' restplace in the sky, perhaps I'll find myself in just such a room, where God (with St Peter on his right hand and a member of a television trade union on his left) will tell me whether I'll be making good current affairs programmes for the rest of eternity or whether I will be condemned to game shows...

I hurried back to the judges' hotel for a meeting with them to go over all the myriad details having to do with procedure. Among other things, we agreed that all witnesses would be called by Sir Frederick Lawton as chairman of the panel. Every morning he would be provided with a list of witnesses' names, with an indication beside each of which counsel – 'presenting' or 'challenging' - would lead them (i.e. take them through their testimony first); this had been agreed by all the lawyers. The judges also decided that, except for Sir Frederick Lawton, they didn't want to take part in the press conference, set for the following morning.

We also had our one and only 'red star treatment' - when all five judges had to rule on a disagreement between counsel. At issue was the use of testimony from Werner Plume, who had been a ranking German officer above Waldheim and was now 92 years old and living in East Germany. He was in hospital and couldn't come to London, but had agreed to be interviewed by Nick Goodrick-Clarke, one of our researchers. Allan Ryan objected to this interview being allowed as evidence as he wouldn't have the opportunity to cross-examine Plume. However, the judges, in closed session, decided that, since they had agreed to admit hearsay evidence, they would allow Lord Rawlinson to call Nick Goodrick-Clarke as a witness, balancing his testimony about Plume against the fact that Allan Ryan wouldn't have the chance to challenge it.

Lord Rawlinson countered with an objection to two expert witnesses that 'presenting' counsel wanted to call − another two of our researchers, Hans Schafranek in Germany and Mark Mazower in Greece, both qualified historians − not only to report on their expert knowledge but also to draw conclusions. Sir Frederick pointed out that, as experts, this is precisely what one would expect them to do, and that there really wasn't anything wrong with calling them, even if they had worked for the programme. However, before the judges could again withdraw to consider this, Lord Rawlinson accepted Sir Frederick's point with very good humour and withdrew his objection − 'To preserve my dignity,' he said with tongue in cheek.

In the afternoon, the judges came down to Teddington to try on their robes and have a look at the set. As they walked around the 'room', I could see that they were impressed. All of us − production team and jurists alike − were becoming infected with the same excitement; at long last, the programme was almost a reality.

Lord Rawlinson and Allan Ryan spent the rest of the day going through their cases and trying to give us some idea of how long they would spend with each witness − i.e. 10 minutes with this one, 15 minutes with that. However, I suspected that the examination of each witness would take somewhat longer than both our counsel had planned.

The problem with getting all the required documents on to the Paintbox graphics device was proving to be an increasing headache, and I had to warn the judges that some of them might not appear on their monitors. This would, of course, be rectified in post-production, but when I left at 9.00 that night, there were still plenty of people in the office worrying about this problem.

In addition, our researcher James Walston was in from Italy, having 'proofed' many of the Italian witnesses, and as darkness enveloped the studios, he was dictating statements for Allan Ryan to a very tired Kate Johns. These came from eyewitnesses who, if all went to plan, would be among the first to appear at the Inquiry.

As I drove the short distance home, I mentally previewed the coming day. I really was *not* looking forward to having to chair the press conference. With so many programme problems that could still occur, I felt that I couldn't afford to be distracted; on the other hand, I supposed it was important to get publicity for the programme.

And so the big day arrived – the 13th of April 1988 – the day we'd been working towards for the previous nine months, the beginning of the recording. I felt a curious mixture of sheer naked fear and great relief.

I arrived in the office at 7.45, but everyone else was already there. Before the press conference and the actual recording, there was still a number of things we had to do. Most important was the rehearsal which would tell us if all our systems were working. For this, Peter had written a short script about a fictional World War II incident in which a couple of people had been captured by the Germans and an atrocity had been committed; two witnesses would be called to the stand to give evidence about this. Ed Braman and Veronika Hyks played the witnesses – Ed speaking German and Veronika speakng Italian – so that we could test at least two pairs of the simultaneous interpreters.

We began the scene with Allan Ryan examining Ed. Straightaway, there was a problem: when Ed was asked a question, he immediately started answering in German, cutting across the interpreter's German translation of the English question. The result was a shambles, so we tried lowering the sound level of the interpreter's voice, raising it and then delaying him speaking. Perhaps it was simply the early hour, perhaps our brains were more occupied with what was to come

188

– in any event, we finally realized that Ed was the problem: any non-English speaker would have to wait to hear the translation. When this finally sank in, we reverted back to our original system, making sure that Ed kept quiet until the interpreter had translated the questions, and everything was fine. Well, that's why we have these rehearsals – to sort out just these kinds of problems!

By the time we'd established that all else on the set worked correctly, the people we were going to be recording began to arrive. The actors and actresses turned up to take their places as extras in the public gallery, with a few for the press bench. The judges, now in their robes, waited for their entrance. Lord Rawlinson looked very impressive in an immaculate suit, his long silver hair combed back – every inch the very eminent Queen's Counsel. Allan Ryan was very smart in a dark blue suit, his beard and hair trimmed by our makeup department – as impressive as Lord Rawlinson, but in a completely different way.

The two clerks of the 'court', one of whom was our multi-lingual researcher Veronika Hyks, were both gowned. They would be performing any tasks that needed doing on set once the Inquiry began, such as passing documents to witnesses, notes from counsel to judges and so on. Veronika would also act as the link between the control room and the chairman of the Commission, Sir Frederick Lawton; she wore an earphone to listen to the production team's 'talkback'. Also gowned were the two ushers, who would lead witnesses into and out of the Inquiry.

Pride of place was taken by inanimate objects – the enormous 'bundles', eight huge ringed binders to a set, each set containing 2000 pages of every conceivable document that the lawyers might need, out of which we would probably only refer to 200 or 300.

Then came the photocall. More than 30 photographers poured on to the set, followed close behind by a number of TV camera crews. With this invasion, I felt as if I'd suddenly lost control of the programme, and I had to remind myself how many times in the past I'd been behind just such a camera, telling my cameraman what to film.

In the midst of the fray, Austrian television requested a

quick interview. The lights went on, a microphone was stuck under my nose, and I was asked why we were doing the programme, if we thought it right to hold an inquiry about the president of a friendly country, and what would happen if we found that there was a case to answer. After trying to reply to these questions satisfactorily, I pointed out that it was apposite that Austrian television was asking them: we would be delighted if Austria agreed to take the programme, and as for what would happen, whatever the result, that was surely in the hands of their own people.

The photocall begat the press conference. HBO's Nancy Lesser and Thames Television's Keith Nurse marshalled Colin Callender, Allan Ryan, Lord Rawlinson, Sir Frederick Lawton, Telford Taylor and me in the 'green room', told us where we would be sitting at the top table and then duly lined us up in the correct order and marched us out into the studio.

As I was chairing the conference, I sat in the middle, and surprised myself, given my propensity for forgetting names, by introducing everyone correctly. Then the questions came. I was told later by various people, including Barrie Sales, that the press had been a bit antagonistic, but personally, I found them far easier than the ones I'd encountered at HBO's press launch in California.

There were a couple of awkward moments. One particular journalist from a British daily newspaper kept having a go at me, asking whether, beneath all the fine words and all the evidence we'd gathered, wasn't this just a cover-up for a cheap 'trial by television'?

That really riled me and I rounded on her somewhat ferociously. 'There are 5000 to 6000 newspaper stories in the computer database,' I said, 'and of those, all but perhaps two have used such words as "murderer" and "war criminal" in the headlines, not to mention the text of the stories. In fact, 99.9 per cent of them have assumed that Waldheim is guilty. *We* are bending over backwards to be fair, providing top counsel to challenge – in an open court – all the evidence against Waldheim, and using real facts rather than a lot of unsubstantiated evidence or suppositions that are frequently wrong.'

This seemed to go down quite well, and after the conference,

190

I was warmly congratulated by some of my colleagues, including Lord Rawlinson. Time had passed so quickly that I was surprised that it was all over.

All the Inquiry participants (except those needed on the set) then had lunch on the *Sir Thomas More*, a beautiful boat owned by Thames Television, which they keep moored at the quay at Teddington. They were joined by Sir Ian Trethowan, chairman of Thames TV, and his wife, who had come down specially for this 'launch' and to watch the afternoon session. As for me, I was only able to grab about seven minutes, just time enough to eat a mouthful, before it was 2.00 and time to begin.

In the studio, there was the usual air of expectancy (heightened for this particular programme). The floor manager called for quiet, everyone settled down, there was silence. On cue, one of the ushers said: 'All rise,' and as everyone on set stood up for the entrance of the judges, the recording — the result of nine months of extreme effort — began.

Part II

The Commission of Inquiry

The following are extracts of verbatim testimony taken down directly from witnesses or through the simultaneous translations given during the days of the Inquiry. They contain some of the evidence upon which the judges — now called 'Commissioners' — had to base their judgement. They also struck me as being particularly relevant, interesting and/or graphic in their descriptions of war-torn Europe, and of Waldheim's war experiences.

In addition, every night throughout the nine days of the Commission of Inquiry, I tried to record my own impressions of that day's evidence.

Day 1: afternoon

As everyone on the set stood up, the judges solemnly entered from the back and took their places behind their wide desk, each of the five seats having its own individual TV monitor and a set of the eight volumes making up the 'bundles'. Sir Frederick Lawton, as chairman of the judges' panel, began the proceedings by reading out the terms of reference that had been decided at the seminar in January:

Whether this Commission − restricting their consideration solely to statements, documents and submissions presented at the hearing − are of the opinion that there is enough evidence to warrant an answer by Dr Kurt Waldheim to allegations that he wrongly participated in acts which were contrary to the international laws of war.

This was followed by the opening statements of both counsel. Allan Ryan spoke first.

Mr Chairman and honourable members, forty-two years ago, the Office of the American Chief Counsel at Nuremberg wrote: 'The conviction that has constantly animated the American prosecution is that only a part of its duty would have been done if it succeeded in persuading the judges of the international military tribunal. Its full task will be accomplished if the world is also convinced of the justice of the cause.'

As this Commission of Inquiry convenes, I shall present evidence animated by that same conviction, that not only this Commission but the world should see what that evidence is and what it means...

Allan Ryan then talked about the difference between Nuremberg and the Commission of Inquiry. One was a governmental judicial procedure, while our Inquiry was a television programme. He explained that the Commission would not be delivering a verdict of guilt or innocence. He continued:

I do not represent that you will find that his [Waldheim's] was the hand that held the smoking pistol. In the days ahead, I shall present...evidence that, taken bit by bit, may seem suggestive rather that compelling, but when taken as a whole, will lead you to conclude, I submit, that the case against Mr Waldheim deserves – nay, demands – an answer.

I shall present evidence that Mr Waldheim – a man trained in diplomacy, languages and the law – held positions of increasing sensitivity and importance in coordination, logistics, operations and intelligence as an officer in the German army – not in combat but on the staffs of generals. I shall present evidence that those officers to whom he reported, those officers with whom he worked, sometimes literally side by side, were responsible for the murder of civilians in Yugoslavia and Greece, for the deportation of civilians and prisoners-of-war in Yugoslavia and Greece, for the deportation of Jews from Greece to mass murder at Auschwitz, for the mistreatment and murder at the hands of the SS of Allied commandos.

All of these acts were crimes under the law of war. All of these acts were outlawed by civilized nations in the Hague Convention and Geneva Convention. But these enlightened treaties, these pleas of the civilized world that bound soldiers to act as decent men even as they waged war, were ridiculed and trashed by Hitler's forces from 1939 to 1945.

Justice Robert Jackson, Chief of Counsel for the United States at Nuremberg, told the international military tribunal: 'This trial's mad and melancholy record will live as the historical text of the 20th century's shame and depravity.' Forty-two years later, these words stand stark, unchallenged and unimpeached.

The international tribunal wrote in its judgement simply: 'War crimes were committed on a vast scale.' They were committed by those men whom Waldheim served and served with, and by those who were joined in common cause with him, and there will be no doubt in your mind, I submit, that Waldheim knew that the crimes were taking place. Does this make him guilty? We reject guilt by association as we reject guilt based on knowledge alone, but I shall show to you that Kurt Waldheim did not make coffee for these men, nor, as he has claimed, was he some junior clerk, some low-level messenger with insignificant duties. He assisted these men; he informed them so that they could carry out their deeds. His acts facilitated their crimes. Here we cross the line from being an associate, a bystander, a companion, to being an accomplice.

The criminal laws of countries around the world recognize that one need not fire the pistol to be an accomplice to murder. Those laws were the basis of Control Law No. 10 of the Allied powers at Nuremberg, and that law says that a person has committed a war crime if he was an accessory to it or if he aided and abetted it, or if he took a consenting part in it, or if he was connected with plans or enterprises involving its commission. That is precisely the evidence you shall hear.

When it is done, I shall ask you to apply the law to that evidence, to conclude that 1st Lieutenant Kurt Waldheim stood too close to those crimes to justify a verdict of exoneration, that his hand may have been the hand of the accessory to crime and, therefore, the hand of the criminal.

Lord Rawlinson then spoke:

I should like to say straightaway that I do not defend Kurt Waldheim; I do not represent him. I've received no instructions from him, and I have not been in contact with him or any of his organizations. My role, I wish to make clear, is to help the Commission in its task by probing and challenging the evidence and, when invited by the Commission, to examine some of the persons who will be called before you.

I think it is impossible to ignore that Dr Waldheim has become a very controversial figure. He has been accused of concealment, of misleading – indeed, even of lying. Conversely, some of his accusers have been guilty of gross exaggeration, of misinformation or even of suspected forgery. The task of this Commission is to examine the nature of his service as a young officer over 40 years ago, and that and that alone.

The years of the war, World War II, were years noted for savagery, when millions were slaughtered in the name of an evil system, an evil empire. Some of us are still proud that we were able to bear arms against it and contribute modestly to its destruction. But the war nowhere was more savage than it was in the Balkans, a place with a tradition of civil strife, and where there was no frontline, where there were ruthless policies of reprisal and deportation.

Either, then, you indicted a whole army, as some would have wished, or, as the Allies chose, seek out and punish those who bore responsibility for what had been done to the peoples of Europe. That included the soldiers, and included the soldiers in the Balkans. It included the Field Marshal List, the commander-in-chief, sentenced to life imprisonment. It included Colonel General Löhr, executed. It included General Lantz, who you will later hear about, sentenced to 12 years. It included the officers who gave the actual orders for any of the massacres that were

197

executed. But a second lieutenant, who became a lieutenant, who never fired a shot, who never gave a command – how is he guilty of crimes against laws of war?

There were two particular officers who were tried for war crimes in the Balkans between 1941 and 1945. Their names were Herman Foertsch and Kurt von Geitner. Both were accused of some of the crimes alleged against Lieutenant Waldheim: the murder of civilians in Greece, Yugoslavia and Albania by hanging and shooting without trial; the execution of 100 hostages for each German; the destruction and pillaging of villages; the denial of status to prisoners-of-war; the herding into slave labour camps of Greeks, Yugoslavs, Albanians and Jews. Those two men were among those accused of those crimes. The men were there in that theatre of war. They knew everything the German army did in that theatre in the same years. They knew of the murders, the reprisals, the deportations, and to use Mr Ryan's words, they facilitated the passage of those orders which ended in those crimes – because Herr General Herman Foertsch was Chief of Staff of the Army Group South-east of the Balkans, and Kurt von Geitner was General Chief of Staff to the General Officer Commanding Serbia (General Bader, of whom you will hear) throughout the period.

Both generals were tried by United States military tribunal. These chiefs of staff were tried with their commanders. The commanders were convicted, the chiefs of staff were acquitted – men who knew everything, who bore key positions in the military hierarchy, acquitted by the United States military tribunal. What then of the lowliest of all staff officers? What then of this lieutenant, when the United States military tribunal acquitted the chiefs of staff of the same accusations in the same theatre?

You will, of course, listen with the greatest of care to what is alleged. But surely you will have to examine very carefully what, it is said, makes this lieutenant different from the generals, colonels, majors and captains. What makes him different? I know that you will... judge this lieutenant, not for what he now is or once became, not for what he has said or he has not said, but for what he did 40 years ago.

My country, and all the countries represented by the distinguished jurists of this tribunal and the distinguished advocate on my left – none of our countries hold with lynching. Maybe – and I stress the word 'maybe' – that is what has been happening over the past months: the lynching of a reputation, the justification of all of us here trying to assist you to get to the truth. Here

198

is the opportunity for a tribunal of people of judicial experience and training to examine the whole controversy, to seek to get out the facts carefully and responsibly, and above all, to examine them judicially and fairly.

Both of these were, I felt, epic opening statements. Both counsel had set the context of their own positions, the role of the Commission and what it was trying to achieve.

Charge 1: War crimes committed in Yugoslavia with Kampfgruppe Bader in connection with the massacre and deportation of prisoners, including the civilian and partisan population, and the indiscriminate burning of villages.

The first witness was Stephen Pavelovich, Reader in Balkans History at the University of Southampton. After a brief description of the history of internecine fighting that has characterized this region for centuries, he gave an overview of the roles played by both the partisans and the Axis forces, and the brutality on both sides.

Dr Pavelovich was followed by Detlev Vogel of the military history department at the Freiburg Institute in West Germany. Dr Vogel described the various 'cleansing' or 'mopping-up' operations carried out by *Kampfgruppe* Bader, to which Waldheim was first posted following his recovery from his injuries in 1942.

ALLAN RYAN: Is that ['cleansing' or 'mopping-up' operation] the translation of the German phrase *Sauberungen*?
VOGEL: Yes, it is, but if I may explain this word *Sauberungen* . . . It is a somewhat colourful concept which, during the operations and during the reprisals against partisans, was handled in a different fashion time and again. But what in general it meant was the following: First of all, the main centres of resistance were to be crunched and done away with. After that, certain territories were to be encircled and 'cleansed'...of the enemy, of those residues of the enemy who were still there – i.e. partisans or those who were suspected of being partisans, those who helped them. Finally, there would be a further step, which was not always undertaken . . . The territory was to be cleared of all male inhabitants so that only children and women and old people remained. Those who

199

were suspected of being partisans – i.e. whole villages – were frequently blown up.

ALLAN RYAN: So in fact, *Sauberungen*, despite its literal translation of 'cleaning-up' or 'mopping-up' operations became, in day-to-day use, a term that meant murders and terrorism, did it not?

VOGEL: Yes, you could express it in that way.

Allan Ryan then took the Commission and Dr Vogel through a number of German documents to establish that Kurt Waldheim had been, in the absence of a superior officer, the German liaison officer dealing with the Italian Pusteria Division, who in turn were involved in the 'cleansing' operations. Since the latter were initiated by the Germans, Allan Ryan was working towards getting Dr Vogel to agree that such orders must have come through Waldheim as interpreter, or would simply have been made known to him in his position as the liaison officer. Responding, Dr Vogel said that, as well as the German liaison team's duties of transmitting messages back and forth between *Kampfgruppe* Bader and the Pusteria Division, they were also to report to the German command their impressions of the Italians and what actions they were taking. According to Dr Vogel, the Italians were known by the Germans not to have a great deal of stomach for the 'cleansing' massacres.

Allan Ryan also pursued the question of Waldheim's involvement in transporting Yugoslav prisoners to concentration camps outside Belgrade, as well as to holding camps there from which they would be sent onwards as slave labour to Germany or Norway.

ALLAN RYAN: My question to you, Dr Vogel – and all my questions are based on the assumption that Kurt Waldheim was doing the duty that he was sent to do – it is possible, is it not, that Kurt Waldheim, in his capacity as a liaison officer, requested assistance from the Bader headquarters in beginning the transfer of this group of prisoners?

COMMISSIONER LAWTON: [interrupting] I must object to that. Anything is possible, of course.

ALLAN RYAN: I'm asking this witness, in the context of this case, Mr Chairman, if it is possible. I'm sure he will tell me.

COMMISSIONER LAWTON: How far does it get you, Mr Allan Ryan, if he says it is possible?

ALLAN RYAN: I will pursue that line of questioning if I may.

COMMISSIONER LAWTON: I think it would be more helpful if Dr Vogel would tell us, as far as he knows from his studies, what was the way in which Italian military commanders communicated with German military commanders above them.

ALLAN RYAN: Dr Vogel, focusing your attention on the liaison command in which Lieutenant Waldheim served, is it possible that his duties would have included requesting assistance from

THAMES TELEVISION LIMITED
BROOM ROAD
TEDDINGTON
MIDDX
01 977 3252

STUDIO ONE, TEDDINGTON

PROD NO C2790   VT 42782

RUNNING ORDER

" W A L D H E I M "

DAY FIVE . . . . MONDAY 18 APRIL 1988

SCHEDULE

0830 - 0930   Lineup Makeup
0930 - 1245   RECORD
              (Coffee approx 1100)
      - 1345 LUNCH
      - 1400 Check lineup
      1245   RECORD
              approx 1530)
              clear

Sir Frederick Lawton, as doodled on the daily Schedule by set designer
Bill Palmer

Bader headquarters to set in motion the transfer of those prisoners from the 5th [Pusteria] Division up to Bader headquarters and beyond?

It was rather significant that this was immediately looked upon as a controversial question, because elsewhere – the Waldheim Commission of Historians, for instance – it had been discussed in great detail.

Here, Allan Ryan was trying to argue that it was likely that any request for the transportation of prisoners or any organizing of transportation would have gone through Waldheim in his liaison capacity. However, Dr Vogel said that, while that may have been possible, there was another way that it could have happened: through the Italian liaison commander direct to *Kampfgruppe* Bader.

One of the real problems that Allan Ryan was undoubtedly going to have was already obvious: although we had found an enormous number of documents, the fact was that it was difficult to cross every 't' and dot every 'i'. Personally, I wondered if, at the end of this first day of recording, he had succeeded in convincing the judges that Waldheim was directly involved in either passing illegal orders or in the deportation of prisoners.

Indeed, after Allan Ryan had finished examining Dr Vogel, Lord Rawlinson, with just a few deft questions, pinpointed some of the gaps in the evidence which we all knew existed.

Day 2: morning

Despite the anti-climax that we all felt at the end of the first day's recording, when we reassembled the following morning, there was a great mood of enthusiasm again. It was quite amusing the way people went straight to their places. The judges were ready, as were the clerks, the court ushers, and the people on the press bench and in the public gallery – extras as well as journalists and other 'real' people with an interest in the programme, such as Professor Telford Taylor who had come over from New York. And everybody knew where they were to go. It reminded me of a protracted court case I'd been involved in once: for three or four weeks, we'd lived in our

202

own little world, as if we were in a play without an audience.

The first witness called was Gualtiero Piatti. In the spring of 1942, he had been an officer with the Italian Pusteria Division operating in the area around Foca in Yugoslavia. Allan Ryan asked him if he could recall any Communists being shot in a forest. He said yes, they did kill soldiers, but it was during battle. A few times, he'd refused to carry out an order to execute civilians – people who'd just been taken to the camps, picked up just like that. Two had been denounced by a boy who was a Muslim. 'He [the boy] started by saying that these men had been Communists, and the captain had them shot. He turned to me and I refused to do it. Fortunately, he did not insist, so someone else had to do the job.' Asked if another member of the Pusteria Division had carried out the execution, he said yes.

Piatti was only questioned very briefly (Lord Rawlinson did not cross-examine). Allan Ryan had used him to prove that the Italians, the Germans' allies, weren't too fussy about who they regarded as being a partisan and who they therefore shot.

The next witness was a man called Michele Bibalo; in the spring of 1942, he was a lieutenant in the Pusteria Division stationed in the town of Visegrad. His main evidence related to the deportations of partisans and civilians. He talked about a train carrying about 500 people, all packed together, which he had guarded for a time. He said that, during that night, the Alpino (i.e. Italian) soldiers were put on guard outside, and one of them opened a wagon. Bibalo had looked inside, and found 30-40 people from Visegrad, packed 'like sardines'; they were there all night and 'very, very hungry'.

The next witness – Vera Pavicevic – had a deeply moving story to tell. In the spring of 1942, she was a 17-year-old girl living in Plevlje. She said her father hadn't been a Communist, nor indeed a Communist sympathizer, but two of her brothers had joined the partisans. The family were imprisoned for a time because of the brothers. Before that, she and her mother had been under house arrest.

PAVICEVIC: In April '42, they let me go home, and I was placed under house arrest again.

203

ALLAN RYAN: Shortly after they let you go home, they forced you out of Plevlje, is that right?

PAVICEVIC: A week later, at 8 a.m. in the morning, they came, the Italian gendarmes came together with an interpreter, and told us that we must be chased out of town. My brother and I and two of our younger brothers tried to take some of our things with us, but they wouldn't let us.

ALLAN RYAN: Were you later told that, on the 4th of May '42, your father had been executed?

PAVICEVIC: We found this out 15 days later, that my father had been executed, together with 31 other hostages. It was a very painful time − probably the saddest thing I've ever experienced in my life.

Mrs Pavicevici said they were never able to recover her father's remains − that much later, after the partisans had liberated her part of the country, they found there had been a communal burial.

The next witness was called by Lord Rawlinson: Zola Genezzini. Serving in the Alpino artillery, he'd been in Plevlje from April to November 1942. He said that he remembers a German liaison team stationed at Plevlje, consisting of a second lieutenant and a radio truck and a few operators. (That was almost certainly Lieutenant Waldheim, who was the liaison officer with the German command from Belgrade.

GENEZZINI: He was the first young German officer I'd seen. I'd never seen one before, and that's why I remember him well.

LORD RAWLINSON: Did he speak Italian well?

GENEZZINI: No. He could manage to make himself understood, but he could not speak it well.

Waldheim, it will be remembered, has always claimed to have been only an interpreter at this point. Fortunately for the Italian soldiers, Genezzini spoke German well because, although of Italian origin, he came from the part that is near Alsace Lorraine, where German was spoken.

He said that he'd had two conversations with Waldheim − one which was fairly mundane, and another which was of interest to the Inquiry.

GENEZZINI: On Easter day, after the famous Easter banquet at the divisional headquarters in the presence of all the officers... he asked me whether it was true that officers had effected killings. He asked me because he had heard that Major Ricci, who was the adjutant to the Alpino artillery, had killed partisans – 'Communist rebels' as they were called, because they were practically all Communists at that time... He asked me about this episode, and I told him that most certainly I was present, at that type of event. I don't know whether I should describe it at this stage, because I remember this was a really nasty period.

LORD RAWLINSON: What did 2nd Lieutenant Waldheim say when you told him about Major Ricci and what he had done?

GENEZZINI: He told me that these were not things that could be tolerated, and it seemed that General Esposito, the commander of the Alpino artillery... had not taken the necessary disciplinary provisions, measures, against those officers – because, according to him [Waldheim] and according to myself, [it was] not possible that people could be killed like that in cold blood.

In cross-examination, Allan Ryan asked Senor Genezzini if Lieutenant Waldheim had been introduced to him as the liaison officer.

GENEZZINI: I was told that he was the liaison officer with the German Command.

ALLAN RYAN: I gather from what you say that he was not much use as an interpreter, is that right?

GENEZZINI: No, no, he certainly was not an interpreter – he was a liaison officer. That is a very different thing.

Charge 2: War crimes committed with Kampfgruppe West Bosnia in connection with the massacre and deportation of prisoners during operations in the Kozara region of Yugoslavia. The aim of these operations was to destroy the partisans illegally and to terrorize civilians.

Allan Ryan opened this segment by explaining the point of his questioning:

If I may take perhaps two minutes to explain to the Commission the significance of the evidence. Following the Trio and Foca campaigns that we have just heard about, Kurt Waldheim was assigned as the assistant, the O2 officer, to the 1b officer of *Kampfgruppe* West Bosnia...He became the assistant to the quartermaster...Unfortunately, all the records of the 1b section of that task force have been lost, and perhaps destroyed at the end of the war, so that we do not have a document like the Commission saw yesterday, or earlier in this proceedings, that establishes that Waldheim was posted to a particular place at a particular time.

He went on to say that Waldheim was told to report to the 1b in the town of Banja Luka. His immediate superior was Captain Plume.

It is our submission that the 1b section was responsible, among other things, for the deportation of prisoners, and that Kurt Waldheim would therefore have been quite closely or intimately involved in the deportation of prisoners. It is clear, I trust, that the deportation of prisoners-of-war is a war crime, and surely that is true if the deportees are merely suspects, supporters or other civilians, as I submit our evidence will show.

The involvement of Waldheim is particularly significant because after the 18th of July 1942, Captain Plume, his superior, was posted elsewhere, and Waldheim carried out all (from all the evidence that we can deduce) the functions of the 1b by himself.

The result of this, Allan Ryan was implying, was that, after the Kozara campaign, large numbers of prisoners were deported, and the deportations resulted in many tens of thousands of deaths, and that Waldheim must have been involved in their transport.

Lord Rawlinson, addressing the Commission, added:

The only point that I would make would be one about the deportation of prisoners. I will, at the proper time be submitting that the removal of prisoners from the battlefield clearly is not a war crime, and that any army has a responsibility to remove from the scene of operations the prisoners-of-war.

What is at issue is whether people were really being removed from the battle front for their own safety, or whether, as Allan Ryan argues, these were prisoners who were being moved into prison camps, into death camps, into slave labour camps –

206

so-called 'Sauckel camps', named after Fritz Sauckel, the man who organized slave labour for the Nazis (he was tried at Nuremburg and was hanged).

The historian, Dr Vogel, was recalled to give evidence about the 'cleansing' operations that occurred after operations Trio and Foca, when the partisans moved into other parts of the Kozara region. Dr Vogel explained that these cleansing operations (*Sauberungen*) continued to destroy not only the partisans, but also potential partisans – i.e. anybody who could be a partisan.

ALLAN RYAN: To destroy them in what fashion? That is to say, to destroy them by killing them and deporting them?

VOGEL: Yes, yes. As it was done with the Bader group, the same method, a combined action of killing...if you were partisans, and if you weren't suspects, deported. Of course, from some areas, some actions, potential partisans were also deported. For instance, male inhabitants of large areas, over the age of 40 – they were all deported.

ALLAN RYAN: A potential partisan is not a partisan at all. Is that fair to say, Dr Vogel? If someone is a potential partisan, one is a civilian and not a partisan at all.

VOGEL: Well, I can imagine, based on experience and reading the documents, the designation of 'partisan', of 'suspected partisan', I mean – the Germans were very generous in the interpretation of that.

ALLAN RYAN: 'Very generous in the interpretation' - which is to say that it was interpreted very, very broadly indeed, to include not only partisans, but anyone who might become a partisan or support a partisan or sympathize with a partisan. Is that not correct?

VOGEL: Yes, in general, I think – not always, but in general, you could certainly put it that way.

In answer to a question from the Commission, Vogel said, 'The 1b plays an important part in the matter of prisoners. Basically, 1b was the department for the organization of deportation and setting up prisoner-of-war camps. It was responsible for the organization of that.' But because the 1b department only had a very small staff, Vogel said, they would call on the people in Ic (intelligence) and other departments to help them.

Allan Ryan's next witness was Druga Rade Savkovic who, in the spring of 1942, lived in a village about three miles from Jazenovac, a Croatian Ustachi concentration camp. He was a miller, and milled grain for partisans and for others: 'In the spring of '42, the Germans arrived in our part of the country. The Kozara offensive started at the beginning of May; this offensive lasted for some 53 days. After that, I was taken prisoner and sent to a camp.' He escaped and went to the Kozara mountains, but was eventually recaptured by the Germans.

SAVKOVIC: They sent us to a village where we were separated from our wives and children.

ALLAN RYAN: How would one in your village be known or recognized as or be suspected of being a partisan by the Germans?

SAVKOVIC: They were not able to recognize them. For example, they noticed that one of the people in our village was wounded, so they assumed that he'd been at Kozara, and he was shot on the spot.

ALLAN RYAN: Because he was wounded?

SAVKOVIC: Yes, because he was badly wounded.

ALLAN RYAN: Is it your testimony that the Germans had no way of knowing who was a partisan and who was not?

COMMISSIONER LAWTON: [interrupting] He's not saying that, Mr Ryan.

ALLAN RYAN: That is what I'm trying to clarify.

COMMISSIONER LAWTON: He made it perfectly clear what they did, [which] was to separate women and children, and then to look to see for those that they suspected of being a partisan.

ALLAN RYAN: That is the point I am at at this stage, Mr Chairman − to see on what basis they decided who was a partisan and who was not.

COMMISSIONER LAWTON: He told us one reason was that people were wounded.

COMMISSIONER HUFSTEDLER: [interrupting] Mr Chairman, if you please, I would like to have the witness answer Counsel's question.

ALLAN RYAN: [to Savkovici] Did the Germans have any way of knowing who among you was a partisan and who was not?

SAVKOVIC: Well, the partisans joined the Kozara offensive and we had to get out. The partisans were wearing ordinary peasant clothes, civilian clothes, there was no way of recognizing them. The only way they [the Germans] would recognize somebody is

208

when they would notice that somebody was wounded and they would just kill such people. I suppose that was their orders.

ALLAN RYAN: Did you know whether there were people who were accused of being partisan supporters when they were not partisan supporters?

SAVKOVIC: That did happen when we came to the Jazenovac camp, when they separated out people who [they thought] were partisans. Among them were quite a number of people who had not been partisans. On this basis, 1600 or so people were shot.

Savkovic said he was taken to the camp at Zemun near Belgrade, transported there in cattle wagons.

SAVKOVIC: Conditions were more than terrible. It was very hot, it was the middle of July, the temperature was very, very high, over 30-35 degrees, it was really terrible. A lot of people fell unconscious. We were packed in like sardines.

ALLAN RYAN: Were you given anything to eat?

SAVKOVIC: No, of course not.

ALLAN RYAN: Were you given anything to drink?

SAVKOVIC: No water even.

ALLAN RYAN: Did some among you die on the train?

SAVKOVIC: Yes, that did happen.

ALLAN RYAN: What happened when you arrived at the camp at Zemun?

SAVKOVIC: When I got into that camp — Simista, it was called — what I found there [were] living skeletons, people who looked liked living skeletons. It was only then I realized where I'd been brought. I'd not realized until that moment that I'd completely lost my freedom — when I, in fact, had lost it.

He said that, for 20 days, they lived on boiled water and swedes. To get a bit extra, they had to dig graves, and then they were only given a tiny amount of food, and they had to fight with each other to get it.

There was a dramatic moment when Allan Ryan asked, 'What happened at the camp at Jazenovac?'

The witness put his head in his hands. 'My goodness, what a story,' he said. 'I was not in Jazenovac, but I know all the terrible things that went on there.' He talked about the village next to the camp, where 360,000 people were buried.

Subsequently, he was sent on a month-long railway journey, which took him to a slave labour camp in Norway.

ALLAN RYAN: Would you describe what you were put to doing when you arrived in Norway.
SAVKOVIC: When we got to Norway ... on the 11th of April ... there was a lot of snow. The SS met us. They gave us a very bad time. We had to walk 2 or 3 kilometres on foot to the camp. There were 70 or 80 of us in one small place, and when dawn broke and they opened the windows, and we got a view of this terrible sight, where we could see living human skeletons out in the yard.
ALLAN RYAN: Did you know the living skeletons?
SAVKOVIC: They were the people who'd been brought over there in '42, before us. They'd been living there with the SS people.

He had used the expression 'our people', and was asked by Allan Ryan, 'What do you mean by "our people"?' Savkovic replied that a majority of camp inmates were from Yugoslavia – from Serbia, Croatia and, especially, Bosnia: 'That's what I mean by "our people", people from Yugoslavia.'

ALLAN RYAN: Were you forced into labour in these camps in Norway?
SAVKOVIC: Yes, they made us work so hard, they wanted to destroy us. When we found our old friends there who were now living skeletons, they told us immediately, 'It would have been better if you had drowned yourself in the Atlantic.'
ALLAN RYAN: Did you know how many people died there, how many you saw die?
SAVKOVIC: Oh, I saw three or four people shot by the *Wehrmacht*, right beside me. But I know that of some 4000 who went out, only 1700 came back. All the rest were killed.

He said that, every day, you had to lose a certain amount of weight so that you could become a skeleton as soon as possible:

I went down to 37 kilograms. I was condemned to be among those who either died or disappeared in a certain way. I suppose thanks to the fact that I'm of small build, I managed to survive with the minimum to keep alive. But at that time, when I weighed only 37 kilograms, death was a much nicer and more beautiful prospect than life, not just for me, but for all of us.

Lord Rawlinson chose not to cross-examine Mr Savkovic.

Next into the witness box was Druga Stepan Pistignjatovic, who had been 17 and living near Sarajevo in 1942, when he was sent to the camps at Jazenovac — for reasons he never discovered. Allan Ryan asked him to describe the conditions there.

PISTIGNJATOVIC: We lived without any kind of hygienic facility, with the minimum of food, which consisted of two potatoes. We were beaten daily, regardless of where we went. Whether we were around the camp or if we were in a group which was taken to work outside, we were beaten. The conditions were extremely difficult. As I said, the people were dying massively and being killed.

ALLAN RYAN: Did you see people being killed, sir?

PISTIGNJATOVIC: Yes.

ALLAN RYAN: How were they killed?

PISTIGNJATOVIC: Shooting from the side by various Ustachis or in the camp itself by pistols. . .

ALLAN RYAN: Were these young men or were they old?

PISTIGNJATOVIC: The group that was brought to the camp, or rather the two groups that were brought to the camp, among them there were both old and young, and also women and children. But in the camp where we were, inside, there were mostly men, while old people, women and children were taken elsewhere.

ALLAN RYAN: How young were the children that you saw?

PISTIGNJATOVIC: Well, the ones I saw — the ones who did not actually enter the camp but were brought there — were about 10 or so. They were the youngest.

ALLAN RYAN: How old were the old men?

PISTIGNJATOVIC: It's difficult to say, but some were over 60, certainly, in my judgement. . . I saw people dying, probably both from hunger and thirst. I could not tell who died of thirst and who of hunger. Most people would die in the night. At the barracks, every morning, we would have to take out 10 or 15 dead bodies and pile them up outside. We were taking out corpses.

Like the previous witness, he had been taken to the Sauckel slave labour camp in Norway. He said that they were made to walk 12 kilometres when they got off the boat at Narvik.

PISTIGNJATOVIC: We worked in the quarries, we built roads, fixed up old roads which already existed. We loaded sand into lorries which was taken I don't know where. We worked almost day and night. In northern Norway, in summer, there is little 'night'.

ALLAN RYAN: Did you see people die in these camps?

PISTIGNJATOVIC: Yes, an awful lot of them, both dying and being killed. That was one of the worst camps of the Second World War. In just one single night, between the 17th and 18th of July, over 300 people were shot at the camp.

He was shown a grainy black-and-white photograph of a great many nude men running under guard. He said it showed how they had been forced to strip naked and run a few hundred metres to an icy lake where they had to bathe – and this was near the Arctic Circle. 'It was very, very cold,' he said. They were given daily rations of 500-600 grams of bread between five of them.

The next photograph that Allan Ryan asked him to look at showed people being executed by a firing squad. 'They didn't need much reason to put you in front of the firing squad,' said Pistignjatovic.

They'd give different reasons. Sometimes a prisoner on the way back to the labour site found either a potato or some kind of vegetable, or something to eat along the way, and put it in his pocket. Or if you were able to get hold of a piece of paper or newspaper – it was forbidden under pain of death to bring any kind of paper into the camp, not even German newspapers. . . that was sufficient to warrant a death sentence and be shot, as is shown in the picture.

Very often, there were cases where if somebody was wounded while working, if they hurt their hand or foot or finger, they were also condemned to execution, because the Germans said that anybody who was unable to work didn't need to live. They used to pick out what they called the 'sick' men, so when people went out to the open latrines, the Germans would check and watch to see whether anybody had dysentery. That would be a sufficient reason for them to be immediately – without any kind of trial – sent to the other side of the wire, beside the communal grave, where they were liquidated.

'Out of the 1000 or so of your group that went to Norway, do you know how many survived?' Allan Ryan asked him.

'In 1945, there were 150 survivors,' he replied. 'Today there are still 67 alive in Yugoslavia.

212

During this dramatic testimony, you could have heard a pin drop.

There was no cross-examination by Lord Rawlinson. The Chairman, Sir Frederick Lawton, then intervened and said that, while he was aware of the appalling things that had gone on, he wanted to know to what extent Dr Kurt Waldheim was responsible for any of them. The latter was, after all, in a particular section of the quartermaster's department of the force which was in West Bosnia – how did that make him responsible?

Allan Ryan replied:

> Our case against Waldheim and his relation to this, Mr Chairman, is very simple. His responsibility, first as the deputy and then as the 1b officer in the *Kampfgruppe* West Bosnia, which was charged with the responsibility of taking thousands of people from the Kozara down to the labour camps at Zemun, from where many of them went to Norway, will have made him responsible for the commission of war crimes – in that the deportation of civilians, for whatever reason, is a war crime.

Day 2: afternoon

After we came back from lunch, Drugamirko Pekic, another Yugoslav, came into the witness box. In 1942, he had been 27 and a partisan officer – commander of the 3rd Kozara Battalion of the Kozara forces.

He said that, during the battle of Kozara ('one of the most brutal attacks ever in human history'), the Ustachis would set light to buildings and kill people and, in this way, force the people to flee to the mountains, grabbing their children and anything else they could, in order to save their lives. The partisans were helped by this increase in their numbers, but they in turn had to supply the people with food.

The Inquiry now got bogged down in a lengthy discussion about what constituted a uniform. Allan Ryan asked Pekic, 'Did your forces, and other partisans you served, wear the Red Star while you were engaged in combat?'

'Not only in combat,' he said, 'but we had these emblems while we were training, patrolling, carrying on our military life.' He made the point that wearing the Red Star, the Communist symbol, was an act of faith for a lot of them.

ALLAN RYAN: Do you know, sir, approximately how many of the people who had fled were there at the time when the attack took place?
PEKIC: Well, today we know that...there was a total of 68,000 people deported from Kozara – mostly women, children and older people. A lot of young people were separated out and sent to a camp near Belgrade.

Then it was Lord Rawlinson's turn to cross-examine. Pekic, having accused the Germans of killing just about everybody, was asked by our 'challenging' counsel: 'What did the partisans do with the prisoners that they took?'

PEKIC: They would interrogate their prisoners and take their arms away, then let them go home. Anybody we suspected, both the Ustachis and the Germans, were sent to the headquarters of the unit.
LORD RAWLINSON: What happened to the Ustachi and German prisoners who were captured? What happened to them, where were they kept?
PEKIC: We did not keep them because we did not have anywhere. We sent them straight to the unit headquarters.
LORD RAWLINSON: Were they shot? They were shot, were they not?
PEKIC: No.
LORD RAWLINSON: What did you do with the German and Italian prisoners?
PEKIC: They were interrogated. There was a military court at the headquarters at that time.

A few exchanges later, Lord Rawlinson asked Pekic, 'During this battle, did you send back your prisoners to join their forces, the Germans? Is that the truth?'

'Yes,' he replied, 'we did let them go, except for those who were suspected of having committed some crime; then they would be taken before a military court.'

Lord Rawlinson then pointed out that he, Pekic, had previously signed a statement that did not appear to coincide with what he was now saying.

214

LORD RAWLINSON
ALLAN RYAN

LORD RAWLINSON: Did you make a statement to a lady, an English solicitor, Miss Susan Aslan, and say that you were not able to keep the prisoners and that they were shot?
PEKIC: No, no.
LORD RAWLINSON: Would you look over at this table, the lady there [pointing to Susan Aslan, Allan Ryan's briefing solicitor]. Is that the lady who took the statement from you?
PEKIC: Yes.
LORD RAWLINSON: Did you tell that lady that, as you could not keep the prisoners, they were all shot?
PEKIC: Listen, I never said that, nor can I ever imagine saying such a thing. If that is what she understood, then she must have misunderstood what I was saying about it, or else there was an incorrect translation or something like that, maybe. But it's not correct, and such things were never done at Kozara.

I have to say that I don't think too many people in the court necessarily believed him!

Day 3: morning

Charge 3: War crimes committed while in Athens, in connection with the indiscriminate killing of Greek civilians, and with the deportation of Italian prisoners-of-war following Italy's surrender to the Allies.

The day's proceedings began with a statement by Allan Ryan about the nature of the charge he would now be dealing with. This related to the time when Waldheim had been transferred to the German General Staff, a small liaison group attached to the Italian army and based in Athens.

Allan Ryan addressed the Commission:

Mr Chairman, in this segment we shall present evidence on the massacre that occurred in the pre-dawn hours of 16 August 1943 in the village of Komeno, near Arta in Greece. This village was in the region of Greece known as Epirus.

At this time... Kurt Waldheim was the O1 officer to the 1a (or operations) officer, Lieutenant Colonel Willers, in the German General Staff attached to the Italian 11th Army. The [latter] was officially – but, we contend, not really – responsible for German units in this area. Indeed, German army forces were sent in specifically because the Italians, in the last stage of the Axis, were no longer trusted.

Our evidence will focus on the 1st Mountain Division, the German unit that carried out the slaughter [at Komeno] – one of the infamous German *Sauberungen*, or 'cleansing' operations. This was indisputably a war crime, with over 300 innocent victims in the village ruthlessly murdered. It could not be any the less a war crime were the village a centre of partisan activity. Our evidence will show that it was not even that.

The connection with Kurt Waldheim is this: the 1st Mountain Division carried out this action, we submit, with the authorization and approval of the German General Staff in Athens. We submit that Waldheim was one of two officers in the section; indeed, as the only assistant to the 1a himself (Colonel Willers), he took part in the authorization of this tragedy. Although there is no single

216

piece of paper that will show that he or the 1a, Colonel Willers, specifically ordered the massacre himself, we contend that Waldheim's actions in that 1a section were sufficiently close to the crime that he is therefore sufficiently complicit in it to hold him answerable for his conduct.

After we have presented our evidence, both Lieutenant Colonel Willers, the 1a himself, and Captain Rothfuchs, the 1c or intelligence officer of the division that carried out the so-called cleansing operation, will testify that they deny any knowledge, complicity, guilt or whatever.

Allan Ryan brought Dr Vogel back to the witness box to describe the structure of the German army, with particular reference to the 1a section to which Waldheim was assigned when he was moved from Yugoslavia to Athens.

According to Dr Vogel, 'the 1a was the core' of the commanding general's staff.

[This was] where the operational orders for the subordinate units were prepared. Instructions from superior authorities were reformulated and passed on. And in this section, the war diary was prepared – all the information was gathered into this diary. In addition, this section was tasked to inform the staff about the general situation, to maintain communications to all subordinate authorities and those sections which were necessary in terms of cooperation – in other words, the air force, the navy and, especially, those in occupied territories.

Dr Vogel was asked to explain what the war diary was.

This war diary was a mixture of activity reports and certain registers from the 1a section which applied to the whole staff ... The various orders were condensed and then reported, and all the reports were recorded, and in the annex of this war diary, the various reports and all this were recorded word by word.

As O1 to the 1a officer, Lieutenant Waldheim's functions and duties included the maintaining of this war diary.

Dr Vogel then described the relationship between the Italian and German armies in Greece during this period. A large part of the country was under the control of the Italians, who at that stage had more divisions there than the Germans. The liaison staff to which Waldheim was attached was appointed by the Germans to work with the Italian 11th Army command. It had a double function. First of all, it was to liaise between the Germans and the 11th Italian Army; but it also had a control function.

Now, this control function is interesting, because during that period, towards the middle of 1943, the Germans were finding the Italian army increasingly suspect because there was a possibility that they were going to capitulate to the Allies. If they did, the Italians would either become non-combatants or, as they did indeed do later, throw in their lot with the Allies, and would then, of course, become the enemy. Given that there were more Italians than there were Germans in occupied Greece, this obviously created a problem for the Germans. So Waldheim's liaison unit were told not only to liaise with the Italians, but also to monitor them and prepare a plan for the disarming and imprisonment of the Italians if and when they capitulated; this plan was codenamed 'Case Axis'.

After Lord Rawlinson's cross-examination, there was an interesting exchange between Dr Vogel and the Canadian judge, A. Gordon Cooper, who was interested to find out what would happen to a German officer if he didn't pass on an order.

COMMISSIONER COOPER: Let's take an example about what Dr Waldheim was allowed to do − his function, for instance. Let's assume... that Lieutenant Waldheim would have had the task of carrying out an order to shoot partisans, prisoners-of-war and so on, and pass that on to the 11th Italian army division. And let's say he'd thrown this all in the waste paper basket.

VOGEL: ... If such an order came from the Army Group E and was passed to the German General Staff of the Italian army, then of course, it gets a receipt stamp on it. If it was not done by Waldheim but from the administration there, Waldheim in his position can't make it disappear; he couldn't do that, and he doesn't have the opportunity either. Once the order exists, he doesn't have the chance not to pass it on. So, at best, he could perhaps slightly reformulate this order on the part of the 1a; he might assist him in reformulating it...

... Certain cases *are* known where such orders weren't passed on, or they weren't carried out. I personally do not know of any case where brutal measures were carried out against such an officer who ignored such an order; he might have been disciplined, he

218

might perhaps have been removed from the staff and put into the front line or something; he might have been sent to the Eastern Front – those things are possible. But as far as him being shot or arrested for what he'd done, I don't know of any such cases.

The Chairman, Sir Frederick Lawton, next questioned Dr Vogel. He asked, 'What chance do you think that a temporary officer aged 23 would have had of influencing decisions made by a lieutenant colonel of the General Staff [i.e. Willers] who had staff training and considerable experience?'

VOGEL: . . . It very much depended on . . . the confidence that the 1a had towards his O1, his assistant. It wasn't so much to do with training, or staffing, or age or anything; it was more a question of what experience was brought to the post. We can assume that the 1a, due to his rank, had more experience in his staff position than the O1 – i.e. Waldheim . . . It certainly doesn't exclude the possibility that the O1 might have had a considerable number of staff positions and staff experience.

The next expert witness to the stand was Professor John Hondross, professor of history at the American University of Worcester, Ohio. He described the way in which the German army operated in Greece during this period.

ALLAN RYAN: In the period of time from summer '43 through October '44 – when the retreat began, the German retreat that is – the Germans carried out a number of operations, ostensibly at least against partisans, called 'mopping-up' or 'cleansing' operations, did they not?
HONDROSS: Yes.
ALLAN RYAN: Would you describe to the Commission . . . the way in which these operations were carried out, what actually happened, who was killed and so forth?
HONDROSS: Until the Italian collapse, Italy was responsible for most of the warfare [in Greece]. The first German anti-partisan activities were in March of '43 and were generally very light, small operations.

He explained how the Germans would go out on a sweep and throw 'skirmish lines' 10-12 kilometres on each side of a road or railway line. 'They would try to kill as many of them as they could. They drove them away from the lines of communication. And they would also destroy homes and villages which they thought supported the guerrillas, and also they seized guerrilla suspects.'

ALLAN RYAN: When you say, Professor Hondross, that the German troops... tried to kill as many as they could and seized guerrilla suspects and so forth, was that limited to people who had taken up arms in combat against the Germans?

HONDROSS: No, no, it was whoever was caught, whoever was a suspect.

ALLAN RYAN: What did it take to be a suspect?

HONDROSS: That was in the eyes of the person who did the seizure.

ALLAN RYAN: Did that classification include civilians and bystanders?

HONDROSS: Oh, certainly.

ALLAN RYAN: Did it include women and children?

HONDROSS: Yes... Say, there was a guerrilla attack, the Resistance had blown a bridge, attacked a German unit – there was a 48-hour period when they [the Germans] would attempt to find the individuals responsible. And if they couldn't find the individuals responsible, then they would take hostages and shoot or hang the hostages according to whatever they thought the crime required.

ALLAN RYAN: Hostages being, by definition in this situation, whoever was caught in the sweep? If they couldn't find the people who'd attacked them in 48 hours, they hanged anyone else they could find. Is that fair to say?

HONDROSS: Right.

ALLAN RYAN: Now, you have examined, have you not, Professor Hondross, the war diaries from Army Group E, particularly those from the 1a section (the operations section) and the 1c section (the intelligence section)? Have you reached a conclusion as to approximately how many Greeks were killed between March '43 and October '44?

HONDROSS: The records are incomplete. All I did was to take, as you say, the records of Army Group E, the sections of 1a and 1c, and total what appeared in the records, although there are gaps. But it comes to something like 20,000 Greeks who were shot or hanged in that period. And another 25,000 were seized as suspects.

Allan Ryan

Day 3: afternoon

Allan Ryan now brought Mark Mazower to the stand. Mark
had, of course, been working for us as a researcher, and had
had a doctorate in modern Greek history conferred upon him
by Oxford University during the making of this programme.
His involvement with the Waldheim project did mean that any
question of bias had to be dealt with before he could proceed
to give evidence. To this end, Allan Ryan asked him, 'Did you
pursue any particular hypothesis in doing your research for
Thames Television?' Mark replied that he had not.

He was asked about the *Kriegestagebuch*, or war diary, of
the German General Staff in Athens for the period 19 July
through 14 October 1943, which had been kept by Waldheim.

221

Allan Ryan quoted from part of the entry for 8 August 1943:

ALLAN RYAN: 'Appropriate directions go out to 1st Mountain Division regarding treatment of bandits. By new order of the Führer, bandits taken in battle are to be shot. Other suspected bandits and so forth are to be apprehended and transported to Germany for labour services.' Dr Mazower, was the 1st Mountain Division a German unit in Greece operating at that time in Epirus?
MAZOWER: It was, indeed.
ALLAN RYAN: Dr Mazower, I call your attention to the signature line in this message which states that the new Führer Order is that bandits are to be shot. Would you read the signature line, please, sir, in English.
MAZOWER: [reads] 'German General Staff with the Italian AOK 11, 1a no. 222/43, secret command dated 8th August.'
ALLAN RYAN: The 1a with the German General Staff AOK 11 was the office in which Kurt Waldheim was the O1 officer. Is that correct?
MAZOWER: That is correct.
ALLAN RYAN: This message transmitting the Führer's order [and referred to in the war diary entry] would have been transmitted by Lieutenant Waldheim to the 1st Mountain Division. Is that a fair inference to be drawn from the facts?
MAZOWER: There is a strong probability that he would have transmitted that order.

Prior to the massacre at Komeno, Operation Augustus had been carried out by the Germans. Allan Ryan's next line of questioning was about this.

MAZOWER: Operation Augustus took place roughly between the 10th and 15th of August. It involved a number of regiments under the command of the 1st Mountain Division who reported back to Athens. These regiments moved in.
ALLAN RYAN: When you say 'reported back to Athens', do you mean to the German General Staff with the Italian 11th Army?
MAZOWER: I do.

Mark Mazower explained that the 1st Mountain Division of the German army had attempted to squeeze the guerrilla bands, but had found it extremely difficult. 'They judged the operation [Augustus] as a relative failure,' he said.
He was then referred to an entry in the war diary, written by

Lieutenant Waldheim. Allan Ryan quoted from a translation of this: 'Mopping-up operations by the 1st Mountain Division in the Parga area completed...Enemy losses: 80 dead.' Allan Ryan asked, 'This is a reference to the completion of Operation Augustus?'

MAZOWER: That's right.

ALLAN RYAN: When you say the operation was judged a 'relative failure', is that in part because only 80 people were killed?

MAZOWER: I don't know what casualties they expected, but they expressed a view at the conclusion of the operation that they had not come to grips with the guerrilla bands in the way they had hoped.

ALLAN RYAN: Did the 1st Mountain Division go on from this, eventually, into the village of Komeno?

MAZOWER: A detachment of the 1st Mountain Division did, yes.

Allan Ryan asked for photographs of Komeno, taken by Mark Mazower, to be shown on the monitors on set. Mark agreed with Allan Ryan that the photographs showed the extremely flat terrain of that area, a flatness that was particularly remarkable in the way that it related to any partisan warfare.

Mark was asked to look at another of the documents from the enormous 'bundles'.

ALLAN RYAN: This is the daily report of the 1c, or intelligence section, of the 1st Mountain Division sent to the German General Staff in Athens. The translation [into English, for the benefit of the Inquiry] is the 1c report; the original is the identical text but sent by the 1a. In other words, there were two reports with an identical text. This was sent to the 1a in the German General Staff in Athens – that is, Lieutenant Waldheim's office. Does this document notify the 1a in Athens that the village of Komeno, of which we have just seen photographs, is occupied by a resistance group of 30 men?

MAZOWER: Yes. If you look at the bottom of the document, section 1c, you will see the item.

ALLAN RYAN: So at this point, the 1a in Athens was aware of this report from the 1st Mountain Division?

MAZOWER: It was. And Waldheim himself sends on the information in a report the next day, which he initials and which contains the information.

ALLAN RYAN: [referring to another document] Is this the report that [was] sent by Lieutenant Waldheim?

223

MAZOWER: This is the same information.

ALLAN RYAN: Would you explain what this is?

MAZOWER: This is the entry in the divisional war diary for the 12th of August '43, which reports the same sighting of a resistance group in Komeno. The same information which was transmitted to the 1a office in Athens.

ALLAN RYAN: Would you turn to another page? Is that the signature of Lieutenant Waldheim on the bottom line, under 'German General Staff 1a'?

MAZOWER: It is.

Mark also agreed that the third paragraph in the same document states: 'Komeno, occupied by approximately 30 bandits.' So it had now been established that Waldheim had been aware of the first message alleging the presence of partisans in this village.

Allan continued his examination: 'Dr Mazower, did Lieutenant Waldheim then send a message to Army Group E at the high command [based at Arsakli/Salonika] – above the German General Staff – stating that a cleansing operation in Komeno was scheduled?'

'Waldheim certainly signed this particular document,' Mark replied.

Lord Rawlinson then intervened: 'I notice, Mr Chairman, that the original has *Für die Richtigkeit der Abschrift*, which does not seem to appear on my English copy, unless it just [means] "signature authenticated", if that is the correct translation.'

There was then some discussion about the meaning of these words. Commissioner Petrén, who speaks fluent German,

Walter Hübner

said, 'It means it is a right copy, it has nothing to do with the content, it is just certifying it is a right copy.'

Walter Hübner, the German commissioner, adds, 'I think [that] in German we use these words if we mean this is the right copy from the original, or the right content from the original.'

Allan Ryan then referred to another document. 'This is a report, is it not, Dr Mazower, after the event. A report of the 1st Mountain Division describing the events of that day in Komeno?'

MAZOWER: That's right. This is a report of the regiment's description of the incidents to their divisional superiors.

ALLAN RYAN: . . . It is true, is it not, that on that day – 16th August '43 – some 300 people were killed in that village by German forces of the 1st Mountain Division?

MAZOWER: Yes.

Allan Ryan asked Mark Mazower about the significance of the particular report filed immediately afterwards by the 1st Mountain Division.

MAZOWER: . . . After a description of their version of the battle, they give a casualty tally in which they explicitly refer to 150 dead civilians. There do not appear to be any people captured or wounded, and if there had been, you would have expected them to be entered. They also appear to have captured only five Italian carbines and one machine pistol.

COMMISSIONER LAWTON: Before we go any further, Mr [Allan] Ryan, I think there is the matter of the record. It may or may not be a tissue of lies, but I think one, in fairness, ought to look to see what the regiment taking part is reporting to the *Wehrmacht* [about] what is happening.

ALLAN RYAN: This is the report: [reading] 'Twelve companies surrounded Komeno from three sides this morning. They received heavy gunfire from all houses. Thereupon the companies fired with all arms; the place was stormed and burned down. In this battle as it appears, one part of the bandits succeeded in escaping in the south-west direction. 150 civilians estimated to have died in this battle. The houses were stormed with hand grenades and went up in flames as a result. All the cattle and wool were captured and taken off. A great deal of munitions went up in smoke due to the burning down of the houses, and hidden weapons presumably burned along with them.'

That is what the report says. We will have evidence from a survivor who will testify that there was no gunfire of any kind, and furthermore, the fact that only five rifles were captured, as appears at the top of the next page: [reading] 'Captured some 150 dead civilians. Cattle, horses, wool, five carbines, one apparently a machine pistol.'

LORD RAWLINSON: With respect to my learned friend, as I understand it the importance of this evidence and these documents is to show what was told to Athens. Therefore, it is what is coming to Athens (where Lieutenant Waldheim was) that is important for the purposes of this Inquiry, as opposed to what actually happened.

As Lord Rawlinson pointed out, what Waldheim would have known about Komeno would not necessarily have been the truth. He would have read only what the officer in charge of the soldiers who perpetrated that massacre would have said in his report.

After agreeing that a number of other documents concerning Komeno had been initialled by Waldheim and passed on to the German High Command at Arsakli/Salonika, Mark was then shown another photograph, a rather touching one, of an elegant monument that now stands in the village of Komeno in honour of the victims of the massacre.

ALLAN RYAN: Did you take this photograph?
MAZOWER: Yes, I did.
ALLAN RYAN: How many names are there on that memorial?
MAZOWER: Over 300.
ALLAN RYAN: Do you know the ages of the victims that were killed at Komeno?
MAZOWER: They range from between several months to over 70.

Allan Ryan paused for quite a long time, then sat down with the words, 'I have no further questions.'

Sir Frederick Lawton then asked Mark Mazower, 'It looks, does it not, Doctor, that the divisional staff of the 1st Mountain Division told Athens a pack of lies?'

MAZOWER: You would not expect them to tell the truth.
COMMISSIONER LAWTON: Maybe. What I am saying, it looks from your investigation and the number of names on that

226

Lord Rawlinson of Ewell, former UK Attorney General (1970 – 74) and 'challenging' counsel. Lord Rawlinson's role was to challenge the evidence and allegations presented to the Inquiry.

Allan A. Ryan Jr, 'presenting' counsel. A former Director of the Office of Special Investigations of the US Justice Department, and now a iawyer for Harvard University, his role was to present the allegations and evidence to the Inquiry.

Allan Ryan, with his briefing solicitor Susan Aslan.

The Commissioners for the Inquiry: *Back row* (*left to right*): Walter Hübner (West Germany), A. Gordon Cooper (Canada). *Front row* (*left to right*): Shirley Hufstedler (United States), Sir Frederick Lawton (United Kingdom), Gustav Petrén (Sweden).

Lord Rawlinson and his briefing solicitor, Tim House.

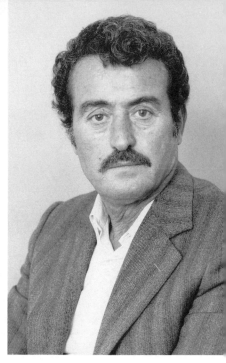

Four key witnesses: *Above*, Vera Pavicevic (left), whose father was executed by the Germans on 4 May 1942, and Alexandros Mallios (right) whose family was killed in the massacre at Komeno in Greece, 16 August 1943.

Below (left), Lt Colonel Bruno Willers, Waldheim's superior officer in Athens, and (right) Karl-Heinz Rothfuchs, Intelligence Officer with the German 1st Mountain Division in Greece.

memorial that, on reporting to headquarters, somebody in the 1st Mountain Division told a pack of lies.

MAZOWER: Certainly.

Lord Rawlinson stood up and began his cross-examination. The first thing he tried to do was to call into question Mark's credibility.

LORD RAWLINSON: Dr Mazower, you conducted this investigation of the documentation, but did you not start with a hypothesis . . . that Lieutenant Waldheim may have known about or have been a party to the planning of an operation which was conducted against the civilian population?

MAZOWER: I assume that you are referring to the analysis that I wrote [for Thames Television] on 13th March.

LORD RAWLINSON: That is what I have been supplied with, Dr Mazower. That was, therefore, the hypothesis. I do want to get clear − you started with that hypothesis, and you examined the documents in the light of that?

MAZOWER: That analysis was written approximately a month and a half after I started looking at the documents.

Mark was giving as good as he was getting − a very impressive witness.

LORD RAWLINSON: Well, you did have some hypothesis in your mind? That is all I wanted to make clear.

MAZOWER: I had no hypothesis in my mind when I started.

LORD RAWLINSON: Why did you write the hypothesis?

MAZOWER: At the time I wrote that report, I had collected about 60 or 70 documents, and I felt the most useful thing to do would be to examine what possible connection there might be with the events at Komeno. It does seem to be the most succinct form of expressing a possible connection. . . I would like to make it clear that I did not start with a hypothesis.

LORD RAWLINSON: Very well. . . [Is it] your suggestion that. . . the lieutenant [i.e. Waldheim] ordered [the general] to attack Komeno? Is that the suggestion, or can we exclude that?

MAZOWER: I think we can exclude that.

LORD RAWLINSON: So there was no question he told the divisional commander to attack. Is it the suggestion that he knew the general intended to attack?

MAZOWER: There is certainly a suggestion that he knew the troops intended to attack, yes.

LORD RAWLINSON: That they intended to attack a village called Komeno?

MAZOWER: That is right.

LORD RAWLINSON: Let us look and see what he actually saw, shall we – what he was actually informed about? ... [Refers to a telegram sent by 1c section of the 1st Mountain Division]. To whom [was] that telegram sent?

MAZOWER: It [was] sent to the German General Staff of the Italian 11th Army.

LORD RAWLINSON: At this time, is it not right to say [that] – after Colonel Willers had made certain representations – reporting from [the] 1st Mountain Division was to Athens, the general liaison staff at Athens, as well as to the army command [i.e. the 11th Italian Army] in Athens. Is that right?

MAZOWER: Reporting was solely to the German General Staff of the Italian 11th Army. There was no direct reporting to the Italians.

The question of whether reports were sent by the 1st Mountain Division to the army command at Athens as well as to the general liaison staff was an important one. This was because the liaison staff were German, and the army command, to whom (at least in theory) they were subservient, were Italian. The events under discussion occurred shortly before the Italians capitulated to the Allies.

LORD RAWLINSON: The command structure [of the Axis in the Balkans] – whatever may be thought to be the reality, as has been suggested – ...was that the Italian general commanded the 11th Army, did he not?

MAZOWER: He did.

LORD RAWLINSON: There was in that army the 26th Corps [based in Jannina], which we see in the documents?

MAZOWER: That is right.

LORD RAWLINSON: There was in that army the 1st Mountain Division, is that right?

MAZOWER: That is right.

LORD RAWLINSON: So we have a division, a corps, an army.

MAZOWER: If you seem to imply by that that the division came under command of the corps, I would have to disagree.

LORD RAWLINSON: How do you know it did not?

MAZOWER: Because it is quite clear from the documents that the division was reporting directly to the German General Staff at

228

Athens — and indeed, on several occasions, actually sought the support of the German General Staff in Athens in changing plans of the 26th Army Corps, which was an Italian corps.

LORD RAWLINSON: I accept that, Dr Mazower, but the German liaison staff were particularly influenced — indeed, there are the orders of the command. But nevertheless, there was a 26th Corps between the [German] Mountain Division and [Italian] army headquarters.

After Lord Rawlinson's cross-examination, Allan Ryan came back for a few questions.

ALLAN RYAN: Regardless of the responsibility that they may have had on paper, did you find any indication in your research on this period that the Italian 26th Army Corps actually ordered the 1st Mountain Division to do or not to do something?

MAZOWER: They tried to order, and generally they appeared to fail. They were certainly not customarily giving orders to the 1st Mountain Division, no.

ALLAN RYAN: The 1st Mountain Division, [when] looking for higher instructions as to what it should do and where it should go, looked to where?

MAZOWER: To Athens.

ALLAN RYAN: And what in Athens? Do you mean the German General Staff in Athens?

MAZOWER: I do.

ALLAN RYAN: Do you mean, for operational purposes, the 1a office of the German General Staff in Athens?

MAZOWER: That's right.

Then the Chairman opened up the questioning to his colleagues. Commissioner Hübner referred to a message which, he said, Mark claimed had been sent by Waldheim.

COMMISSIONER HÜBNER: Please suppose it was Waldheim who sent this message. If he would not send it here, would there be any chance that the order in the message would not be carried out?

MAZOWER: This was an important message for setting guidelines for the future conduct of operations. If he had thrown it away, I'm sure somebody else would have delivered it.

Mark was suggesting that the authority for carrying out the massacre probably came through the 1a section, probably in

229

line with the order that came from division headquarters itself for Operation Augustus, which says:

> All armed men are to shot on the spot. Villages in which shots are fired or in which armed men are found are to be destroyed. All able-bodied men between the ages of 16 and 60 are to be arrested and sent to Jannina as prisoners. The following are to be held as hostages: all prominent people – teachers, priests, mayors. They will vouch with their lives for the peaceful behaviour of the local population.

Allan Ryan's next witness was Alexandros Mallios who, as a young boy of 13, lived in the small Greek village of Komeno.

> ALLAN RYAN: I want to call your attention to the 15th August 1943. Was your sister married on that day?
> MALLIOS: My sister Karmita.
> ALLAN RYAN: Was that a festive day in the village of Komeno?
> MALLIOS: In the village, it was a festival on the 15th of August and the village was celebrating on that day. Celebrations – they had musical instruments according to the Greek tradition.

Mr Mallios said that there was singing and dancing late into the night – they were celebrating a lot that evening. He and the other children were sent to bed while the celebrations were still going on.

> ALLAN RYAN: What did you hear when you woke up?
> MALLIOS: In the morning, my father woke me up because a group of Germans and Italians came, and they surrounded the village. [My father] asked us to take the animals out of the village so the Germans will not take them from us.

He told how he and his younger sister, aged 9, had only been walking a few minutes when they heard shooting. Then he saw the German soldiers beating and shooting the people. Someone called to them, 'They are killing people, go away, leave the animals and go away because they are killing people here!'

> ALLAN RYAN: Who was killing people there?
> MALLIOS: The Germans.

ALLAN RYAN: Did you and your sister throw yourselves on the ground to avoid the bullets?

MALLIOS: No, we were running. People were shouting at us to leave the animals and go away. We were trying take the animals to an estate belonging to us. They [the Germans] saw us running and they started shooting us. I hear that, during the war, when they are shooting, it is good to fall down. After a little while, we fell into a yard.

Alexandros
Mallios.

Holding his sister, he managed to cross a river, and people on the other side helped them get out. 'Then I left,' he said. 'I went to a village called Nerharion...'

ALLAN RYAN: What did you hear about your family when you reached the other village?

MALLIOS: From the wedding nobody was left.

ALLAN RYAN: What do you mean 'nobody was left'?

MALLIOS: They were all killed, but nobody had seen them. When

231

I heard this, I started crying and running. I fell into the river again. I came to the entrance to the village.

ALLAN RYAN: And this is the village of Komeno you went back to?

MALLIOS: Yes, Komeno. It was about 12 or 12.30. The Germans were leaving. I could not see the people, but I saw their vehicles. As a small innocent child, I went into the village. I was going through the village, when I saw the first houses – everything was burning, dying people. I was afraid to proceed to the square of the village, and I came from a narrow street to go to my house, of course. When I arrived there, within 20 metres, I saw everybody killed, especially my father with a baby in his arms. Then I fainted.

ALLAN RYAN: Your father and the baby in his arms were both dead?

MALLIOS: My brother had just died; he was hit at the back of his head. From there, the people took me to the river and they washed the blood.

ALLAN RYAN: Mr Mallios, except for you and your sister, who escaped by swimming across the river, did anyone else from your family survive?

MALLIOS: Nobody.

ALLAN RYAN: How many of your brothers and sisters were killed, Mr Mallios?

MALLIOS: Four sisters and three brothers.

And, of course, his parents were killed.

He was asked by Judge Petrén, 'How old were you at this time?'

'I was 13 years old.'

'How many people lived in the village on this occasion?'
'About 650.'

Alexandros Mallios left the stand, and Allan Ryan's final witness of the day was called. Georgios Babeorgios had been a partisan – a colonel with the Resistance, which he had joined in 1943.

He said that he had not been stationed at Komeno on the 16th of August 1943, the day of the massacre, but at the partisan headquarters at Arta, some distance away. According to Babeorgios, Komeno wasn't a centre of partisan activity – in fact, it was totally unsuitable for partisan activities.

232

This was because, as our photographs showed, Komeno was in the middle of a plain, and partisans preferred mountainous terrain for their headquarters because they were easier to defend.

Day 4: morning

The first witness of the day was Bruno Willers, now 79 years old. He told the Commission that he had joined the German army in January 1928, had seen service in a variety of different places, and finished up as the 1a (operations) officer of the liaison group in Athens, with Kurt Waldheim as his number two.

LORD RAWLINSON: What was the principal reason in the minds of the [German] military at that time with regard to their relationship with the Italians, and the fear of what might happen to the Italian army?

WILLERS: Well, the uncertainty of the Italians became more and more evident because the Italian government evidently had the aim to get out of the Axis, and certainly this was felt by the army. So that we were very uncertain whether it would happen quite quickly and rapidly. Therefore, the military command wanted to establish a staff section there which would take care of German interests and the German units, bearing in mind that some of the German units were working with the Italians.

Lord Rawlinson asked him to look at some documents. He was shown the war diary entries for 19 July 1943 and 8 September 1943.

LORD RAWLINSON: Is this the *Kriegestagebuch*, the war diary of your unit, the German General Staff attached to the German/Italian army?

WILLERS: Yes.

LORD RAWLINSON: And that was kept from 19th July '43 until 23rd August '43 by a 1st Lieutenant Waldheim?

WILLERS: Yes, that's correct.

LORD RAWLINSON: Who was 1st Lieutenant Waldheim?

WILLERS: 1st Lieutenant Waldheim came from Army Group E to me, and was a young, very well-educated 24-year-old 1st lieutenant. He came and reported to me, and I must say, he made a very impressive but modest impression.

LORD RAWLINSON: How many did the liaison staff amount to?

WILLERS: It was a very small liaison staff. It wasn't any kind of command staff or anything; it was just a staff which represented the interests of the German units. It was to supervise and look after them, as it were. The main task really was to prepare and to plan the disarming of the Italians who wanted to capitulate and get out. This was our task, for which we were used then.

LORD RAWLINSON: It appears on a document [which is contained in one of the 'bundles'] that there were 24 officers and men on that staff, of which there were captains, majors and lieutenant colonels, and the lowest ranking were the two 1st lieutenants, Waldheim and Krohne.

WILLERS: Yes, that's right.

LORD RAWLINSON: You said, Herr Willers, that one of your tasks was looking after the interests of the *Wehrmacht* German division. Does that mean you had command over these troops?

WILLERS: No, heavens, certainly not. The commander over these German troops were the Italians, the commanding officer of the Italian army. We were there ... to cover any problems from day to day, any complaints. I certainly didn't have any command authority. We were not a headquarters command or anything like that. We were just an organization of planning staff, planning headquarters ...

LORD RAWLINSON: What did you use him [Waldheim] as primarily?

WILLERS: The main task really was this question of interpreting. He had the task not only to take part in my conversations with the Italians, but also in discussions with the Chief of the General Staff, Major General Gyldenfeldt. He was supposed to be there as an interpreter. Now these notes which he made during those conversations, they were then ... written down by him and presented to us ... He also had the job of keeping and maintaining the war diary ... And he had, of course, certain administrative functions. He was my assistant ... He was a sort of office chief, as it were, who looked after all those people who were in his office. Those were his duties.

LORD RAWLINSON: We have heard that his Italian, certainly earlier, was not very good Italian, that he was not very fluent or even very comprehensible in Italian. Was he speaking Italian as far as you could see in the summer of '43?

WILLERS: I, of course, cannot really say anything derogatory about his ability. He seemed to function all right, to work all right. His Italian, certainly for our purposes, was adequate ...

LORD RAWLINSON: As 1a officer of the office liaison staff, did you have daily meetings with General Gyldenfeldt?

WILLERS: Yes.

LORD RAWLINSON: Would 1st Lieutenant Waldheim come to those meetings?

WILLERS: No, he would not.

Lord Rawlinson then referred Willers to a document which states: '1a is the head of the command section, and is concerned with all matters relating to the commanding of the troops; he reports to the Chief of General Staff, and is usually present when the Chief of Staff reports to the Commander-in-Chief.'

WILLERS: That is possible, but only in extreme cases, if both command forces or operation forces no longer exist, but in principle, not.

LORD RAWLINSON: This is the general staff of a command, is it not? Not liaison?

WILLERS: Yes, command, yes.

LORD RAWLINSON: [quoting from the document] 'No officers other than those mentioned ... above are entitled to ask any questions regarding military actions without explicit authority to do so.' Was that a strictly enforced order?

WILLERS: Yes, it was.

LORD RAWLINSON: Would any of these paragraphs invest Lieutenant Waldheim, as your O1, with power to take any decision regarding military action?

WILLERS: No, certainly not.

LORD RAWLINSON: [referring to another document] ... 8th August transmission to the 1st Mountain Division concerning the shooting of bandits: 'A new Führer Order is at hand which will be transmitted: Bandits taken in battle are to be shot, other bandits, suspects and so forth are to be arrested and evacuated to the Sauckel labour service.' That was from the 11th Army head-quarters ... Was that order, which had apparently come from Adolf Hitler, strictly adhered to?

WILLERS: This order – which I do not remember all that well – but usually it was ignored because, quite honestly, we rejected that. But, of course, on the other hand, certainly in many attacks which took place on the columns ... there were dead. But the Führer command in this sense, I have to say quite clearly, certainly was not observed by us.

235

Lord Rawlinson referred him to another document — a monthly situation report — and asked him to look at the name 'Waldheim (*Oberleutnant*)' at the bottom of it.

WILLERS: Yes, it was a situation report which comes from the 1st Mountain Division, which was then passed on.

LORD RAWLINSON: Did Lieutenant Waldheim have any part in drafting it or writing anything into it?

WILLER: No, it was purely a copy.

LORD RAWLINSON: I want to turn now, Herr Willers, to an operation which took place on the 16th of August 1943, which resulted in the massacre of many innocent men, women and children at a place called Komeno. Did you give any order that there should be a massacre at Komeno?

WILLERS: I've never heard anything about Komeno. It's a completely new word for me. I simply cannot imagine that this might have happened.

LORD RAWLINSON: When did you first hear about Komeno?

WILLERS: When I got here.

LORD RAWLINSON: Do you recollect being asked about it by people who came to see you in preparation for this ... Commission?

WILLERS: Yes, I do, yes. I do not know when it was, but at that particular time ...

LORD RAWLINSON: It does not matter which month it was, but had you heard about Komeno — which, after all, was a very serious matter; it was a massacre — before all the people came to ask you questions in preparation for this Commission?

WILLERS: No, the answer is no.

Lord Rawlinson referred him to a report of 16 August 1943 from the Mounted Rifles Regiment of the 1st Mountain Division.

LORD RAWLINSON: [quoting from the report] 'This morning, 12th Company received very heavy gunfire from all houses during the surrounding of Komeno, which was carried out on three sides. Thereupon, fire was opened with all weapons by the Company. The place was stormed and burned down. During this battle, as it appears, the bandits succeeded in escaping in a south-east direction. 150 civilians are estimated to have died in this battle.' That was quite a substantial battle, was it not, for this time, or was it not very substantial?

236

WILLERS: I cannot imagine that the figures here are really right. It does not make sense to me. I simply do not believe that this is the way it happened. I am really assuming it is somewhat exaggerated reports based on the emotional situation behind it at this particular period.

LORD RAWLINSON: You do not think there could have been a battle – is that what you are saying? Do you not think there could have been a battle, that there might have been, indeed, there *was* a massacre, is that right?

WILLERS: I cannot imagine it. Quite honestly, I have to reject this as something that happened.

LORD RAWLINSON: This is a report that came to you.

WILLERS: I do not know this report. I've never seen it.

Lord Rawlinson then quoted from another report: 'The report of that day, of the 16th of August 1943: "Result of cleaning-up operation in Komeno: 150 enemy dead, several head of cattle, wool, weapons of Italian origin, explosions of large quantities of ammunition during the burning down of the village." That is a report that came in. Would that have been brought to your attention?'

'Well, I cannot remember it, I'm afraid,' replied Willers. 'I simply cannot remember it.'

Lord Rawlinson now turned to the question of the treatment of the Italian prisoners-of-war.

LORD RAWLINSON: I come now to September, the Italian armistice, which was concluded with the Allies on September the 9th. From a military point of view, to the German forces, what was the consequence of this?

WILLERS: Well, of course, it meant that the [German] troops that were still available, we had to secure and fill out the coastline, and also the interior – what was left of us after the Italians capitulated.

LORD RAWLINSON: Then the Italian soldiers were effectively disarmed by the *Wehrmacht*, is that correct?

WILLERS: Yes, they were disarmed, that is right. When they were not prepared to fight on any more ...

LORD RAWLINSON: What happened to them after they'd been disarmed? Was that a matter for the *Wehrmacht* or for some other authority?

WILLERS: Oh, it was a matter for the commanding officers, really. It was up to them.

LORD RAWLINSON: Who dealt, though, with the sending of the Italians from Greece elsewhere?

WILLERS: It went via the military commanding officer (operations) or OKW [Armed German Forces High Command] in Berlin.

LORD RAWLINSON: I just want to get clearly from you . . . whether Lieutenant Waldheim could have had, or did have, any authority to give the commands, or make plans or influence plans, while he was your O1 in that period of August to September '43.

WILLERS: No.

Allan Ryan now began his cross-examination: 'Colonel Willers, you have never heard of the massacre at Komeno?'

WILLERS: No.

ALLAN RYAN: And you widely disregarded the Führer Order [describing the treatment to be meted out to partisans]?

WILLERS: Correct.

ALLAN RYAN: And Kurt Waldheim had no authority to assist you in making policy?

WILLERS: No.

ALLAN RYAN: Those are the three things that you ask this Commission to believe?

WILLERS: Yes.

ALLAN RYAN: Let us go back, Lieutenant Colonel Willers, to the summer of '43 when you were sent to the German General Staff, to the 11th Army command in Athens. This was a time, was it not, when it was perfectly clear that the Italian forces were in a state of near collapse, and had to be shored up by the German forces? Is that correct?

WILLERS: Well, I would not put it like that. Perhaps they had to be supported, yes, and the German forces were there. I mean, they were already deployed when we entered the Balkans; the German troops were already there, the others were pulled back. And then the Italians came along later on.

ALLAN RYAN: I am sorry. Let me ask the question again and give you another opportunity. Was it not true that, in the summer of '43 – July '43, when you were posted to Athens – the Italian forces were in a state of great uncertainty and turmoil, and the Germans wanted a very strong presence there to safeguard its position. Is that correct?

WILLERS: Yes, it is right to the extent that the Italians were just about to capitulate, and the German units would be there on their own to take over all the tasks which had to be carried out in the area.

ALLAN RYAN: You were there as 1a of the German General Staff until the capitulation, and then you became 1a of Army Group Southern Greece. Correct?

WILLERS: Yes.

ALLAN RYAN: And you knew, from the time that you went there, that would be the course of events: the Italian defeat and capitulation were inevitable, and you were there, along with your other officers on the German General Staff, to make sure there was a [German] military presence that would be there when the Italians fell?

WILLERS: That is correct.

ALLAN RYAN: Is it your testimony that in the final three weeks before the capitulation of the Italians, the German military units were taking orders from the Italians?

WILLERS: Correct.

ALLAN RYAN: Surely you cannot be serious, Lieutenant Colonel Willers? Is it your testimony that the Italians were telling the German units in the field where to go and what to do?

WILLERS: Yes, yes. To the extent that they were subordinate to the 11th Army, they had to carry out the orders of the 11th Army.

ALLAN RYAN: Who killed all those people in Komeno? It was not the Italian troops, was it?

WILLERS: Well, that is it, I do not know. I do not know this name. It's quite new to me, as I've already said. I'm very sorry, but I cannot say anything on that.

ALLAN RYAN: You know the 1st Mountain Division, do you not, sir?

WILLERS: I had no connection with the 1st Mountain Division. All we did was planning with the 11th Italian Army. We had no liaison; only telex or telephone information. Reports we got – no personal contacts or any questions or any orders.

ALLAN RYAN: Is it not a fact that, on the 6th and 7th of August '43, in the town of Jannina, you had a meeting with the commanding general of the 1st Mountain Division? Did you not, on 6th August, Colonel Willers, attend a meeting in Jannina with the commanding general of the 1st Mountain Division?

WILLERS: No, not that I can remember. I do not think so.

Allan Ryan then referred him to a document dated 6 August 1943, and read from it: 'This is a notice of a meeting held on 6 August 1943 from the Field Marshal General Baron von

239

Richt to the General of the 1st Mountain Division, and it says: "Present: Field Marshal General Baron von Weitz ..." He was the commanding general of Army Group F, was he not?'

WILLERS: Yes, that's true.

ALLAN RYAN: He was a very senior general, was he not?

WILLERS: Yes, he was indeed.

ALLAN RYAN: [continuing to read] '... General of the Mountain Troops, General Lanz; Major General von Stedner, Commander, 1st Mountain Division; and Lieutenant Colonel Willers, 1a Army High Command.' You were at a meeting with three generals, including the most senior general in the entire south-east area of Europe, and you do not remember that, sir?

WILLERS: I'm sorry, I cannot change it. I am sorry. I do not seem to remember.

There is a short recess, after which Allan Ryan continued his cross-examination of Bruno Willers.

ALLAN RYAN: I call your attention to another document. If you look at the very bottom line of the message, it says '1st Mountain Division 1a', does it not, sir?

WILLERS: Yes, I see that it does, now, yes.

ALLAN RYAN: On the bottom of page 472, the signature is from the 1a of the 1st Mountain Division.

WILLERS: Yes.

ALLAN RYAN: On top of the document, it is addressed to the German General Staff with the 11th Italian Army. Do you see that?

WILLERS: Yes, it is written there.

ALLAN RYAN: So this is one of those documents that would have come to you and to Lieutenant Waldheim in the 1a office of the German General Staff? Is that correct?

WILLERS: Yes, that's correct. But I should add that, at the same time also, it went to the Corps of the 26th Italian Army.

ALLAN RYAN: I'm only interested in your office at this point, Colonel Willers. Paragraph 1 of that communication reads as follows: 'Result of the *Sauberungen*, the "cleansing operations", at Komeno: 150 enemy dead, a number of cattle, small arms of Italian origin, explosions of large quantities of ammunition when the settlement was burned down.' Is it your testimony, Lieutenant Colonel Willers, that you have no memory of this event whatever?

WILLERS: I can't at all ... I don't remember it at all, in any shape

240

or form. There were such a lot of goings-on during this period, that these individual memories of individual events simply . . . it is not possible. You must imagine that, during all this period – namely, from August to the end, to the dramatic close in '45 – there was constantly such battles going on. The number of dead, killed, deportations and so on. I mean . . . I very much doubt it.

ALLAN RYAN: The fact is, Lieutenant Colonel Willers, that in this one incident alone, 150 were reported killed. That was twice as many as had been killed in the whole of Operation Augustus, that lasted for eight days. Is that not correct?

WILLERS: Oh, please imagine those 150 dead. How are you going to count them? No one is going to count them. It's a report which you simply can't accept at face value . . . Well, I can't remember, and that's all I can say about it.

ALLAN RYAN: I put it to you, sir, that the number of 150 killed in one *Sauberungen* operation was such an unprecedentedly high figure that it ought to have caused you to investigate immediately, assuming you did not already know what had happened.

WILLERS: It wasn't my job. As I said, we couldn't have any influence in those matters. It was to do with our superior authorities, and this was the Italian 11th Army.

Allan Ryan brought out another document and asked Willers if he recognized it. He said he did: 'This is the *Kriegestagebuch*.'

ALLAN RYAN: The war diary which was kept by your O1 officer, Lieutenant Waldheim, was it not?

WILLERS: That's correct.

ALLAN RYAN: And he kept that diary from the 19th July '43 until the 21st of August of that year?

WILLERS: Correct.

Allan Ryan referred Willers to part of a war diary entry, which says: 'Appropriate directions go out to the 1st Mountain Division regarding the treatment of bandits. By new order of the Führer, bandits taken in battle are to be shot. Other suspected bandits and so forth are to be apprehended and transported to Germany for labour services.'

ALLAN RYAN: That message was sent out to the 1st Mountain Division by your O1 officer, Lieutenant Waldheim. Is that correct?

241

COMMISSIONER LAWTON: You're making an assumption there, Mr Ryan. Ask him first who sent the message to the 1st Mountain Division ...

ALLAN RYAN: Who sent the message to the 1st Mountain Division, do you know?

WILLERS: No, I don't.

COMMISSIONER LAWTON: You don't remember who sent it out? As a matter of routine in your department, who would normally have sent it out?

WILLERS: Well, it went through the office.

COMMISSIONER LAWTON: What does 'through the office' mean? Who decided to send the message through *Der Führer* of the 1st Mountain Division?

WILLERS: Well, it was the Chief of the General Staff of the headquarters, the liaison staff. It was ordered by them.

ALLAN RYAN: Is it your testimony, sir, that your Lieutenant Waldheim — that is to say, the 1a office of the German General Staff — would not have sent out such an order?

WILLERS: No, no, they couldn't do that.

ALLAN RYAN: They couldn't do that?

WILLERS: No.

ALLAN RYAN: Ever?

WILLERS: No, never, never.

Willers was then referred to another document.

ALLAN RYAN: [quoting from document] 'A new *Die Führer* order is at hand, dealing with the shooting of bandits, and will be sent soon. Bandits caught during battles are to be shot. Other suspected band members are to be arrested and sent to Sauckel work details.' Do you see the signature line on that, Colonel Willers?

WILLERS: No, I don't, no. It doesn't seem to be on there, the signature.

ALLAN RYAN: Right there, that is what I'm referring to. It says '1a of the German General Staff', does it not, sir?

WILLERS: That doesn't mean anything.

ALLAN RYAN: Am I not correct, sir, that that it is you or Lieutenant Waldheim?

WILLERS: Well, this onward transmission of the various orders was passed through normal official channels.

ALLAN RYAN: The 1a of the German General Staff was you or Lieutenant Waldheim, am I correct or am I not correct, sir?

WILLERS: Yes, 1a was us, but only with the approval, of course,

242

of General Gyldenfeldt. He signed it at the top; his approval was necessary. He says, up there at the top, 'As ordered by the Chief of the General Staff'. It says so there . . .

ALLAN RYAN: Who gave the order that the order of *Die Führer* was to be disregarded?

WILLERS: There was no order. It was simply not carried out. It was ignored.

ALLAN RYAN: It wasn't ignored at Komeno. It wasn't ignored at Kalavrita. Does that mean anything to you?

WILLERS: I don't know. I've never heard anything about Komeno. I've never heard of it.

ALLAN RYAN: Have you ever heard of Kalavrita?

WILLERS: Nothing.

ALLAN RYAN: Have you ever heard of Distomon?

WILLERS: No.

ALLAN RYAN: Have you every heard of Kalimnios?

WILLERS: No.

ALLAN RYAN: Those are four massacres that took place at peasant villages in Greece where innocent men, women and children were slaughtered by German troops. The *Die Führer* order was not ignored in those villages?

WILLERS: I don't believe it, I don't believe it. I am sure that wasn't the case. Perhaps there is a report for Croatians or Greeks.

ALLAN RYAN: We are in Greece, Colonel Willers. We are not talking about Croatians. Those are villages in Greece.

WILLERS: I simply don't believe it − I don't believe it.

COMMISSIONER LAWTON: Look at these initials − GKDOS. What do they mean?

WILLERS: That is a secret staff matter, a secret command letter.

COMMISSIONER LAWTON: When you have a secret command letter, who sent it out?

WILLERS: It goes through 1a.

COMMISSIONER LAWTON: Through anybody in 1a or are there only some people who can send out a secret staff message?

WILLERS: Only 1a itself.

COMMISSIONER LAWTON: Yes, but 1a consists of you, Lieutenant Waldheim and a number of NCOs. Who can send it out?

WILLERS: The 1a.

COMMISSIONER LAWTON: Who is the 1a in this particular?

WILLERS: That is me − in fact, that is me.

COMMISSIONER LAWTON: Could Lieutenant Waldheim send out a secret letter which required the initials GKDOS?

WILLERS: Well, only with the permission of the chief − that is,

243

General von Gyldenfeldt – only with his permission.

COMMISSIONER HUFSTEDLER: If you were away, Lieutenant Waldheim being the only person there, would he have had to wait to send out a secret message until you returned?

WILLERS: Yes, of course, he had to wait, certainly.

COMMISSIONER HUFSTEDLER: Let's talk about Lieutenant Waldheim for a moment, shall we, Colonel Willers? He and you were the only two officers of the 1a section of the German General Staff. Is that correct?

WILLERS: Yes, that's correct.

COMMISSIONER HUFSTEDLER: And you depended on him, did you not, to carry out such functions of your office as you might deem necessary?

WILLERS: He was my subordinate and he had to carry out the tasks I gave him to do.

COMMISSIONER HUFSTEDLER: And he carried out those tasks, did he not?

WILLERS: Yes, the tasks he was given he did, in fact, carry out.

COMMISSIONER HUFSTEDLER: And in carrying out those tasks, he made it possible for you to carry out your tasks correctly.

WILLERS: Undoubtedly.

COMMISSIONER HUFSTEDLER: In fact, you could not have carried out your own tasks and duties to the extent you did without his assistance. Am I correct?

WILLERS: Well, it wasn't absolutely necessary in certain cases, but as I said, his terms of reference were very clearly defined. We didn't have a lot of problems.

COMMISSIONER HUFSTEDLER: But in doing what he did, he made it possible for you to do what you did. Is that right?

WILLERS: I don't understand the question.

COMMISSIONER HUFSTEDLER: Lieutenant Waldheim had certain things to do in the office, right?

WILLERS: Yes.

COMMISSIONER HUFSTEDLER: These things that you'd assigned him to do?

WILLERS: Correct.

COMMISSIONER HUFSTEDLER: How many of the things that he did were necessary to the operation of the 1a function? He kept the war diary, for example?

WILLERS: Yes.

COMMISSIONER HUFSTEDLER: He saw that orders were brought in and sent out.

WILLERS: As I said, we did not issue any orders, any reports, messages and so on; we just had to pass those on.

COMMISSIONER HUFSTEDLER: So he passed those on, such as the reports that you had to pass on, he passed on in your place?

WILLERS: Yes, that's right.

COMMISSIONER HUFSTEDLER: If he was not there, that job would not get done, I take it?

WILLERS: Well, then I did it.

COMMISSIONER HUFSTEDLER: When you were not there, he did things that you sometimes did?

WILLERS: The Chief of General Staff, General Gyldenfeldt, did it. Someone was always there.

COMMISSIONER HUFSTEDLER: If it was not you, it was somebody else?

WILLERS: Of course.

COMMISSIONER HUFSTEDLER: And one of those, sometimes, was *Oberleutnant* Waldheim?

WILLERS: No, not on his own, he couldn't do it.

COMMISSIONER HUFSTEDLER: He continued to keep the *Kriegestagebuch*, the war diary, did he not?

WILLERS: Yes, that's correct.

COMMISSIONER HUFSTEDLER: And he continued to send out such reports or orders or whatever it was the 1a's duty to send out?

WILLERS: Correct. Yes, [they were] passed to [him] to see that they were in order. He did not have the authority to make his own decisions, and to pass on reports and so on, not without initialling or agreement of the 1a.

COMMISSIONER HUFSTEDLER: He, in any event, made it possible for you to carry out your functions?

WILLERS: Correct.

Bruno Willers was again questioned by Allan Ryan.

ALLAN RYAN: I'll put it to you, sir, that you learned about Komeno when it happened, that it was you in your office, with the assistance of Lieutenant Waldheim, who authorized and approved the massacre of civilians – men, women and children – at the village of Komeno.

WILLERS: I have not understood the question. Perhaps you could repeat the question?

ALLAN RYAN: I would be glad to repeat the question. I put it to you that you learned about Komeno when it happened, and in fact, you and your office, Lieutenant Waldheim included, authorized and approved the operations of the 1st Mountain Division to go and kill everybody in Komeno.

245

WILLERS: I told you, I knew nothing about it. Surely I don't know. This is completely new to me.

Willers was then asked a number of other questions by the members of the Commission.

COMMISSIONER PETRÉN: [referring Willers to a document dated 17th August] You've actually signed this. Did you normally read through the daily reports? You must have read about Komeno?
WILLERS: I simply don't remember it. I don't remember it any more.
COMMISSIONER PETRÉN: Well, who put together this report? Did you put it together or somebody else?
WILLERS: Of course, the O1 put that together.
COMMISSIONER PETRÉN: Was it done personally by you, this order?
WILLERS: It was presented by the O1 and then I signed it. This is a report. It was not an order. It was purely a report.
COMMISSIONER HUFSTEDLER: When the order of the Führer was disregarded, do you know of any consequences that occurred to those officers who disobeyed the Führer's order?
WILLERS: I don't know.
COMMISSIONER HÜBNER: ...As far as your function is concerned, did you have any repercussions, especially in terms of what Herr Waldheim did, did it have any repercussions on whether such an order was followed or not? Herr Willers, what were your actions, what did you do in order to ignore this order?
WILLERS: By verbal discussions, conversations with the Chief of General Staff, and [which] he had with the commanding officers. It was usually the Chief of General Staff − he did it personally.

Commissioner Hufstedler took the testimony back to the time just before the Italian capitulation, and asked Willers if his assignment had been basically to take the necessary steps in the event of an Italian capitulation. 'You did not have anything to do with ordnance or with transportation. What kind of plans were you brought there to formulate in the event of an Italian capitulation?'

WILLERS: The plan was laid down in detail. Every German authority in Greece, where there was a German unit stationed, had an order in his pocket, as it were − a secret order in his pocket that, on Day X, so and so many Italians should be disarmed. That held good for the whole of Greece. Then Day X took place, and all the preparations were already made in advance, and where, indeed, the Italians should be concentrated, and then the camps were set up. This was our task. . .

COMMISSIONER HUFSTEDLER: I do not think my question was quite clear. . . I'm trying to find out what kind of plans [you were assigned to make] with respect to the expected collapse of Italy.

WILLERS: Well, there was a very big plan. I can't tell you the details about it.

COMMISSIONER HUFSTEDLER: I certainly do not want the details.

WILLERS: It is a huge, enormously comprehensive plan, and tremendous details. I cannot reconstruct those details.

Day 4: afternoon

The next witness was Karl Rothfuchs, now a 77-year-old lawyer. During World War II, he served with the 1st Mountain Division of the *Wehrmacht* in France, and later on the Eastern Front. Then in April 1943, the division moved to the Balkans.

LORD RAWLINSON: Were you serving with the 1st Mountain Division at the end of July and through August 1943?

ROTHFUCHS: Yes, indeed I was.

LORD RAWLINSON: Were you under the command of the Italian 26th Army Corps?

ROTHFUCHS: At that point, yes.

He was shown a document and asked if his initials appeared at the bottom of it. He agreed that they did.

LORD RAWLINSON: Does it read. . . 'Company Group Salminger stormed Komeno north of Gulf of Arta against heavy resistance. In the course of burning down the town, large amounts of munitions destroyed. 150 dead bandits; one part of the bandits escaped to the south-east'? That is the report by this officer, with your initials on it. Does that mean you saw the report, the fact that your initials are upon it?'

ROTHFUCHS: I have seen it, yes. Obviously, I must have done.

LORD RAWLINSON: Did you, apart from that report, know anything at all about that action which is being reported in this report?

247

ROTHFUCHS: No, this report is purely a report about the result of an action...

LORD RAWLINSON: In an operation involving a company of 90 to 110 soldiers, would the German liaison staff at Athens be involved in ordering that company to storm a particular place, or do a particular operation?

ROTHFUCHS: I consider totally excluded that such an army group gives orders to a group within a division. I consider totally excluded that even the division could order this action...

Lord Rawlinson then handed over to Allan Ryan for the latter's cross-examination.

ALLAN RYAN: What happened at Komeno on the 16th of August?

ROTHFUCHS: I do not know. What is known to me is only the report of the Group Salminger, to be handed on to superior command.

ALLAN RYAN: Let me ask you, based on everything you know today – not what you knew in '43, but based on everything you know today – what happened at Komeno on the 16th of August?

ROTHFUCHS: No idea, I do not know. Obviously, according to this report, it's a place that had been taken, had been stormed, and during the storming of it, there were losses on both sides. As a consequence, such villages, where they were attacked, they were full of ammunition, in every corner, and every house was on fire, then that house exploded...

ALLAN RYAN: Do you deny, on the 16th of August '43, in the village of Komeno, 300 men, women and children were slaughtered by the troops of the 1st Mountain Division? Do you deny that, sir?

ROTHFUCHS: Well, first of all, our soldiers did not murder. Our soldiers fought...

ALLAN RYAN: ...Do you deny, sir...

COMMISSIONER LAWTON: Let him finish. Mr Rothfuchs, you may continue your answer.

ROTHFUCHS: ...The situation is such, the village was obviously occupied and was stormed by this company. There were losses on both sides. I cannot say more because I only have the report. I was in Jannina, and that happened down below at the Gulf of Arta, some 120 kilometres away.

ALLAN RYAN: Is it your testimony, sir, that you only know what is in this report and nothing else, even today?

ROTHFUCHS: Yes.

ALLAN RYAN: So if there was a massacre committed by the

248

soldiers of the 1st Mountain Division – your division – in the village of Komeno, you know nothing about it, even today?

ROTHFUCHS: No, there were always actions.

ALLAN RYAN: You were the 1c officer for the 1st Mountain Division in August '43?

ROTHFUCHS: Correct, yes.

ALLAN RYAN: And as the 1c officer, like any 1c officer, you were responsible for the intelligence function, were you not?

ROTHFUCHS: The intelligence officer only had to deal with the enemy information, information about the enemy.

ALLAN RYAN: The enemy at that time were the partisans, were they not?

ROTHFUCHS: Yes.

ALLAN RYAN: Komeno was a village where, according to all the documents coming out of your division, the partisans were attacked. Is that not right.

ROTHFUCHS: Probably – otherwise they would not have stormed the village.

ALLAN RYAN: In fact, there were no partisans in Komeno. Is that not correct, sir?

ROTHFUCHS: I do not know. If there had been no partisans there, the company would not have stormed the village.

ALLAN RYAN: So the fact that the company stormed the village is proof that there must have been partisans in the village, is that your testimony?

ROTHFUCHS: ...There was fighting there...so that means that the village was occupied.

ALLAN RYAN: That report is false from top to bottom. Do you acknowledge that? It's a phoney from top to bottom?

ROTHFUCHS: No, I do not. We normally used to report what was being reported to us.

ALLAN RYAN: Do you acknowledge that this report is false and fraudulent from top to bottom, or do you not, sir?

ROTHFUCHS: No.

ALLAN RYAN: [referring the witness to another report] This was a report written by the regiment that was in Komeno. It was written to the 1st Mountain Division, its higher echelon, is that correct?

ROTHFUCHS: Yes.

ALLAN RYAN: That report says, '150 civilians died in the battle.' Do you see that?

ROTHFUCHS: Yes, I see it. What comes earlier on, you do not say that, because it's what it says beforehand: 'The 12th Company was attacked with rifles from all the houses of that village.' ...

You must also read that out if you wish to be just.

ALLAN RYAN: It says '150 civilians', does it not, Captain Rothfuchs? It does not say 'partisans' − it says *civilians*. Correct?

ROTHFUCHS: Yes, it is correct. The partisans opened fire...

ALLAN RYAN: The only thing in this report that is true − I put to you, sir − is that the victims were civilians. They were men, women and children who had been celebrating at a wedding party. Everything else in this report − from the heavy gunfire that was received to the losses of your own troops − I submit to you, sir, is phoney.

ROTHFUCHS: I can't imagine that the wedding opened fire on German troops...

ALLAN RYAN: Is it your testimony, sir, that the troops of the 1st Mountain Division, during the time that you were attached to them, never killed an innocent civilian?

ROTHFUCHS: No.

ALLAN RYAN: They never did?

ROTHFUCHS: No, never. Why should they kill civilians?

ALLAN RYAN: You do not acknowledge that any civilians at all were killed?

ROTHFUCHS: It may have happened, yes, could have happened, because frequently one couldn't differentiate... between civilians and bandits.

ALLAN RYAN: Well, one could tell the difference between partisans and babies, could not one?

ROTHFUCHS: No, you can't tell. In those days, if you went into a Greek village, you didn't know who was an opponent, who was a civilian. You couldn't recognize it.

ALLAN RYAN: Could a 5-year-old boy be a partisan?

ROTHFUCHS: No, but a 10-year-old boy could be a messenger.

ALLAN RYAN: So, a 10-year-old boy, if [he's] a messenger, could be...

ROTHFUCHS: [interrupting] Only as an example, only as an example.

ALLAN RYAN: What do you mean 'as an example'?

ROTHFUCHS: No, he wasn't shot, but he was taken prisoner.

ALLAN RYAN: Is it your testimony, Dr Rothfuchs, that there were no crimes at all committed at Komeno, to your knowledge?

ROTHFUCHS: I don't know. I only reported what happened. It could well be that crimes occurred. I can't prove it, and you can't prove it.

ALLAN RYAN: We had a witness in here...Dr Rothfuchs, who

250

could prove it. He had seven brothers and sisters, his mother and father were slaughtered by the 1st Mountain Division. Don't say 'it can't be proven', sir. It has been proven in this [Commission of Inquiry].

Did the 1st Mountain Division take its orders from the Italians? By that I mean, did the Italians tell the 1st Mountain Division where to go and what to do?

ROTHFUCHS: Very rarely, very rarely. But I could imagine it happening.

ALLAN RYAN: I'm not talking about imagining. I'm saying, in August '43, three weeks before [the capitulation of the Italian Army].

ROTHFUCHS: Yes, in theory, yes.

ALLAN RYAN: I'm not interested in theory. I'm interested in reality. Did the Italians really direct the German units and tell them where to go and what to do?

ROTHFUCHS: As a rule, no. But if... then they would have to ask via 1a. I can't tell you. I don't know with the Italians.

ALLAN RYAN: The fact is, is it not, that the 1st Mountain Division was told where to go and what to do by the German General Staff in Athens? Is that so, sir?

ROTHFUCHS: I don't know. It need not be, I cannot tell you. You have to ask somebody from 1a.

ALLAN RYAN: You were the intelligence officer for the division. You were on the general staff of the division, sir, and you don't know where the orders came from?

ROTHFUCHS: Who or if Athens gave us the orders, to what degree the 26th Italian Corps gave us the orders – I don't know, I can't tell you. You must have found orders. You've got everything else, haven't you?

ALLAN RYAN: We have the documents. I'm asking you, Dr Rothfuchs, for your recollection and your testimony before this Commission.

ROTHFUCHS: I cannot reliably confirm this – it is 50 years ago now. I would like to know what you will say about this case if I could ask you in 45 years' time.

ALLAN RYAN: Is it your testimony that, after 45 years, you have forgotten where the orders have come from?

ROTHFUCHS: I don't know any more. You've got to ask the 1a. They were the right authority. I cannot tell you. I can imagine, but I cannot say 100 per cent.

ALLAN RYAN: I have nothing further, Mr Chairman.

Various desultory questions were put by the members of the Commission, but then, as that particular day's hearing came to an end, it did so on an extraordinary note.

Sir Frederick Lawton said that he wanted to ask Karl Rothfuchs a few questions. and pointed out that the German was, like himself, a lawyer.

COMMISSIONER LAWTON: You know, do you not, that accusations have been made against Dr Waldheim? That while he was serving in Athens on the General Staff, he participated in war crimes? You know that, don't you? You know, do you not, that the allegations have been made? Whether they are true or not is another matter, but the allegations have been made, have they not?

ROTHFUCHS: I have only heard it [here]. I didn't even know that Waldheim was [the] army group O1 in Athens...

COMMISSIONER LAWTON: Are you telling us that, despite the publicity which has been all over the world, certainly during the past 12 months, until you came here, you did not know that any allegations had been made against Waldheim, that he'd taken part in war crimes?

ROTHFUCHS: Well, let me tell you something: O3 or O1 is in no position to go in for war crimes. [This answer may be the result of a mistranslation of Commissioner Lawton's question.]

COMMISSIONER LAWTON: Herr Rothfuchs, do answer my question. Are you saying that, until you came here, you had no idea that allegations were going round the world that Dr Waldheim had been participating in war crimes?

ROTHFUCHS: I heard it, with this reproach: the accusation is so absurd, based upon the position of Mr Waldheim, that you could not take it seriously, in my opinion.

COMMISSIONER LAWTON: That is what we are here to discover — if there is an allegation of that kind, and if it has got any basis of fact. The first thing anybody has to do is to find out if there was a war crime. Do you accept that as a lawyer?

ROTHFUCHS: It is alleged that he could not have participated as an O3 or an O1 because he did not have the powers to give orders.

COMMISSIONER LAWTON: Herr Rothfuchs, did you hear my question?

ROTHFUCHS: Yes.

COMMISSIONER LAWTON: Did you understand it?

ROTHFUCHS: Yes.

COMMISSIONER LAWTON: Why didn't you answer it? I'll put it to

252

you again. If anyone is investigating an allegation that Dr Waldheim participated in war crimes, the first thing to discover is whether there has been a war crime. Would you agree with that?

ROTHFUCHS: Yes, correct.

COMMISSIONER LAWTON: You say that you have no knowledge that a war crime was committed at Komeno. If German troops killed over 300 people in that village, including a large number of women and children, would you accept that that was a war crime if they did it?

ROTHFUCHS: Yes.

COMMISSIONER LAWTON: We have seen a photograph today, which was taken by an English academic historian, of a war memorial in Komeno with over 300 names on it. Would you accept that as a fact?

ROTHFUCHS: Yes.

COMMISSIONER LAWTON: You were the intelligence officer of the 1st Mountain Division. Would you have been likely to have heard of anything of that kind happening within the divisional area of the 1st Mountain Division?

ROTHFUCHS: I only know what I reported.

COMMISSIONER LAWTON: I didn't ask you that. I'll put it to you again. If there had been a massacre at Komeno in August '43, would you, as the intelligence officer of the 1st Mountain Division, have expected to learn about it?

ROTHFUCHS: I would have reported it then to the commander.

COMMISSIONER LAWTON: I didn't ask you that. If there had been a massacre in that area, would you, as the intelligence officer, have expected to hear of it − if you were doing your job properly as an intelligence officer?

ROTHFUCHS: I reported to the Group Salminger and I passed them on in an abbreviated form to Athens.

Sir Frederick, totally exasperated by this stage, said: 'Well, I don't think there is any point in asking you any more questions. We'll finish now.'

Everybody had been so wrapped up in this cross-examination that there was a strong feeling that we had all been involved in a real trial. There were jokes from the public gallery that, had this been a real court, Sir Frederick might have been inclined to deal rather harshly with Karl Rothfuchs for failing to answer his questions. There certainly appeared to have been what, at best, could be described as 'crossed wires'!

253

Day 5: morning

This was Monday, 18 April. Only a few of us had had the Sunday off, but I hadn't been one of them. Instead, on Sunday morning, director Roger Thomas and I had a meeting with Allan Ryan and Susan Aslan to sort out one or two problems. Then Roger and I went into the studio and worked for the rest of the day, marking up the transcripts to make an initial cut. This was to enable videotape editor Alan Ritchie to make a start on the preliminary edit, so that, the following week, when the Inquiry was all on tape and we began to edit in earnest, we would not have to look through the entire programme – that would take at least a week. Roger and I retained everything that was relevant to the Inquiry, as well as anything that might prove to be contentious, deleting only those things that had been repetitious or not specifically relevant. We were still left with far too many hours of tape, but at least it was a start.

The days were now falling into a pattern. We worked through the day in the studio hearing evidence. After we came off, in the early evening, I would call a production meeting of all my team. First, we would hammer out the witness list for the following day, the names coming from Caroline Blackadder and Jacqui French, who'd got them from their respective legal teams. We'd work out an order of appearance, and any amendments that I might suggest would then be cleared with Tim House and Susan Aslan. We'd also discuss any other problems we'd encountered. For example, initially, we'd had delays of a couple of minutes getting witnesses into a sort of 'holding room' before going into studio, but we were beginning to sort that out.

We were getting our transcripts from the stenographers very efficiently at the end of each day, and Roger and I spent every evening cutting them, working most nights until midnight or later. As we were usually back in the office by eight o'clock the following morning, ready for the next day's recording, we were putting in 16-hour days. As a result, we were both tired, but as we entered our second week of recording, the atmosphere of the studio penetrated even our exhausted brains and we were up and running.

254

Allan Ryan began the fifth day with a statement:

Mr Chairman, in our evidence on Komeno, we showed that the troops of the 1st Mountain Division committed an enormous war crime. At that time, they came under the control, for all intents and purposes, of the German General Staff in Athens. That is so, despite the contention of Colonel Willers, the 1a officer of the German General Staff, that 'our staff was merely a liaison operation and it was the Italians who were giving orders to the German units.'

The point is important, Mr Chairman, because the 1a officer was responsible for this or any other German General Staff matter having to do with the operations of troops in the field, and because Lieutenant Waldheim was Lt Colonel Willers' O1 officer. Indeed, the two of them were the only officers in the 1a section. Thus, we must submit, it is entirely likely they not only had advance knowledge of, but very possibly planned or authorized, the operations that killed 300 men, women and children in the predawn hours of the 16th of August '43 as they slept after a late-night wedding celebration in that flat and open village.

Lord Rawlinson followed Allan Ryan's summary with a few comments of his own.

I believe I should have the opportunity, in view of those words, to make the opposite comments, if I may. I would submit that the Commission should look with great care at those documents to establish what was the actual sphere of responsibility, first, of command and, secondly, of the responsibility of those officers Colonel Willers and Lieutenant Waldheim. I will suggest there is no evidence that the liaison staff with which they were concerned was at all involved in the orders before what was undoubtedly a terrible massacre at that village.

Secondly I would submit that the Commission must look carefully at that witness Colonel Willers, and look not only at what he said but also at the personality of the man. Whether, in the view of the Commission, that is a man who would have taken instruction from a lieutenant. I would suggest to you that, when you look at Colonel Willers' evidence as the 1a...if you came to the conclusion that he played any part in the orders – which, I suggest, there is no evidence of – but if you did come to that conclusion, I would suggest that the demonstration of the personality of Colonel Willers was such as to make quite clear that, if there

255

had been any responsibility in that department, it was the responsibility of that man and certainly not of his subordinate officer.

After this interpolation, Allan Ryan continued with his statement, which looked forward to the next part of the allegations:

We will now show the Commission that Komeno was not the end of it, that the killing of innocent people continued. And this time, there can be no attempt to foist the blame upon the Italians, because the Italians capitulated and laid down their arms on the 8th of September 1943, as everyone had known for a month they would eventually have to do. Overnight, the German General Staff to the 11th Italian Army became what they had been sent to Athens in July to become: Army Group Southern Greece, answerable to Army Group E in Salonika.

But more importantly for our purpose are the commanding units of German soldiers in southern Greece. Nobody missed a beat: Lt Colonel Willers automatically becomes the 1a of [Army Group] Southern Greece and Lieutenant Waldheim is the O1, as he has been since July. Within a few days, the 1st Regiment of the Brandenburg Regiment go into the town of Lavidia, some 350 miles north-west of Athens, take some 200 civilian prisoners − careful, of course, to call them 'suspects' − hang many of them, burn the village. Kurt Waldheim writes this all down and signs it. And more than this, we submit, as with Komeno, this Commission may properly find that he and his boss, the 1a, knew of it in advance, and that Waldheim may well have assisted the 1a in whatever planning or support for these crimes was necessary for the general staff in which they served.

The second part of our evidence for this period will have to do with Lieutenant Waldheim's role as the coordinator or assistant coordinator, we'd submit, for Army Group Southern Greece of the forcible and inhumane deportation of thousands of Italian officers and men.

The next witness is Dr Gerhard Schreiber, an historian in the research office of the West German military archives in Freiburg. His area of research and expertise is the period of World War II dealing with the Italian role and events surrounding that.

ALLAN RYAN: 12th September '43, [in a] daily report, under 'The 1st Regiment of the Brandenburg Regiment', the following appears: 'Clean up [in German, '*Sauberungen*'] Lavidia. In Lavidia, 200 civilians, suspected bandit prisoners. Explosives found in houses. Ten hostages hanged in retaliation for the murder of a German soldier. Part of the village burned down.' That report also bears the signed 'W' of Lieutenant Kurt Waldheim ... Dr Schreiber, I ask you, sir, is it possible that the 1a of Army Group Southern Greece would have assisted in or authorized this operation in Lavidia?

SCHREIBER: Due to the fact that the Brandenburg descended from the Army Group Southern Greece, it is possible, but we cannot prove it ... We can't prove that the details were drafted by the Army Group Southern Greece, but surely they were informed. They had knowledge of this operation. In general ... (and this means that there are exemptions) ... these operations were ordered by the Army Group Southern Greece or by the Army High Command or something like this. It is not likely that a regiment starts by itself [but] it could happen.

ALLAN RYAN: Lt Colonel Willers has testified that his O1, Lieutenant Waldheim, merely supervised the clerks and played no part in the planning or operation function of the 1a office. Is this all an O1 officer would normally do in the 1a office at that time? Is this your opinion?

SCHREIBER: Well, I wouldn't like to say this gentleman is a liar. I don't intend that − the problem with the human memory is a

257

central one – but due to the organization of the German staff, it is not likely. Supervising the internal affairs of the office is actually a duty of the 2a. This is the man you call 'adjutant'. It's quite a different job. It could happen, due to the fact that the Germans were short of officers at this time, that such a task was within the competence of Herr Waldheim, but it was surely not his main task. As O1, he was the one who was drafting the tactical operations for the German units, as the right hand of the 1a. I would not exclude that, if one officer [was missing], he'd do this job, but it was not his main job and it was not only this he did. This I am absolutely convinced about.

ALLAN RYAN: [reading from a document] 'Unless missing weapons are handed over by 4th October, five hostages from Limnos will be hanged.' His [Waldheim's] signature, his signed initial, is at the end of this text as well ... [Dr Schreiber nods in agreement] I call your attention to a document, dated 9th September '43, to the District Transport Commander (Athens) from Army Group E. It reads (paragraph one): 'Every available empty train is to be made use of for the removal [or] transport ... They have to be loaded as tightly as possible with no concessions to comfort.' To what is that paragraph referring, Dr Schreiber? Who was being removed or transported ...?

SCHREIBER: The Italian ... prisoners-of-war ... It refers to the Italians in the area of the Army Group E. This means about 200,000 Italian former soldiers.

ALLAN RYAN: [reading paragraph 3 of the same order] 'Transport Commander (Athens) is requested, with reference to the removal/transport of the Italians from the Peloponnese [i.e. southern Greece], to contact immediately Army Group Southern Greece.' I refer you to the reference line in this cable, the second line: ... does it not say 'Army Group E/1a'? Do you see that, sir?

SCHREIBER: That is Arsakli, yes.

LORD RAWLINSON: [interrupting] I'm sorry, but just for the information, this seems to be *from* Army Group E ... That is, Arsakli, nothing to do with Athens?

ALLAN RYAN: Yes, it is from Army Group E to the district commander in Athens. And it is from the 1a office in Army Group E. It is *not* from the 1a office of Army Group Southern Greece, but you will see the significance momentarily ...

After some questions from the Commissioners, Allan Ryan continued to question Dr Schreiber.

258

ALLAN RYAN: Dr Schreiber, on paragraph 5, returning to the text of the document, it states: 'Italian soldiers are to be told that the destination of the transport is Italy. The transport is actually to go initially to Belgrade and is to be reported in advance to the Transport Command.' Paragraph 6: 'Of primary importance, Greece must be cleared of Italians as soon as possible.'

I call your attention, sir, also to the fact that this document was distributed or copied to the 1a office of Army Group E in Salonika, was it not? (Arsakli [and] Salonika [are] the same.)

SCHREIBER: Yes.

ALLAN RYAN: Now, if you turn to the Athens bundle — that is, the bundle of documents called 'Athens' - [referring the witness to one document] Dr Schreiber, have you seen this document before?

SCHREIBER: Yes.

ALLAN RYAN: With particular reference to the question of liaison with the Army Group Southern Greece, to which the earlier transport order refers, would you describe this?

SCHREIBER: It's a record of a long-distance telephone call from *Oberleutnant* Frei to *Oberleutnant* Waldheim, and it's signed at the bottom with the 'W' of Lieutenant Waldheim.

ALLAN RYAN: Would you describe, Dr Schreiber, what this document is or what it appears to be?

SCHREIBER: The document obviously talked about the transportation of or the removal and transportation of Italian prisoners-of-war in the area of Army Group Southern Greece to the north, in general terms.

ALLAN RYAN: I call your attention, sir, to the top of the document that states 'Army Group E/1a/O1' and, on the right-hand side at the top, 'Army Group Southern Greece/Department 1a', signed by Waldheim whom we know is the O1. Can we reasonably infer from this, Dr Schreiber, that this is a record of a telephone conversation between Lieutenant Waldheim, the O1 in the 1a section of the Army Group Southern Greece, to his counterpart in the higher command, the O1 in the 1a department of Army Group E?

SCHREIBER: Due to my interpretation, it is the information that Waldheim gives to Frei.

ALLAN RYAN: Calling your attention specifically to the cable [i.e. the written report of the telephone call] — at the end of the first paragraph where it states: 'Withhold approximately 2000 rank and file as workers. Total of transport to be completed within three to four days.' To what does that refer, Dr Schreiber? Who are the '2000 rank and file' and what are they being withheld for, if you can tell from this document and your knowledge?

SCHREIBER: As far as I know the situation at this time, they were held for the *Wehrmacht*, to work within the German armed forces. You will find them working in harbours for the navy, you will find them working in the airfields for the *Luftwaffe* and so on. There was a special sort of forced labour, I would say, because they were not volunteers. They did not do it voluntarily. We should not consider forced labour only those who had to go to the mines. Even those who worked in the German armed forces were forced to do it and they risked their lives.

If I can mention here that working for the armed forces in Russia when the Army Group Central was destroyed in June/July '44 were 5365 Italian soldiers, prisoners-of-war, working there against international law, who lost their lives. And [Italian prisoners-of-war] lost their lives, of course, even in the Greek harbours, where they were being attacked by British planes.

Asked by Sir Frederick Lawton if he were saying that it was illegal to retain disarmed soldiers to work in an area of danger, Allan Ryan replied, 'Under the conditions in which these workers were to be held, these POWs ... yes, Mr Chairman, that is true.'

Turning back to the witness, Allan Ryan then referred Dr Schreiber to another document, dated 1 October 1943 and signed by General Gyldenfeldt, the Chief of General Staff of Army Group Southern Greece, and he asked the historian about the significance of this document.

SCHREIBER: What is important is, indeed, the first paragraph because it says clearly that one of the tasks of the General Staff [on which Waldheim was serving] was to prepare for the capitulation of the [11th] Italian Army High Command and to prepare to disarm the Italians.

The report went on to say that, because the General Staff had prepared for this in such detail, they had been able to carry it out within two days.

ALLAN RYAN: The Chief of the General Staff would not sit down and write a report like this in his own hand from scratch, would he?

SCHREIBER: No.

ALLAN RYAN: It would be prepared for his own signature by some part of his staff, would it not?

SCHREIBER: Most probably.

ALLAN RYAN: That would be the office and the staff with responsibility for that particular function, would it not?

SCHREIBER: That is exactly what was mentioned already, and was truly one of the tasks of the O1.

ALLAN RYAN: If one looks at the top left-hand side of page 1, it states: 'Army Group Southern Greece/1a office', does it not?

SCHREIBER: Yes.

ALLAN RYAN: Is it your testimony that this would have been written by the officer responsible for coordinating [the report] – that is, the O1 officer in that section?

SCHREIBER: It is not true.

ALLAN RYAN: It is possible, is it not?

SCHREIBER: It is possible.

ALLAN RYAN: And the O1 officer in that section on the 1st of October 1943 was *Oberleutnant* Waldheim. No more questions.

Lord Rawlinson then began his cross-examination of Dr Schreiber.

LORD RAWLINSON: ... By the withdrawal of Italy, the Italian forces, after the armistice they'd made with the Allies, that fact was a severe blow to the German military position. Wasn't it? It must have been?

SCHREIBER: Of course.

LORD RAWLINSON: [In] this situation on September 8th/9th, they [the Germans] were in grave jeopardy ... the Germans [on] the borders and in Greece ... They reacted in accordance with a plan – '[Case] Axis' - which they had been preparing for many months previously?

SCHREIBER: Yes.

LORD RAWLINSON: And had the people who had been mainly concerned in the preparation of those – not the preparation of the plans, but carrying them out – were they the general staff attached to Athens under General Gyldenfeldt? Is that correct?

SCHREIBER: Yes.

LORD RAWLINSON: A man called Willers who was the 1a said that that was the prime task of that staff, that they were to prepare for 'Axis', which was [the plan] to take over the Italian positions ... Was there a *Der Führer* directive as to how the Italians should be treated, which came from him [Hitler] through OKW [i.e. Supreme Command]?

261

SCHREIBER: First, we had ones of the 9th, 10th and 12th. Then we had a summary of the 15th September, [giving] more details . . .
LORD RAWLINSON: Can we look at the document dated 15th September? . . . It [appears] to come from Hitler's headquarters, concerning treatment of the Italian armed forces militia. It sets out the principal three groups of Italian soldiers: those who are loyal to the alliance, those who don't want to assist in any way, and those who offer active or passive resistance. Then it talks about Italian officers, [who could] keep their weapons [if they wished] to fight on. It then deals with employment: [the Italians were] to be employed in the German forces still fighting with the alliance and used as voluntary assistants, and so on.

The report goes on: 'Italian soldiers who do not want to help us in any way . . . are to be disarmed and become prisoners-of-war, and the armed forces High Command prisoners-of-war chief is to take charge of that . . . Italian soldiers who offer active or passive resistance are to become prisoners-of-war . . . Officers who don't persuade their troops to put down their arms are to be put straight before a firing squad. Non-commissioned officers . . . are to be sent to the East. Thirdly, Italian troops and other persons who are still offering resistance will receive a brief ultimatum. All others will be shot if they have not complied with the order to hand over their weapons.'

That was the order exactly that came down from the supreme head of the German forces? Is that right?
SCHREIBER: Yes.
LORD RAWLINSON: The position was that the Germans reacted very swiftly in a very critical situation and managed to keep . . . on balance by having acted so swiftly in disarming the Italians.
SCHREIBER: That is so. Correct. The only point I can add is that you can understand the German reaction from the military point of view, but you cannot have any understanding — and this is the only critical point — about the criminal orders that they issued.
LORD RAWLINSON: Certainly, I understand that. I just want get to the facts that the soldiers in the field and the staff of that time, what they did was to carry out those orders which ended with the Italians being disarmed and being evacuated from the theatre of battle.
SCHREIBER: I'm sorry, I cannot agree with this point of view because there was something in addition. Even a general like Löhr made the orders of Hitler — the criminal orders — even sharper because he said . . .
LORD RAWLINSON: [interrupting] What I just want to get from

262

you, Professor ... is that the Germans from the military point of view had to remove those Italian soldiers whom they disarmed [away] from the theatre of operations. Wasn't that sensible for them to do?

SCHREIBER: OK, I agree.

LORD RAWLINSON: How they did it was another matter ... From the document you produced earlier, there seems to be a transport commander who's in charge of the transportation of these Italians out of the theatre of operations.

SCHREIBER: This transport commander was responsible until Belgrade [i.e. Army Group F] took over the same office of the High Command South-east.

LORD RAWLINSON: Can we look again at the documents which you yourself handed to Mr Ryan and which Mr Ryan handed to me this morning. This document – to District Transport Command (Athens) from the Plenipotentiary Transport Office, Army Group E in Arsakli ... Just to make quite clear so that everyone appreciates – Lieutenant Waldheim is in Athens, and this comes from Arsakli *to* Athens. Is that correct?

SCHREIBER: Yes, to Athens from Salonika ...

After a few more exchanges, Lord Rawlinson ended his cross-examination, and questions were asked by members of the Commission.

COMMISSIONER HUFSTEDLER: During the course of your historical studies, did you have any occasion to study the treatment by the British of the French after the French capitulation?

SCHREIBER: I haven't studied it, but I have come across certain cases.

COMMISSIONER HUFSTEDLER: Are you aware of any direct parallel between the treatment by the Germans of the Italian soldiers who surrendered and the treatment of the French prisoners by the British after the French surrendered?

SCHREIBER: Obviously, you can't compare the two because the French soldiers were not treated by the British as the Italians or other prisoners-of-war were treated by the Germans. The Germans just said that they were not used for forced labour, for example. Meanwhile, the Italians *were* used for forced labour, and the Italians *were* killed: 6000 Italian prisoners were massacred, 17,000 died on the transports because of a criminal order personally issued by Hitler, about 40,000 died in the camps, almost 6000 died in the area of operations, the zone of the army.

All this did not happen to the French.

COMMISSIONER HÜBNER: Dr Schreiber, you refer to the deportation of the Italian soldiers by the Germans ... If there was another officer who had the function and the rank of Waldheim, did such an officer have the possibility to influence matters in such a manner that a detailed order such as how individual transports are to be undertaken, how many prisoners are to be transported – did he have a possibility to influence such detailed orders ...?

SCHREIBER: Basically no, because the 1a department, as far as transport was concerned, was not directly involved with the execution of the transport. This is why we had the transport officer ... But an *Oberleutnant* – who is, after all, a subordinate of the 1a – can only in the most audacious case make proposals to a 1a. But it does not prove anything. One cannot even speculate about it. A clear reply to your question is 'no'.

Allan Ryan completed this interview with Dr Schreiber by asking a few final questions. Then he summed up what his position was at that point:

It is not our submission that the 1a officer issued direct orders to the commanding general of the Brandenburg Division to do something; much less his first lieutenant would have issued such an order. Rather, our position is [that] the 1a officer – being the commanding general's staff officer for matters of command, operations, planning ... with his O1 officer, as Dr Schreiber testified – could well have been involved in the planning, the preparation, the building up of that incident in the course of advising his commanding general. Dr Schreiber quite rightly points out that we have no proof of precisely that role; indeed, we don't. The point is that, given the responsibilities of the 1a at that time, this could have well come within his duties ... I think it is clear that the Brandenburg Division, the commanding general of that division, reported to the commanding general of the 68th Army Corps who in turn reported to the commanding general, Army Group Southern Greece, General Felmy, on whose staff Lt Colonel Willers and Lieutenant Waldheim were – it is not a command authority we are talking about here; [rather] the operations section, the 1a section, and the role that they might have played.

COMMISSIONER LAWTON: I'm glad you said that. I got the impression, when you opened your case, that you were suggesting that the 1a branch gave specific directions as to what was done in the field.

264

With Commissioner Lawton's point in mind, Allan Ryan decided to ask Dr Schreiber for clarification.

ALLAN RYAN: Where did the 1st Regiment of the Brandenburg Division in fact report to? Directly to Army Group Southern Greece?

SCHREIBER: Yes, exactly, this is the case ... I have checked through my documents and diagrams that I've worked out, the German documents, and it shows that, after the new organization or installation of the Army Group on the 9th of September, [there were] under the direct command of General Felmy ... several groups and even regiments, and one regiment was the 1st [Brandenburg] Regiment. This regiment was detached; it was not under the command of the divisional commander who belonged to the Army Group E, but was given to Felmy for special tasks. Looking at the military hierarchy, it is highly probable that the orders (or operations) that were executed by this 1st [Brandenburg] Regiment − always independently mentioned in the daily reports − [came] directly from the Army Group High Command. Since it is a matter of fact that the military engagement of troops came from the 1a section through the Chief of Staff to the units, we can state − I repeat, it is highly probable that the 1st [Brandenburg] Regiment was engaged directly by the staff.

ALLAN RYAN: We can therefore conclude, Dr Schreiber, with a high degree of probability that the only 1a section above the 1st [Brandenburg] Regiment was the 1a section of Colonel Villers and Lieutenant Waldheim?

SCHREIBER: Yes.

LORD RAWLINSON: But the orders that were given to that regiment then were the orders given by General Felmy?

SCHREIBER: Most probably by the Chief of Staff, sir, as normally happened.

LORD RAWLINSON: Through the Chief of Staff, but the commander is Commander Felmy, is it not?

SCHREIBER: Yes.

LORD RAWLINSON: Felmy directed, through his staff, what his regiment should do?

SCHREIBER: Yes.

Day 5: afternoon

The first witness of the afternoon was Carlo de Luca, a former lieutenant in the Italian army, involved in the motor department. He had been serving with the Germans, and after the surrender on 8 September 1943, he became a prisoner-of-war — and the fate of the Italian prisoners-of-war was the subject of the second part of Allan Ryan's third charge.

ALLAN RYAN: Mr de Luca, I call your attention to 11th September '43 when you were arrested. Do you recall that, sir?

DE LUCA: Yes, in the morning there arrived some Germans. They took us and some other officers . . . and lined us up.

ALLAN RYAN: Were you ever told that you would be going back to Italy?

DE LUCA: Yes. Our superiors said so . . . that the Germans would have taken us back to Italy.

ALLAN RYAN: You were told by your superiors that the Germans would take you to Italy?

DE LUCA: Yes.

ALLAN RYAN: Where, in fact, did you go? Where were you sent?

DE LUCA: They took us to cattle cars. The first time they opened it, in Belgrade, they stopped there and let the officers descend. And at that point, they asked us who wanted to fight alongside the Germans.

ALLAN RYAN: What were the conditions like in the cattle car from Athens to Belgrade? How many people were in the car? Did you have any food to eat?

DE LUCA: During the journey, we were five days without eating . . . They opened the door and just threw some pieces of bread into the car, made from wood shavings . . . We were about 60 people in the cattle car.

ALLAN RYAN: Is your testimony that the food you were given to eat was composed of sawdust, of wooden shavings?

DE LUCA: Yes. After the Liberation, we had it analysed and doctors found it contained 70 per cent sawdust.

He was taken from Belgrade to Germany, then to Poland and back to Germany. They separated the officers from the other ranks.

DE LUCA: Since we did not belong to the Fascist army [i.e. De Luca and his compatriots had refused to fight for the Germans], they asked us who among us wanted to go to work. You will remember that, according to the Geneva Convention, officers were not supposed to work, but the Germans had already taken

266

the doctors to work and some other specialists.

ALLAN RYAN: What were you made to do, Mr de Luca?

DE LUCA: Sometimes we tried to recite the Geneva Convention, but the Germans did not even know what it was — at least, that's what they told us.

COMMISSIONER LAWTON: Signor de Luca, did the Germans make you work?

DE LUCA: No, I never had to do any work, but other officers worked. In February, they came to the hut and took the whole hut away, but when they came to me, I could not stand up because a few days before, I'd been shot at — I was under shock and I could not even eat. So the German who was supposed to take me — he chased me away and I never had to do any work.

COMMISSIONER LAWTON: But they tried to get the Italian officers to work. did they?

DE LUCA: Yes, many had to go to work, some of them voluntarily, but others were forced.

The next witness was Christiano Garaguso, who had been a captain in the Italian army. He'd held a variety of posts and, finally, served in the office of the general staff of the 11th Italian Army in Athens.

LORD RAWLINSON: On the 8th of September, in the evening, was an announcement made about the armistice which Marshal Pietro Badoglio had effected with the Allies, with General Eisenhower?

GARAGUSO: Yes. In the afternoon towards the evening of the 8th of September, we heard on the radio that announcement, and it surprised us greatly because there was no previous news that would have made us think of the possibility of an armistice. The following morning, General Veccherelli called us and told us that he had reached an agreement with the Germans, based on which we should all leave for Italy with our individual arms, handing over to the Germans all heavy arms in our stores.

He said that he left Athens around 23 September 1943 with the Army General Staff, travelling on a train commanded by Colonel Armatucci, the Assistant Chief of Staff. It was supposed to be going to Italy.

LORD RAWLINSON: Where did you think you were going when you boarded that train on the 23rd of September?

GARAGUSO: We had many doubts, many well-founded doubts

267

that we might be taken to Italy. Our country at the time had no chief of state, no government; [they] had all fled for southern Italy, leaving the country completely abandoned. The idea that a military authority like the Germans would bring us back into Italy, 100,000 soldiers — to hand us over to whom?

GARAGUSO.

Although they were very doubtful about this, there was no protest. It was all fairly peaceful. 'The soldier's always happy when he can smell peace,' said Mr Garaguso, 'when he no longer has to shoot and nobody would shoot at him. There was a certain satisfaction in what was going on.'

LORD RAWLINSON: Was there any feeling by the officers that they had been betrayed or that they'd betrayed the Axis powers?
GARAGUSO: Well, we were not very satisfied. The soldier has a sense of honour which, of course, in that moment, had not been respected correctly ...
ALLAN RYAN: [beginning his cross-examination] After the

capitulation, Signor Garaguso, if I understand your testimony correctly, you were put on a train, and in Vienna, you were told that you would be guests of the *Reich*, and you later went on to the Olympic village in Berlin, and you went on from there to a camp called Luchenwalder. Am I correct in that, sir?

GARAGUSO: Yes ... [Luchenwalder] was a concentration camp, mainly for French soldiers.

ALLAN RYAN: If this was a concentration camp, were the officers allowed to play tennis? ...

GARAGUSO: There was a tennis camp, and there were some Indian officers who could play tennis with their turbans on their heads.

ALLAN RYAN: So you, yourself, were not in any way mistreated by the Germans, if I understand you correctly?

GARAGUSO: Never.

ALLAN RYAN: I see, in fact, as you put it, you ended up the war in April '45 fighting with the ally you started off with.

GARAGUSO: Yes.

ALLAN RYAN: But you would not deny, I take it, that thousands of your fellow officers and soldiers were not so fortunate and were, in fact, treated very severely by the Germans. Am I correct, sir?

GARAGUSO: I do not know. I have no news about this. When we were in the concentration camp, there was never any bad treatment of anyone.

This brought to an end the Commission's examination of Charge 3, comprising Waldheim's time in Athens. After the capitulation of the Italians, Army Group Southern Greece was dissolved on 4 October 1943, and Lieutenant Waldheim was sent to be the O3 (i.e. the assistant) to the Ic on the staff of Army Group E in Arsakli/Salonika.

Charge 4: War crimes committed while in Arsakli/Salonika, in connection with the deportation of Jews from Crete, Corfu and Rhodes; and in connection with the capture, interrogation and subsequent execution of various commandos (British, Greek and others), following Hitler's illegal order of 18 October 1942 with reference to captured commandos.

Allan Ryan set out the background to his next allegations:

Army Group E was headquartered in Salonika and was subordinate to Army Group F in Belgrade. It was the highest command in Greece itself [having within its sphere of command all the major Greek islands including Corfu, Crete and Rhodes].

Our evidence in this final section is that Lieutenant Waldheim served in this section as the O3 officer, and we will have evidence as to what that means. He served from October '43 till the end of the war, although our evidence will take us primarily through [Waldheim's military career until] the withdrawal of the German forces from Greece in October and November of '44.

He showed on a map that Arsakli was the headquarters of the Ic/A0 section. Arsakli was just on the outskirts of Salonika.

Our evidence will focus on two . . . areas, one having to do with the deportation of Jews from the Greek islands of Corfu, Rhodes and Crete in the year of '44, and secondly, the interrogation of commandos, including commandos who, we submit, the Commission will find were turned over to the SD for execution during this time.

Lord Rawlinson spoke briefly:

Might I be permitted to add just further to that agreed statement, that the Commission should bear in mind the dates of leave that Lieutenant Waldheim had during this period. From 23rd November '43 to Christmas '43, he was on leave and out of the theatre. He was on leave again on 25th February '44 to 16th April '44. [The latter] is an important date, principally because it relates to one of the charges. Lieutenant Waldheim was again on leave from 13th August until the 3rd September 1944.

Lord Rawlinson asked the Commission to bear in mind that Waldheim was actually away during a great deal of the relevant time.

Dr Schreiber returned as a witness, this time to give expert evidence as a military historian about Waldheim's role as the O3 officer at Army Group E's headquarters at Arsakli.

ALLAN RYAN: The chief of the section Ic is a Colonel Warnstorff and his deputy, a Major Hammer?
SCHREIBER: Yes.
ALLAN RYAN: [referring to an organizational chart showing the structure of the Ic/AO office of Army Group E] Dr Schreiber, in

270

the left-hand column where we find Warnstorff's name and under his name that of Major Hammer, if we follow over to the second column which is captioned 'O3', we see the names of *Oberleutnant* Waldheim and *Oberleutnant* Poliza .... Do you take it from this table of organization that as Major Hammer was Colonel Warnstorff's deputy, so Poliza was Waldheim's deputy in the O3?

SCHREIBER: I would understand it this way — that is, the deputy is always in the second line of the diagram.

ALLAN RYAN: Could you describe to the Commission, please, generally what were the functions and duties of the Ic department at Army Group E in that year, late '43 through '44?

SCHREIBER: In general, of course, Ic in the army group is the officer employed on an evaluation of the situation of the enemy. This means, in the special case of the Balkans, that he was engaged with the partisan warfare, the anti-guerrilla warfare.

... It's important that the Ic was cooperating with the 1a in the question of ... mopping-up operations and sanctions as far as regular troops were engaged. This is one point because we had to give details of the enemy evaluation to the 1a, so there is a connection between the two of them which one has to keep in mind.

ALLAN RYAN: The section is called 'Ic/AO'. Would you explain what the 'AO' stands for and its significance with the function in the office?

SCHREIBER: The AO is, in English, the counter-intelligence officer. There was something like rivalry between the Ic and the AO ... The AO was the counter-intelligence officer and was concerned with the inner affairs. He was working together with the SD, the SS and the police concerning the territory where the army was stationed. Meanwhile, the Ic was concerned with the operations ... It happens, if the Ic was not available, that the AO took his job for a certain while and the other way round.

ALLAN RYAN: In this case, we find Major Hammer wearing two hats, so to speak — as Colonel Warnstorff's deputy as head of the Ic section, and he is also head of the AO section. Is that fair to say?

SCHREIBER: According to this diagram, that is correct.

ALLAN RYAN: So if Colonel Warnstorff were away for some reason, then Major Hammer as his deputy would presumably run the shop. Otherwise, Major Hammer was the head of the AO section?

SCHREIBER: Yes.

271

ALLAN RYAN: Looking at the first column – that is, the general description of the duties of the Ic – do you find there, Dr Schreiber, the interrogation of prisoners? Is that one of their duties? . . .

SCHREIBER: Yes. That is true.

ALLAN RYAN: Will you explain to the Commission what the O3 designates in a Ic operation? What does the O3 do?

SCHREIBER: . . . He kept a book of all the entries and outgoings of classified material. So all orders, writings with a higher classification, and including confidential, he has seen. This shows that any O3 was one of the best informed officers in the staff.

ALLAN RYAN: Do you mean to say, Dr Schreiber, that the book contains the most secret and sensitive messages of the entire Army Group staff?

SCHREIBER: Of the whole military, whatever it is. Even of the Army Group staff because he has to see the documents. He writes down the number, the date and so on. He registers the document, the number on the document, so he sees it . . .

ALLAN RYAN: The Ic section, I suppose, depending on how you look at it, was also responsible within the Army Group staff for communications and liaison with the SS and the SD, was it not?

SCHREIBER: As far as the operations were concerned.

ALLAN RYAN: In fact, the Ic or the Ic section, depending on how you look at it, also exercised control over the *Geheinfeldpolizei*, the secret field police, did they not?

SCHREIBER: Actually, it's a question that I can't answer.

ALLAN RYAN: Can I direct your attention, Dr Schreiber, to the very last paragraph, the last task, if you will. Listed under the Ic's responsibilities, there is a reference there to the GFP – the *Geheinfeldpolizei*.

SCHREIBER: There is a misunderstanding between the two of us. I will explain. I talked about the *band* of *Geheinfeldpolizei*. Of course, there were troops of the GFP in the area of the Army Group E (south) and so on. So it means that, only for certain tasks, he had the right to engage this police group and, yes, to give some orders for their engagement . . .

ALLAN RYAN: So it is your testimony, do I understand you correctly, that the *Geheinfeldpolizei* were at least attached to the Army Group E and that, in a sense, were directed by the Ic officers?

SCHREIBER: This is correct . . .

ALLAN RYAN: Will you describe, please, in general terms, the relationship between those who did the Ic and those who did the

AO? To what extent they might have deputized for each other or crossed through the fences?

SCHREIBER: I think the most important fact is that the AO, for example, was deputy for Ic, and if the Ic was away, the AO took over his task. There was not really a strict division between these two sections. At the very moment when he [the AO] took over, he did all the jobs that were described on the second page ... I can only say that the two sections were very closely related to each other, and officers in these two sections changed to revise the job in the AO and the job in the Ic ...

ALLAN RYAN: Would it be fair to say also for those who were in this office at this time, that everybody knew pretty much what everyone else was doing? ... Would it be a fair inference to be drawn that much of what was going on was known by ...

SCHREIBER: If we are talking about the officers, I would say yes.

Allan Ryan had no further questions, and it was Lord Rawlinson's turn to cross-examine.

LORD RAWLINSON: In retrospect, when you were talking about what everybody knew, this is all reconstruction, isn't it? Talking with other people and looking at documents, how do you make a statement such as that? I just want to know the basis ...

SCHREIBER: I have two bases for my answer. The first one is that I am engaged with German military documents for now 20 years and that I've read a lot of documents and reports about the staff. The second is my personal experience of 25 years in the armed forces — I served 25 years in the staff. So it's my conclusion and my interpretation, and I have seen the summaries.

LORD RAWLINSON: Has it not been your experience that different staffs under different commanders, different chiefs of staff, sometimes act in different ways?

SCHREIBER: That is true.

LORD RAWLINSON: It depends a lot [on] personalities, doesn't it?

SCHREIBER: Yes.

LORD RAWLINSON: I suppose, if you have a very dominant, strong, emphatic colonel, he's more likely to dominate than someone who is not?

SCHREIBER: That is the case.

After some more questions from Lord Rawlinson, Dr Schreiber was finally released from his long stint in the witness box, and the Commission of Inquiry was adjourned until the following day.

273

Day 6: morning

The first witness of the day was Dr Werner Schollen, a 72-year-old retired lawyer, who had specialized in drafting commercial contracts. During the war, he had been Kurt Waldheim's immediate predecessor as O3 officer serving in the Ic department of the general staff of Army Group E in Arsakli. Lord Rawlinson began the questioning.

LORD RAWLINSON: [Was] it the role of the Ic department to produce the enemy situation report each day?

SCHOLLEN: Correct...

LORD RAWLINSON: Those daily reports would be sent up to the Supreme Command, from Army Group E, to the Supreme Command, OKW, through Belgrade?

SCHOLLEN: Well, first of all, it went immediately to OKW, but later on, it went from Army Group E to Army Group F [in Belgrade].

LORD RAWLINSON: As an O3 officer in the Ic department at Arsakli, did you very rarely have meetings with the 1a?

SCHOLLEN: Very infrequently.

LORD RAWLINSON: Did you have daily meetings with the Ic, who was Colonel Warnstorff?

SCHOLLEN: Yes, that is right...

LORD RAWLINSON: ...When an operation in the theatre [of war] was planned against some partisans, would it be the Ic's input or contribution to set out information with regard to strength, etc. of the partisans in that particular area?

SCHOLLEN: Well, these facts were made available to the 1a.

LORD RAWLINSON: I want to ask you about the involvement of the Ic/AO department in March to May 1943, when you were the Ic...at Arsakli. Were you conscious, did you know about, or did you see any report about the deportation of the Jews of Salonika in March to May 1943?

SCHOLLEN: Well, what I knew was − I once went by train from the north to Salonika, and there was a covered goods train coming the other way. I saw frightened faces in the small windows, and I told myself, those are probably, this is likely to be a transportation of Jews. But this is the only personal knowledge I had as far as what happened in Arsakli and the persecution of the Jews.

LORD RAWLINSON: [Who] carried [it] out, that deportation of the Jews from Salonika?

Schollen

SCHOLLEN: It must have been the SD section.
LORD RAWLINSON: Did the Ic/AO department have anything to do with it?
SCHOLLEN: No.
LORD RAWLINSON: Did you go often from Arsakli into Salonika?
SCHOLLEN: Very infrequently.
LORD RAWLINSON: Did you never notice the deportations which were taking place in March to May of 1943?
SCHOLLEN: No...
LORD RAWLINSON: When you say you went very infrequently into Salonika, do you mean by that once a week, once a month, once a quarter?
SCHOLLEN: I can't answer that on the strength of my memory.

We went to Arsakli and we lived well there. Salonika was not a very nice place ...

LORD RAWLINSON: Did you have any telephone conversations with Lieutenant Kurt Waldheim ... in the summer of 1943, some three months before he came and succeeded you in your present position?

SCHOLLEN: Well, the first time I telephoned Mr Waldheim was after I decided to try to leave the staff.

LORD RAWLINSON: During the course of the summer of 1943, did you find that you wished to leave the staff of Army Group E and go back and be a gunnery officer in some fighting division?

SCHOLLEN: That is what I wanted to do. That is what I thought about, yes ...

LORD RAWLINSON: Do you remember the announcement of the armistice of the Italians with the Allies? ...

SCHOLLEN: Yes.

LORD RAWLINSON: At the time when you heard about that, were you the O3 for the Ic at Arsakli?

SCHOLLEN: Yes, sir ...

LORD RAWLINSON: Were you at Arsakli at the time when the Italians on the island of Cephalonia resisted the German demands to disarm, and a battle took place on the island of Cephalonia? Were you then at Arsakli in your post of O3 to the Ic?

SCHOLLEN: Correct. Yes, I was in Arsakli.

LORD RAWLINSON: Do you remember being delivered to you rucksacks full of the personal belongings of a number of Italian soldiers whom you had been told had been shot?

SCHOLLEN: ... [I heard about] this order that Hitler issued, that [Italian] officers of units which were not interned or did not surrender voluntarily, that they were to be shot, so when I opened these rucksacks, I realized that it must have been the belongings of Italian officers that were shot. I was very depressed then, and I tried – this is why I wanted to get away from the staff.

LORD RAWLINSON: ... This must have been after the 22nd September 1943. How long after that incident was it before the arrival, as your successor, of Lieutenant Waldheim?

SCHOLLEN: It must have been a few weeks later, I guess.

LORD RAWLINSON: You wanted, you say, to get away from the Balkans theatre. How did you go about achieving this aim?

SCHOLLEN: Well, the Ic went to the Chief of Staff. I wanted to get to the front lines, I wanted to fight. So that I would get fit for this, I wanted to go to the artillery school, but the situation was such that, afterwards, this was only to be granted if I could introduce a successor. That's when I got into contact with Waldheim ... Waldheim was not fit for front-line duty, not at that time anyway ... Of course, I was quite sure he would be a suitable successor for me. Waldheim was a diplomatic chap, he was an excellent linguist, he had staff experience and so on, so Waldheim was accepted by my superiors as my successor ...

LORD RAWLINSON: Did Waldheim join you in October 1943, and did you stay with him for some time to show him the duties?

SCHOLLEN: Yes ...

LORD RAWLINSON: Was the group of officers with whom you were connected at this time, were they strongly pro-Nazi or were they anti-Führer and anti-Nazi?

SCHOLLEN: Well, in the Ic section, there was a very open and free manner. We were relaxed in our section. There was nobody there, as far as I knew − I certainly wouldn't have taken anybody there for a Nazi.

LORD RAWLINSON: Did you know anything about Waldheim's reputation?

SCHOLLEN: Excellent reputation. He was generally recognized among his comrades ... that he was a very good chap, a clean fellow.

LORD RAWLINSON: Did you think he would fit into the Ic department that you were just about to leave?

SCHOLLEN: Certainly ... We could work well with him. He worked hard and he was very knowledgeable ...

LORD RAWLINSON: ... Was he strongly pro-Nazi or anti-Nazi or what? ...

SCHOLLEN: He certainly didn't have a reputation that he supported the Nazis. He was very critical about the Nazis.

LORD RAWLINSON: In the role which he then took up from you of the Ic/O3 officer, would that officer, as a lieutenant, have any influence on the orders given to the troops carrying out operations against partisans?

SCHOLLEN: Practically no, I don't think, because the O3 is only an auxiliary officer, a helper, an assistant, for those people who make the decisions ... He didn't have any kind of authority to issue commands, and he had no influence on what happened.

LORD RAWLINSON: When you were the O3 officer of the Ic, did you know of the standing orders relating to the taking of hostages and the use of reprisal measures?

SCHOLLEN: Yes. I didn't know the order, but he [the Ic] heard about this order and I knew that it existed.

LORD RAWLINSON: What was generally the attitude of the

department to the order?

SCHOLLEN: Well, I personally didn't once hear that this order was made use of, but I heard repeatedly – we said it jokingly, perhaps – that those who are captured, they should never be commando troops [but] normal prisoners.

LORD RAWLINSON: The taking of the reprisals, the hostage killing and the cleaning-up operations – were they decisions usually of the local commanders in the area?

SCHOLLEN: Shooting hostages in the Balkans was the task of the local commanders. They made the decisions.

After asking the witness about the classification of secret documents, Lord Rawlinson continued.

LORD RAWLINSON: ... There was, in the Ic department, a radio-monitoring unit which was monitoring all the radio from the Allies and elsewhere. Was that a very secret area? Were you allowed into that as the O3? ...

SCHOLLEN: Yes, I had access, but there were very few people who had access here, because there was an order from Hitler, too, that the listening in of information, of broadcasting stations, was something which was punishable by death. So only those people in terms of their job, who had to find out about these things – and O3 was allowed, he listened because of getting information about the enemy ...

Allan Ryan now began his cross-examination, first asking the witness about a report he had written on possible moves of the Allies. He had been ordered to write this by the Chief of Staff of the army group, General Winter, but when the latter had received it, he found it too pessimistic and wrote 'Defeatism!' on it. However, when events turned out as Lieutenant Schollen had predicted, the General had apologized to him. The Commission heard that Schollen and the relevant person in 1a (operations) had joined forces and tried to persuade those in command that Schollen's theories should be taken seriously.

Then Allan Ryan turned to the subject of Schollen's decision to leave the general staff at Arsakli.

ALLAN RYAN: Did I understand you correctly, Mr Schollen, that you decided to leave your assignment in Ic, if you could get

278

permission, after you saw the rucksacks of what you thought were the personal effects of murdered Italian soldiers?

SCHOLLEN: Yes, that is right ...

ALLAN RYAN: Do you know why the personal papers and wallets of murdered Italian soldiers – if that is, in fact, what they were – were sent to you? Do you know why they came to you?

SCHOLLEN: Well, what I am saying is I have suspicions, [that] these people that collected these papers, they did not know what to do with them ... [I asked], 'What am I going to do with this stuff?' I went to Ic about this and also the Chief of Staff, and they said, 'Send them to the exiled government in Munich.' So we took the two rucksacks and we sent them to Munich ...

ALLAN RYAN: What did you tell the Chief of Staff, General Winter, were your reasons for wanting to leave?

SCHOLLEN: All I told him was that I want to leave because I want to go to the fighting units. It would have been very dangerous to outline the true reasons why I wanted to leave ...

ALLAN RYAN: You testified, I believe, that you were aware that he [Waldheim] had a reputation as being anti-Nazi. Did I understand you correctly?

SCHOLLEN: That is the way it is, yes.

ALLAN RYAN: But you had no basis for judging this by yourself – you did not know him personally. Am I correct?

SCHOLLEN: But I got to know him for a few weeks when he worked in this new job, and this was confirmed by this personal contact ...

ALLAN RYAN: But he perceived, perhaps, that you were not enthusiastic about the Nazis, so he, too, told you he was not enthusiastic. Is that it?

SCHOLLEN: Yes, correct.

ALLAN RYAN: The manoeuvre, if you will, was successful, and Lieutenant Waldheim was named as your successor. Is that right?

SCHOLLEN: Yes ...

ALLAN RYAN: In the course of your service with the Ic section from the spring of 1943 until the autumn of that year, did you interrogate any prisoners-of-war or any commandos, you yourself?

SCHOLLEN: No.

ALLAN RYAN: Do you remember whether any commandos were brought to the Ic officer for questioning?

SCHOLLEN: I cannot remember any kind of interrogation of commando troops. I simply cannot ...

After some more questions, Allan Ryan told the Chairman

that he had nothing further to add. The next witness was Mrs Perla Soussi.

ALLAN RYAN: ... Were you born on Corfu in 1920?
SOUSSI: Yes.
ALLAN RYAN: And are you Jewish, Mrs Soussi?
SOUSSI: Yes.
ALLAN RYAN: And do you remember, in 1943, when the Germans took over on Corfu from the Italians?
SOUSSI: Yes, I do.
ALLAN RYAN: And could you tell us, please, what happened ... to your daily life and the life on Corfu in the Jewish community when the Germans took over?
SOUSSI: The Germans came in September as an occupation force. They started writing inscriptions on the shops, saying that we are Jews. Our lives changed because we felt fear when we saw the Germans ...
ALLAN RYAN: Were the men of Corfu, the Jewish men, required to register with the German authorities?
SOUSSI: Yes, they had to be present − all men, from the younger men to the old people, including the sick people.
ALLAN RYAN: How many people [i.e. Jews] were there living on Corfu at this time, Mrs Soussi?
SOUSSI: About 2800, including children.
ALLAN RYAN: Do your remember, in June of 1944, when you and all of the other Jews on the island were made to assemble near the fort on Corfu?
SOUSSI: Yes, I do ... They said everybody − including old people, mental people − everybody should go there.
ALLAN RYAN: By 'everybody', they meant everybody who was Jewish, correct?
SOUSSI: Yes ...
ALLAN RYAN: Did you go with your family, Mrs Soussi, that morning as ordered to the fort on Corfu?
SOUSSI: Yes, exactly. We all went, all the family, young and old, we went to the fort, outside the fort. Then they took us inside ...
ALLAN RYAN: How many were in your family, Mrs Soussi, at this time?
SOUSSI: About 25 people, grandchildren, married, everybody, 25.
ALLAN RYAN: And did all 25 of you, were you all forced to go to the fort that morning?
SOUSSI: Yes ...
ALLAN RYAN: Were you frightened at the time?

280

SOUSSI: Of course. We were panicked. We were terrified.

ALLAN RYAN: Did you know what was going to happen?

SOUSSI: ... [We thought] they were going to take us to labour camps. We didn't know they were going to burn us, the crematorium, we never imagined that. We couldn't understand that it is possible for a human to reach this degree of barbarism.

ALLAN RYAN: Mrs Soussi, were you herded on to boats in the harbour at Corfu?

SOUSSI: Yes, they put us into boats, yes ...

Allan Ryan established that the Jews of Corfu left in about six small boats, and sailed from the island to Igoumenitsa, Lefkas and Patras, from where they were taken to Athens.

ALLAN RYAN: Would you describe the conditions of your travel? What was it like on the boat during this journey?

SOUSSI: They were terrifying. We were beaten. Hunger, everything, during this voyage.

ALLAN RYAN: Were you given food to eat?

SOUSSI: Especially in Lefkas, something happened. A gentleman of ours asked for a cigarette; [a Greek Orthodox priest] offered him one and the German beat him and killed him ... and people were afraid to come to us to give us a piece of bread because they were afraid for their lives.

ALLAN RYAN: Were you then taken to Athens and put on a train by the Germans?

SOUSSI: Yes, on the train for Hebreii. We arrived at Hebreii; there we stayed for eight days. After Hebreii, they put us into a train like animals, and they took us to Gagenau.

ALLAN RYAN: Hebreii was a prison in Athens, was it not, Mrs Soussi?

SOUSSI: It wasn't a prison; perhaps it was a military camp. There were rooms there, large rooms, and all of us assembled there, all people who came. Then in wagons, carrying animals, they put us there. They gave us black liquid, some bread, some water ... We were overcrowded, and the people who died were [used by others] as pillows or they threw them from the windows.

ALLAN RYAN: This was on the train going out of Athens?

SOUSSI: Yes.

ALLAN RYAN: The Germans that drove you in this way, were they German soldiers, do you know?

SOUSSI: Yes, they were German soldiers. We couldn't lift up our eyes; we could hear their boots and panic overtook us. They were wearing a green uniform.

281

The witness said that, from Athens, the Jews of Corfu were taken by train to Birkenau and Auschwitz. Allan Ryan asked what happened to them there.

SOUSSI: As we came out of the wagons, the trains, ... they took us to have a bath naked, they shaved our hair (where there was hair), they put us in line, they gave us some kind of clothes like mad men ... There we stayed for 40 days.

Everyday, they took us out to count us. They gave us in the morning ... some kind of coffee and, at lunch, gave us carrot soup. Evening meal: one slice of bread [and] margarine, cheese or salami.

ALLAN RYAN: What were you forced to do at Auschwitz? Were you put [into] the fields to work?

SOUSSI: ... In a forest nearby, they gave us a knife, very small ... to cut trees. We tried to cut, but it was torture for us − 28 kilometres to go and 28 kilometres come back, it was raining, the wind, naked as we were. We couldn't lift our shoes to reach this forest to cut the trees. [There] was a small bridge; we had to walk in fives and someone was falling into the river ... We were in the line, they used to beat us, everything, humiliation, everything ...

ALLAN RYAN: Were you liberated finally from Bergen Belsen in 1945, Mrs Soussi?

SOUSSI: From northern Germany I was liberated. The Americans liberated − I can't remember − French and English.

ALLAN RYAN: Did you return to Corfu, and do you live in Corfu today?

SOUSSI: Yes. I was liberated, and in September, I returned to Corfu.

ALLAN RYAN: Of the 2000 or more Jews who lived on Corfu until 1944, how many returned to Corfu?

SOUSSI: About 120 persons.

Lord Rawlinson did not cross-examine the witness. Sir Frederick Lawton asked her to show the tattoo of her prison number on her forearm, which she did.

The next witness was Armandos Aron, another Jewish survivor from Corfu.

ALLAN RYAN: Would you describe, please, the change that came about when the Germans took over the island in September 1943? ...

282

ARON: The change was terrible, against the people of Corfu, but mainly against the Jews ... Two or three days ... after the occupation of Corfu by the Germans, they put posters on the walls. One [included an] order from the commandant at the time, of the Gestapo of Greece: This ordered a curfew and Jews were not allowed to move, not to be away from the town of Corfu ...

ALLAN RYAN: Were you and other Jews on the island of Corfu made to assemble on the 9th June 1944 by the fort?

ARON: Exactly. They gave an order. After many humiliations against the Jews of Corfu, including the order on the 9th June 1944 in the morning, for us to present ourselves at the great square of Corfu, which is next to the old castle.

ALLAN RYAN: Were you held there, and then later put on boats and sent across to Igoumenitsa?

ARON: Exactly. When they went inside, all the Jews of Corfu, they brought them by force. They put us inside disgusting rooms – a terrible life, from the point of view of water and cleanliness and food. As soon as we went inside the castle, they forced us to give whatever precious things or money we had, and the keys of our houses, and they destroyed them. The Jews were separated into three groups [and sent by boat to the mainland] ...

ALLAN RYAN: When you yourself were in Patras, Mr Aron, you were able to escape from the rest of the group, or you were cut away from the rest of the group, and you were taken by a Greek farmer. Correct?

ARON: Exactly. Gioris Mitsavos helped me to escape. In the evening, where we were living, life was very bad – beating, hunger ... Somebody whom I never met before, he took me to his house .... Of course, a lot of people helped me, and then I fought in the Resistance against the Germans ...

ALLAN RYAN: Did you ever see your mother, father or two brothers again after that, Mr Aron?

ARON: No, I have never seen anybody from my family. I lost my father, my mother, and two [brothers] – there were three brothers, but one had been killed before [by the Germans] on the 13th September [1943]. The other two were lost in the concentration camps in Poland.

Mr Aron was the last witness of the morning. The Commission went into recess for lunch.

Day 6: afternoon

The next witness was Hans Wende, a retired schoolteacher of 83.

LORD RAWLINSON: I want to take you back, if I may, before the Second World War. Had you, between 1934 and 1938, worked in Athens as a schoolteacher and [did you] speak fluent Greek?

WENDE: I worked as a teacher at the German school and I could speak Greek ...

LORD RAWLINSON: ... You served in Athens as a teacher, then were you called up into the Army at the start of the war, and in 1942, at the age of 37, were you posted to Army Group E at Arsakli, in Salonika?

WENDE: Yes ...

After establishing that Wende had been posted to the Ic section at Army Group E, Lord Rawlinson took him through the organizational chart, seen by other witnesses and showing all the occupants of the various jobs in the Ic/AO department and their duties.

LORD RAWLINSON: ... Did you stay in the department and serve under four different O3 officers – an officer called Merren, another called Schollen, Lieutenant Waldheim and an officer called Zieger – during the course of your service?

WENDE: Yes, indeed.

LORD RAWLINSON: Was it your duty to receive the incoming information about the position of the partisan bands in Greece?

WENDE: Yes.

LORD RAWLINSON: When you had got that information, what did you do with it?

WENDE: The information I checked, and then I processed it, and made a draft for the state-of-the-day situation report ... which then went forward to Ic.

LORD RAWLINSON: Forward to whom?

WENDE: Via O3 to Ic.

LORD RAWLINSON: Of the officers you served under, did you, in fact, know more about Greece than they?

WENDE: Well, yes. That is why, at first, I always got the reports, because I had become the specialist who knew almost every partisan group, knew about its armaments, its weapons, because all this we had from troop reports and from intelligence reports

284

... It was a very painstaking job to ... [as if I were taking] little pebbles ... and [making] a mosaic of them in order to set them up into a fairly credible picture.

LORD RAWLINSON: That picture you presented to the O3. At one time, it was Lieutenant Waldheim?

WENDE: Yes ... It came about that [information] went to O3, but mostly before it got to O3, it went via myself, because I could make comments ... which were informative for O3 ...

LORD RAWLINSON: Did, each morning, the O3 have an 11 o'clock meeting with the Ic officer, which was Colonel Warnstorff?

WENDE: Yes.

LORD RAWLINSON: And to prepare the O3 for the meeting with his colonel, did you brief the O3?

WENDE: Indeed ...

LORD RAWLINSON: Were there meetings you had with the O3, Lieutenant Waldheim, in the afternoons, as well as that brief meeting in the morning?

WENDE: Yes, of course, because the evening reports had to be prepared ... I always had a telephone next to me, and sometimes I got from the intelligence centre urgent messages, even by telephone, and I noted it ...

LORD RAWLINSON: Did you prepare in-depth reports – for instance, on the situation of the bands in Greece? ...

WENDE: Yes, of course, I did prepare that, and later on, too, I had the summary reports which I wrote ...

LORD RAWLINSON: Did, in your view, Lieutenant Waldheim make any substantial contribution to any proposals or suggestions as to action that should be taken against the Greek bands?

WENDE: No. Lieutenant Waldheim only sometimes corrected my reports, because I was somewhat too meticulous and I mentioned everything. He used to say, 'Well, this is unimportant.' But any kind of proposals as to how or what measures were to be taken, Lieutenant Waldheim has never given to me – has never spoken to me about it.

LORD RAWLINSON: ... From your experience and knowledge of working with him at this time, what would you say if it was suggested that Lieutenant Waldheim, aged 23, was making a contribution to the debate as to what operations should be taking place in which part of Greece? What would you say to that?

WENDE: I hardly think so, because he could only hand over to Ic and tell them, and then, during the discussions of the general staff with 1a, they would process it further. They would come up with proposals and go in for planning, but we had no influence upon that whatsoever, not Lieutenant Waldheim either, not in my opinion.

LORD RAWLINSON: Have you read the various books and articles which invest Lieutenant Waldheim with considerable importance as an expert in the field of counter-partisan operations and intelligence? What would you say to that, Mr Wende?

WENDE: I do not know it precisely, but I believe that *Oberleutnant* Waldheim was well informed about the enemy position – I emphasize, the enemy position. He was well informed, but that he independently concluded for himself and handed on to others – not as far as I know ...

LORD RAWLINSON: The department in which you were – Ic department – did it have any responsibility at all for operations?

WENDE: Perhaps indirectly, because on the basis of the reports, we tried to find out where partisans had their focal points, their concentrations. You can imagine that these concentrations, of course, were of interest to the troops – the supplies, the transports – because it was a source of danger to them. If we were of the opinion that there was a strong partisan unit which had gathered itself there, then we – I myself was not present, but I would assume Ic, among the deliberations, would have proposed to start something there.

LORD RAWLINSON: Did you learn about the reprisals, actions which were being taken by the Germans against the Greek bands?

WENDE: In no manner whatsoever. We were only informed if proper military activities were intended, and afterwards, we were told whether we had done our research well, whether the strength of the enemy forces was correct, where here or there the kind of resistance came up – but of reprisals and so on, I know nothing ...

LORD RAWLINSON: I want to take you forward now to 1944. Did the Ic department at Army Group E have any responsibilities for the interrogation of any Allied – that is, British or American – troops which fell into the custody of Army Group E?

WENDE: Yes. The situation was such that we found that the activities of the Allies became more and more pronounced. Whereas earlier on, they only went in for sabotage and sent sabotage troops who blew up bridges and so on, we now found more and more English and, later, American officers were either landed or were dropped ...

LORD RAWLINSON: Where was the interrogation or the interviews of any of these Allied prisoners conducted, do you know?

WENDE: The interrogations of prisoners were already partly handled by the divisions aโ.d by the individual army staffs. We only got reports about it, what they had said about the interrogation itself. I can only assure you, on my word of honour, only in one [case] I can tell you what happened, and that was done by order. Here, I am no longer quite clear. I think it was by order of *Oberleutnant* Poliza and *Oberleutnant* Waldheim.

LORD RAWLINSON: I stop you, if I may. Did Lieutenant Waldheim, to your knowledge, ever conduct any interrogation of Allied prisoners?

WENDE: I can't say.

LORD RAWLINSON: You took part in one interrogation, did you, of prisoners?

WENDE: Yes, indeed.

LORD RAWLINSON: When was that, Mr Wende?

WENDE: It was in the spring of 1944 . . . My friend Wollschläger, who was also on the staff of Ic . . . and I myself were asked to go down to the prison of the secret field police – the *Geheimfeldpolizei* – in order to interrogate two British prisoners . . . I can remember precisely: one of the gentlemen, one of the officers, came in a Scottish kilt, and the other, my friend Wollschläger, who had an excellent command of English . . . soon found he came from South Africa . . .

We made it clear to both [Allied] officers what our superiors had told us: that for medical treatment, they would have to be taken to a hospital, because we knew that then they would be in the sector of the Red Cross and therefore would not be handed over to the SD, the security service. Because we ourselves said quite openly, 'The Führer, the order of the Führer which has ordered . . . '

LORD RAWLINSON: [interrupting] Did you know about that order of the Führer?

WENDE: Officially, no, we did not have it read officially, but . . . we were a small group. We were the so-called sub-staff, or lower staff. We were all academics, all of us knew several languages, all of us had a certain level of education, and we met, of course, frequently after we had done our duty.

As far as Hitler's order was concerned . . . we certainly did not take any notice of it. We had an exchange of views, of thoughts, and we became more and more aware of the difficulty of the situation . . .

LORD RAWLINSON: . . . The interrogation of prisoners that you conducted with this officer in the kilt and the other officer – just explain, if you will, to the Commission, was that a formal military, polite interrogation as is permitted, or was it something different?

WENDE: It was a purely official military interrogation, but — it is difficult to express this — with human intentions ...

Lord Rawlinson referred the witness to a number of documents, which had been classified as 'secret' by the Germans.

LORD RAWLINSON: ... Let us look at this. It is a secret command cable ... dated 26 April from High Command E ...
WENDE: Yes, I have it.
LORD RAWLINSON: That is a text that reads: 'To High Command South-east. Further interrogation of British commando Alimnia. Decision whether prisoners are now to be delivered to SD. Proposed Greek sailors be exempted because forced.' ... So when we look at this telex, which was from Army Group E to [Army Group] F, from what you say, it must have come with the authority of the colonel, Colonel Warnstorff, and only of him?
WENDE: In my opinion, yes ...
LORD RAWLINSON: Would you look now over some other documents? ... [This] is a telex from Army Group F to the superior of Army Group E ... It says: 'The English Captain Blyth captured near Alimnia was transferred directly from Rhodes to Camp 7a, Moosberg. This is now instructed to place Captain Blyth at the disposal of the security service [i.e. the SD] for their command headquarters. Captain Blyth could well be informed about strength, distribution and possible deployment of ranking forces ... The first results of interrogation by *Sturmdivision* Rhodes will be forwarded later.'

Lord Rawlinson then referred the witness to other documents, quoting from some of them. All of them referred to the commandos captured near the island of Alimnia.

LORD RAWLINSON: I want you to look at those documents, Mr Wende. Would you agree that the presence of such commandos — the existence of them — was clearly known not only at Army Group E, but at Army Group F, at Supreme Command OKW and, conceivably and possibly, by the Führer himself? That appears from the documents, does it not?
WENDE: On the basis of the documents, yes ...
LORD RAWLINSON: [referring to another document; reads] 'High Command, 6th of May 1944, to High Command Army Group E: the following English prisoners have been passed on, captured during the morning of 6/5 near Asproangeli, 22 kilometres west

of Gradmanini: Captain Bluett, Captain Hamilton, Private Davies, Private Bennett.' ... Those were the two officers whom you saw at Salonika, when they arrived in Salonika.

Now, Mr Wende ... when you saw these officers, what did you want to do after you had questioned them about the situation where they had been operating, what did you want to do to ensure that they were safe from illegal action?

WENDE: [Wollschläger] pointed out to them [the British officers] that their state of health [left] something to be desired, and that he would see to it in some shape or form that they would be taken to a hospital, which would mean that they would be handed over to the Red Cross ...

LORD RAWLINSON: When you saw those two officers at that prison, was any ill treatment given to them by you or the man with you?

WENDE: In no shape or form whatsoever because we had from above − I don't know, *Oberleutnant* Waldheim or Poliza − we received the order (I will call it good advice) to deal with them in a humane fashion ...

LORD RAWLINSON: In fact, we will hear that Captains Hamilton and Bluett ... did survive. Do you think anything you said or did to their prison authorities helped in that survival?

WENDE: Well, I am of the firm conviction that our requests and our advice were taken up, and they went in the right direction.

After a number of other questions along these lines, Lord Rawlinson completed his examination of Hans Wende. Allan Ryan began his cross-examination.

ALLAN RYAN: Mr Wende, were you at any time a member of the Nazi Party?

WENDE: ... In Germany, I was never in the Party. In [Athens], I was only in the so-called National Socialist Association of Teachers, which was an automatic thing if one was a teacher ... I couldn't have remained in Athens had I not been a member ...

ALLAN RYAN: When did you become a member?

WENDE: Beginning or in the middle of 1935, it could be ...

ALLAN RYAN: Greece was not, at that time, under German occupation, was it, sir?

WENDE: No. We lived in total harmony with the Greeks ...

ALLAN RYAN: You were with Army Group E in the Ic section from 1942 until the end of the war ... Now, your duty, your job at that time, Mr Wende, was to gather information about the movements of Greek civilians and partisans, was it not?

WENDE: I wouldn't like to say 'civilians', but only about those partisan . . . movements which . . .

ALLAN RYAN: [interrupting] Whether you like to say it or not, sir, is it not the fact that much of the information that you collected and passed on dealt with civilian movements?

WENDE: As soon as civilians took up arms, we looked upon them as partisans, but civilians, as such, themselves did not come into what was our orders to deal with.

ALLAN RYAN: Is it not a fact that you collected and passed on information about uprisings in the Jewish community at Salonika?

WENDE: About uprisings of the Jewish populations, I know nothing about that. Only with great horror, I saw the exit of the Jewish population . . .

ALLAN RYAN: Well, I had the impression, from your testimony, Mr Wende, that it was your duty to be expert in the smallest detail about the Greek population, and that you carried out that duty to the best of your ability. Did I misunderstand your testimony?

WENDE: . . . I had . . . got it confirmed that . . . the view was that the Jews or the Jewish population, correctly speaking, was going to Poland in order to be sent to labour camps . . .

ALLAN RYAN: Is it your testimony that, in the course of your duties, you came across no information, no intelligence about the deportation of tens of thousands of Greek Jews from Salonika?

WENDE: That is my testimony. Officially, I never had anything reported about it to me.

ALLAN RYAN: Salonika was about 3 miles from your office, was it not, Mr Wende?

WENDE: Yes, Arsakli, yes, 3 to 4 kilometres.

ALLAN RYAN: Is it your testimony that you knew about the deportation of the Jews from Salonika only because you happened to talk to a friend of yours who lived in Salonika? . . . Did you actually see the Jews of Salonika being deported?

WENDE: Yes, I have seen it. I was in Salonika, I had some kind of job to do there − I no longer remember what. I went along the road, and there were long columns of the Jewish population who had loaded the luggage on to carts and which were escorted by Jewish police. That is the only thing I know about the Greek population − sorry − the Jewish population. That is all I can say about it . . .

ALLAN RYAN: Why did you not give any report [of the deportation] in any way officially, Mr Wende?

WENDE: Well, because it was not my job. The armed resistance movement, [I] was there to get information about it and report about it. About anything else, what I personally saw, I did not have to officially report, it wasn't my job, it wasn't my province. But I am aware that I wasn't the only one – that many had also seen it. The inhabitants of Salonika, they had seen it and, of course, were aware of it because it happened in the middle of the day.

Allan Ryan asked the witness whether he was aware that Jews were deported to Auschwitz from Salonika, Corfu, Rhodes and Crete – all on the orders of Army Group E, section Ic. The witness answered, 'No,' to all four questions. Allan Ryan then turned to a different subject.

ALLAN RYAN: There were two sections in the Ic office: military intelligence and counter-intelligence. Is that right?
WENDE: Yes.
ALLAN RYAN: You were in the section that dealt with military intelligence – am I correct in that?
WENDE: Only with that.
ALLAN RYAN: Did you have any responsibilities in the counter-intelligence field?
WENDE: In no manner.
ALLAN RYAN: Yet there was a time, was there not, when you left your office and infiltrated with the Greek population to determine what intelligence you could get? Is that not correct, sir?
WENDE: Once I got the order . . . to get informed about the mood among the population of Athens . . . that was in 1944 . . .
ALLAN RYAN: When you went down into the population in this fashion, did you identify yourself as a German soldier, a non-commissioned officer who was seeking information?
WENDE: No, I did not do that, but I had permission to go in mufti. Since, earlier on, I had been a book dealer, I camouflaged myself as a field book dealer, because there was in Salonika a library for soldiers. In this camouflage, I went among my Greek acquaintances [in Athens for four days] and talked to them . . .
ALLAN RYAN: In other words, Mr Wende, you were a spy on those occasions?
WENDE: I was not a spy, because I did not work against the enemy in any way. I do not work as a spy. I wouldn't like to call myself that . . .
ALLAN RYAN: Who was it that gave you the order to [go to Athens], Mr Wende?

291

WENDE: This order came from Ic ...
ALLAN RYAN: Who in Ic gave you that order, Mr Wende?
WENDE: [Colonel] Warnstorff, who was then Ic ...
ALLAN RYAN: Did the order come to you through any inter-
mediate officer, through a lieutenant or any officer other than
Colonel Warnstorff?
WENDE: Well, possibly, that may be. I do not know whether
Oberleutnant Waldheim was there at the time ...
ALLAN RYAN: In April of 1944, Lieutenant Waldheim was present
in that office, I can assure you of that ... So [to] the best of your
recollection ... it is possible that Lieutenant Waldheim gave you
that order. Is that accurate, sir?
WENDE: I prefer to say that he transmitted the order, because the
order came from Ic, and the O3 could only transmit it to me.

The Chairman called a recess. When the Inquiry recon-
vened, Allan Ryan addressed the Commission: '... I said
earlier in my questioning of Mr Wende that Lieutenant
Waldheim had been at Army Group E in April of 1944. In
checking the detailed chronology, I find that we accept that he
was on leave from 1 March through either the 8th or 16th − it
is not clear − of April 1944. I do not want to be misunderstood as representing something that is not in evidence. My
learned friend [Lord Rawlinson] quite correctly pointed out
those dates to me.' He then resumed cross-examining the
witness.

ALLAN RYAN: Mr Wende, you used the analogy in describing your
duties that you were like a man who picked up stones, but you did
not make the mosaic. Do I recall that accurately, sir?
WENDE: I would say that they were stones. A fairly large part of
the total picture was composed by me, but time and again − I
must emphasize that − we are dealing only with so-called enemy
positions, only those.
ALLAN RYAN: What exactly do you mean by 'enemy', sir?
WENDE: Well, as enemies, we have the movement of the Greek
armed resistance ...
ALLAN RYAN: So your responsibility was that section of the
enemy picture that dealt with Greek partisans or insurgents?
WENDE: Yes ...
ALLAN RYAN: ... You were bringing him [Waldheim] the stones,
if you will, for the Greek situation; somebody else was bringing

292

him stones dealing with other aspects of the enemy picture. Is that right?

WENDE: Correct.

ALLAN RYAN: From those stones that were being brought to Lieutenant Waldheim, he had to select which were the most important and which ones went into the mosaic. Is that right?

WENDE: Correct ...

ALLAN RYAN: When Lieutenant Waldheim brought the information – brought the mosaic, if you will – to Colonel Warnstorff, you were seldom, if ever, present at those meetings. Do I understand you correctly?

WENDE: Very, very rarely.

ALLAN RYAN: So you are in no position to testify as to what Lieutenant Waldheim might have said in those meetings to Colonel Warnstorff, or what the Colonel might have said to the Lieutenant?

WENDE: No, I am not in that position ...

ALLAN RYAN: Mr Wende, returning for a moment to the mission you undertook to go into Athens disguised as a bookseller to determine the feelings of the Greek citizenry, among the people you talked to on that occasion were counter-intelligence troops of Army Group E, correct?

WENDE: Yes.

ALLAN RYAN: In fact, you met with agents of counter-intelligence troop 376, did you not?

WENDE: Yes.

ALLAN RYAN: And those troops were attached, were part of Army Group E, is that right?

WENDE: Correct ...

ALLAN RYAN: Those troops reported to the counter-intelligence officer in the Ic section, did they not?

WENDE: Yes. Athens had its own command, but I was entitled to also talk to those gentlemen and even get together with those people in the presence of so-called 'V-men'...

ALLAN RYAN: If I could just stop you there for a minute? A 'V-man' was an informer for the SS, was he not? That is what 'V-man' means?

WENDE: No, certainly not. But the counter-intelligence troops purely militarily also had connections, certain people – i.e. Greeks who made themselves available to them. Mostly, they were nationalist Greeks who came and testified at the courts about the force of the Communist groups and so on.

ALLAN RYAN: They were, in effect, Greeks who were agents for the German forces?

WENDE: Yes, one could say 'collaborators'.

ALLAN RYAN: And your gathering of information in this way, on at least this one occasion, was consistent, was it not, with the policy of section Ic, which is that the line between military intelligence and ... counter-intelligence was sometimes quite flexible?

WENDE: It could be that one could see it in this light ...

ALLAN RYAN: So ... the line between the Ic — that is, the military aspect, if you will — and the AO — the *Abwehr* officer — was not a hard-and-fast line?

WENDE: No, not in that sense ...

ALLAN RYAN: ... Did you know that, in fact, innocent hostages were being shot in Greece by German forces?

WENDE: That I can no longer remember. I believe that I have never heard anything concrete about it.

ALLAN RYAN: May I read to you, sir, from the third paragraph of the report that you wrote that went to General Löhr? [Reads] 'I nearly always got the impression that any Greek with nationalist leanings saw in every hostage who was shot an innocent countryman murdered.' Did you write those words, sir?

WENDE: Yes, I can remember now ...

ALLAN RYAN: Do you wish then, sir, to amend your testimony earlier wherein you said you knew nothing about the shooting of hostages?

WENDE: I repeat once again: officially, I did not know here or there hostages were being shot. I only got this from speaking to Greek acquaintances.

ALLAN RYAN: Did you not know, sir, from information that was coming to you from German units in the field, that they had carried out cleansing operations in this village or that village the day before?

WENDE: ... I had always believed that this was regular fighting ... between the armed resistance and our troops ...

ALLAN RYAN: These operations are known as *Sauberungen*, is that correct?

WENDE: Well, *Sauberungen*, one understood it to mean that certain localities — roads, railway tracks which were threatened by the partisans and possibly even occupied by them — that those would be freed by our troops ...

ALLAN RYAN: Is it your testimony that, at no time, did it come to your attention that innocent people were being killed in these *Sauberungen*?

WENDE: I have never heard anything about it, neither officially, nor otherwise . . . I always thought in terms of honest fighting . . .

ALLAN RYAN: You were aware, Mr Wende, were you not, that commandos were to be handed over to the SD, which is part of the SS, for 'special handling', correct?

WENDE: That I know, yes . . .

ALLAN RYAN: And the meaning of 'special handling' was widely known to mean just one thing, was it not?

WENDE: Officially, no, but we assumed it. We had an inkling but there was no clear order . . .

ALLAN RYAN: If not precise information, Mr Wende, you assumed, did you not, that *Sonderbehandlung* meant murder?

WENDE: *Sonderbehandlung*, 'special treatment', could also mean that they might go to another camp or that they were, once again, interrogated [and] so on. It can also mean that the worst had to be feared . . .

ALLAN RYAN: Did you not state, sir, that the first time that you learned that commandos were to be handed over to the SD for 'special treatment' – which was a euphemism for execution – you were horrified by the knowledge?

WENDE: Yes.

After a number of other questions about the treatment of the commandos, which primarily repeated previous testimony, Allan Ryan concluded his cross-examination. Lord Rawlinson rose to ask a few final questions.

LORD RAWLINSON: Mr Wende, you were asked about your joining the National Socialist Association of Teachers in 1935, when you were a teacher at the German school in Athens?

WENDE: Yes.

LORD RAWLINSON: I just want to make clear: . . . would you have been able to teach at all unless you had joined that national association of teachers?

WENDE: I would have been dismissed immediately, and I was happy, as an unemployed teacher, to get a job.

LORD RAWLINSON: You were asked about your visit down to Athens in April 1944. I suggest that Lieutenant Waldheim was on leave until 16 April 1944. Can you say when it was at all that you went down to Athens to go and talk with your acquaintants, when you were in plain clothes, to find out information?

WENDE: . . . It was in the period from the 2nd April until the 6th April.

LORD RAWLINSON: So . . . if Dr Waldheim was on leave, as I

suggest he was – and it is made quite clear in the [Commission of Historians'] report – he could not have given you the instructions, could he?

WENDE: Well, as I said earlier on, I honestly don't know ...

LORD RAWLINSON: You were asked about the deportation of the Jews from Salonika, which took place on 24 March 1943. If Dr Waldheim was on leave until 16th April, he could not have had anything to do with that, could he?

WENDE: In my opinion, no ...

Lord Rawlinson completed his questions and, thanking the witness, sat down. The Commission was now invited to examine the witness.

COMMISSIONER HUFSTEDLER: You have informed us that, when you came to interrogate the commandos, that you could not fully participate in the interrogation because you did not speak English?

WENDE: Yes.

COMMISSIONER HUFSTEDLER: What was your role in that interrogation when you could not speak the language?

WENDE: My job was to ask the concrete questions. I told my friend Wollschläger: 'Please ask whether the groups or bands have had munitions some time ago, because of air drops' and similar questions. These he translated, and he passed them on to the [British] officers, so it was the technical military questions I asked ... They [the officers] then – astonishingly, I would like to say – spoke comparatively openly with us ...

COMMISSIONER HUFSTEDLER: Do you know whether or not your interpreter asked questions of the commandos independently of what you asked him to translate?

WENDE: No, no. He had only passed on what I asked him ...

COMMISSIONER HUFSTEDLER: With respect, therefore, to any reference or lack of it to turning the prisoners over to the SD, it would therefore have been you that put those questions, or made those statements to the prisoners, would it not?

WENDE: Well, I could not say that, because I did not speak English. What the prisoners were asked, or what was told to them, went via my friend Wollschläger ...

COMMISSIONER HÜBNER: Herr Wende, you have already said, through the official channels – that is, the military information channels – that you had not heard anything about reprisals. Had you unofficially heard anything in a private conversation at one time with Herr Waldheim?

WENDE: I speak specifically of Herr Waldheim. I have certainly not discussed this question with Herr Waldheim, because Waldheim was very precise, officially. But in personal terms, he was distant, very distant. Please do not misunderstand me: I cannot remember having discussed anything personally with him ...

The Commission of Inquiry then adjourned until the following day.

Day 7: morning

The first witness of the morning was Karl Mueller-Mangeot, now a 68-year-old retired precision instrument manufacturer. He had joined the German army in 1939 and, in July 1943, was posted to *Sturmdivision* Rhodes, as the O1 officer to the Ia there.

Lord Rawlinson led the witness.

LORD RAWLINSON: I ask you now about the commando raid on Alimnia. If you look at the map, you'll see the small island of Alimnia. We have heard that, on the evening of 7th April [1944], there was a commando raid on that island. As a result, two officers – Captain Blyth and Lieutenant Tuckey of the Royal Navy – and [Radio Operator] Carpenter, [Gunner] Reiss, [Gunner] Evans, [Gunner] Jones and [Sergeant] Miller, together with three Greek sailors, were captured. Did you hear of the capture of these men?

MUELLER-MANGEOT: We had heard that the British commandos' two boats, I think, were supposed to be on the island of Alimnia. And our coastal guard company Brandenburg was sent over to the island of Alimnia, which overwhelmed the British commandos in the harbour there. Both officers, certainly on the 8th April, they went to the division headquarters at Papania, where they appeared, and the unit 1c interrogated them. I myself was present during the interrogation, and afterwards, I went with both officers to the officers' mess in order to have lunch with them.

LORD RAWLINSON: How were those interrogations carried out? In what spirit and manner?

MUELLER-MANGEOT: The interrogation? I won't say it was done in a sort of comradely form, but it was by way of a conversation, more informal than it is here, as I am testifying.

LORD RAWLINSON: After it was completed, you then said you took the two officers to the officers' mess to have lunch. Did you walk with them from where they'd been interrogated to the mess?

MUELLER-MANGEOT: Yes, I went over with the two officers.

LORD RAWLINSON: Had Lieutenant Lockner conducted the interviews, the interrogation?

MUELLER-MANGEOT: Present were Lieutenant Lockner, who was the 1a, Major Kronstein and myself. I think the major questions came from *Oberleutnant* Lockner; his job as O3, among others, was also to interrogate prisoners and officers.

LORD RAWLINSON: You said you walked with them to the officers' mess. Were you by yourself?

MUELLER-MANGEOT: Yes, I was by myself. It was a distance of some 150 to 200 metres. I had thought, 'Now what happens if those two "take a powder"?' I wasn't armed.

LORD RAWLINSON: I don't follow 'take a powder'. Would you explain what you mean?

MUELLER-MANGEOT: I went with the two gentlemen to the officers' mess, there was no armed guard, and I was rather concerned lest both officers tried to run away. There was not much I could do about it; everything was shut − at one o'clock, everyone was in bed on the island of Rhodes.

LORD RAWLINSON: Where were the officers detained after they had been at the officers' mess having lunch?

MUELLER-MANGEOT: I don't know where they spent the night because, after that, they only spent a few more days on the island.

LORD RAWLINSON: At this time, in April '44, were you aware of the infamous Hitler order concerning what should happen to commandos captured in uniform?

MUELLER-MANGEOT: No. We knew of the existence of the commando order as regards British commando units, but only after the war did I see the commando order in its totality.

LORD RAWLINSON: Did you know the effect of an order which had come [from] Hitler − that commandos, even if taken in uniform, should be handed over to the SD for special treatment?

MUELLER-MANGEOT: We did not know any details. We only knew [that] the so-called 'commando order' of Hitler was decreed in order that British commandos should be deterred. Some kind of deterrence was intended.

LORD RAWLINSON: What was the deterrence, did you know what the deterrence was . . . ?

MUELLER-MANGEOT: The deterrence consisted in the fact that . . . [whoever] is taken prisoner and who is a commando or is over-

298

whelmed during a fight, that he would immediately be killed. We were of the opinion, if I may say so, that if . . . that was known to them [the British commando units] . . . that the purpose of this order was that this illegal type of warfare would be stopped. I could say more if you like about what we looked upon as illegal warfare . . .

LORD RAWLINSON: Do you think it illegal warfare to shoot people captured in uniform?

MUELLER-MANGEOT: No [it is not legal], neither did we practise it on the island of Rhodes.

LORD RAWLINSON: Where you present at any of the interrogations of any of the other commandos than the ones you have told us about?

MUELLER-MANGEOT: All other members of those commando troops were inevitably interrogated by the GFP [*Geheimfeldpolizei*; we only had the two officers. So the interrogations, they would be handled by Lockner and others. I would assume that Lockner went to Rodi [near the town of Rhodes] and was present there.

LORD RAWLINSON: [referring the witness to a document] It is [a report of] the interrogation in Rhodes of Captain Blyth. That appears to have been done by Lockner because we see his signature in several places?

MUELLER-MANGEOT: Yes.

LORD RAWLINSON: Were those interrogations the interrogations that took place in which you were present or not?

MUELLER-MANGEOT: Yes.

LORD RAWLINSON: [They took place] on 8th April, and [this is] the assessment of 8th April by Lockner: 'Captain Blyth is an experienced professional soldier who withheld important information in his interrogations so far. He evaded questions with specific military content, but could be fairly well informed about composition, disposition of forces and possible deployment of raiding forces. He himself does not admit to taking part in other military operations, but this could be assumed with a considerable degree of probability. (See interrogation of Private Reiss.)' That was Captain Blyth maintaining his position which he was entitled to maintain, was he not?

MUELLER-MANGEOT: Yes. If I may say so, there was no need for us to urge both officers to tell us more because we had testimonies from the NCOs, which were complete, about this commando structure, its wireless information, its travel routes and where they were to go.

299

LORD RAWLINSON: Then they were sent to [Army Group] E and that was the last you were concerned with, as regards these prisoners?

MUELLER-MANGEOT: Yes.

LORD RAWLINSON: I want to turn now to the deportation of the Jewish community from Rhodes. [Refers to a document dated 13 July 1944 and signed 'Kleemann'. That is the German commander]. Is your signature to the left, under the FDR initials [*Für die Richtigkeit*, 'correct copy'], of which we have heard?

MUELLER-MANGEOT: That is my signature, yes.

LORD RAWLINSON: [This order says:] 'The Jews of both sexes, all age groups, required with immediate effect to take up residence in four villages. These moves must, as far as they have not taken place, be completed by 10.00 on 17th July, and Jews thus moving are required by noon for the purposes of having their names entered in a special register. Non-compliance with this decree will be punished by fine and prison sentence and, in serious cases, by hard labour.' How did it come about that General Kleemann was signing that order on which your initials appear? How did that happen?

MUELLER-MANGEOT: Well, these are two different fields. First of all, it could only have happened by the appearance of two SS officers on the island.

LORD RAWLINSON: May we take this in stages? They arrived on the island. Did the commanding general of the *Wehrmacht* know they had arrived, or what they were doing on the island?

MUELLER-MANGEOT: No, we did not know. We heard about it, and we saw to it that these two SS officers immediately had to go to the commandant office, that they had to report there.

LORD RAWLINSON: Where you present at the meeting between the general commanding, General Kleemann, and these two officers?

MUELLER-MANGEOT: Yes, I was present.

LORD RAWLINSON: What was the General's reaction to the demands of the SS officers that the Jews should be deported from the island?

MUELLER-MANGEOT: Well, Kleemann was very annoyed about it, and he told the two SS officers that it was a presumption to ask that of him. 'Here on the island of Rhodes,' he said, 'I lead.' . . . We shared his opinion completely . . .

LORD RAWLINSON: From what happened, did you gather that General Kleemann had been overruled, and that he must do that which these two SS officers demanded?

MUELLER-MANGEOT: Well, the consequence [will] have been [that

300

he was under orders to prepare for] the deportation of the Jews.

LORD RAWLINSON: In a matter such as that, can you tell us from your experiences as an O3 officer, a lieutenant, would he have had any part to play in deciding whether such a decision was made or not?

MUELLER-MANGEOT: An ordnance officer could have no influence upon what happened around him, his immediate environment, or what moved his superiors – as, for instance, General Kleemann or the 1a ...

LORD RAWLINSON: [referring the witness to another document; reads] 'Deportation of Jews at the end of July 1944. Deportation of Jews who are not Turkish subjects of the total command area on the instruction of the High Command, Army Group E 1c/A0. Implementation in the hands of the SD (Greece) who provided *Sonderkommando* in the command area. Documents have still been retained because they are required further.' That is a paragraph on page 3 of that report. First of all, when was that report made?

MUELLER-MANGEOT: I know this report. It was the 22nd of September '44. That's an activity report of the department 1c. It was set up and also probably sent to Army Group E. It was, therefore, dated in September, three months after the event which it describes.

LORD RAWLINSON: Yes. As far as I know, the activity reports went to 1c every quarter. Who wrote that report?

MUELLER-MANGEOT: Dr Brenner was at least responsible for the report. His signature is also on page 4.

LORD RAWLINSON: Is that an accurate description of the deportation of the Jews and what happened?

MUELLER-MANGEOT: Well, yes, it's a summary of matters in which 1c was involved ... Well, that is what 1c had to deal with – in this case, the deportation of Jews.

LORD RAWLINSON: Finally, was General Kleemann indicted in 1957 on the charge of being an accessory to the murder of some 1600 Jews who were deported from Rhodes, but that the charges were dropped and he never stood trial?

MUELLER-MANGEOT: That is correct. There was no indictment. The examination was stopped twice.

Lord Rawlinson concluded his examination of Mr Mueller-Mangeot, and Allan Ryan began his cross-examination.

ALLAN RYAN: As far as the commandos that were captured on

301

Alimnia, Mr Mueller-Mangeot — I was interested, really, in only one fact: were they in uniform?

MUELLER-MANGEOT: They wore a uniform.

Allan Ryan refers Mueller-Mangeot to a document dated the 13th of July 1944.

ALLAN RYAN: That is an order, is it not, Mr Mueller-Mangeot, that requires the Jews of the island of Rhodes to live in certain places and to register with the Command Staff, with the military authorities? Am I right? Do you recognize the signature on the bottom of this document as being General Kleemann's?

MUELLER-MANGEOT: Yes.

ALLAN RYAN: I call your attention to the 3rd, 4th and 5th paragraphs of this order, particularly the 3rd and the 5th. Let me read it in the English translation: 'I request that necessary steps be taken immediately' - and 'immediately' is underscored — 'to remove all doubts among our groups concerning the treatment of the Jewish question, and issue the following guidelines to that effect.

'Nazi ideology is an essential and natural pre-condition and the basis for the handling of all political, economic and other issues within the Command. The Jewish question can, in the Dodecanese, be handled only by reference to the overall situation, and be brought to a radical solution only if a number of conditions currently being worked on are met.'

I ask you, Mr Mueller-Mangeot, is it your testimony that General Kleemann was forced by the SS to sign that decree?

MUELLER-MANGEOT: No. The SS cannot have forced him.

ALLAN RYAN: Precisely.

MUELLER-MANGEOT: They could not force Kleemann, but something could be said . . .

ALLAN RYAN: The only person who could require and command Kleemann to sign that decree would be someone from his own miltary command, could it not, Army Group E?

MUELLER-MANGEOT: Yes, it could not be the SS. It could not be any civil authority, only Army Group E. Yes.

After Mr Mueller-Mangeot finished giving evidence, Allan Ryan addressed the Commission, summing up the previous testimony.

Mr Chairman, with the Commission's permission, I would like to

302

make a short statement that might tie things together, some of the matters on Corfu. I will be referring to all of the documents relating to Corfu, some of which have been referred to and some not. I hope this will tie it together. Perhaps in doing this, it will demonstrate our submission that the deportation of Jews from Corfu, as from Rhodes, could not have been carried out without the full involvement of military resources controlled by Army Group E, and will show more particularly that the Ic officers at all levels – from the lowest up to the Ic/AO section at Army Group E – were intimately involved in that operation. We do not contend that Army Group E or anyone in it actually ordered – in the sense of deciding upon – the deportation of the Jews. That decision clearly was made by the SS. But our position is that the Army Group E then carried it out in cooperation with the SS.

I will go through these documents in chronological order.

Allan Ryan referred to a report dated 27 April 1944. (The Jews were deported from Corfu on or about 9 June.)

This is a report dated the 27 April 1944, from the GFP – the *Geheinfeldpolizei* – on Corfu to Corps Group Jannina, which was the intermediate group of command between High Command at Army Group [E] at Arsakli and the Corfu outpost.

The paragraph is captioned 'Jews', [and] states: 'According to reports by the Jewish community, there is a total of 1700 Jews on the island. Apart from a very few families that live in the town of Corfu, no limitations have been placed on their personal freedom, apart from the duty to make a weekly report of their presence. They are not being pressed into service for any labour, and there is no evidence to support the opinion of the island's commandant that deportation of the Jews would cause unrest among the Greek population.' We shall see more about the attitude of the island's commandant in a moment.

'It is well known that the deportation of the Jews from the Greek mainland was, on the whole, met with approval by the Greek population.' The final sentence states: 'Difficulty in effecting the deportation will only arise given the shortage of shipping capacity.'

Allan Ryan then referred to a report of 28 April – a report on Corfu island written after an official visit by the Ic on 23/24 April 1944. He quoted from this:

'There are still about 2000 Jews on the island, who mostly live within the precincts of the town. Their deportation would equally represent a not inconsiderable alleviation of the food situation. The SD and the secret military police are currently engaged in making preparations for the deportation of the Jews.' The final paragraph states: 'The measures outlined under paragraphs 1-3 must be carried out urgently. In order to settle the Jewish question, the Corps Group requests that the measures to be implemented be referred to the SD.'

He then quoted from a document of 13 May, written by Colonel Jaeger, the commandant of Corfu:

'SS *Obersturmführer* von Manowski reported to the island commandant with an order from the *Reichsleader*, *Reichsführer* SS Heinrich Himmler to despatch the Jews from Corfu. Since this measure is connected with the provision of shipping capacity – there are some 1800-2000 Jews involved – it was requested from the Admiral Aegean Operations, but up to now has not been forthcoming. In the meantime, the SS captain has departed.'

[The report] concludes at the bottom: 'Militarily, Corfu is in the front-line territory. It cannot be desired to pay for the evacuation of the Jews at the cost of lowering the morale among the troops, effectively strengthening enemy intelligence and setting up increasing guerrilla activity and an ethical loss of prestige in the eyes of the population. For that, and for the good reason that the unavoidable brutality involved can cause repugnance, to this is added the inability to carry out this operation briefly and painlessly.' He concludes as follows: 'Suggestion: the operation should be postponed indefinitely.'

Allan Ryan refers the Commission to Army Group E's war diary. Under the entry dated 26 May 1944, it says that a telex went out saying: 'High Command Army Group E is in agreement with the deportation from Corfu, provided that troop transports for supplies to the island will not suffer, and provided that the transportation will be effected quickly and without interruption.'

The next witness was Charles Bluett, a South African. It is likely that he was one of the captured commandos seen by Hans Wende and his friend Wollschläger at Salonika. During the hour that he gave his evidence, the room was absolutely

304

silent. He answered precisely, without any sort of self-aggrandizement – a totally self-effacing man.

Captain Bluett had volunteered for service in the Second World War, fighting his way through El Alamein and various other places with David Stirling (founder of the SAS) in his long-range Desert Group. Finally, he became part of the commandos.

In May 1944, he was the commanding officer of over 100 troops who landed on the Greek coast north of Corfu, bringing with them equipment that was to be distributed to the partisans.

ALLAN RYAN: During this mission, Mr Bluett, were you and your men wearing insignia or a device of any kind on your uniform to identify you?

BLUETT: We were wearing military uniforms and badges of rank – sergeants, corporals, 2nd lieutenants, lieutenants, captains. We were properly dressed in military uniform.

ALLAN RYAN: Would you describe, sir, the events leading up to your capture? You were captured at Asproangeli, north of Jannina. Is that correct?

BLUETT: We were captured right on the edge of the lake of Jannina.

ALLAN RYAN: Can you explain how you were captured?

BLUETT: We were crossing this range of hills – the Mitsikeli. Captain Hamilton, who was with me...he was hit in the head. The bullet hit him straight above the bridge of the nose and went through. I only found this out afterwards. The bullet went round the interior of his cranium and came out just above his left ear. Naturally, it put him down. I got across to him and I tried to move him, but it was quite useless because I was exposed all the time. There were two other men who could see me, but I could not get any instructions to them, and the next thing, we were jumped on by a group that had come round from the eastern section, down a bit of low ground, which they obviously knew about. They got Hamilton and myself.

ALLAN RYAN: This was a group of German soldiers?

BLUETT: Yes, it was...

Captain Bluett, Captain Hamilton and two non-commissioned soldiers were taken to Jannina and then to a prison in Salonika.

ALLAN RYAN: What uniforms were being worn by those who ran the prison?

BLUETT: The ordinary German uniform, the *Wehrmacht*...

ALLAN RYAN: So it was, from where you could see, being run by the army?

BLUETT: Yes.

ALLAN RYAN: What happened to you when you were brought into the prison? Where were you put?

BLUETT: I was put into a cell on the ground floor. Where Jock Hamilton went, I do not know. The other two vanished. We never saw them again.

Captain Bluett's cell was roughly 8 foot by 6 foot, with a stone floor and walls 4 feet thick. The building itself looked as if it had been built, according to the former officer, 'before Christ', with huge, heavy stonework. The cell into which he was put had no bed, chair or sink, and only what looked like an old meal tin for a latrine.

ALLAN RYAN: What were you given for food and drink on a daily basis in this cell, Mr Bluett?...

BLUETT: I asked for water, and they said, 'You can't drink here. You get malaria.' I told him he was talking a lot of bull, because I come from a malaria area... You don't get malaria from drinking water.

ALLAN RYAN: What sort of food were you given?

BLUETT: None.

ALLAN RYAN: At all?

BLUETT: Those first few days.

ALLAN RYAN: How long did this period go without any food or water?

BLUETT: Four days.

ALLAN RYAN: What happened after four days? Were you then fed?

BLUETT: A man came along dragging a sanitary bin. He scooped out a helping about the size of a small jam tin of boiled cabbage, and the water it was boiled in. That was your meal.

ALLAN RYAN: Did there come a time, Mr Bluett, when you were interrogated in this prison?

BLUETT: Yes.

ALLAN RYAN: Can you describe, sir, where you were taken and who interrogated you on that first occasion?

BLUETT: There were these two SS there: an interpreter and one of the prison guards.

ALLAN RYAN: What sort of uniform was the interpreter wearing? Was it an SS uniform?

BLUETT: No, he was *Wehrmacht*. He was allegedly an interpreter, but he had a very, very poor command of English.

ALLAN RYAN: How tall was he?

BLUETT: 5 foot 9.

ALLAN RYAN: Enlisted rank?

BLUETT: No, I'm unsure of his rank. I think he was just an ordinary private.

ALLAN RYAN: We have heard testimony that a South African and a man in a kilt were interrogated in a prison, and that the questioning was civilized and informal, even friendly. Is that fair description?

BLUETT: No.

ALLAN RYAN: Would you describe the interrogation itself?

BLUETT: These two SS chaps, at the slightest whim that they had, produced these heavy truncheons. They kept hitting on the nape of the neck, and predominantly on your left side, which we knew from unarmed combat training was the place where, if you really applied it, you could kill a man immediately. What they achieved was they put me into a state where, if you stood up, you fell over.

ALLAN RYAN: While the questioning that was carried on, while you were being beaten during a normal conversation, how would you describe that?

BLUETT: They would raise their voices. They shout at you all the time. They swing these batons round. They even got a bit rough with the interpreter because they said he did not know what he was doing.

ALLAN RYAN: How long did the interrogation last, Mr Bluett? To the best you can recall.

BLUETT: About half an hour.

ALLAN RYAN: When it concluded, what happened then? Did you stand up and walk away?

BLUETT: They pulled me to my feet and led me away. I went back to my original cell. . .

ALLAN RYAN: Were you interrogated a second time, Mr Bluett. . .?

BLUETT: Yes.

ALLAN RYAN: Will you describe this questioning session, sir? Who was there and what happened?

BLUETT: The same two SS and one Gestapo chap. And the same interpreter.

ALLAN RYAN: The interpreter was wearing a *Wehrmacht* uniform?

BLUETT: Correct.

ALLAN RYAN: Were you again beaten with a truncheon?

BLUETT: It was used.

ALLAN RYAN: Was there someone else present in the room at that time, sir, standing behind you?

BLUETT: Yes. I was sitting on this low stool – it was barely a foot off the ground – and the others were sitting on chairs at a table. They were looking down on me. Someone walked in behind. I had no view of him at all, but when he spoke, he spoke in a soft voice, as opposed to the shouting and yelling that was going on normally. These chaps at the table immediately kept silent when he spoke to them. I could not really hear exactly what he was saying, but he was speaking in what I would call a civilized tone of voice. I believe the term is 'peripheral vision', but to the side of my face, there was a man there, who was, I should say, over 6 feet and in officer's uniform. He must definitely have been an officer because the reaction of the interrogaters was immediate. They said, '*Zu befehl*,' or '*Jawohl*,' and they kept quiet while this man spoke.

ALLAN RYAN: This man was standing straight behind you, and you did not get a straight on look on his face? Is that correct?

BLUETT: Correct.

ALLAN RYAN: You were able to discern that he was taller than you?

BLUETT: Yes.

ALLAN RYAN: How tall are you, sir?

BLUETT: 5 foot 10.

ALLAN RYAN: Do you have any estimate of how much taller than you he was?

BLUETT: If...I had stood up, I would have been looking at his shoulder.

ALLAN RYAN: Do you have any sense of his build? Was he stocky, slim?

BLUETT: He was slim.

ALLAN RYAN: Were the beatings going on? Were you actually being beaten during the time that this officer was standing behind you in the room?

BLUETT: As soon as he spoke, everything stopped.

ALLAN RYAN: When he came into the room, before he spoke, were you being beaten at that point?

BLUETT: Yes.

ALLAN RYAN: Did the beatings continue at all while he was in the room?

BLUETT: No.

ALLAN RYAN: Did they resume when he left?

BLUETT: No. The whole session stopped, and I was taken out and put into the cell again.

Captain Bluett maintained that he had been given little food, even afterwards. Once, when one of his guards gave him the daily bowl of cabbage with a bit of water and then deliberately kicked it over, Bluett flew at him and wrestled him to the ground: the South African survived that little dust-up. Finally, he was taken by train to Munich, and then put in an extermination camp. However, in the end, he finished up in Moosberg prisoner-of-war camp until he was eventually released by the Allied forces.

Neither Lord Rawlinson nor the Commissioners had any further questions to ask Mr Bluett.

The next witness was Albert Davies, another survivor of German interrogation techniques. He had volunteered for the Royal Armoured Corps in 1941 when he was 19 years old, and had served in North Africa. Then he joined the Raiding Support Regiment, and trained in Palestine for missions behind enemy lines in the Balkans.

ALLAN RYAN: In 1944, sir, were you on a mission under the command of the then Captain Charles Bluett?

DAVIES: I was with Captain Bluett.

Allan Ryan asked him to describe the circumstances of his capture. With great modesty, this extremely brave man explained how they had been in a mule column; they'd completed a march of over 100 miles, and their ultimate aim was to get beyond the mountain range of Jannina before sunrise.

DAVIES: Unfortunately, we were still climbing the mountain range near the Jannina valley when the sun came up and we were exposed to a German military unit in the valley. They opened up with their mountain guns. The whole column was brought under fire from the guns in the valley . . . In those days, the rule was that every man looked after himself, and I went over the top. Subsequently, I walked into a machine-gun ambush, and I was taken prisoner.

I was taken to a rallying point of the German troops. That was where I first saw Captain Bluett, who had also been taken prisoner. He was faking injury at the time and supporting himself on a large stave he'd got hold of. There were three or four partisans – civilian men – there. That's all I can remember.

ALLAN RYAN: Were you put into a prison at Salonika?

DAVIES: Yes, I was.

ALLAN RYAN: Please describe the conditions in that prison.

DAVIES: It was late at night when we entered this prison, and all I saw at that time was nine flights of stairs up to the first floor. The cell door was open and I was told to go in and the state was unbelievable – it was a dirty, filthy cell. I thought to myself, 'Well, I shan't be here very long.'...I was in four walls with a small iron window about nine feet up from the floor, and that was the cell. The smell was from the bugs and insects that had been squashed against the walls in there, and it was infested with filthiness in there. That was the accommodation [in which] I spent the next 3½ months.

ALLAN RYAN: Would you describe, sir, what sort of rations you received for the next 3½ months?

DAVIES: We were going through the high summer period and the heat was unbearable, yet the only rations I had was a small bowl of cabbage or potato soup each day, and an empty meat tin of water. That water, I could drink it, wash in it, or save it; so, you could say, the next 3½ months I didn't have a wash. Some of the water I soaked in my boots to try and keep the leather soft. I was worrying about going out and putting them on quickly. [The rations] never varied that I can remember; it was either potato soup or cabbage soup.

ALLAN RYAN: About how much soup did you have in a day?

DAVIES: Maybe half a pint.

ALLAN RYAN: Did you see any civilians in the prison from time to time?

DAVIES: I saw two civilians. One was put in my cell to try and question me; he was a stooge of some sort, which I quickly became aware of. On another occasion, on the way back from slopping out in the morning, I saw an elderly man standing on the landing. He'd been very heavily, badly beaten up. His face was heavily contused with blood...I could see him all the time I walked up the last flight of stairs. He was standing there and I was looking at him, and his face was so badly beaten, it was difficult to recognize any salient features on his face. His face was just a mass of pulp. He was just standing there – a bedraggled figure.

310

Eventually, Davies was taken to a work camp in Salonika, occupied by Italian prisoners-of-war. In the fullness of time, he was released.

Again, neither Lord Rawlinson nor the Commissioners had any more questions, and Mr Davies left the witness box.

The next witness, Bruce Ogilvie, had been specifically called by the Commission. He had claimed in the British press that his life had been saved by an officer called Waldheim. On the basis of this, the Commission had decided to hear him. Lord Rawlinson led him through his main evidence.

Mr Ogilvie had been in the Royal Air Force as an air support officer for the raiding forces in that theatre of war. On 15 October 1943, he had been shot down near an island off the Turkish coast.

LORD RAWLINSON: After you had been arrested, where were you taken?

OGILVIE: Only a short distance, a few hundred yards, to what appeared to be some form of police or security barracks.

LORD RAWLINSON: Were you interrogated with brutality there?

OGILVIE: Yes. For a short time, we were knocked about, strip searched, kicked and that kind of thing. There was no attempt to interrogate us constructively. The people who were doing this were, in my view, quite clearly not Germans. They appeared to be Eastern European troops of some sort.

LORD RAWLINSON: What happened on the following day?

OGILVIE: While it was still dark, a patrol arrived at the police station or police barracks, and they appeared to have some authority to visit and search police buildings or other forms of holding areas. They said they were looking for escaped British prisoners and escaped British commandos. In the end, with some reluctance, we were released on this particular officer's signature, released into his custody.

He and the other British officers, as well as a wounded American airman, were taken to an airfield and placed in a building which looked like an old-fashioned canteen.

LORD RAWLINSON: Tell the Commission of Inquiry what happened.

OGILVIE: The escort officer from the truck came into the building with us and told us that we were, in fact, now to be transferred to

311

Salonika ... and our prisoner-of-war status would be assured. We [were] told to expect an escort officer and guard to take us by air to Salonika, which was the railhead to Germany.

When this officer arrived, he came through the door with his guard and introduced himself simply as 'Waldheim' ... He proceeded to speak to us in English, in rather stilted English. I felt this was something of a prepared speech. He informed us once again that our prisoner-of-war status was now assured, in spite of events up to that time, and that he was our escort officer in the normal course of events and would be accompanying us by air to Salonika.

LORD RAWLINSON: Describe the officer and what he was wearing.

OGILVIE: He was very young looking. I ought to mention that this was a long time ago, and this officer was about my own age at that time − 23. He was a very young-looking man and, I thought, very much a college-boy type. This was the general impression he gave: a tall, gangling, young man. I use the word 'gangling' because this is the impression he gave, both with his stance and the fact that he was tall and slim. He spoke to us in English [for] this rather stilted speech, assuring us of our position.

LORD RAWLINSON: What happened then, after he had spoken to you? ... What happened to you?

OGILVIE: He told us we would be leaving immediately for Salonika by air. The aircraft was outside. He then said that he'd be taking from us our identity discs because it was likely that our safety had already been compromised by our identity and our association with the operations in Leros ... He'd be taking our discs from us to disguise our identity while we were still in Greece, before we left for Germany.

The thrust of Ogilvie's evidence centred around the removal of these discs (i.e. 'dogtags'). If the airmen's names had already been given to the SD or the SS as commandos, or as being involved in commando operations, then plainly, under the Führer Order, their safety would have been prejudiced. Mr Ogilvie was suggesting that by changing their identity discs − presumably for the discs of ordinary servicemen, whose names would not have already gone to the SD or SS − this officer had probably saved their lives.

When Bruce Ogilvie returned to Britain after the war, he was debriefed by the RAF. He told the Commission that he had been keen to have the Allies recognize that some Germans

312

had, in fact, acted correctly during the war, and to that end, he personally contacted the British security services so that he could be debriefed by them. He did have one meeting with someone from the security services, at which he told his story about the officer Waldheim who had been so helpful.

When his turn came to cross-examine, Allan Ryan asked just one question.

ALLAN RYAN: If I understand your testimony correctly, that name that you gave [the RAF and the security services] does not appear in any contemporary documents at the time. Am I right on that, sir? In other words, in your debriefings and so forth, the various reports that issued out of that, none of those contains the name that you gave of Waldheim?

OGILVIE: No, although I inquired about this, I have seen no record of my own.

The Commissioners were very interested in Mr Ogilvie's testimony, and asked a number of questions.

COMMISSIONER HUFSTEDLER: Did you ever see the person who identified himself as Waldheim [after] the time when you left his presence, when he escorted you from Athens to Salonika?

OGILVIE: Yes, I saw him once more in the building which we had been led to believe was the headquarters of the unit.

COMMISSIONER HUFSTEDLER: You did not talk to him, if I understand it correctly – you saw him?

OGILVIE: I saw him, he acknowledged us and went on down the passage.

COMMISSIONER HUFSTEDLER: Did you connect the name given to you at that time upon seeing photographs of Dr Waldheim which appeared in the international press?

OGILVIE: Yes, but very much later.

Mr Ogilvie made the point that, for quite a long time, Waldheim had claimed that he had not been in Salonika during the war – in fact, he had said that the war had ended for him when he had returned to Austria after being wounded on the Eastern Front. It was only when Mr Ogilvie had subsequently read that Waldheim had indeed been in Salonika, and obviously at the same time that he'd been there, that he had put two and two together.

313

COMMISSIONER HÜBNER: Would you tell us, when did you first realize from press photographs that it was this Mr Waldheim who helped you?

OGILVIE: I recall seeing pictures of Dr Waldheim on the occasion of his acceptance [as Secretary-General] to the United Nations. The name was familiar . . . [but] his appearance – I must say, very much changed from the young officer I remember in style, stance, appearance and everything else. He could have been the same one, but there was such a lack of clarity as to whether Dr Waldheim could have been the Waldheim I knew in Greece. And . . . what finally made me sure was that he had been, in fact, stationed in Salonika; it was, in fact, the word 'Salonika' that told me it was quite the same person. That was quite recently.

After Mr Ogilvie left the stand, the next witness was led into the Commission of Inquiry. This was James Doughty, who'd come from the States, and from whom the Waldheim project team had initially hoped for some spectacular evidence. However, it transpired that the very honest evidence he gave did not match up to the sensational treatment that had been given by the press to his story.

During World War II, he'd been an ambulance driver, and had been landed in Greece with the commandos as a medical orderly. He had been among a party of 12-15 commandos who had carried out a raid on the island of Calino, the objective being, thought Mr Doughty, a place called Port Baden.

DOUGHTY: There was shooting, and . . . two of our men were wounded – one of them very seriously and one less seriously. We decided that I would stay behind with the wounded men and treat them while the others went back to the cave [which they were using as a base].

ALLAN RYAN: You stayed with the wounded?

DOUGHTY: We took the wounded soldiers into the basement of a little house, and I treated them, and we stayed there the night. Early the next morning – the Germans, I presume, had been told we were there – two soldiers came and escorted us to their barracks.

Mr Doughty and the wounded soldier had been taken from Leros to Rhodes, and then by train to Salonika. Once there, he was taken to some sort of institution that had been turned into a jail, and was put into solitary confinement. Later, he was

314

taken to an upper floor where he was questioned. He said that he really couldn't remember the interrogator at all; he was questioned in English. The subject of the questioning was 'Was there an operation?' He could not give any real description of the person who had interrogated him. Afterwards, he was transferred to a prison containing Italian POWs, and treated quite well.

Lord Rawlinson established, in cross-examination, that one of the wounded soldiers had died – a Private Fishwick. Lord Rawlinson also expressed what we all felt, when he asked, 'Was the other wounded soldier with whom, if I may say so, you gallantly stayed, was that Sergeant Dryden?'

DOUGHTY: Yes.
LORD RAWLINSON: After the war, you had a reunion with the man with whom you stayed?
DOUGHTY: Yes.

That reunion had taken place in London after both Doughty and Dryden had been released from prisoner-of-war camps. That was the end of Mr Doughty's evidence, and he was able to return to his peaceful life on board his boat in Florida.

Lord Rawlinson then gave a summary of the evidence concerning Waldheim's involvement with the fate of the commandos:

...May I seek to assist the Commission with this resumé to put before you? First, that Lieutenant Waldheim was on leave when, on the 7th April, those ten commandos were captured on the island of Alimnia. Of those ten, all but one, we must assume, were executed. When Lieutenant Waldheim was still on leave, the Supreme Command of the German forces were aware of the existence of these commandos and of their capture, and announced it in the *Wehrmacht* communiqué. When Lieutenant Waldheim was still on leave between the 14th and 15th of April, there must be an irresistible inference that Adolf Hitler, the Supreme Commander, was aware of the existence of these commandos. From that time on, the Commission may think that the possibility of anyone using any ruses – as has been suggested was in the past used or could have been used, a ruse to save their lives – was at an end.

Lieutenant Waldheim returned to the headquarters on the 16th

315

April. On 27th April, Army Group F, which was the superior command to the Army Group E, on the staff of which Lieutenant Waldheim was serving, ordered their transfer which led to their deaths: the deaths of all save two, whose fate came weeks later, on June the 5th. Therefore, the Commission might think, on recital of the facts and examination of the documents, that Lieutenant Waldheim had nothing to do with the fate of those men who disappeared, presumably executed. It was in the hands of those far senior in command to the lieutenant. In any event, this lieutenant never had custody of the prisoners, nor did he have the power or the command to dispose of them. If any responsibility rests, it rests in Army Groups E and F, it must rest with the chiefs of staff, and it must rest with Colonel Warnstorff and his equivalent in Army Group F.

I would suggest to the Commission [that] they will think long and look hard before it is found that it could have rested with the lieutenant, who was, in fact, absent at the time when the fate of these men in reality was concluded.

Allan Ryan responded:

Mr Chairman, if I may respond briefly. Lieutenant Waldheim may have been on leave when the Alimnia commandos were captured, but there is nothing illegal about their capture. The war crime here is that those commandos were turned over to the SD for execution. Somebody carried that order out in Army Group E, and it was Kurt Waldheim who was in charge of the interrogation of prisoners, if one follows the table of organization – the *Führerabteilung*). He was back, indeed, from leave in plenty of time to sign the transmission reports, sending the interrogation reports up to Army Group F.

I submit there is no evidence that Hitler himself knew of any of this. The only suggestion we have in this regard is a message back from Army Group F, which says, 'The Führer has not authorized raids on Turkish...' [It] is beside the point, whether it was known at [Army Group] F or Berlin or at any other level. The question is: somebody at Army Group E turned those commandos over, both in April and in June, the latter group when they were killed. Somebody in Army Group E committed a crime as far as Mr Bluett and Mr Davies were concerned. Their testimony can leave no doubt whatsoever that they were subjected to the most vigorous and horrifying war crimes that could still leave one alive, in the course of their imprisonment at the *Geheimfeldpolizei*

316

prison in Salonika. Again, we call attention to the fact that the 'interrogation of prisoners' falls in the O3 column under the names of Lieutenant Poliza and Lieutenant Khrone, both of whom answered to Lieutenant Waldheim.

With that, the Commission adjourned until the following day.

Day 8: morning

Helmut Poliza was the first witness of this, the penultimate day of the Inquiry. Now 69 years old and a retired insurance executive, he had been posted to Arsakli in November 1943 to work on the general staff of Army Group E. Here, he had served with Lieutenant Kurt Waldheim in the Ic section.

Lord Rawlinson's initial line of examination led him to ask about the character and reputation of Poliza's superior – the Ic himself, Lt Colonel Warnstorff.

POLIZA: Warnstorff was a very intelligent young officer. In fact, he was only 32. Each morning, Waldheim would go to Colonel Warnstorff and take this written synopsis with maps and sketches; all three of them were put together.

LORD RAWLINSON: Why did Dr Waldheim get such long periods of leave? Do you know?

POLIZA: It was said there was a kind angel looking after him. Because he wanted to study, this was leave for studies. If I remember correctly study leave could be taken longer and granted more frequently than normal leave.

LORD RAWLINSON: After the meeting which Lieutenant Waldheim, or whoever was deputizing for him, attended with Colonel Warnstorff, was there then the superior meeting with the Chief of Staff held, at which sometimes the commanding general appeared later in the morning?

POLIZA: Yes, that is correct.

LORD RAWLINSON: Was that a meeting at which Lieutenant Frei [of the 1a (operations) section] invariably attended and Waldheim, or whoever was deputizing for Waldheim, came to if required?

POLIZA: Well, *Oberleutnant* Frei, as far as I know, was always present as the O1 ... As for the rest, it was *Oberstleutnant* Warnstorff, and possibly *Oberleutnant* Waldheim additionally was present. Waldheim may have been there from time to time or once in a while. I hardly ever participated in these discussions on the situation, so I can't say much from my own experience.

LORD RAWLINSON: Who, in the absence of Warnstorff, was deputy?

POLIZA: Hammer.

Poliza

LORD RAWLINSON: What would happen if both Warnstorff and Major Hammer were away?

POLIZA: Well, the deputy was *Sonderführer* Schlenker.

LORD RAWLINSON: So if Warnstorff is away, Major Hammer takes over responsibility. What happens if Major Hammer is also away, does Lieutenant Waldheim take on the responsibility?

POLIZA: No, he cannot. We did not have the responsibility.

LORD RAWLINSON: With regard to the decision-making process which emerged from Army Group E, did you ever submit proposals or suggestions as to what operation or actions should be taken by the fighting troops?

POLIZA: No.

LORD RAWLINSON: Did you ever hear Waldheim make any such proposals or suggestions?

POLIZA: No.

LORD RAWLINSON: Any intervention or comments or interjections made by a lieutenant at the meeting with the Chief of Staff, would they be limited to his area – namely, enemy positions – or might they be extended into other areas?

318

POLIZA: No, only enemy positions...

LORD RAWLINSON: The Commission has heard from a gentleman, Mr Wende ... that he played a substantial part in the preparation of that new type of report. What do you say to that?

POLIZA: I think Herr Wende invented that, in a manner of speaking, this type of monthly report about the enemy situation [but] I do know that Herr Wende worked very well and was very informative...

LORD RAWLINSON: That was very much to the benefit, perhaps to the credit, then of Lieutenant Waldheim that Mr Wende had such expertise and knowledge.

POLIZA: That was very good for Herr Waldheim.

LORD RAWLINSON: Lieutenant Waldheim took advantage of that, did he?

POLIZA: Well, I do not think that he would call it 'taking advantage' in the sense where it is exploitation.

LORD RAWLINSON: As far as you are aware, did Waldheim conduct any interrogations of prisoners of any nationality?

POLIZA: He did not.

LORD RAWLINSON: Did Lieutenant Kurt Waldheim have any command authority whatsoever over any *Wehrmacht* troops, SS personnel or GFP personnel or any other active serving people?

POLIZA: No – that is, *Oberleutnant* Waldheim, Khrone and the ordnance officer had no power to give any orders.

LORD RAWLINSON: [referring to a map that shows the island of Rhodes and a very small island north-west of Rhodes, Alimnia] On or about 10th or 11th April, one of the officers, Lieutenant Tuckey and other ranks – Rice, Miller, Jones, Evans and three Greeks – were taken from Rhodes, where they had been taken after capture in Alimnia, to Salonika in the area of [Army] Group E. Is that correct?

POLIZA: Yes.

Lord Rawlinson then referred to a document to High Command Army Group F from Army Group E, one of the daily *Wehrmaçht* reports that went through Army Group F. He pointed out that, as a result of these documents, Poliza was aware that the information about the capture of these prisoners was, in fact, known right up to OKW, the top of German high command. Poliza agreed that that was correct.

LORD RAWLINSON: [reading from a document in the war diary of Army Group E] 'High Command South-east [i.e. Army Group F]

319

has indicated that it is necessary, as a result of the increased commando activity in the Dodecanese, to bring in members of commando troops as prisoners, and to compile documentation concerning the departure point for commando activities and the further intentions of the enemy. To complete this order, an order is being issued to General Commanding, 68th Corps, Jannina Corps Group, Salonika, Commandant of the Fortress Greece *Sturmdivision* at Rhodes:

Information for the Admiral of the Aegean: Recent experiences have shown it is necessary to hand over to the High Command of Army Group E for interrogation members of the commando troops or prisoners of whom there is doubt concerning their membership of commando troops. A preliminary interrogation is to be carried out by Division or General Command. A decision on treatment in accordance with the Führer directive will then be made from there.'

What was the 'Führer directive', Mr Poliza?

POLIZA: The Führer directive had as its contents that English commando troops, British commando troops, should not be taken prisoner in Germany, but that they should be killed in battle. I think that was the original version; I myself have never seen it.

LORD RAWLINSON: What was to happen if they were not killed in battle?

POLIZA: What is afterwards apparent and of significance here, if somebody was taken prisoner in some shape or form or by the police, he should immediately be handed over to the SD for further treatment − the security services.

LORD RAWLINSON: What does that mean?

POLIZA: Whatever that may mean, it has not been laid down in writing.

LORD RAWLINSON: What did it mean?

POLIZA: I would interpret it to mean that, certainly, also it comprises the possibility that an execution would take place at the end. But as I said, nobody knew precisely.

LORD RAWLINSON: . . . On the 16th April, Lieutenant Waldheim returned from leave. By the time he returns from leave, not only does [Army Group] F know about the existence of these commandos which have been captured, but OKW − that is, German High Command − knew of the existence of the commandos which have been captured, and an inference can be drawn that the Führer himself, Adolf Hitler, knew that these commandos had been captured. Is that right?

POLIZA: I was just going to say it is quite clear here, quite clear, that they knew about this matter of the commandos.

LORD RAWLINSON: Would it be right to say that there was very little that could be done to save these unfortunate soldiers from being handed over to the SD in accordance with Adolf Hitler's infamous order?

POLIZA: I do not think there was any possibility once it was known right to the top of staff, that there could be any possibility of circumventing it, it would be impossible.

LORD RAWLINSON: [quoting from another document] 'The High Command South-east requests that Captain Blyth, the commander of this group of commandos who were captured at Alimnia, and who was transferred from Rhodes to be held at the SD in accordance with the Führer's orders. The SD should be advised Captain Blyth is initially to be kept available for the OKW interrogation to take place in accordance with instructions of OKW.' Captain Blyth had been separated from Lieutenant Tuckey and the other soldiers, who had been sent direct to Germany, to Moosberg Stalag, I believe.

POLIZA: Yes, Moosberg Stalag.

LORD RAWLINSON: That is the 16th of April and it is on the day that Lieutenant Waldheim returns from leave?

POLIZA: Yes...

LORD RAWLINSON: Did you interrogate any of these British prisoners who were captured at Alimnia?

POLIZA: I can't remember.

LORD RAWLINSON: These were the first commandos who were captured since you had taken up your duties?

POLIZA: That is correct, but I would assume that, if they were interrogated there, that was Wollschläger because he spoke very much better English. I assume therefore the interrogation was not very successful.

LORD RAWLINSON: Why were you present when the Greeks were interrogated when you don't speak Greek, and not present when the British were interrogated when you did understand some English?

POLIZA: On the first interrogation of the Greeks, it showed that the results of the interrogation of those Greeks – above all, Laskari – [were of great] interest... because there would also be the Turkish problem. [The Germans believed that the British commandos were using Turkish bases, thus violating the sovereignty of neutral Turkey.] Also, the Allied troops opposing us, although they were Greeks, [had with them] the British commando unit that had been taken prisoner. Hence, it was of particular interest to us.

321

LORD RAWLINSON: After Lieutenant Waldheim came back from leave on the 16th April, did he interrogate any of the commandos who were still in Arsakli at that time?

POLIZA: No, certainly not.

LORD RAWLINSON: I turn to the officers Captains Bluett and Hamilton who were captured in May '44. Did you interrogate them?

POLIZA: No.

LORD RAWLINSON: Did you know that they were in custody in Salonika?

POLIZA: I cannot remember.

LORD RAWLINSON: The group that was captured in Asproangeli in May '44 – Captain Bluett, Hamilton, Davies and Bennett – they have all survived, have they?

POLIZA: Yes, they have survived...They must have come to a prisoner-of-war camp. They have survived which proves – I mean to say that if they followed the normal procedure that they were also handed over to the SD, which would again prove the fact that, [since] they have survived, that in general, special treatment need not mean execution. But I don't know. I can't say.

LORD RAWLINSON: Did you have any part in the interrogation of Allied commandos captured at Calino – a British sergeant, Dryden, and an American private, Fishwick [and an American medical orderly, Doughty]?

POLIZA: No, but I know about it. But I was at that point on leaving Germany.

LORD RAWLINSON: ...These gentlemen survived?

POLIZA: Yes, they have also survived. One of them died in an army hospital in Athens and the other two survived.

LORD RAWLINSON: Who were they interrogated by?

POLIZA: I am not sure, but it was probably Wollschläger.

LORD RAWLINSON: Who gave the actual order to hand over the Alimnia prisoners, the ones who didn't survive, to the SD?

POLIZA: I think it must have been Herr Hammer because he could give orders to the Secret Field Police, but I cannot state that with authority because I do not know.

LORD RAWLINSON: Someone must have given the actual order which handed them over. Was it Warnstorff or Hammer?

POLIZA: Correct, yes. In my view, it must have been Hammer because Hammer was the direct superior of the Secret Field Police. Ic matters such as interrogations had been dealt with in the meantime, and now it's up to the *Geheinfeldpolizei*, the secret field police, and what happened there, it seems to me, is a matter for Hammer.

Sir Frederick Lawton and Gustav Petrén, two of the Commissioners, framed under the programme 'logo'.

The members of the Commission of Inquiry overlooking one of our researchers, Veronika Hyks (middle left), who not only knew every document in the eight 'bundles' but was our conduit for messages to the Chairman. The other 'clerk' was an actor, but the court shorthand writer was there 'for real'.

Yugoslav prisoners forced to strip nude and bathe in an
icy lake in a slave labour camp in northern Norway.

Below: Captain Charles Bluett (*left*) and Gunner Albert Davies, members of a British
Commando unit captured in Greece and re-united after 44 years at the recording
of the 'Waldheim' programme. Their last meeting was in a German prison.

1100 - VERY URGENT. Lieutenant Kurta Waldheim from General Stal's Headquarters requests that 4,224 prisoners from Kozara consisting mainly of women and children, and with about 15% old men, be sent to Grubišno polje (3,514) and Zemun (730).

TELEGRAM

09
22.VII.42.

Address: Command of the First GR ZDRUGA

Above left, the so-called 'Plenca' document, sold to and printed by *Der Spiegel*, which we believed to be a forgery; an English translation of the document is given beneath it. *Above right*, what we believe to be a genuine version of the Plenca form. It was found by one of our researchers based in Yugoslavia, Pierre Vicary.

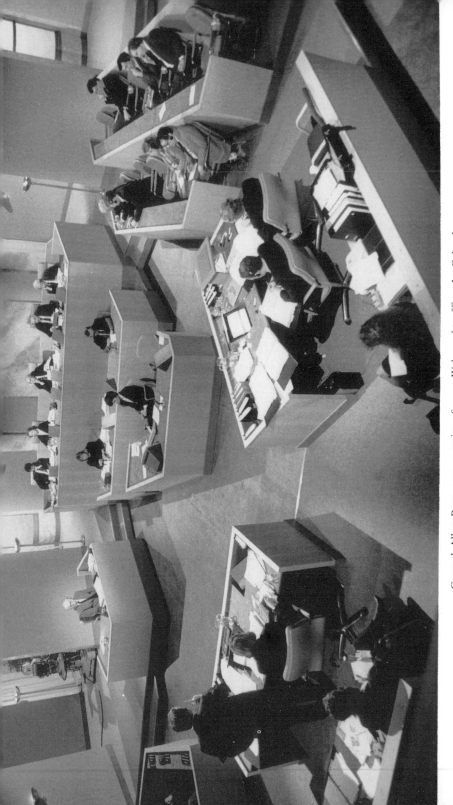

Counsel Allan Ryan cross-examines former Wehrmacht officer Lt Colonel Bruno Willers, who was Waldheim's superior during his service in Athens in 1943.

LORD RAWLINSON: Did Lieutenant Waldheim play any part in the actual order of handing over of the Alimnia commandos to the SD?

POLIZA: Most certainly not because he had no possibilities as an *Oberleutnant* to give any orders of any kind; he had no possibility.

LORD RAWLINSON: I come to ask about the deportations of the Jewish population from the Greek islands during the time you served with the Army Group E in Greece at Arsakli. Do you recollect the Jewish deportations from those islands?

POLIZA: No. I mentioned this to the historian in the Commission in Vienna. I had no information in my time about the deportation of Jews. How dreadful it was! I knew nothing about it.

LORD RAWLINSON: Did you know that there were deportations, that they had taken place? The deportations of Jews or deportations as such, deportations of the Jewish population from the Greek islands?

POLIZA: That is exactly what I did not know.

LORD RAWLINSON: Would not the Ic department be involved in arrangements for the deportations?

POLIZA: No, in my view, not. If at all, it would have been the 1a or the AO. It was either a matter of 1a because it was more an operational matter: deportations for reasons I would assume, questions of supply – other ethnic groups, as I saw afterwards, have also been deported. Or AO possibly as well, but only marginally because, as such, it was not a matter for the *Wehrmacht* or for the Army.

As Allan Ryan rose to question Poliza, there was certainly an air of expectancy, everyone remembering his fairly strenuous cross-examination of Willers and Rothfuchs. However, it seemed that he had decided to play this one very differently.

To begin with, Allan Ryan went through the structure of the command with Poliza, establishing the fact that Colonel Warnstorff was the head, Major Hammer was his deputy and Lieutenant Waldheim was the 03, and that, of the three lieutenants – Waldheim, Khrone and Poliza – Waldheim was the first among equals, *primus inter pares*.

ALLAN RYAN: You assisted him? You were one of the equals who was a little less equal than he was, is that right? [This was one of the very few remarks in the entire nine days of recording that brought a little laugh.]

323

POLIZA: Well, if you like it, yes.

ALLAN RYAN: I take it there is no question, Mr Poliza, that the responsibility for matters dealing with the interrogation of prisoners-of-war was within the Ic section, correct?

POLIZA: Yes, that is correct.

ALLAN RYAN: More specifically, within that Ic section, it came under the supervision of the O3 officer, who is Lieutenant Waldheim?

POLIZA: No, that is not correct because, as far as interrogation of prisoners were concerned, he had nothing to do with it. He had to do with the evaluation of what they said but not the interrogation because that was under Khrone and myself, all supervision. The results he got afterwards.

ALLAN RYAN: So you were in charge of interrogation of prisoners dealing with Great Britain and the United States and the Allies, and Lieutenant Khrone was in charge of the interrogation of prisoners dealing with the partisans, the Balkans and so forth, is that right?

POLIZA: That is correct.

ALLAN RYAN: Let's get another matter cleared up. The Führer Order of 18th October, you are surely aware of what the order said?

POLIZA: I would say so. Yes, I would say so.

ALLAN RYAN: The way that order was implemented, it was that the commandos would be turned over to the SD, the police arm of the SS...They would be turned over for *Sonderbehandlung* – 'special handling'. Was that your understanding as well at that time?

POLIZA: Yes, it was.

ALLAN RYAN: 'Special handling' meant murder, let's face it, right?

POLIZA: I don't know whether it meant 100 per cent because, otherwise, some would not have survived. I don't know.

ALLAN RYAN: We don't know of any case where someone, turned over to the SD, ever survived, I take it? You don't know of anyone who survived the SD, do you?

POLIZA: Well, here, for instance, it seems obviously that this commando operation with Bluett and Hamilton and so on...

ALLAN RYAN: *They* were never turned over to the SD, Mr Poliza, I can tell you that. They were never turned over to the SD. My question to you, just so we understand the basis for your testimony, is that you don't know of any case of anyone who was turned over to the SD who made it out alive?

POLIZA: That is correct. I don't know that.

Allan Ryan referred Poliza to a memorandum about two telephone conversations in which the latter was involved.

ALLAN RYAN: What it says essentially is this: 'I got a telephone call from *Oberleutnant* Heinicke who wants answers by ten o'clock tomorrow morning to the following questions concerning the Alimnia prisoners: (1) Where are these people? (2) Have they already been interrogated? (3) When is interrogation to be completed? (4) When is the *Sonderbehandlung* [the 'special treatment'] to start?

You tell them: 'These people are indeed at Army Group E; we have these people.' Secondly, 'the interrogation is not yet completed because they are being very obstinate, very stubborn.' Thirdly, you say to them: 'These people should be handed over to the SD tomorrow morning, but should be continued to be interrogated by the SD.' The duration of 'special treatment' or the time of the 'special treatment', the end of the 'special treatment', if you will, 'is to be determined by the SD'. Would that be a fair reading of that memorandum?

POLIZA: That would be a fair interpretation of this note whereby this is not something that we could say by ourselves independently. There must have been some kind of planning via Warnstorff, or undertaken by Warnstorff or Hammer because the decision...

ALLAN RYAN: [interrupting] Good, so we have a conversation on the 14th of April '44 in which you tell the Ic office at Army Group F that these prisoners are being very stubborn, very obstinate, if you will. What do you mean by that phrase, Mr Poliza, 'very stubborn'?

POLIZA: Well, that they did not spontaneously tell us all kinds of things, but time and again, one had to ask: 'Was it like this?' or 'How was it done?' or 'Where did you have in the Turkish waters your base?' It was not an interrogation which was in a sort of friendly spirit, where we had backwards and forwards. It was difficult to get something out of them.

ALLAN RYAN: Did you say it was not a friendly interrogation or it was friendly interrogation?

POLIZA: No, I think that would give a wrong picture, 'friendly'. What I mean, not very spontaneous. There are interrogations which are like conversations, backwards and forwards, question and answer, backwards and forwards, but in this case, I think

325

what is meant that, time and again, questions had to be asked twice or had to be pursued because the interrogated person did not reply very spontaneously but only if one put the questions.

ALLAN RYAN: Did you ever mention the SD at all to these prisoners you interrogated?

POLIZA: No.

ALLAN RYAN: Let me see if I follow you, Mr Poliza. You were trying to get information from these captive commandos. The information, I take it, is of some value to you. They are not giving it, they are being obstinate, you want the information and you never said, 'Look, give me the information or else you will be handed over to the SD.' That never happened?

POLIZA: No.

ALLAN RYAN: Did it ever occur to you to do that?

POLIZA: No, of course not.

ALLAN RYAN: You didn't think that, perhaps, if the prisoners knew they faced a very dangerous situation with the SD, they might be more willing to give the information to you?

POLIZA: No, I don't think so. I don't believe that they knew what the SD was.

ALLAN RYAN: That's the whole point. Didn't you tell them what the SD was and what could happen to them if they didn't cooperate with you?

POLIZA: No.

ALLAN RYAN: The next day, Kurt Waldheim comes back from leave − 16th of April, I believe the date is. Can we safely assume that, when he comes back, you give him a briefing on the situation, what has gone on in his absence and where things stand on the day he came back? That would be a fair assumption, I think?

POLIZA: That is correct, yes.

ALLAN RYAN: So as of the 16th April, when he comes back, he knows that there are some captured commandos, some prisoners that you have interrogated but without great success, and that they are being very stubborn, very obstinate. Did he give you, at any point, any instructions, any directions on how to proceed with those commandos?

POLIZA: No, because he couldn't give me any instructions. He didn't have the right to do that. He had no cause.

ALLAN RYAN: Are you saying he didn't suggest, maybe, 'Try this tactic or try that tactic'? I'm not asking you if he was your commanding officer − we know he wasn't your commanding officer − but he was first among equals and he was the first and you were

326

the equal. Did he give you any suggestion as to how you could get some information out of these prisoners?

POLIZA: No.

ALLAN RYAN: [showing the witness a telegram sent on 26 April from Army Group E to Army Group F] Do you see in the lower right-hand corner the 'Received' stamp of Army Group F? It was received by the O3 officer up there. Telegram says: 'Further interrogation of the British Alimnia commandos fruitless. Decision requested if prisoners are to be handed over to the SD.'

POLIZA: Yes.

ALLAN RYAN: On that very same day, another message comes back from Army Group F to Army Group E Ic/AO, to your office, and the message says: 'The British radio operator' - Carpenter, we assume – 'and the Greek sailor' – we can assume this is Laskari – 'are to be kept ready there under the strictest guard as possible witnesses. The remaining prisoners are to be handed over to the SD for interrogations, possibly still of interest to us, and *Sonderbehandlung* afterwards according to the Führer's order.'

You testified that Major Hammer carried out this order, in your view, and turned over the prisoners to the SD for 'special treatment'. Is that right?

POLIZA: I must correct this. I did not say that Hammer had done it. I do *assume* that Hammer had done this because he was in a position to order the secret field police where the prisoners were kept.

Allan Ryan talked about the fact that the prisoners who were not turned over to the SD on 26 April remained under close guard, as the telegram says, for many weeks.

ALLAN RYAN: Are you suggesting that Waldheim, having been back for ten days after the 26th of April, could be there for another six weeks while these prisoners were there and not be aware of them? You don't mean to suggest that, I trust?

POLIZA: Well, I do not wish to say that. I would imagine he did know.

ALLAN RYAN: You would imagine he did?

POLIZA: Yes.

ALLAN RYAN: I would imagine he did, too. A British radio operator being held under lock and key was not an everyday occurrence at Army Group E, I would take it?

POLIZA: No, he certainly would have heard of it – from me, too, because I knew it.

327

ALLAN RYAN: You knew it, and you were one of his assistants, one of his sort of equals?

POLIZA: Yes.

ALLAN RYAN: What did you tell him about it, do you remember?

POLIZA: No, we certainly must have talked about it, but I cannot say what I said.

ALLAN RYAN: I would think you did talk about it. Do you recall — I know it has been a number of years; I don't expect every detail — but do you recall any of the substance of the conversations you had with Waldheim about Carpenter and Laskari.

POLIZA: Well, it could well be [that] we talked about it, whether one would have the possibility — after the fact of their having been taken prisoner, this commando operation where that was known right up to Hitler — that there was no possibility whatsoever in any shape or form to try to make the attempt to subvert somehow this handing over to the SD. It was totally impossible.

ALLAN RYAN: So by early June, Mr Carpenter and Mr Laskari had been in the secret police prison, I take it, for almost two months. Would that be accurate?

POLIZA: Yes.

ALLAN RYAN: What were conditions like in the secret police prison, Mr Poliza?

POLIZA: Well, as far as I can judge it, they were perfectly normal cells with a wooden bunk. Nothing special about it, no barred windows.

ALLAN RYAN: Were the prisoners who were kept there given adequate food and drink, to your knowledge?

POLIZA: As far as I'd know, yes, they had normal provisions. They were like rations, army rations, the same thing as the soldiers.

ALLAN RYAN: Did you visit the secret police station in that two-month period, do you recall?

POLIZA: During those two months, no, I don't think I was there during the two-month period.

ALLAN RYAN: So you are in no position to testify to the treatment they actually received, is that correct?

POLIZA: Well, I wasn't there, that is correct.

ALLAN RYAN: [referring to a document of 5 June 1944] A message is sent from Army Group F to Army Group E Ic/AO. It says: 'Re. British radio operator Carpenter, Greek sailor Laskari. On the orders of OKW in Berlin, Carpenter and Laskari were captured, they are "no longer required" and are made available for "special treatment" in accordance with the Führer's order.'

328

POLIZA: That is correct, yes.

ALLAN RYAN: Your belief is that the person who delivered them was not Lieutenant Waldheim but his immediate superior, Major Hammer, is that your belief?

POLIZA: But that [Major Hammer] was not Mr Waldheim's superior, Hammer – yes, that is correct. My view is that the person who caused these two people to be given to the SD . . . was Mr Hammer because he was responsible for the SD, but he was not the superior of Herr Waldheim. Herr Hammer had the AO group under him and that was only if necessary he was the deputy of Warnstorff.

ALLAN RYAN: Whatever capacity he was acting in, it probably made no difference to Mr Carpenter or Mr Laskari, don't you think?

POLIZA: [speaking in a very soft voice] That is correct. But that is correct for those two, it didn't make any difference, but it had nothing to do with Waldheim and not with myself.

ALLAN RYAN: It was Hammer who was doing it only on the instructions from Army Group F?

POLIZA: That was the case.

ALLAN RYAN: So whatever he was, he was just 'following orders'?

POLIZA: Yes, he followed orders from the Army Group South-east – that is, [Army Group] F High Command or Supreme Command South-east.

Allan Ryan then changed tack and introduced the subject of the deportation of the Jews.

ALLAN RYAN: You were present at Army Group E, the Ic office, during that period of time, but you had no knowledge about the deportation of the Jews?

POLIZA: That is correct.

ALLAN RYAN: Since you are the most senior officer from that office that the Commission is likely to hear, I would like to show you a few documents and see if you can explain them to the Commission. [Refers to a document] Look at the bottom of the page. Do you see the words '*Judenfrage* – The measures to be implemented be referred to the SD'?

POLIZA: That is correct. I've got what you were referring to.

ALLAN RYAN: That says the Jewish question should be carried out quickly, does it not? If you look up a couple of sentences in that same paragraph, Mr Poliza, the sentence that refers to paragraph 133 above. . . , it says: 'The measures outlined in the Paragraph 1

329

and 3 must be carried out urgently.' So this is the Corps Group Ic telling Army Group E Ic that the measures concerning the deportation of the Jews should be carried out urgently?

POLIZA: ...It would have been a matter which one would have passed on to the 1a for them to take the necessary steps, because it would have been an operational matter and not a matter for Ic. Ic did not cause active measures; it only collected reports.

ALLAN RYAN: Is it possible that it went first to the postal department at Ic?

POLIZA: It is possible ... but I think that, after 1b, it would have been handed on to 1a because it was not to be dealt with by Ic. Possibly AO, always I must add, but I think rather to 1a.

ALLAN RYAN: Is there some place in there that it says it is not to be handled by Ic?

POLIZA: I did not see that.

ALLAN RYAN: One more document, Mr Poliza. If you will read along with me the first sentence – this is from the activity report of the Commandant East Aegean. That was also part of Army Group E, was it not, Commandant East Aegean?

POLIZA: Yes, that is correct.

ALLAN RYAN: Let me show you the entire report. That sentence, Mr Poliza, reads as follows: 'Deportation of Jews' - this is being written in September – 'At the end of July '44, deportation of Jews not of Turkish nationality from the entire area under the orders of the headquarters Army Group E Ic/AO.' That would seem to indicate, Mr Poliza, that it was Army Group E Ic/AO that ordered the deportation of the Jews in so far as the Army was concerned. Is that the way you read it, too?

POLIZA: Yes, you are certainly correct up to a point, but it was not a Ic matter, but if it was done by AO – I had already said, AO or 1a – and in this case it must have been caused by AO. AO, of course, had the rights to give certain orders.

ALLAN RYAN: That would have been Major Hammer?

POLIZA: Yes, that would have been quite clearly [Major] Hammer.

ALLAN RYAN: But it would not have been Lieutenant Waldheim?

POLIZA: Definitely not.

ALLAN RYAN: Just so the record is clear, it would not have been you?

POLIZA: No.

ALLAN RYAN: In fact, this was not your job at all, nothing to do with it?

POLIZA: None of us.

330

ALLAN RYAN: Thank you, Mr Poliza.

With the conclusion of the cross-examination of Helmut Poliza, the next witness was Theodor Lauber, a 73-year-old lawyer in the town of Neuberg unter Donau in West Germany. He had been a member of the *Geheinfeldpolitzei*, or secret field police, with Army Group E in Salonika in 1943.

ALLAN RYAN: You were stationed with Army Group E from the fall of '43 up through the retreat, is that correct?

LAUBER: Yes, apart from some small interruptions, I was seconded to Army Group E from September '43 — I think possibly October — to the end of the war.

ALLAN RYAN: And you were the liaison, were you not, between the *Geheinfeldpolitzei* and the Ic/AO section of Army Group E?

LAUBER: Yes, I was the liaison man. But not only a liaison man.

ALLAN RYAN: And in that capacity, you. . . were stationed at the staff headquarters in Arsakli, is that correct?

LAUBER: It is.

ALLAN RYAN: What did the GFP do, the *Geheinfeldpolitzei*? What was the GFP in Salonika in '44?. . . What were its functions?

LAUBER: Well, all I know basically is one task, and that is to engage the partisans, to fight against the partisans, not the military partisans, but to clear partisan movements, to prevent partisan groups from forming, of course, the collaboration with the Greek population.

ALLAN RYAN: Mr Lauber, the *Geheinfeldpolitzei* ran a prison in Salonika, did it not? Primarily to interrogate Greek citizens — those suspected of supporting the partisans. That is correct?

LAUBER: That is correct.

ALLAN RYAN: Those members of the *Geheinfeldpolitzei* who were at the prison wore the regular army uniform, did they not?

LAUBER: Yes.

ALLAN RYAN: That was the prison where commandos were also kept on those occasions when commandos were interrogated, correct?

LAUBER: Well, I cannot talk about the numbers. I only know of one case. That is all.

ALLAN RYAN: In the one case you know of, the commandos were held at that prison, correct?

LAUBER: Yes, they were held in that prison. Yes, I'm sure they were held there. I was only present during the interrogation which took place there.

331

ALLAN RYAN: Mr Lauber, were the interrogations that were carried out at the GFP prison sometimes accompanied by beatings of the prisoners?

LAUBER: Well, there were people with the GFP who did practise this, but there were also people with the GFP who did not practise force. Later on, this beating was prohibited, not allowed. This beating, of course, where I myself only saw hands and fists, I never saw any kind of instrument being used. Only once I remember that. I came into a room, and there was a stick on the table, but it was not used. It was a threat, as it were, the stick on the table. Certainly that is the way I interpreted it myself.

ALLAN RYAN: But that stick could have been picked up and used if the interrogator had thought it advisable?

LAUBER: Yes.

ALLAN RYAN: In other words, there is no question in your mind that the stick you saw there could have been used for beating prisoners?

LAUBER: Yes, could have, but I think it was only a threat.

ALLAN RYAN: Could you describe that stick for us, Mr Lauber – how big and how heavy?

LAUBER: So, like that.

He made a shape with his hands. It was about the thickness of a thumb, and he extended his hands to show that the stick had probably been 14 to 16 inches long.

ALLAN RYAN: What was it made of?

LAUBER: Wood.

ALLAN RYAN: Was it a thick stick, the size of your fist maybe?

LAUBER: Oh, about my finger there, or my thumb maybe, if you like.

ALLAN RYAN: But it could have inflicted pain had it been used as a weapon to beat prisoners?

LAUBER: Yes.

ALLAN RYAN: Mr Lauber, in your time in the Ic/AO section at the headquarters of Army Group E, would it be fair to say that there was no sharp distinction between the Ic function and the AO function, from your observation?

LAUBER: Well, in this case I was a simple soldier myself. I did not notice any difference myself – no, I noticed no difference. For me, it was one authority, one office. Of course, I may be wrong, but it's my impression.

ALLAN RYAN: I'm just asking you for your observations, what

you saw over a period of time. As far as the division between the two functions, your testimony is there was no sharp distinction that you were aware of?

LAUBER: Absolutely none, no.

ALLAN RYAN: Mr Lauber, were you aware of an order — in fact, it was a Führer Order — that commandos were to be handed over to the SD for *Sonderbehandlung*, 'special treatment'?

LAUBER: Yes, I was.

ALLAN RYAN: In your mind, what did you think 'special treatment' really meant?

LAUBER: Well, I'm afraid, usually it was termination, the end, death. Yes, indeed, as a rule, but I'm sure there were exceptions, but as a rule...

ALLAN RYAN: And as far as you are aware, was this order, or this policy, common knowledge in the Ic/AO department?

ALLAN RYAN: Well, everybody knew that, I think, anyway. Of course, there are some people who never know anything, but generally, this was known. Soldiers have a special information system, you know. It is on the grapevine, as it were; you hear about these things. I did not read [the order], but on the grapevine, I found out about it.

Allan Ryan said that he had no further questions, and Lord Rawlinson then cross-examined Mr Lauber.

LORD RAWLINSON: You witnessed beatings. Did you take any steps to try and stop those beatings?

LAUBER: No, I did not. I just passed by, as it were, but I was never at an interrogation where beatings were used. I just heard about it very briefly when I was in the Zimiski Road 72 [the authority office, not the prison where these beatings took place].

LORD RAWLINSON: You just passed by, is that what you are saying, Mr Lauber?

LAUBER: Yes.

LORD RAWLINSON: You were in the GFP. That was your role, was it not?

LAUBER: Yes.

LORD RAWLINSON: You were liaising with the staff at Army Group E?

LAUBER: Yes.

LORD RAWLINSON: On reflection, are you not ashamed to have worn a uniform indulging in beatings of defenceless prisoners in your interrogation rooms?

LAUBER: No, I did not do anything like that.

LORD RAWLINSON: Are you ashamed that your colleagues did it?

LAUBER: Of course, I am, yes.

That was the end of Theodor Lauber's testimony. The next witness was Wolfgang Sattman, now 65 years old and still employed as a civil servant. He began his wartime service at the age of 19, and in 1942, he was assigned to a regiment as a radio operator. On 19 July 1942, he went to Arsakli to serve with the radio communications regiment.

LORD RAWLINSON: Were you assigned to the *Abteilung* Ic/AO?

SATTMAN: Yes.

LORD RAWLINSON: Was your direct superior Lieutenant Colonel Warnstorff?

SATTMAN: No, the immediate superior was an NCO, then came 1st Lieutenant Waldheim, and then *Oberstleutnant* Warnstorff.

LORD RAWLINSON: His deputy was Major Hammer, who was in charge of the AO officers and staff. Did you get into contact with Major Hammer at all?

SATTMAN: Yes, I did.

LORD RAWLINSON: What was your exact task? What were you doing at the headquarters?

SATTMAN: From the basis of my knowledge of shorthand, which I could write very quickly, from 6 o'clock in the morning until 12 o'clock at night, we had to listen to Radio London and Radio Moscow, also the Swiss and others, and the United States. We had to listen to it round the clock: six times London, six times Moscow. We had to take it down in shorthand and type it out.

He said that he also listened to the speeches of Stalin, Roosevelt, Churchill and the Pope. He recorded these programmes, the reports were typed up and they were distributed to the staff officers with the nomenclature 'Top Secret'.

LORD RAWLINSON: Were they regarded as highly confidential?

SATTMAN: There was a thick red stamp 'Strictly Secret'.

LORD RAWLINSON: Was the ordnance officer, the O3, was he entitled to have access to these reports?

SATTMAN: No, no, no, he didn't get them.

LORD RAWLINSON: Was he prohibited from even entering the office in which you worked, without authority?

334

SATTMAN: Indirectly, yes. On the door, you had a sign 'entry', also for officers prohibited without exception. If Dr Waldheim sometimes came to me to find something out or to know something, he knocked at the door. Although he was superior to me in rank, it was a somewhat grotesque situation...

LORD RAWLINSON: Before he [Waldheim] arrived at Arsakli, in between March and May of '43 there was the deportation of the Jewish population from Salonika. Were you aware of that Jewish deportation from Salonika in these months before Waldheim arrived?

SATTMAN: Yes, nothing at all. I knew nothing at all.

LORD RAWLINSON: Did you see the deportations taking place?

SATTMAN: No, I didn't see anything.

LORD RAWLINSON: There were a considerable number of people involved in the deportation. Are you saying you saw nothing?

SATTMAN: Yes, I saw absolutely nothing. We were 4 kilometres outside Salonika, at Arsakli. We knew nothing about it. We saw nothing of it. And Radio London and Moscow did not say anything about these matters, nothing of that kind.

LORD RAWLINSON: I come to the autumn when Lieutenant Waldheim arrived in Arsakli – the 4th of October '43. Did you have any direct contact with O3, 1st Lieutenant Waldheim?

SATTMAN: Very little, only sometimes he came in and asked me if Radio London had already reported this or that, or if there was some kind of military event, but not otherwise. I only saw him in the corridors.

LORD RAWLINSON: Did he ask you on any occasion to stand in for one of his regular assistants who was away for some reason?

SATTMAN: Yes, but only once.

LORD RAWLINSON: What did that involve you having to do?

SATTMAN: He dictated to me several military reports which had arrived, and I typed them up on the typewriter for him.

LORD RAWLINSON: That must have been, what?, late '44 or early '45?

SATTMAN: November '44.

LORD RAWLINSON: And you were up at Sarajevo. The reports that you have typed, the dictation you took from him, were they concerning the enemy situation – the losses of the partisan brigades and so on?

SATTMAN: Yes.

LORD RAWLINSON: Were they predominantly concerned with the battles that were going on between the partisan brigades and the *Wehrmacht* in the area of Banja Luka?

335

SATTMAN: Yes.

LORD RAWLINSON: Were you aware that Lieutenant Waldheim frequently attended meetings with Colonel Warnstorff?

SATTMAN: It was to be assumed. It was likely that he was frequently together with his superior.

LORD RAWLINSON: You said that you had to hand your reports personally to Commander-in-Chief General Löhr's adjutant. Did you hand them personally to the Chief of Staff as well?

SATTMAN: Yes.

LORD RAWLINSON: In your assessment, could Lieutenant Waldheim exercise any command authority over anybody?

SATTMAN: Never, in my opinion, never.

LORD RAWLINSON: I want to ask you now about the GFP. From what you saw of the Ic department and the A0 department, would it be right that the Ic department dealt with military matters, and the A0 department dealt with the police matters?

SATTMAN: Yes, correct.

LORD RAWLINSON: Now, I want to ask if you were aware of any prisoner interrogation that was taking place at all at that headquarters.

SATTMAN: I didn't see a single prisoner. I'm prepared to say that under oath.

LORD RAWLINSON: Did you know of the terms, or if not the terms, the effect of the infamous Hitler Order about commando prisoners?

SATTMAN: No, not really. I was not with the fighting troops. We only dealt with the radio station. We had a great deal to do. We never took notice of these things. Nobody told us anything.

Allan Ryan now began his cross-examination.

ALLAN RYAN: Are you telling this Commission that you had no knowledge of the fact that commandos were under orders to be turned over to the SD for 'special handling'?

SATTMAN: I knew nothing about it, I wasn't interested in it, it was not within our field, it wasn't our job, and I can't remember it having been broadcast. They only talked about the Jews being gathered in Poland. There was one report − I don't know whether it was London or Moscow. We didn't believe it. We thought it was probably propaganda. We wrote it all down.

ALLAN RYAN: Let's stay with the commando order for a minute. There has been testimony before this Commission that the lowliest soldier, the lowliest stenographer knew about it and said

336

it was common knowledge in the headquarters. You are saying, as the foreign radio monitor, you knew nothing about it?

SATTMAN: There is a difference, because I only listened to the radio, which is different.

ALLAN RYAN: Well, you also had those who wanted telegrams and so on.

SATTMAN: Which was not within our field. It was not our job. We only dealt with the radio.

ALLAN RYAN: Now, I don't suppose that you would have been aware that the Jewish community in Salonika was the largest Jewish community in all of Greece? You wouldn't have known that?

SATTMAN: I didn't know that.

ALLAN RYAN: You wouldn't have known that it took three months for the forces of the *Wehrmacht* and the SS to move all of those Jewish men, women and children out of Salonika? You didn't know that?

SATTMAN: No, we didn't know that. We were not interested in it.

ALLAN RYAN: I'm sure you weren't interested in it. You were only 4 kilometres away, correct?

SATTMAN: Yes, that is correct. That I had my job to do, then I had my private life, and I went to the social club or I went for walks.

ALLAN RYAN: Or you went sailing in Salonika harbour?

SATTMAN: Of course.

After Wolfgang Sattman left the witness box, he was followed by a very interesting witness, Joachim Lützow. He was an active officer in the *Wehrmacht* during the war. He told Allan Ryan, who was examining him first, that he entered Army Group E on General Löhr's staff in January/February 1945. He was seconded as an assistant to the 1a.

ALLAN RYAN: Army Group E was in retreat during this period, was it not, and was in the area of Yugoslavia generally?

LÜTZOW: Yes, shortly before I arrived it came from Sarajevo.

ALLAN RYAN: At this time, Lt Colonel Warnstorff was still the Ic officer and Lieutenant Waldheim was still the O3 officer on that staff. Is that correct?

LÜTZOW: Yes.

ALLAN RYAN: I ask you, sir, did you attend meetings of the General Staff at that time?

LÜTZOW: Yes, almost regularly, really. During the week, there

337

were one or two large meetings that took place ... with the Commander-in-Chief. The Chief of the General Staff was there as well. The Ia was there and, of course, I was accompanying him. The Ic was there, and of course, the quartermaster was there as well.

ALLAN RYAN: Did Lieutenant Waldheim attend these meetings regularly, too?

LÜTZOW: Well, these major discussions with the Commander-in-Chief, I was only there three times. Waldheim was there twice, and he gave a resumé, a situation report on those bands, those gangs in the Balkans.

ALLAN RYAN: Do you recall the nature of his statements and discussions in these meetings, Mr Lützow? I am referring particularly to his contributions and suggestions about policies and ideas. Do you have any recollections about that?

LÜTZOW: Yes, I said expressly, earlier, you must understand this, that I myself was never a witness in any way... I only met him on the staff. These presentations, especially these presentations when the Commander-in-Chief was there and the Chief of General Staff, as far as I'm concerned he made an impression of someone who was rather keen on his job. He was almost religious in his keenness, as it were, because everything he said, he said with a certain passion, a certain conviction of a National Socialist kind. This is the way I [heard] it, of course. I was not there then.

But also, in the way he talked and so on, the way he expressed himself, it seemed to reflect the old period, the old Austrian period at the time of the emperors of Austria. It seemed to be the attitude he was reflecting vis-à-vis all the other nations in the Balkans. He had a certain arrogance about his manner towards these other races.

ALLAN RYAN: Was he putting forward specific ideas and suggestions or not? How would you characterize that aspect?

LÜTZOW: At those meetings, the situation always was that there was some kind of command or order for base support. And then, of course, those cleansing operations as well. Based on his knowledge of the Balkans, he made his proposals, and this is quite customary in staff meetings. They were taken by the Ia and included in any orders — as it were, translated into these orders.

ALLAN RYAN: I ask you to focus on Lieutenant Waldheim. My question is: is it your testimony that at these meetings he readily put forth his own ideas or suggestions or comments as to what ought to be done in particular situations?

LÜTZOW: No, he did not actually present them. I mean, he

338

always tried to put them through, to get his way. The Chief at those meetings was not always happy with these meetings. I will put it like that. But he did seem to get his own way.

Allan Ryan concluded his examination. Lord Rawlinson then launched into a fairly strong attack on Lützow.

LORD RAWLINSON: Are you getting quite used to appearing on television?
LÜTZOW: It's not easy; indeed, it's not easy, but I am trying to get used to it anyway.
LORD RAWLINSON: I'm merely going to ask you some questions about your previous appearances on television. You have made previous appearances on television, have you not, about what may be described as the Waldheim controversy?
LÜTZOW: Well, yes.
LORD RAWLINSON: Have you or have you not?
LÜTZOW: Yes, I was on television once, a brief section appeared on German television, but I mean, three minutes or something – it was not very much.
LORD RAWLINSON: You have adopted, have you not, a particular position with regard to Kurt Waldheim? One of criticism of him, is that not right?
LÜTZOW: Yes, that is my position ... He was a man who was rather keen and ambitious in his nature.

Lord Rawlinson asked Lützow about the so-called 'Plenca document', the forged Ustachi telegram that implicated Kurt Waldheim in the illegal transport of Yugoslav civilians to death camps, and which *Der Spiegel* had printed.

LORD RAWLINSON: I suggest that you publicly defended the Plenca document by saying, in your view, that it was genuine. Is that not correct?
LÜTZOW: No, it is not true. I said it was possible. I did not say it was true.
LORD RAWLINSON: Were you on the side that was arguing in the television debate [in West Germany] that this document was a genuine document, and shortly after, *Der Spiegel* apologized for having published it, did they not?
LÜTZOW: No, I did not say that; I did not say it was genuine. I said that an ordnance officer could sit on the periphery of all the orders given, so that he could have some kind of influence on the

339

population, the soldiers and so on. I said it was possible, based on my experience when I was a quartermaster.

LORD RAWLINSON: I suggest to you that you are consumed by personal dislike of Dr Waldheim, and you are totally distorted in your views about Dr Waldheim, totally partisan. Is that not correct?

LÜTZOW: OK, I am going to say something on that as well. Since 1934, I've been a German officer, and especially, I was in very high staffs and I was heavily wounded. I worked for people of a very high calibre...

COMMISSIONER LAWTON: You thought Waldheim was rather, what we in English call, a pushy young man?

LÜTZOW: Yes, OK, but with this kind of very, very ambitious background.

COMMISSIONER LAWTON: I think we have the picture...

COMMISSIONER PETRÉN: Is it customary that an officer of the Ic section should make suggestions or proposals when it is a question of tactical actions, tactical measures of the 1a section?

LÜTZOW: Well, as you see, it is part of his duties to do that ... That was his duty – to make proposals – which he considered to be right. Of course, it was his Balkan knowledge which was always called upon.

COMMISSIONER HUFSTEDLER: From your testimony, it appears that you had a wide variety of duties when you were in the post at the same time that Herr Waldheim was. Is that correct?

LÜTZOW: Yes, yes. I was assistant to the 1a before I became the 1b in the High Command – before, in the last few weeks of the war, I became head of 1b. But before that, I was an assistant who might represent 1a in small matters, but I was just an assistant to someone in the office. I made telephone conversations and so on. That is why I was there.

Following Joachim Lützow's evidence, the Commission heard from Peter von Meissner. During World War II, he had served as a private on the Eastern Front and then had undergone officer training. On completion, he was posted as a company leader to the 23rd Tank Division, fighting on the Eastern Front until seriously wounded at Stalingrad in 1943.

ALLAN RYAN: Based on your experience as a staff officer, if an officer found his duties to be unpleasant or personally repugnant to him, could he request a transfer to front-line duty without suffering adverse consequences for making the request?

VON MEISSNER: That was certainly possible. It could be held against him, but in general, it depended with what energy and what force of conviction, with what argument he could prove it. Certainly, I do not know of any one individual case where an officer had been disadvantaged if he acted in this manner.

ALLAN RYAN: Would your answer apply to even an officer who served on a Ic section at army group level?

VON MEISSNER: Well, I would also include him in what I've said.

ALLAN RYAN: Mr von Meissner, in your experience might an army corps or a group commander seek the views of a staff officer, if that staff officer was particularly well informed on a particular area – recognizing, of course, the final decision rests always with the commander?

VON MEISSNER: Yes, certainly.

ALLAN RYAN: So it would not be unusual, in your experience, for a senior-level commander to seek out the views of even a relatively junior staff officer, if the commander thought the officer would be helpful in some way?

VON MEISSNER: That was the rule. Every officer of a higher rank depended upon the work of the officers below him. He had to rely upon what they reported to him, what they said to him, their planning, their evaluation. So, therefore, he also had to be able to take notice, and be forced to take notice, of their opinion.

ALLAN RYAN: Thank you, Mr von Meissner.

Lord Rawlinson began his cross-examination.

LORD RAWLINSON: On which staff did you serve during the war?

VON MEISSNER: I was, first of all, with an infantry division as a young soldier, then I went to an armoured department, then I was with the regimental staff.

LORD RAWLINSON: Was there in the German army, as in other armies, a view of the fighting soldier [who was] rather critical or contemptuous [of] the staff officer?

VON MEISSNER: Well yes, that is correct. That was the general view of the practitioner *vis-à-vis* the theoretician. The one sat at his desk, and the other one had to do the work up at the front.

LORD RAWLINSON: You never served in Greece, did you?

VON MEISSNER: No.

LORD RAWLINSON: You never served in Serbia, did you?

VON MEISSNER: No, I have not.

LORD RAWLINSON: And you have never met Dr Waldheim?

VON MEISSNER: No, I have not.

LORD RAWLINSON: Thank you.

341

Peter von Meissner's testimony was useful because, during his service with the German army, he had served at staff level as Waldheim had, and could talk in principle about what had been expected of an officer in that position, and what he could and could not do.

Then came the last of the eyewitnesses. This was Dietz von dem Knesebeck. He was 76 years old, and his last employment had been as Special First Secretary at the West German embassy in Athens. During World War II, he had served as a Ic officer with the 2nd Panzer Army in Yugoslavia during 1943 and 1944.

LORD RAWLINSON: Did you remain as the Ic officer in the 2nd Panzer Army until you left the Balkans in September '44?

VON DEM KNESEBECK: Correct.

LORD RAWLINSON: In your 2nd Panzer Army, was it the same as we've heard elsewhere that the Ic officer had reports brought to him, and he then analysed [these] and took a report to the Chief of Staff at [a] daily meeting?

VON DEM KNESEBECK: Yes. Usually this report was first of all given verbally, and then afterwards it was formulated in writing if it was demanded.

LORD RAWLINSON: What was the relationship between your O3 officer and yourself as Ic? Was that a relationship of a superior officer to a junior officer, [or] was it something closer?

VON DEM KNESEBECK: No, quite normally it was a relationship between a superior officer and a subordinate. Of course, the daily close collaboration naturally would create a certain closeness.

LORD RAWLINSON: Did you ever have any command authority over any troops?

VON DEM KNESEBECK: No.

LORD RAWLINSON: Did you ever give any orders to any operational group, division, regiment or battalion to carry out a particular operation?

VON DEM KNESEBECK: No.

LORD RAWLINSON: Did you know Adolf Hitler's infamous order of 18th October '42?

VON DEM KNESEBECK: Well, I knew about it from the rumours, but when this order was issued, I was in Russia. In Russia, this command was not of interest because...no Allied commandos appeared there.

LORD RAWLINSON: When you took over your staff post, was that

342

order, in its exact terms, specifically brought to your attention by the officers from whom you took over?

VON DEM KNESEBECK: No, only later, when there was a necessity that I should familiarize myself with details of this command.

LORD RAWLINSON: Though you had not, at that stage I am asking you about, seen or looked at the exact terms, did you know the general import of that order, which was that Allied commandos, even if captured in uniform, should be handed over for what was in effect execution?

VON DEM KNESEBECK: The significance and, of course, the specific details of this order — I did not know those at all, because up to that particular point [in] the Balkans, we had not really occupied ourselves with this particular subject...

LORD RAWLINSON: I come now to the operations in the summer of '43 to, perhaps, the summer of '44. Was that theatre reasonably quiet in the sense there were not many operations during those months?

VON DEM KNESEBECK: It was a kind of colonial war in a sense, when the enemy perhaps suddenly appeared for two hours and then suddenly disappeared again. There was no demarcated front.

LORD RAWLINSON: Where there had to be an operation against a partisan or a Chetnik band which was suspected of being in a town or village or part of the mountains. Who would give the orders with regard to the operations?

VON DEM KNESEBECK: Well, basically the order was issued by the supreme commander, the Commander-in-Chief, or the Chief of the General Staff, but in terms of execution, of course, that was dealt with by the 1a, the implementation of that order.

LORD RAWLINSON: What role did the Ic have in those kinds of orders?

VON DEM KNESEBECK: The Ic supplied that part of an order which concerned the enemy: his strength, the weapons he was carrying, where he was and so on.

LORD RAWLINSON: What part would the O3 — the lieutenant to the Ic — in your experience, do [to formulate] these operational orders?

VON DEM KNESEBECK: Formulation . . . of the enemy strength . . . that was my task, my job. The O3 supplied the background, the material, for me to do that.

That was the end of Lord Rawlinson's questions. Now it was Allan Ryan's turn to cross-examine.

ALLAN RYAN: Mr von dem Knesebeck, this Commission has heard testimony from a man who was a soldier in a tank command and a staff officer, and he said that the Ic officers were the best-informed officers in the army. Would you agree with that statement, sir?

VON DEM KNESEBECK: I wish it had been so. I wish it had, but in fact, I don't think that it was like that, certainly not for the Ic officers of the staff with the front-line troops. [At] headquarters, if you like, it might have been like that.

ALLAN RYAN: Mr von dem Knesebeck, I would like you, if you would, to turn to page 45 of the 'Commandos' bundle. I would ask you, Mr von dem Knesebeck, if your Ic chart looked anything like that? Did you have functions listed on the *Führungsabteilung* as this one does?

VON DEM KNESEBECK: No.

ALLAN RYAN: Did you have a list like this at all, a breakdown of the functions within the Ic group?

VON DEM KNESEBECK: Yes, I did. I had a double sub-division. The one part dealt only directly or indirectly with the procurement of information, and the other part, a smaller part – this was called the A0 part – dealt with all the other matters to do with security and espionage and possible collaboration with the local police [and] . . . with the territorial military commander in Serbia or, in special cases, with the SS police. At his disposal for such tasks . . . was the GFP, the *Geheinfeldpolitzei*.

ALLAN RYAN: All these functions came under your concern, your responsibility as the Ic officer for the army group?

VON DEM KNESEBECK: That is correct, yes. The AO, too, was, in the final analysis, under me.

ALLAN RYAN: Do I understand you correctly when you said that the only time that your O3 officer attended Chief of Staff meetings was when you were absent? Is that right?

VON DEM KNESEBECK: He was only there during the daily briefings, with the Commander-in-Chief, he was only there if I personally was not there.

That was the end of Mr von dem Knesebeck's evidence. The Commission then adjourned for lunch.

Day 8: afternoon

We had come to the final witness of all: Christopher Greenwood, a fellow of Magdalene College, Cambridge, a lecturer in international law of the University of Cambridge and a barrister-at-law. He had been called by Lord Rawlinson, as 'challenging' counsel, to give expert opinion on international law as it applied to war crimes.

First, Lord Rawlinson asked Mr Greenwood to tell the Commission the rules regarding complicity in war crimes and the liability of staff officers, and the defence of 'superior orders' – that is, a soldier of a lower rank committing a war crime by obeying an order of a superior – to a charge of committing war crimes, as reflected in the reports of the United States military tribunals and the law reports of the trials of war criminals.

GREENWOOD: Certainly, there are no rules of international law as such regarding complicity in war crimes, in the sense there is no treaty that expressly deals with the matter. It is left to the national law of each tribunal. In the case of tribunals which have an international or part-international composition, it tends to be dealt with in the charter which establishes them.

LORD RAWLINSON: Though that scope was wide, what was the practice of the prosecutions as reflected in the reported cases?

GREENWOOD: The practice was considerably more restrictive than the theory. In theory, Allied Control Council Law No. 10 in particular would have enabled anyone who had knowingly taken a consenting part in the commission of a war crime or been connected with plans which resulted in the commission of a war crime – any person in that category would have been liable. In practice, however, the tribunals took a more restrictive view – in particular, in relation to some of the senior staff officers who had been involved.

LORD RAWLINSON: I was going to ask you about the liability of staff officers. In the Von Leeb case [a leading case of the liability of staff officers], what was the ruling in that case with regard to the intermediate administrative function of transmitting an order?

GREENWOOD: The tribunal rejected the prosecution's suggestion that transmittal of any criminal order was necessarily a criminal offence in itself. Such transmittal is a routine function which, in

345

many instances, would be handled by the staff of a commander without being called to his attention. The commander is not in a position to screen orders so transmitted.

LORD RAWLINSON: Then in the United States v. List – the hostages trial – did the US military tribunal go on to consider the positions of the Chiefs of Staff in the Balkans?

GREENWOOD: Yes,indeed.

LORD RAWLINSON: Who were those Chiefs of Staff?

GREENWOOD: General Foertsch, who was the Chief of Staff for the 12th Army from May '41 to August '42. The other Chief of Staff was General von Geitner from '42 to October '44, to the military commander in Serbia.

LORD RAWLINSON: In the judgement of the three American judges in that case, what was the basis for their judgement of acquittal of these two officers?

GREENWOOD: The US tribunal acquitted both the Chiefs of Staff on the grounds that they had not played a sufficient part in any of the crimimal offences which the tribunal found had been committed by other defendants.

LORD RAWLINSON: Then after the case of Foertsch and Von Geitner, in the light of the duties or responsibilities or liabilities of subordinate staff officers, have you looked at the Stalagluft case?

GREENWOOD: Yes, I have.

LORD RAWLINSON: Is that the case of the British prisoners-of-war who made a mass breakout from their prisoner-of-war camp, and later, half of them were recaptured [and] were murdered?

GREENWOOD: Yes, that is right. [This case was the basis for the famous film *The Great Escape*.]

LORD RAWLINSON: Who were the people then indicted and convicted in that case?

GREENWOOD: They were mostly members of the Gestapo, responsible for ordering or carrying out the execution of individual officers.

LORD RAWLINSON: What about the staff officer in the criminal police headquarters who admitted to handling the order to execute half of the prisoners-of-war?

GREENWOOD: He appeared as a witness but was not charged.

LORD RAWLINSON: From your study of the cases, are you aware of any case of a staff officer of Lieutenant Waldheim's rank being charged or convicted of a war crime?

GREENWOOD: None.

LORD RAWLINSON: In regard to the defence of 'superior orders', was that unanimously rejected by the tribunals after trying the

346

cases just after the conclusion of the Second World War?

GREENWOOD: Yes, it was the defence most frequently raised, and as far as I'm aware, it was never accepted that obedience to a manifestly unlawful order constituted a defence.

LORD RAWLINSON: I would like to ask you about the cases. I think there is a case, 'Buck', which you looked at as well as the Stalagluft case.

GREENWOOD: Buck and a number of other defendants were the commandants of various guards at a prisoner-of-war camp. They took a number of prisoners-of-war out into the woods and murdered them. They were all convicted. When I say all, all [against] whom ... there was any significant evidence were convicted.

LORD RAWLINSON: Of participating in that killing?

GREENWOOD: Yes.

LORD RAWLINSON: Was anybody tried who had, as it were, further up the line transmitted the orders?

GREENWOOD: Not as far as I'm aware.

LORD RAWLINSON: To what degree does the United States tribunal judgement in List help at all with the law regarding knowledge?

GREENWOOD: Yes, it makes it clear that knowledge and the fact that the defendant knows that troops are committing war crimes is not in itself enough to make him guilty, with the one exception of the commanding officer, who may be held liable for violations of the laws of war committed by troops under his command.

LORD RAWLINSON: Turning to deportations, the High Command case, again the United States military tribunal, what did that hold with regard to deporting prisoners-of-war?

GREENWOOD: The High Command case held that there was nothing unlawful in deporting prisoners-of-war from one country to another. As for what happened to the prisoners-of-war after they had been deported – in many cases, of course, they were deported to be used as slave labour – but in the High Command case, the United States military tribunal took the view that the commanding officer who was responsible for the deportation itself, sending prisoners within his custody back to the Reich, could not be held responsible for what happened them afterwards.

Lord Rawlinson asked him about transportation or deportation of civilians from the field of operation.

GREENWOOD: I think there is a distinction that has to be drawn between their removal from the combat zone, because it was perfectly legitimate for a belligerent occupant to remove this civilian population from an area where fighting was taking place. Indeed, in some circumstances, it might be his duty to do that, but you must distinguish between that and deporting them from the country of which they were residents to the territory of the occupying power or to some other occupied country. The first is lawful, but deporting them out of the country *per se* was not.

LORD RAWLINSON: What [is] the position of partisans with regard to capture if they are not in uniform? What are the provisions under international law with regard to uniforms?

GREENWOOD: Partisans at the time of the Second World War would have been covered by provisions of Articles 1 and 2 of the Haig Regulations on Land Warfare of 1907. The Haig Regulations laid down four conditions which had to be met if combatants were to be entitled to prisoner-of-war status. [They] had to belong to an organized group responsible to a commanding officer. That group had to conduct its activities in accordance with the laws of war. The members of the group had to carry arms openly, and they had to wear a fixed distinctive sign recognizable at a distance.

LORD RAWLINSON: Have you examined the law reports to discover if there was any case in which a liaison officer of junior commissioned status had been charged with participation in war crimes?

GREENWOOD: Yes, I have looked for that. I have not found a single case in which a junior liaison officer was convicted.

LORD RAWLINSON: I come to ask your position on the Italian soldiers following Italy's surrender — the armistice, the terms of which were signed in Sicily on the 3rd September 1943. There are passages in the decision in List which deal with the execution of certain Italian officers, including, I think, two generals who were in command of the Italian troops that resisted the German attempt to disarm [them].

GREENWOOD: I see no reason at all why the German authorities should not have disarmed the Italian troops. Indeed, there was every reason for them so to do. They were quite heavily outnumbered by the Italians, and they had every reason to believe the Italian troops might join with the Allies and turn their weapons on Germany.

LORD RAWLINSON: Therefore, this army of the Italians, [their] removal from the theatre of operations, the authority you quoted, would that be a war crime?

348

GREENWOOD: No, it couldn't.

LORD RAWLINSON: The treatment thereafter of prisoners-of-war, of those who had been deported [to] slave labour camps, would that be a war crime?

GREENWOOD: Yes, most certainly. The murder of some of the Italian officers was a war crime for which several of the defendants in List were convicted.

LORD RAWLINSON: With regard to the cases in international law and your submission with regard to reprisal measures, who were entitled to take reprisal measures under the laws of war?

GREENWOOD: There are some suggestions, particularly by the United States military tribunal in the List case, that even the shooting of reprisal prisoners and the execution of hostages could be lawful in certain circumstances. That is a very controversial decision. It is very heavily criticized by Lord Wright, the President of the United Nations War Crimes Commission.

LORD RAWLINSON: Have you looked at the allegations which are alleged against Kurt Waldheim, that he was a staff officer in the general groups to which General Foertsch and General von Geitner were the Chiefs of Staff? Have you looked at those allegations?

GREENWOOD: I have, sir.

That brought Lord Rawlinson's examination to an end. Allan Ryan picked up the questioning.

ALLAN RYAN: You were retained by 'challenging' counsel to advise him, [and] to present your conclusions to the Commission?

GREENWOOD: Yes.

ALLAN RYAN: I would suggest that one of the distinctions you can draw here is the distinction which you draw throughout your day, between practice and the law — to put it differently, between who is guilty and who is prosecuted. Now you would agree, I would hope, that prosecutors every day must make decisions as to who among the guilty they will prosecute?

GREENWOOD: Yes, of course.

ALLAN RYAN: Prosecutors by their office have only so much money and so much staff and so much space and so much time to represent the public interest in prosecuting criminals, and they must necessarily decide who they will prosecute and who they won't, or what categories they will prosecute. Correct?

GREENWOOD: There is a big difference between people committing offences and necessarily being prosecuted for them.

349

ALLAN RYAN: Let's say that the charge was stealing five dollars. If the question before this Commission was: Is there a case to believe, a case to answer that Mr X might have stolen five dollars, you would not find it particularly helpful to say, 'Well, wait a moment, no one will prosecute for stealing five dollars.' Would you?

GREENWOOD: No, I wouldn't.

ALLAN RYAN: You would agree that Telford Taylor [one of the US prosecutors at Nuremberg] and [his] counterparts – the British forces, the other Allied forces – faced the same sort of decision that any prosecutor faces, right?

GREENWOOD: Yes.

ALLAN RYAN: OK. And you have also testified quite accurately, as far as I know, that of the 2000 or more cases that were prosecuted after World War II by the Allies for the violations of the laws of war, the most complete compilation of all those is found in the UN War Crimes Commission reports, and that there are only some 200 cases summarized.

GREENWOOD: Yes.

ALLAN RYAN: Even under the best of conditions, we can only talk about, look at 10 per cent of the cases that [the] prosecutors decided to go with, among the many choices they had, is that right?

GREENWOOD: Yes, it is.

ALLAN RYAN: Whether a staff officer is guilty or not, [his] guilt of a crime is determined the same way any one else is found to be guilty or not guilty of a crime – that is, you look at the evidence and apply it to the law. Is that right?

GREENWOOD: Yes.

ALLAN RYAN: In fact, there were 1st lieutenants and 2nd lieutenants prosecuted after the war just as there were staff officers, right?

GREENWOOD: Correct.

ALLAN RYAN: So, what one comes to is that whether a person has violated the laws of war or, if you prefer, whether there is a case to answer or reason to believe, whatever you choose the standard to be, depends upon the evidence that can be deduced against a defendant [and] measured under the law...

GREENWOOD: Yes.

ALLAN RYAN: Now, another point ... that would [perhaps] be useful to clarify is the question of complicity – being an accomplice or an assistant. You testified, quite accurately as far as I'm aware, [that] there is no treaty that addresses the point specifically.

350

The point I am trying to make is this. I think it is the laws of every country – virtually every country that we might recognize as having developed a legal and judicial system – recognize, do they not, that [you] don't have to pull the trigger to be guilty of a crime. Am I correct so far?

GREENWOOD: Yes, certainly.

ALLAN RYAN: That is, the laws of every country recognize something called the 'degree of complicity', or degree of being an accomplice, that makes a person guilty of a crime as a principal for his role in the commission of the crime. To take a commonplace example, if three people decide to rob a bank and one says, 'I'll buy the gun,' and the other says, 'I'll hold the gun in the bank teller's face,' and the third one says, 'I'll keep a lookout and drive the getaway car,' and they all three do exactly that, then all three are guilty of bank robbery. Is that correct?

GREENWOOD: Yes, of course. The entire enterprise. . . is criminal.

ALLAN RYAN: And they are all accomplices to the crime, therefore. They have committed a crime, is that right?

GREENWOOD: Yes.

ALLAN RYAN: Now, you point out quite correctly that, in the List case – the South-east generals case – the tribunal there, which was an American military tribunal of three generals, acknowledged the possibility that, under the laws of war, there might be a situation in which hostages can be taken and might lawfully be executed. Is that right?

GREENWOOD: Yes.

ALLAN RYAN: But they certainly didn't find that those conditions had been followed in the case before them.

GREENWOOD: Absolutely not. The scale of the killing made it clearly unlawful. No question about that whatsoever.

ALLAN RYAN: Precisely. In fact, there was never a case as far as you know or I know where any German or Axis war criminal, war defendant was ever acquitted because he had shot his hostages lawfully. Right?

GREENWOOD: I'm not aware of a case of that kind.

ALLAN RYAN: I think we can conclude for all practical purposes, can we not, that the killing of a hostage is murder just as was said in the OKW [i.e. High Command] judgement?

GREENWOOD: Quite so.

ALLAN RYAN: Let's move on to your discussion of 'superior orders'. I take it that you would agree that the defence of a superior order in the context of war crimes is an absolutely and thoroughly discredited defence?

GREENWOOD: Yes, if the order was clearly unlawful and was known by the defendant to be unlawful, then a 'superior order' does not constitute a defence.

ALLAN RYAN: That is my point. Since 1944, the defence of superior orders by itself – in other words, 'I was just following orders' - is not a defence to a crime. One has to go beyond that.

GREENWOOD: Yes, certainly, not if the order was manifestly unlawful. But in both List and the High Command cases, as well as a number of other decisions after the war, the tribunal did draw a distinction between those orders which any soldier could tell were unlawful, and those orders which were unlawful as it happened but which the ordinary soldier could not be expected to realize were unlawful.

ALLAN RYAN: The question then becomes the ordinary soldier not having training in the law?

GREENWOOD: Yes.

ALLAN RYAN: Or in languages or diplomacy.

GREENWOOD: I do not know that training in languages and diplomacy would be particularly helpful.

ALLAN RYAN: Training in the law might?

GREENWOOD: Yes.

Here, Allan Ryan was making the point that, whether or not you (as a junior officer) knew an order was unlawful could make the difference between being found guilty or innocent of a war crime. Kurt Waldheim, it may be remembered, studied for and eventually received his doctorate in law during the years under examination.

ALLAN RYAN: I take it that it is clear that the 'commando order' is manifestly unlawful and that it has been so held.

GREENWOOD: Undoubtedly so.

ALLAN RYAN: This is one of those cases where there is no defence of 'superior orders' under any conditions because it is such a manifestly unlawful order that no defence can be made to the carrying out of it.

GREENWOOD: Certainly. Somebody who ordered the execution of prisoners-of-war under the term 'commando' would have no defence based on 'superior orders'.

ALLAN RYAN: In fact, one of the points that you raise both in your testimony and in your paper [a paper that Greenwood submitted to the Commission in advance to speed up testimony] is the case of the two Chiefs of Staff who were acquitted at subsequent

352

military tribunals, General Foertsch and General von Geitner, yes? It certainly did not say that a Chief of Staff could never be guilty.

GREENWOOD: No, it did not.

ALLAN RYAN: In fact, as you pointed out, staff officers all over the place, including Chiefs of Staff, had been convicted regularly by post-war military tribunals.

GREENWOOD: Yes.

ALLAN RYAN: Let me read two sentences from your paper on this point. You state: 'It has often been held that a commanding officer is responsible for the acts of men under his command and may, therefore, be criminally responsible if he fails to prevent the commission of offences by them.'

GREENWOOD: Agreed.

ALLAN RYAN: The next sentence: 'No such responsibilty attaches to the staff officer.' I suggest to you that the sentence by itself is a little too simple, a little too sweeping. I give you this case: Suppose a private has a prisoner-of-war, or let's call it a suspected partisan or a civilian, down on his knees in front of him, and the private has a pistol to the man's head. The private turns to the lieutenant and says, 'Lieutenant, I will now shoot this prisoner unless you tell me not to.' The lieutenant says nothing, and the private kills the prisoner.

Would you agree in that case that the lieutenant is guilty of complicity in the murder of the prisoner?

GREENWOOD: Yes, on those facts. I am not aware of any case which has ever quite resembled that.

ALLAN RYAN: Regardless, on those facts you would agree that the fact, as we said before, that the lieutenant happened to be a staff officer means nothing at all? Those are the facts. A staff officer's status does not mean anything?

GREENWOOD: No. If the lieutenant on the staff was aware that the troops in the company to which he was attached were committing atrocities, he does not incur criminal responsibilty for failing to take positive steps to put a stop to those atrocities in the way that a company commander would do.

Allan Ryan now switched his questioning to the deportations, and asked Christopher Greenwood, referring to the paper that the latter has already presented to the Commission, to clarify the limits of deportation.

ALLAN RYAN: [quoting from paper] 'Evacuation of civilians from

353

a combat area to another part of the occupied territory, on the other hand, was lawful so long as it was conducted humanely.' I agree with you on that. I think that accurately states the law - though I underscore 'so long as it was conducted humanely'. The point being, you would agree, that deportations or evacuations or transports, whatever term is used, [lose their] protection if those who are carried away are crammed like sardines or are deprived [of] food and water and are sent off under extremely harsh conditions. You would agree with that, would you not?

GREENWOOD: It is not that the transport of civilians in itself is unlawful, [but] the conditions in which they are deported can amount to an offence in its own right.

ALLAN RYAN: I accept that point.

GREENWOOD: It is not a difference without any significance, because the officer responsible for the transport may not have any control over the conditions under which the transportation takes place.

ALLAN RYAN: I think we can wrap all of this up by bringing together the concept, now that we've established that staff officers are not immune from prosecution, that the question of complicity that we mentioned before, when it was brought into a particular situation − that is, whether a particular defendant is or is not an accomplice to a crime − is also a question that has to be decided on the facts of every case.

GREENWOOD: Yes. I think that the decision in the List case suggests very strongly indeed that staff officers in particular would be guilty as accessories to war crimes only in cases where their involvement went beyond that of the two Chiefs of Staff in the Balkans theatre.

ALLAN RYAN: Let me read this ... from the OKW case and ask you if this is an accurate statement, still in your opinion, of international law: 'To prepare orders is the function of staff officers; staff officers are an indispensable link in the chain of their final execution. If the basic idea is criminal under international law, the staff officer who puts that idea into the form of a military order, either himself or through subordinates under him, or takes personal action to see that it is properly distributed to those units where it becomes effective commits a criminal act under international law.' You would agree with that?

GREENWOOD: Yes.

ALLAN RYAN: Thank you, nothing further.

And, with that, the examination of witnesses by the Commission was at an end.

Day 9: morning

This last day of recording – Saturday, 23 April 1988 – had been set aside entirely for the closing speeches by Allan Ryan and Lord Rawlinson. The judgement was to be reserved for later – for 5 June, the day of transmission. Counsel had both worked hard on their closing speeches. They were both keen to make their points, not only to the five learned judges who made up the Commission, but to the worldwide audience that would be watching the programme.

Everyone who was there seemed to sense the dignified atmosphere that these closing arguments warranted, and as Allan Ryan rose, there was a hush and a great air of expectancy. The 'presenting' counsel began:

Mr Chairman and honourable members of this Commission:
In 1942, he was a liaison officer to the Pusteria Division, when innocent hostages were shot at Plevlje and Cajnice in Yugoslavia. He was then the chief assistant to the transport officer in the Kozara mountains, and later, he was the transport officer when thousands of civilians were brutally deported. In 1943, with the German General Staff in Athens, he was the only assistant of the operations officer when German soldiers carried out the massacre at Komeno and reprisal killings at Lavadia and many other places, and when tens of thousands of Italian prisoners were deported under inhumane conditions, some to slave labour. In 1944, he was the third-ranking intelligence officer of an army group staff which oversaw the torture of commandos and turned some over to the SD for certain death, and which coordinated the deportation of the Jews from the Greek islands.

All of this is established by the evidence. The acts that I have cited are, without doubt, criminal under the Hague and Geneva conventions, as the judgement of Nuremberg demonstrates, despite the attempts of Nazis to disguise them with words like 'cleansing operation', 'special treatment' and 'evacuation'.

This hearing has put to rest any claim that Kurt Waldheim did not know of these crimes: the offices he held were in the thick of them, his initials are all over the evidence. Kurt Waldheim's

355

knowledge is not by itself a crime; the office that he held is not by itself a crime. And neither is his age nor his lieutenant's insignia, nor his lack of command authority a defence, nor can it be a defence that other staff officers were acquitted on other evidence in other cases. If it were, the acquittal of a Chief of Staff would confer immunity on every other officer beneath him, and as we have seen, that proposition cannot be seriously put forward.

But the case is more than this. To reach a fair conclusion, this Commission must consider the nature of responsibility for war crimes. We have seen that these crimes took place only with planning and consultation beforehand, with coordination and supervision in the meantime, and with follow-up and reporting afterwards so the results could be analysed and future crimes planned. We have seen not isolated individual crimes, but a continuing criminal enterprise.

And so this Commission should not be lured into a search for the one officer responsible for each of these crimes. It will not find him, for that officer does not exist. And if it goes off on such a futile search, this Commission will fall precisely into the traps set by the array of unrepentant witnesses who came before this Commission. To a man, they said, 'It was not my job,' 'I knew nothing. I was in intelligence, but this had nothing to do with intelligence,' 'I was in operations, but this had nothing to do with operations,' 'I was only on the general staff. What did I know?' You see what they are doing? They are inviting you to search for the tiny black pinhead of malignancy that is responsible for all the cancer. Do not be misled.

History and the evidence show us that Nazi crimes poison the entire system. Germany could not have done it without its collaborators. The SS could not have done it without the military. The commanding general could not have done it without his staff and troops. The 1a could not have done it without the 1b and Ic. The colonels could not have done it without the lieutenants, nor the lieutenants without those who wielded the weapons.

For two years, Kurt Waldheim has been urging the world to do what Nazis have done since 1945: to slice the responsibility into such tiny pieces that no one can be held responsible. If we believe that, what do we believe next — that these millions of dead were victims of a natural disaster?

This Commission saw one witness at least who knew what responsibility means. He was an ordinary Italian soldier —

Pompeo de Poli, the man with the diary*. You heard him here: when ordered to the firing squad to kill innocent civilians at Cajnice, he said to his commanding officer, 'I am not going to do that.' In that moment, decency looked evil in the face, and evil backed down.

If all these lieutenants and captains and colonels had shown the simple humanity of that soldier, the Nazi killing machine would have been brought to its knees. When that most vulnerable of ordinary foot soldiers could refuse to be a part of murder, what defence, what excuse does a lieutenant have?

If this proceeding has done nothing else, let us hope that we have exposed the fallacy of two of the Nazis' most important post-war myths: that only the mighty could influence events; and that the only alternative to obedience of criminal orders was court-martial and execution. They are lies.

Let us not make the mistake, however, of going to the opposite extreme, of saying that *everyone* was responsible, for that distorts history as well. If Kurt Waldheim had been a lieutenant commanding a rifle company on the Eastern Front, or if he had been the intelligence officer for a tank division in North Africa, we would not be here. But he was not that. At Plevlje, at Cajnice, in the Kozara mountains, in Athens, in Salonika, he was the lieutenant on whom the colonels depended to help them carry out the criminal orders that the generals issued to execute the will of the Führer.

Waldheim did not thrust a bayonet into the back of Alexandros Mallios's seven brothers and sisters at Komeno. He did not push Perla Soussi on to the boat at Corfu for her voyage to hell and Auschwitz. He did not crack the rubber truncheon on the neck of that courageous man Charles Bluett of South Africa. Kurt Waldheim did none of these things – that was not his job. His job was to assist the colonels and generals who ordered and authorized the privates and the sergeants. Are we to say that the generals are responsible and the soldiers are responsible, but the lieutenants and colonels who acted between them are not?

This Commission must render its decision on the evidence and the law, nothing else, but you cannot render your decision in disregard of history. You cannot, I submit, base your decision on the testimony of those benders and breakers of history, who sat in that box and said, 'Someone else must have done it.' Should Kurt

---

*This refers to a witness, Pompeo de Poli, who appeared briefly on the programme and who, like the other Italian soldier Gualtiero Piatti (see page 203), refused to carry out executions of Yugoslavs when ordered to do so by an Italian officer.

Waldheim answer for his role on four general staffs, each deeply implicated in the commission of palpable crimes? Should he come forward and, for once, tell the truth? To explain and defend his actions, to answer the evidence that so strongly suggests complicity? Or shall he be let go? The allegations dismissed because he was, after all, just a lieutenant? A lieutenant who did his job. All of them did their jobs. The greatest crime of our time would not have happened except for that.

After that very moving speech by Allan Ryan, Lord Rawlinson came to his feet for his closing speech.

May it please you, members of the Commission, [quoting] ' "Are you," politely inquired Captain Blakely' – who was the creation of Mark Twain – ' "are you going to hang him first and try him afterwards?" ' That is not inapt in the controversy, the whole controversy which has surrounded, over the past months, the case of Dr Waldheim.

But at least, here, we have had an opportunity fairly and rationally to examine what is the real case. To put aside the distortion and rhetoric, the generalizations, to look at the detail. There have been plenty of falsehoods and false documents. There have been people who have come forward who have seen Dr Waldheim beating Jews and tearing their valuables from them in Greece, when he was hundreds of miles away studying in Vienna.

In this Inquiry at one time, it was alleged he participated in the murder and deportation in the summer of 1943, during Operation *Schwarz* – charge abandoned. It was alleged he planned and participated in the 1944 massacre in the village of Distomon – charge abandoned. It was alleged he disseminated and issued propaganda – charge abandoned. It was alleged he participated in a massacre along the Stip-Kocane road in 1944 – charge abandoned.

So what remains in fact, in reality? May we review them together?

Operation Trio, Serbia, April '42. Role: 2nd lieutenant, interpreter, Italian Division, part of the Bader Group. Charge: Participation in murder, deportation of hostages. No witnesses, no documents showed Waldheim ever transmitted any orders to kill those hostages. No witnesses, no documents that Waldheim reported back to General Bader about it. No witnesses, no documents that Waldheim commanded any troops or a radio car.

Rather there was evidence that he had just arrived in the Balkans, shocked when told of the cold-blooded murder by an Italian officer, and the deportations alleged to have been [carried out] by the SS. Result: no evidence to warrant answer.

Second charge: Operation Kozara, summer '42. Role: assistant to captain in charge of supply, West Bosnia, 2nd lieutenant. Involved, the charge says, in murder, ill treatment, deportation of civilians. No witness, no document that he was personally involved in the custody and deportation of the civilians. No witness, no document that he dealt at all with prisoners. No witness, no document that he received any orders of any description. Rather he had no power of command, while the removal of prisoners from the battlefield is a legitimate military duty. No evidence to warrant answer.

Third charge: Athens, Greece, August '43, lieutenant on the General Staff with the Italian 11th Army. The murder of civilians at Komeno. No witness, no document to show the staff with which Waldheim served had command over troops. No witness, no document that this staff had any knowledge of what went on at Komeno, save what was officially reported to them. No witness, no document that this staff acquiesced in an operation against Komeno. No witness, no document that this staff connived at a cover-up by the 98th Regiment of the 1st Mountain Division. No evidence that the troops who committed that massacre reported what was done beyond their regiment or division; if they had, then it was sanitized before it came to Athens. No evidence that Colonel Willers gave the order, but if he did, the personality of that colonel, you may think, makes it unlikely and improbable that a young lieutenant would have had much influence over anything that gentleman decided to do. Result: allegations formed and founded, not on the evidence, but the theoretical reconstruction by academics based on a hypothesis that Waldheim was somehow involved. There is no evidence that he was personally involved, so there is no answer that he should make.

Athens, Greece, September '43, lieutenant, General Staff. Charge: Involved in the deportation of Italian soldiers after the armistice. No witnesses, no documents that he had any responsibility in organizing that deportation to Germany or to Poland. No witness, no document. No responsibility for the conditions in which they were deported to Germany or Poland. This was an operation, the scale and importance of which was far above that of a lieutenant. That a lieutenant could have had any authority is a matter which, to anyone with any experience of military matters, would be greeted with derision.

Arsakli, Northern Greece. Role: lieutenant on the staff of Army Group E. Involved in the deportation of Jews. No witness, no documents that he had any involvement whatsoever, but positive evidence that the orders to deport came from the SS, from *Reichsführer* Himmler in Berlin. Waldheim's department not involved in the actual deportation. Again, that the lieutenant should have any degree of input in policy matters of such importance is derisory. Result: no evidence to warrant an answer.

Arsakli, Northern Greece, summer and spring of '44. Charge: Involved in the maltreatment and transfer to SD for execution of commando prisoners. No witness, no document that Waldheim ever interrogated. No witness, no document that he ever communicated with anyone about the transfer of the prisoners. No witness, no evidence that he communicated any order. He was on leave on 16th April; by the time he returned to that headquarters, the Supreme Command knew of the existence of and the role these commandos had played. The Führer himself knew, for he made a decision not to raid the bases from which these men had come. After that, there was no chance of saving them. But there is positive evidence that Waldheim did not interrogate those prisoners. The decision was taken by Army Group F, given to [Army Group] E. The only officer who could have borne that responsibility in [Army Group] E must have been Colonel Warnstorff. He would not have shared that with a subordinate; that is a responsibility a commanding officer, if he had to do it, must have taken upon himself. Result: no evidence to warrant an answer.

The war, Mr Chairman and members of the Commission, in the Balkans was of unique savagery. Cruelty begat cruelty, murder, reprisal. Hidden enemy, no front line – the situation with all armies in different wars. All armies are put to a very severe test. The German army committed many crimes in that theatre of operations. Therefore, many German officers were later tried and convicted, including Field Marshal List. But those two Chiefs of Staff – and this is the principle which matters – who facilitated

360

those commands, who knew of what was happening, who made it possible for it to happen? The United States military tribunal distinguished their position because they said they had no power to rescind or palliate – and that relieved them of criminal responsibility. That was a decision of the United States military tribunal. If that excuses the chiefs in those positions, then how can it possibly condemn the lieutenant?

Mr Chairman, you are a Commission of five jurists, experienced with five different jurisdictions, all with one common thread, and that is a belief in the rule of law, which is the answer always to the barbaric. I can only speak of one: 40 years of practice in one jurisdiction, at one time having responsibility for all the prosecutions of all the serious crime. But strip away prejudice, as I know you will, and strip away also the sad cries of the victims and the bitter cries of vengeance, as you must. On this evidence, no court would convict, no committal would be made by a magistrates' court or, I would suggest, a grand jury. No law officer would launch a prosecution.

I do not care, Mr Chairman, a fig for Dr Waldheim. It is not for you or me whether he is fit for the office which he now holds, whether he has lied or prevaricated, whether he ought to have been elected as Secretary-General of the United Nations – I care for none of this. But I do care passionately for justice. I recoil at the hounding and the distorting and the generalization. Over 2000 years ago, Cicero said, 'Nothing, nothing can be operable when there is no justice.' And so enter the jurists to examine coolly, fairly, accurately the evidence – not the rhetoric, not the generalizations – to examine the evidence presented to you and, in the great independent tradition of your calling, to do justice. And justice on this evidence suggests – demands – the dismissal of these charges.

And with those dramatic words, the proceedings came to an end.

Part III

Post-production

On the Monday following the last day of recording, I wandered into cavernous Studio 1 at Teddington. It was empty. Bill Palmer's set – our 'courtroom' – had vanished as if it had never existed, gone to a breaker's yard somewhere to be turned into firewood. The set, like most things in television, had been an illusion.

The Commission of Inquiry, on the other hand, had not been an illusion: the evidence, the witnesses, the lawyers, the Commissioners – they had all been very real. At one stage or another, all five of the judges had told me that, within five minutes of the start of each day's recording, they had forgotten that they were involved in a television programme; to them, the set was their own courtroom and the proceedings had a reality all its own.

For nine days, our jurists had heard evidence from 38 witnesses, who'd subjected themselves to legal examination and cross-examination. Some of them, before they had gone back to their respective countries, had thanked Thames Television and Home Box Office for an extraordinary experience. Others, who'd had a bad time in the witness box, departed in a hail of threatened lawsuits, hellfire and damnation.

Why had they allowed themselves to be put through all the questioning, some of which had been quite gruelling? I have no idea. Perhaps it was the 'thrill' of being on television. Perhaps they thought that they were cleverer than any lawyer, or that, after all these years, they could finally set the record straight and tell what *really* happened. For whatever reason, none of them walked out – something they could have done with ease. After all, they weren't there because of any subpoena; no Federal marshal or police officer was standing behind them with a warrant.

Perhaps, like the rest of us, they had become totally absorbed in the 'reality' of the recording. It had truly become, just as we'd planned 10 months earlier, a genuine search for the truth behind the allegations against Dr Kurt Waldheim. In the absence of any real judicial inquiry, created by a government or any other authoritative body, television had stepped into the breach.

But questions remained: Had we done it properly? Was this a proper role for television?

To find the answers, I looked back to the very first day of recording, to the press conference that had preceded it. Faced with the ranks of the mighty media, Sir Frederick Lawton, the Chairman of the Commission, had spelled out his own reasons for taking part, and those of his colleagues on the Commission:

> During the past 12 months, various allegations have been made against Dr Kurt Waldheim, and for my part, they have disturbed my sense of fairness. I am of the opinion that those allegations, unless properly investigated, are likely to endanger historical accuracy.
>
> The allegations have been many and various, and the facts in support of them have been few ... I have got the impression from reading and hearing about the allegations that many of those who have made them and repeated them had only a hazy idea as to what constitutes a war crime ... A war crime is a legal concept under public international law. It has a fairly precise definition ...
>
> Dr Waldheim has never been tried by any court for a war crime, and it's obvious that he never will be. It follows, in my judgement, that no lawyer ought to say that he is guilty or not guilty of a war crime. The most, it seems to me, that it would be proper to do is to say, after having investigated the facts, that there are facts which, had they been known in 1946, could fairly and reasonably have led to Dr Kurt Waldheim being charged with a war crime before a properly constituted war crime tribunal ...
>
> The events which we are inquiring into took place no less than 43 years ago ... Within a very short time, there will be nobody alive who can say, of their own knowledge, what in fact happened. The nearest one's going to get to recording what happened is an inquiry such as we are conducting, and using our best endeavours, we will try to separate rumour, speculation and possibly fiction from fact.
>
> We may not succeed, but it's to be hoped we'll go a long way to establishing what really happened, in the light of our experience as judges and lawyers. It may be, at the end of the Inquiry, that the person who will be most grateful for its setting up will be Dr Kurt Waldheim. There is a possibility, of course, that he may not appreciate our efforts, but what I am sure about is that we will have done our best to serve history and to have done whatever we can to establish historical accuracy.
>
> Those are the reasons why I've agreed to take part, and those are the reasons which have led my colleagues to take part.

To me, Sir Frederick's hopes before the Inquiry started were more than equalled by the recording and by the programme itself. We heard stories of heroism and we heard stories of loss, pain and tragedy. We heard people tell what was obviously the truth, and we heard men tell what were obviously, even to the naïve, untruths of enormous proportions. We heard former soldiers blame everyone except themselves for things that had happened, and we heard counsel – and, on occasion, even the judges – on the verge of losing their patience with witnesses. And, throughout, there was the overriding consideration of the search for the truth.

But apart from the judicial analysis of Kurt Waldheim's wartime activities, what else did we learn from this extraordinary programme? For me, the biggest lesson was the enormous difficulties we encountered marrying the very different disciplines of the law and of television. When the latter is dealing with hypothetical cases or the trials of dead defendants, lawyers will largely play to television's rules. But, in this unique case, we had to let the lawyers work to rules *they* found acceptable.

Take, for example, the expert witnesses that the lawyers used to give background and explanation. To a television producer, these are often best delivered by commentary accompanied by a quick bit of film or some graphics. In the recording, however, our two counsel spent valuable hour upon valuable hour putting the experts in the witness box through their academic paces, to prove points of legal but not audience interest. Then there were the documents. These can be dry and boring to a television audience, but to our lawyers, they were key elements in the building up of their cases. While witnesses' memories may fade with the years, the documents remained untouched by time.

And time itself was becoming increasingly important. Whatever constraints were agreed in advance with the lawyers, they rightly responded to witnesses in their traditional manner. Given a lead, they followed it. Given an obtuse witness, they pursued him relentlessly, oblivious of the studio clock spinning around at double speed – or so it seemed to us in the control room. That problem could be doubled and trebled by the judges who, being free to ask questions if they wished, did so – always with the desire to get at the truth. And being aware of that desire, our own frustrations at seeing the valuable minutes disappear were mitigated. But we were left with the fact that time was not elastic.

We had also made a mistake in allowing our researchers to work right up to the last moment. This meant that, even during the days of the recording, the two counsel and the solicitors were still proofing witnesses, calling up new documents and maps and altering the shapes of their respective cases. In retrospect, I should have stopped the research at least one month before we went into the studio. Carrying on for longer, in the end, didn't change anything, but it did lead to Allan Ryan, Lord Rawlinson, Susan Aslan and Tim House being incredibly exhausted by the time the first day of recording arrived.

However, perhaps the biggest single distinction between the legal process and television was the inherent distinction between what television (and newspaper) journalism generally requires for a story and the amount and quality of the evidence that the lawyers required. The media circus that had surrounded Kurt Waldheim for the previous two or three years was a good example of that. In our Inquiry, using legal criteria, all spurious material was dispensed with, and it was all too obvious which 'evidence' did not hold water – 'evidence' that, in some cases, had produced banner headlines in newspapers.

I think we carried out the Inquiry properly – at least, to the best of our abilities after months of hard work, and at a cost of a small fortune. But is this a proper role for television? Again, I believe it is. The evidence from witnesses who had lived through those terrible years – whichever side they were on – is now on the record, as are the documents, so assiduously gathered and translated. Not only will the people who watched the programme benefit from knowing about them, but when the documents have been placed in an archive, they will be made available to historians and students of that period.

But more than simply making the evidence available, this programme has allowed television to take a small step in a new direction. It was taken with care and thought. It was taken

368

only with a great deal of advice from many capable, experienced and qualified people. It was taken responsibly. *Waldheim: A Commission of Inquiry* showed what, in these exceptional circumstances, a power for good television can be. It is, I believe, a programme of record.

As the lights went out in the studio for the last time, there were handshakes, kind words, little gifts of appreciation for work done above and beyond the call of duty, and then we were finished – finished, that is, all except for the editing. Confronting the Waldheim team was a further five weeks of trying to reduce the 50 hours of tape that had been recorded down to our transmission time of 3½ hours.

In the days and nights that followed, we watched and cut and rewatched and re-cut. Not just footage but *mileage* metaphorically landed on the cutting-room floor. So, I am afraid, did some of the witnesses' testimony – at least, in their recorded image. They had to go, not because they weren't good, but because their evidence repeated facts said by someone else. In this way, we lost the brave Mr Davies of commando fame, who had been held, like Captain Bluett, in prison in Salonika; we lost Mr Doughty, who had flown to London all the way from Florida. We also lost some of our German witnesses – Herr Sattman, Herr von dem Knesebeck, Herr von Meissner and others – squeezed out, like the others, only because of the terrible time constraints that we had to adhere to. But their evidence had been heard by the Commission – and appears in this book – and is thus a matter of record.

The editing process had thrown up yet another area of difference between the law and television. Susan Aslan and Tim House rightly worked hard to preserve the parts of the recording that represented the best of their own cases. On the other hand, director Roger Thomas and I worked just as hard to preserve a good television programme. These two efforts did not always coincide. However, with patience and respect for each other's problems, cuts were agreed and the programme came down to time – preserving, we hoped, the best of both requirements.

During this period, we all wondered what the result of the

369

judges' deliberations would be. But whatever the verdict, it really made no difference to me or to any of the people on the production team. I'm not saying that, privately, we didn't have our own views – that would be totally untrue – but as far as the programme was concerned, we had tried, as far as possible, to be as fair as any properly constituted judicial hearing.

Then the programme was completed. The long hours of editing were over, and the versions for Home Box Office and Channel 4 (lacking only the result) were sent out. Other copies in a variety of languages winged their way as far afield as Australia and New Zealand, the Middle East and a number of European countries.

Like us, they waited only for the result. Personal delivery by air, line feed and satellite were to be used to carry the 15-minute judgement or judgements (if there were a split decision) just minutes after being delivered by the Chairman of the Commission and recorded. Then, and only then, would we all know whether Dr Kurt Waldheim, in the opinion of the five judges from five different countries, had a case to answer in that he wrongly participated in acts contrary to the international laws of war.